BUILDING BILINGUAL EDUCATION SYSTEMS

FORCES, MECHANISMS AND COUNTERWEIGHTS

Edited by **Peeter Mehisto** and **Fred Genesee**

G000078416

CAMBRIDGE
UNIVERSITY PRESS

CAMBRIDGE
UNIVERSITY PRESS

University Printing House, Cambridge CB2 8BS, United Kingdom

Cambridge University Press is part of the University of Cambridge.

It furthers the University's mission by disseminating knowledge in the pursuit of education, learning and research at the highest international levels of excellence.

Information on this title: education.cambridge.org

© Cambridge University Press 2015

First published 2015
Reprinted 2015

Printed in the United Kingdom by Printondemand-worldwide, Peterborough

A catalogue record for this publication is available from the British Library

ISBN 978-1-107-45048-6 Paperback

CONTENTS

ACKNOWLEDGEMENTS

We dedicate this book to the many students, teachers, parents, administrators, politicians, academics and other stakeholders who have worked to develop bi/trilingual programmes around the world. It is their commitment and hard work that have made this book possible.

In addition, we thank Helen Imam and Colin Baker for their insightful comments and advice.

Peeter Mehisto and **Fred Genesee**

NOTES ON CONTRIBUTORS

Fatima Badry obtained her PhD in Psycholinguistics from the University of California at Berkeley, USA. She is a Professor at the American University of Sharjah (AUS) in the United Arab Emirates (UAE) and teaches undergraduate and graduate courses in applied linguistics. She has occupied several administrative positions at AUS including Chair of the Department of English, Director of the MA TESOL programme, and graduate Programmes Director at the College of Arts and Sciences. Her publications include books and articles on Arabic lexical acquisition, English as a second language, identity and migration, global English and local identity, education policy and bilingual education in the UAE.

Hugo Baetens Beardsmore is Emeritus Professor of English and Bilingualism at the Vrije Universiteit Brussel, and of the Sociology of Language at the Université Libre de Bruxelles. He has worked as a consultant on issues connected with bilingualism, bilingual education and language planning for the European Commission, the Council of Europe, the Singapore, Hong Kong and Brunei education authorities, as well as on similar issues for the Basque, Catalan, State of California, Canadian and Kazakhstan authorities. He has collaborated on the Language Education Policy Profiles for the Irish Republic and the Val d'Aosta region of Italy. Most of his publications cover linguistic, educational, sociolinguistic and sociological questions connected with bilingualism.

Raquel Cook is an Associate Professor of Education at Utah Valley University with specialisation in Curriculum Development. She holds advanced degrees from Oxford University and Utah State University. Her research focuses on self-directed learning, internationalisation and teacher preparation. She is particularly interested in efforts of globalising curricula and how teachers' international and intercultural experiences have an impact on their classroom practice. She is the parent of a Grade 6 Spanish immersion student.

Fred Genesee is Professor Emeritus in the Psychology Department, McGill University, Montreal. He has conducted extensive research on alternative forms of bilingual and immersion education for language minority and language majority students. His current research interests include language acquisition in pre-school bilingual children, internationally adopted children, second language reading acquisition, and the language and academic development of students at-risk in bilingual programs. He is the recipient of the Canadian Psychological Associate Award for Distinguished Contributions to Community or Public Service, the Canadian Psychology Association Gold Medal Lifetime Achievement Award for 2014, and the 2-Way CABE Award for Promoting Bilingualism.

Rick de Graaff is Professor of Bilingual Education at Utrecht University, the Netherlands. The chair of bilingual education is co-founded by the Dutch national Network of Bilingual Schools, the European Platform and Utrecht University. He is a member of the Network's accreditation committee, and a coordinator of the international CLIL Research Network (www.clil-ren.org). Rick de Graaff's main fields of interest include Content and Language Integrated Learning (CLIL), language teaching across the curriculum, foreign language pedagogy and teacher professional development. He also holds a professorship in Language Pedagogy at Inholland University of Applied Sciences, Amsterdam.

Antoinette Camilleri Grima is Professor of Applied Linguistics at the Faculty of Education, University of Malta. She has researched and published widely in the areas of bilingualism in education, sociolinguistics in education, intercultural competence, learner autonomy, and the teaching of Maltese as a first and as a foreign language. She has recently edited a Special Issue of the *International Journal of Bilingualism and Bilingual Education* (2013), dedicated to the Maltese context. She has been project leader and team member of several European projects of the European Centre for Modern Languages (Council of Europe), and has also worked as linguistic administrator at the Council of Ministers (EU) in Brussels.

Kathleen Heugh is Associate Professor in Applied Linguistics at the University of South Australia. She is also Extraordinary Associate Professor of Linguistics at the University of the Western Cape and Honorary Research

Fellow at the Human Sciences Research Council of South Africa. She has designed and taught postgraduate courses on language policy and planning, bilingual and multilingual education and language acquisition at the Universities of Cape Town and Antwerp. As a language education policy specialist and field researcher she has undertaken large-scale evaluation and assessment studies on languages and literacy in education in sub-Saharan Africa for various development agencies and governments. Her research interests include linguistic diversity and the education of minority, migrant, marginalised and Indigenous communities.

Jamie Leite is the Portuguese Dual Language Immersion Director for the Utah State Office of Education. She is responsible for curriculum and professional development for Portuguese immersion in Utah. As a member of the state immersion team, she helps with the administration of Utah's Dual Language Immersion Program at the school, district and state levels. She also works as the Dual Language Immersion Coordinator for Provo School District in Provo, Utah. She holds a bachelors degree from Brigham Young University and a masters degree in education from Utah Valley University. She is the parent of a Grade 3 Portuguese immersion student.

Gwyn Lewis was, until mid-2014, Senior Lecturer and Deputy Head of the School of Education at Bangor University, and a former Research Collaborator in the ESRC Centre for Research on Bilingualism in Theory and Practice, also at Bangor. His research interests include heritage/maintenance language education and immersion education, specifically within the context of Welsh-medium and bilingual education where two languages are used in the classroom for teaching and learning. He has held a number of advisory posts with the Welsh Government, and is joint editor of the *Trafodion Addysg – Education Transactions* series and a member of the editorial board of *Gwerddon*, a web-based Welsh-medium research journal. His latest publications focus on translanguaging as an emerging and developing methodology in bilingual classrooms.

Peeter Mehisto is a visiting research associate at the Institute of Education, University College London. He has worked internationally with a wide variety of stakeholders to develop and manage bilingual and trilingual programmes. Generating strategic plans and work plans, building teacher-training programmes, managing public relations and creating learning materials have been integral to these initiatives. He has won several awards for his work. Through the University of London, Peeter Mehisto has researched factors contributing to successful bilingual programme development, as well as potential barriers to their implementation. He has taught at primary, secondary and university levels. He has extensive experience working with teachers in the classroom to support the implementation of best practice in bilingual programmes.

Diane J. Tedick is an associate professor in Second Languages and Cultures Education at the University of Minnesota where she directs a graduate certificate programme in Dual Language and Immersion Education. Her primary research interests involve teacher development and student language development for one-way and two-way language immersion settings. Recent publications include articles in Language, Culture and Curriculum, the Modern Language Journal and Foreign Language Annals, as well as two co-edited volumes on immersion education (Multilingual Matters). She is founding co-editor of a new research journal titled Journal of Immersion and Content-Based Language Education, published by John Benjamins.

Anne-Marie Truscott de Mejía is a Professor at the Centro de Investigación y Formación en Educación at Universidad de los Andes, Bogotá, Colombia. She holds a PhD from Lancaster University, UK, in Linguistics, with a focus on bilingual education. Her research interests include interaction in bilingual classrooms, the construction of bilingual curricula, processes of empowerment, and bilingual teacher development. She is the author of a number of books and articles in the area of bilingualism and bilingual education, both in Spanish and English. Her latest publications include *Forging Multilingual Spaces* (2008) and *Empowering Teachers across Cultures* (2011), both jointly edited with Christine Hélot.

Onno van Wilgenburg is a Senior Policy Officer with the European Platform. Onno van Wilgenburg studied English Language and Culture at Utrecht University and the University of Bristol. He trained as a teacher and taught English in secondary schools for five years before transferring to the European Platform, the Dutch national organisation for internationalisation in primary and secondary education. In his current role of Languages Coordinator, he coordinates the work of the Dutch national network of over 120 bilingual secondary schools.

Yolanda Ruiz de Zarobe is Associate Professor in Language and Applied Linguistics at the University of the Basque Country. She has published on the acquisition of English as a third language, multilingualism, and Content and Language Integrated Learning (CLIL). Her work has appeared in books, edited books, and international journals. Her latest individual publications and co-publications include *Content and Language Integrated Learning: Evidence from Research in Europe* (Multilingual Matters, 2009), *CLIL in Spain: Implementation, Results and Teacher Training* (Cambridge Scholars Publishing, 2010), *Content and Foreign Language Integrated Learning: Contributions to Multilingualism in European Contexts* (Peter Lang, 2011) and the Special Issue *CLIL: Language Policy and Educational Practice* (International Journal of Bilingual Education and Bilingualism, 2013).

SERIES EDITORS' PREFACE

The manifold dimensions of the field of teacher education are increasingly attracting the attention of researchers, educators, classroom practitioners and policymakers, while awareness has also emerged of the blurred boundaries between these categories of stakeholders in the discipline. One notable feature of contemporary theory, research and practice in this field is consensus on the value of exploring the diversity of international experience for understanding the dynamics of educational development and the desired outcomes of teaching and learning. A second salient feature has been the view that theory and policy development in this field need to be evidence-driven and attentive to diversity of experience. Our aim in this series is to give space to in-depth examination and critical discussion of educational development in context with a particular focus on the role of the teacher and of teacher education. While significant, disparate studies have appeared in relation to specific areas of enquiry and activity, the *Cambridge Education Research Series* provides a platform for contributing to international debate by publishing within one overarching series monographs and edited collections by leading and emerging authors tackling innovative thinking, practice and research in education.

The series consists of three strands of publication representing three fundamental perspectives. The *Teacher Education* strand focuses on a range of issues and contexts and provides a re-examination of aspects of national and international teacher education systems or analysis of contextual examples of innovative practice in initial and continuing teacher education programmes in different national settings. The *International Education Reform* strand examines the global and country-specific moves to reform education and particularly teacher development, which is now widely acknowledged as central to educational systems development. Books published in the *Language Education* strand address the multilingual context of education in different national and international settings, critically examining among other phenomena the first, second and foreign language ambitions of different national settings and innovative classroom pedagogies and language teacher education approaches that take account of linguistic diversity.

Building Bilingual Education Systems is an important addition to the literature on bilingual and multilingual education. This is an innovative and exciting collection of analyses of the phenomenon as experienced within different national educational settings. The overall framework of the book consists of a rare combination of vivid, historical accounts of the development of bilingual education policy and practice with a clear and persuasively justified 'tripartite' analytical perspective for understanding the systems: 'forces, mechanisms and counterweights'. We are delighted to publish this volume as part of the language education strand of this series.

Michael Evans and **Colleen McLaughlin**

FOREWORD

Although bilingual and trilingual education existed in some form from the Ancient World onwards, it was the latter part of the 20th century that scientists extensively researched bilingual education. While there was some scepticism and organised opposition to bilingual education (e.g. in some States of the US), the use of two languages to teach the curriculum was empirically tested and found to be successful.

The modern movement in bilingual education is sometimes dated from 1965. As Chapter Three by one of the original Canadian pioneers expertly details, the St Lambert experiment from 1965 was a dream come true for those in Canada and beyond who believed that bilingual education was viable, valuable and vibrant. Along with the experimental dual-language schools for minority-language students in the United States, Canadian 'immersion' initiatives became a well-documented 20th century success story that deserves a chapter in the history of world education.

In the 21st century, there is now less scepticism, and much accumulated data to suggest that bilingual education is effective and advantageous for all students. Many, if not most, countries have some form of bilingual education. The 21st century continues to see new bilingual and trilingual education initiatives, as chapters five, six, seven and eight demonstrate.

This book is a treasury of such 20th and 21st century internationalism in bilingual and multilingual education. Since 1965, there has been an absence of books showing the international spread of bilingual and multilingual education. This gem of a collection helps to fill that gap in the education literature. Apart from case studies of individual countries, it includes 'Voices from the field'. These short contributions make the book grounded and share the experiences of wise educators with long experience of the realities of bilingual education in schools and corridors of power.

For those looking for a highly original element to the book, the chapters are successfully integrated by three over-arching concepts: forces, mechanisms and counterweights. This tripartite framework provides a compelling, comprehensive and creative conceptualisation for bilingual and multilingual education. Such an astute 'prism' framework is the analytical tool for each chapter and is shown in the final chapter to be the spectacles through which to analyse and understand bilingual and multilingual education for students and scholars, administrators and academics, legislators and evaluators, innovators and professional developers.

The tripartite framework engages, almost for the first time, the complex and interacting multitude of variables that initiate, influence and impact the development of such bilingual and trilingual initiatives. By utilising the concepts of forces, mechanisms and counterweights, the book uniquely and innovatively reveals the many powerful forces that shape such initiatives. It also offers substantial detail about common and less common investments. It draws out the interplay of forces and mechanisms, and how programme planners seek out counterweights to the criticism, opposition and occasional conflict that accompany bi/trilingual education. Major language initiatives inevitably go beyond education into politics, ideology and personal beliefs, and these are a challenge to navigate.

Nonetheless, bilingual and trilingual education are destined to blossom and flourish in the 21st century. There are at least three major reasons for this. First, the rise of international travel and trade encourages the spread of language learning. Second, the multiple (e.g. communication, cultural, cognitive, curriculum, and cash) advantages of individual bilingualism appear to make bilingual and trilingual education increasingly attractive to parents and educators. Third, the potential societal and community benefits of bilingualism such as continuity of heritage, cultural vitality, empowered and informed citizens, improved school achievement, social and economic inclusion, social relationships and networking, ethnic group self-determination and distinctiveness are variably being broadcast to win minds and raise awareness of the benefits of bilingual communities. These three factors join to make bilingual and multilingual education no longer an experiment but, as this book abundantly testifies, a highly effective and enlightened form of mainstream education.

Colin Baker

Emeritus Professor of Education, Bangor University

INTRODUCTION:
Forces, Mechanisms and Counterweights

Peeter Mehisto (Institute of Education, University College London)

CHAPTER NAVIGATOR

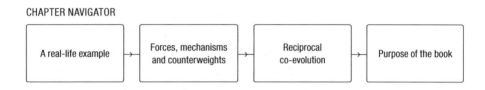

A REAL-LIFE EXAMPLE OF THE COMPLEXITIES OF COUNTERACTING MECHANISMS AND FORCES

In 2006, three United States departments (Education, Defense and State) and the National Intelligence Agency launched the National Security Language Initiative (NSLI). The NSLI aimed 'to increase dramatically the number of US residents learning, speaking, and teaching critical-need foreign languages' (US Department of Education 2008). Learners were expected to achieve fluency – mastery of these languages. The initiative was directed at the entire spectrum of the education system from kindergarten through to university level. Arabic was one of the critical-need languages.

In this context, with a $400 000 grant from the Bill and Melinda Gates Foundation and with the enthusiastic support of some members of the local community, the New York City Department of Education (NYCDOE) opened the Khalil Gibran International Academy in 2007. The Academy aimed to support students, not necessarily of Arab origin, in becoming fluent in Arabic and English by teaching half their school subjects through Arabic and half through English. The decision to name the academy after the Christian Arab poet Khalil Gibran was used to stress that the school did not have a Muslim orientation. Before the school opened, opponents formed a 'Stop the Madrassa Coalition'. Opponents labelled the principal as a jihadist and a radical Muslim. Prior to this, the principal was widely known as a moderate and as an inter-faith activist who had won praise and awards for her work.

Following this controversy and apparent inaccurate quoting of the school principal in the New York Post, the NYCDOE forced the principal to resign and moved her into an administrative role at the Department of Education. The principal filed a charge with the New York State's Equal Employment Opportunity Commission. In 2010, the Commission found that the Department 'succumbed to the very bias that creation of the school was intended to dispel and a small segment of the public succeeded in imposing its prejudices on D.O.E. as an employer' (Elliot 2010 referring to a letter from the Equal Employment Opportunity Commission). NYCDOE did not agree with the ruling. Tensions in the community about the Khalil Gibran International Academy were from the start of the initiative also reflected in the school behaviour of some students. To cut a long and complicated story short, the school has had a difficult history (cf. Elliot 2008, 2010; Zakharia and Mencha Bishop 2013). This difficult history has led the authorities to relocate and reconceptualise the school. The school does not offer content classes through Arabic, but does teach Arabic in Arabic-as-a-second-language classes (Khalil Gibran International Academy 2013).

Although the above is not an exhaustive, multi-perspective empirical review of the case, it does point to several forces and mechanisms that supported or hindered the development of this bilingual education programme. A powerful force in support of bilingual education in post-9/11 America was a belief, at least among part of the higher echelons of the country's government, that improved foreign language knowledge and learning was important for national security and for helping America to cross intercultural divides. Yet, in the case of the Khalil Gibran International Academy, a more powerful force, which was a fear of the initiative felt by a small number of people, was able to thwart the development of the school as originally planned. The 'Stop the Madrassa Coalition' put its energy into opposing the school, instead of building a bilingual school that the Coalition would have deemed acceptable.

Despite having in place: (1) seemingly powerful mechanisms such as a policy prescription from three government departments (Defense, Education, State) and the National Security Agency about the importance of supporting the teaching of critical-needs languages, such as Arabic; (2) financing from the Bill and Melinda Gates Foundation, and (3) a local Department of Education decision to open the school, these mechanisms were insufficient to withstand the force originating in a belief by a small group of highly engaged people that the school needed to be stopped. The coalition to stop the school as it was originally conceived proved to be a formidable force, against which no effective counterweight was found.

Yet the world remains dynamic. In 2013, an Arabic-English dual-language programme was established at the Mary White Ovington Public School in

New York City. The initial impetus for a dual-language programme came from the New York City Department of Education's Office of English Language Learners. The school chose the target language – Arabic. The Arabic-English programme is enjoying broad-based community support. At the time of publication of this book, there was a waiting list of parents wishing to place their children in the programme.

FORCES, MECHANISMS AND COUNTERWEIGHTS

As is the case in the preceding real-life example, this book draws out many of the factors[1] that can contribute to or hinder the development of successful bilingual or trilingual education. It does so with reference to **forces, mechanisms and counterweights.** These terms are defined below.

The book is a hybrid product that (a) offers an academic discussion about building bi- and trilingual education, and (b) captures practical knowledge used by those leading and managing these programmes. Thus, this book is primarily about how to lead and manage the construction of bi- and trilingual education programmes. However, the book is not just for leaders and managers of bi- and trilingual programmes. This book is also for university students, scholars, government officials, programme evaluators, researchers, those delivering professional development, and parents seeking to establish and shape bi- and trilingual education programmes.

For the purposes of this book, bi- and trilingual education refers to programmes that, over several years, teach various content subjects such as Maths and/or Science through at least one or more additional language(s), and that aim to support students in becoming bi- or triliterate.

A force belongs to the ideational realm. It is a form of intellectual power, vigour or energy that has the capacity to affect people and events. A force is more than an idea or principle, for ideas and principles do not necessarily lead to any action. However, despite being on some level intangible, these forces have 'ontological reality' – that is to say, they move beyond the denotative to the performative, and are 'generative-productive' (Scott 2010). Examples of forces are stakeholder inclusion, a belief in the value of and/or a positive attitude toward bilingual education, trust, and concerns about national security and cohesion. Forces can lead to the creation of mechanisms and they fuel or are capable of being harnessed to fuel action. Understanding and managing forces requires considerable knowledge and skill because they are powerful and because one cannot simply command a force such as a belief, an attitude, trust, respect, loyalty or a sense of mission. For those in positions of leadership and/or management, forces require at least as much attention as mechanisms, if not more.

In contrast to forces, **mechanisms are tangible. They belong to the material realm.** A mechanism is part of a system that interacts with other parts and leads to something else being done or created. Mechanisms receive their energy from a force or a combination of forces. Thus, despite being created with a causal purpose in mind, mechanisms are not in and of themselves causally efficacious. Potential mechanisms include agreed-upon policy prescriptions, flexible and adequate financing, opportunities for joint stakeholder learning and discussion, and a centre responsible for managing a national bilingual programme. Mechanisms are a key part of a bi- or trilingual education system, but they are never enough for building an effective education system. It is argued throughout this book that over-stressing the importance of mechanisms over forces is likely to have negative consequences. Forces are often more powerful than any one mechanism and as such need to be carefully identified and managed to ensure that mechanisms operate as intended.

Finally, there is often a tension among mechanisms, among forces and between the two. **Counterweights** are offered as a way of analysing these tensions, and as tools to be used for keeping a bi- or trilingual education system in balance. A counterweight can be either a positive or negative force or mechanism. For example, moral authority (a force) can act as a positive counterweight to the excessive use of positional power or legal authority (a mechanism) that can demotivate stakeholders. Also, assessing programmes based primarily on agreed-upon results or measurable indicators (mechanisms) can act as a positive counterweight against the negative effects of giving too much attention to accountability for process. Excessive accountability for process can undermine people's ability to focus on high-quality results.

Many of the world's success stories in innovation and development of bilingual and trilingual education are represented in the chapters of this book, as are the five continents. The book also represents various political systems (democratic, authoritarian, national, regional), different forms of bilingual education and different developmental patterns. Each country or region is to some extent unique. Forces, mechanisms and counterweights that influence and regulate bi- and trilingual education systems vary. Some of these variations will be described below as a further introduction to the forces, mechanisms and counterweights paradigm. Each country or region mentioned below has a chapter dedicated to it in this book.

The **Basque Country**'s bilingual programme was driven by an initial desire (a force) to right past wrong's committed against the Basque people and language by the Franco regime. Pilot programmes and research initiatives (mechanisms) contributed to the development of trilingual education programmes. Yet, despite having received the majority of their education in Basque, students in major urban areas still tend to use Spanish as their dominant mode of communication in the public sphere. The education system by and of itself appears to be an insufficient counterweight to shift the Basque Country to becoming a Basque dominant society.

Canadian bilingual (language immersion) programmes have been driven by a belief in the value of official-languages bilingualism. This belief has been a powerful force giving birth to grassroots movements that have fuelled programme creation and expansion. Responding to parental demand, local authorities have had to establish their own mechanisms to build programmes. Centralised mechanisms such as the lobby group *Canadian Parents for French* and the *Canadian Association of Immersion Teachers* are more a result of grassroots initiatives than government plans. Despite the fact that immersion programmes are deemed successful by a host of academics and by parents who continue to place their children in these programmes, some powerful forces come into play that undermine programmes. Students seeing restricted options for studying in the immersion stream at the secondary and university levels and believing that bilingualism will not facilitate their entry to university tend to drop out of the programme before the start of high school. Further, Canadian schools have been successful in educating students through their second language, but graduates, generally speaking, tend to infrequently use their second language in the public or private spheres. Counterweights against these tendencies, such as well-structured and frequent bilingual exchanges and other ways of integrating French and English-speaking students, are insufficiently applied probably because they are time-consuming, potentially expensive and require considerable skill on the part of teachers.

In Colombia, bilingualism in high-status or prestigious languages such as Spanish and English is fostered especially in private-sector education. The high status of these languages is a positive driving force. Yet attitudes regarding Indigenous languages underpinned by a lack of belief in their value have been powerful negative forces undermining the creation of education environments that foster biliteracy in an Indigenous and a high-status language. Government mechanisms, be they in the form of legislation, policies or programmes, are currently insufficient counterweights to change the status quo.

Estonia's bilingual and **Kazakhstan's** trilingual programmes have both benefited from substantial investment and foreign input. Estonia's programme is over 14 years old. The Kazakh programme is more recent. Both the Estonian and Kazakh programmes are driven by forces such as stakeholder inclusion and high expectations by all stakeholders. In Estonia, the voluntary nature of participation in the programme has been a particularly powerful positive force driving development. Both Estonia and Kazakhstan have established a large number of mechanisms to support programme development such as centrally-produced textbooks, in-service training and international co-operation. Results-based plans had counterweights built into them to avoid slavish adherence to the original plans. These included research and programme management review processes, the results of which were intended to guide the annual renewal of plans.

The bilingual programme in the **Netherlands** is centrally managed. A central agency has been an important mechanism in promoting programme development. It has been buoyed by forces such as stakeholder inclusion and a widespread belief in the value of bilingual education and internationalisation. Large numbers of stakeholders have jointly created and used mechanisms such as criteria for accrediting bilingual schools that have guided programme development. In addition, English is a linguistic cousin of Dutch and, as a result, the acquisition of English is facilitated in Dutch bilingual schools. Dutch is not widely studied in other countries; therefore, many Dutch people believe English is a basic skill needed for international communication. At the same time, concern for the future of the Dutch language is a major force and a counterweight to the spread of bilingual education into primary schools.

Arabic is disadvantaged in the **United Arab Emirates (UAE)** for numerous reasons including the fact that the majority of the country's population consists of non-Arabic-speaking expatriates. In an effort to change the situation, the UAE government has adopted an Arab Charter. However, many mechanisms will be required and forces harnessed and managed in order to realise the policies in the Charter. If bilingual education programmes are to flourish, a counterweight will have to be found to offset a dominant parental belief that fluency in English is more important than fluency in Arabic.

The **United States of America (USA)** is a highly dynamic society with some strong movements in opposing directions when it comes to bilingual education. For example, **Utah** is systematically establishing and supporting the development of immersion programmes in several languages including Chinese, while several states in the USA have 'English-only' laws that restrict access to bilingual education. In addition, partly based on the need for foreign language skills and the success of bilingual education in states such as Utah, opposition to 'English-only' laws and support for bilingual education are growing. Utah's programme is driven by political vision and the belief that skill in more than one language is central to increasing the state's economic advantage in a global economy. These forces are fuelling the creation and use of numerous mechanisms such as training programmes and employment incentives that have been created to quickly build programmes. The use of several languages in the Utah programmes may also help counterbalance fears in some circles that Spanish may at some point become the dominant language of the state.

In **Wales**, Welsh-English bilingual programmes were developed some years ago and continue to evolve as one way of counteracting the threat presented by English to Welsh. The inward migration of English speakers into Wales, who generally speaking have not learned Welsh, has acted as a force undermining the Welsh language. Yet in recent years considerable progress has been made in slowing down and even reversing the decline of the Welsh language. Mechanisms are in place to inform expectant parents of language learning options for their future child. Many Welsh speakers have for decades believed in the value of their language (a force) and worked to promote it. Co-ordinated protests such as the withholding of public broadcasting licence fees in the 1930s led to mechanisms such as increased Welsh-language radio programming and the establishment of a Welsh regional broadcasting channel in 1937. Another campaign to withhold public broadcasting licence fees and the threat of hunger strikes led to the establishment of a Welsh-language television station in 1982. Quality Welsh-medium education has acted as a counterweight to language decline by attracting significant numbers of native speakers. Concomitantly, Welsh immersion programmes are also attracting substantial numbers of students. Welsh immersion programmes are offered with several entry points. Still, a dearth of learning materials and qualified teachers are acting as obstacles to immersion programme expansion.

RECIPROCAL CO-EVOLUTION

Forces, mechanisms and counterweights, as illustrated in these national snapshots of bilingual education around the world, are in a constant process of reciprocal co-evolution, at societal, systemic and institutional levels. Reciprocal co-evolution[2] is a process where stakeholders, their understandings, actions, and the forces they are subject to and influence, and the mechanisms stakeholders produce, all evolve in response to one another and in response to other external stimuli. That does not mean, however, that every aspect of a complex system such as a bilingual education programme or system nested within society works together in perfect harmony and evolves together at the same pace. At a societal level, policies may be in place to support bilingual education, as is the case in the United States with the National Security Language Initiative. Yet, at the level of the local education system, Khalil Gibran International Academy evolved along a path that was unaligned with the national policy.

Reciprocal co-evolution implies relationality. When one part of a system changes, it has the potential to affect some other part or parts of the system. For example, if a district with a stable population develops a bilingual programme, it will likely over time need to hire more bilingual teachers and fewer monolingual teachers. It may even need to make some monolingual teachers redundant. If a district's population is growing at a rapid pace, existing monolingual teaching positions may be preserved even if the overall percentage of monolingual staff declines. This may mean that existing teachers will feel less threatened by a new bilingual programme and may be more supportive of it. If considerable money is drawn away from a central budget to a bilingual or a trilingual programme for professional development and the creation of learning resources, and if special financial incentives are required to attract bilingual teachers, particularly in a climate of fiscal restraint, those decisions can lead to less money being available for standard programming. This, in turn, could undermine support from the general education sector for the bilingual programme. If the bilingual programme does not provide equal access to all groups in society, this could also fuel resentment that can act as a force that could be used to harness existing mechanisms such as school boards or unions to lobby against a bilingual initiative.

From a planning perspective, various elements of a bilingual education system are best kept in a purposeful and intentional process of guided reciprocal co-evolution. A newly developed bilingual or trilingual education system calls for changes to the curriculum and to learning resources. For new curriculum and learning resources to be implemented, teaching and learning practices would logically be realigned accordingly. In turn, pre- and in-service training of educators and school managers, school inspections, and assessment and evaluation procedures and practices should all be aligned with one another. If any key part of an education system, which is seeking to support students in becoming bi- or trilingual, is unaligned with the rest of the system, it can potentially act as an obstacle to or a drag on the achievement of bilingual programme goals. For example, universities may not have the expertise to train educators and school leaders for bi- or trilingual education. Vested interests and resistance to change in universities can be powerful forces that need to be addressed with counterweights (e.g.

incentives for change) if mechanisms such as new programmes for training teachers for bi- and trilingual education are to be developed.

The long-term effects of certain mechanisms or forces may not be as apparent to all stakeholders as their short-term effects. This calls for those developing bi- and trilingual programmes to analyse the long-term potential effects of existing and planned mechanisms, forces and counterweights within society at large and within the education system. For example, in China, authorities have established a system of secondary schools or classes called *neidiban* that bring Tibetan students to Chinese schools outside of Tibet. Chinese authorities are seeking to have these Tibetan students learn Chinese and better integrate with the mainstream population of China. A decline in fluency in Tibetan among *neidiban* graduates, who generally tend to return to Tibet, has been an unfortunate, intended or unintended, side-effect of this policy. There are many causes of the decline in fluency, but a key factor has been the fact that the unified national test (UNT) score in Tibetan is no longer taken into account in the total score used for admission to Chinese universities. Consequently, students report concentrating their efforts on high-stakes subjects that are taken into account during the university admissions process (Postiglione et al. 2007). This is undermining the value attatched to the Tibetan language.

In other cases, long-term consequences may be at the forefront of a given stakeholder group's thinking and not necessarily at the forefront of a programme organiser's thinking. Prior to the launch of Estonia's national immersion programme in 2000, many Russian-speaking parents who were deciding whether to place their six or seven-year old children in the programme wanted to know in which language their children would take national school-leaving examinations. This was a key factor in some parents' decision whether to choose the bilingual Estonian-Russian language immersion programme or a primarily monolingual Russian-medium school for their children. An issue such as the school-leaving exams seemed 12 years in the future to programme organisers, but it was in the forefront of parents' minds when making their decision.

The main point about reciprocal co-evolution is that societies, systems and institutions are dynamic and in a constant state of flux and, thus, those seeking to develop bi- and trilingual education systems or programmes need to keep a constant eye out for those people, groups and organisations that can be affected by, or that can affect, the planned system or programme. These people, groups and organisations need to be listened to and understood. It is wise to build a constructive relationship with them, to build partnerships.

At a societal level, a political party that is not in power today can be in power tomorrow, so there is much to be gained from building broad-based political support for a bi- or trilingual programme. This can also help to de-politicise bi- and trilingual education and safeguard existing programmes from the potential negative consequences of changes in the political land-scape. Moreover, it is helpful if existing and new governments understand how their actions can support or undermine bi- or trilingual programmes. For example, heavily target-focussed governments may need help in under-standing how success criteria for bilingual schools may need to be adapted in the short-term while students are in the early stages of language learning, and that language and content learning in these programmes needs to be judged based on long-term results.

At a systemic level, if opponents of a bilingual programme are express-ing unfounded fears or beliefs about bilingualism, counterweights need to be brought to bear. Public meetings can be used to discuss concerns, fears and beliefs. During these meetings a major force in winning people's hearts and minds is the ability to maintain and demonstrate respect for opponents and their concerns. By contrast, humiliating anyone during a meeting could fuel resentment and make long-term enemies of the programme. Furthermore, meetings can be used to present current state-of-the-art knowledge about bi- or trilingual education. The sharing of research results, the engagement of experts in the field, and the involvement of parents whose children have been through a bi- or trilingual programme can all act as effective counterweights, helping to assuage the concerns of ill-informed stakeholders. The same can be done at an institutional level to help ensure that teachers teaching through the society's dominant language, or parents of children who are not in the bi-lingual programme, support or at the very least do not actively work against the programme.

PURPOSE OF THIS BOOK

This book maps out many of the complexities of building bilingual and tri-lingual education programmes and systems. Processing these many com-plexities can lead to cognitive overload where programme planners and implementers are simply overwhelmed or where they slip into a state of wilful blindness, ignoring those complexities they do not fully appreciate or feel unprepared to deal with. This book aims to help readers understand, at the societal, systemic and institutional levels, investments required for establish-ing bilingual and trilingual education programmes. It aims to help readers anticipate potential consequences of various programme development decisions and to prepare for both the expected and the unexpected.

More specifically, the book offers a conceptual framework built around forces, mechanisms and counterweights for organising and processing the complexities of bi- and trilingual education (see Table 1). This conceptual framework is used to analyse **case studies** of countries or regions mentioned above as well as others (i.e. Europe, Malta, South Africa). Most case studies illustrate how interacting parts of education systems nested in society are in a process of reciprocal co-evolution, how contexts favourable to those programmes and systems have been built, and ultimately how forces, mechanisms and counterweights have been used to build bi/trilingual education programmes and systems. Other case studies point out why bilingual education for certain groups is having trouble taking root and flourishing.

Following this introductory chapter, the core of the book is organised into four sections. These sections inevitably overlap with one another to some extent:

- Looking at the big picture (USA, Europe)
- Getting started (Canada, Estonia, Utah, the Basque Country, Kazakhstan)
- Looking at the long-term (Wales, The Netherlands)
- Understanding the role of context (UAE, Malta, Colombia, South Africa)

These four sections are followed by a concluding chapter that revisits the paradigm of forces, mechanisms and counterweights and draws conclusions based on the case studies that precede it.

Voices from the field are integrated with the four case-study sections of the book. These are short personal perspectives written by people working in bilingual education around the world. They provide a personal view of what those individuals worked or are working to achieve in their context (Brunei, Canada, England, New Zealand, Spain, Wales). They describe forces, mechanisms and counterweights that are playing an important role in that context.

Finally, the book provides **tools** for planning, constructing and implementing bilingual and trilingual education systems. Some are available in the book, but many more are available on the book's website. These have been, or are being, used in the countries profiled in this book. The tools ultimately serve to build stakeholder understanding, shape behaviour and build context favourable to bi/trilingual education. Importantly, these tools have built-in mechanisms for ongoing learning and change. These tools include: bilingual school accreditation standards; a bilingual education continuum summarising key beliefs and teaching and learning practices that support the development of bilingual education; government and school-level planning considerations; a one-page strategic plan, and results-based management frameworks.

In conclusion, repeatedly in the next chapters of this book, well-informed advocates (a mechanism), who believe in the value of bi/trilingual education (a force), are described as two key factors in the development of successful bi/trilingual education programmes. Yet the book explores many more factors that are part of the critical mix of forces, mechanisms and counterweights, all of which need to be skilfully navigated in order to build successful bi/trilingual education systems and/or programmes. At the very least, it is hoped that the reader will be able to identify forces, mechanisms and counterweights (factors) that they believe may have also had, or could have, an impact on bi/trilingual education in their part of the world, and that the reader gains knowledge about how those factors can be managed to ensure the long term success of their bi/trilingual programmes.

Table 1: Definition of forces, mechanisms and counterweights with examples

FORCES	MECHANISMS	COUNTERWEIGHTS
Definition: • belong to the ideational realm • form of intellectual power or energy • have the capacity to affect people and events	Definition: • are tangible • are part of a system that interacts with other parts • lead to something else being done or created • are fuelled by forces	Definition: • can be either a positive or negative force or mechanism • are part of a complex, emergent and dynamic system • can counteract overly powerful forces or mechanisms or take a system out of balance
Examples: • stakeholder inclusion • status • a belief in the value of bilingual education	Examples: • a centre to manage a programme • learning materials • policy prescriptions	Examples: • information and public meetings countering fear • parental demand countering government or political resistance

NOTES

1   'Factors' are considered entities and quantities that lead to an accomplishment, a result or process.
2   The concept is commonly used in biology (*cf.* Ridley 2004). However, it is redefined here for bilingual education contexts.

REFERENCES

Elliot, A. (2008). 'Critics Cost Muslim Educator Her Dream School'. *New York Times,* 28 April 2008.

— (2010). 'Federal Panel Finds Bias in Ouster of Principal'. *New York Times,* 12 March 2010.

Khalil Gibran International Academy (2014). www.schools.nyc.gov/SchoolPortals/15/K592/AboutUs/Overview/default.htm (retrieved August 2014).

Postiglione, G., Jiao, B., and Manlaji (2007). 'Language in Tibetan Education: The Case of the Neidiban'. In A. Feng, (ed.), *Bilingual Education in China: Practices, Policies and Concepts.* Clevedon: Multilingual Matters, 49–71.

Ridley, M. (2004). *Evolution.* Oxford: Blackwell Science.

Scott, D. (2010). *Education, Epistemology and Critical Realism.* London: Routledge.

U.S. Department of Education, Office of Postsecondary Education (2008). *Enhancing Foreign Language Proficiency in the United States: Preliminary Results of the National Security Language Initiative.* Washington DC: Department of Education.

Zakharia, Z., Menchaca Bishop (2013). 'Towards Positive Peace through Bilingual Community Education: Language Efforts of Arabic-Speaking Communities'. In O. García, Z. Zakharia and B. Otcu, (eds), *Bilingual Community Education and Multilingualism: Beyond Heritage Languages in a Global City.* Bristol: Multilingual Matters.

PART ONE:
Looking at the Big Picture

1   UNITED STATES OF AMERICA:
The Paradoxes and Possibilities of Bilingual Education

Diane J. Tedick (University of Minnesota)

CHAPTER NAVIGATOR

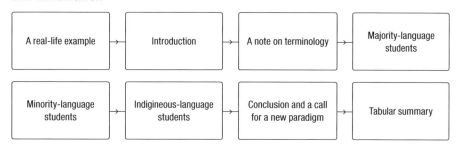

A REAL-LIFE EXAMPLE

'What country is this?' 'America!' 'What language do we speak here?' 'English!' came the rallying cries from the standing-room only crowd at a school board meeting in the small community of Forest Lake, Minnesota. It was the winter of 2003. Two years earlier a new parent, Shannon Peterson,[1] had approached school board officials about establishing an immersion pro-gramme. They asked her to identify 20 other families who would be willing to place their children in a pilot programme. She found 60 families. The school board organised a task force that included Shannon, parents representing the interested families, and local teachers and administrators. The task force worked tirelessly to inform the community of the benefits of immersion and was convinced the district would launch a programme. The 2003 meeting signalled a change. Fear, ignorance and anti-immigrant sentiments served as powerful forces against the proposal.

Shortly after that meeting the school board decided not to open an immer-sion programme, citing a lack of financial resources. The parent group pursued other options – a different nearby school district, a private or charter school.[2] The group's tenacity and stamina were major forces that functioned as effective counterweights to the obstacles they faced. They eventually established a charter school once the Minnesota Department of Education agreed to authorise them.[3] Lakes International Language Academy (LILA), an early total foreign language immersion programme (100% immersion in early grades) with an International Baccalaureate Primary Years Programme curriculum, was launched in September of that same year. LILA opened its doors to 177 children with two Spanish immersion classes each in kindergarten, first and second grade (ages 5–7), as well as third- and fourth-grade classes that received enhanced Spanish-as-a-foreign-language instruction. The latter was phased out as the immersion programme grew. LILA's new director Cam Hedlund had spent years in the community as a principal and was highly trusted and respected, and LILA benefited from his political capital.

Now, in 2014, the highly popular K–6 school serves over 700 students, offering both Spanish and Chinese immersion. The Chinese programme opened in 2011 and currently encompasses Grades K–3. A significant Foreign Language Assistance Program (FLAP) federal grant for 2006–9 provided the stability needed in the Spanish programme to try out Chinese immersion. The Spanish immersion students also study Chinese as a foreign language, and Chinese immersion students have Spanish classes.

Ironically, the school district that opposed immersion in 2003 began losing students to LILA *and* dollars (since state per-pupil funding follows the student). They turned to LILA for assistance in establishing their own immersion programmes. In 2010 the district elected to offer partial immersion (50% in English, 50% in Spanish) at its two elementary schools. The board did not wish to compete with LILA's total programme and wanted to allay parent concerns about English language development. Meanwhile, the district was instrumental in creating public, non-charter junior-high and high-school immersion continuation programmes for LILA graduates.

Important mechanisms support LILA. Initially, the Minnesota Advocates for Immersion Network (MAIN),[4] a grassroots consortium of immersion educators and University of Minnesota researchers/teacher educators, as well as the Immersion Projects at the University's Center for Advanced Research on Language Acquisition (CARLA),[5] were particularly valuable as LILA established roots. LILA responded to parental needs and concerns by offering a pupil before- and after-school care programme, parent language classes, student summer language camps and orientation camps for incoming kindergarteners. Another beneficial mechanism is the Amity Institute (www.amity.org), which provides interns from Spanish- and Chinese-speaking countries to serve as 'language ambassadors' at LILA.

LILA is thriving, yet remains challenged by issues faced by most US immersion programmes. There is a shortage of qualified (according to state licensure standards), highly proficient teachers who are prepared for immersion settings. Per-pupil funding for charter schools is lower than in regular public schools, and there are few federal and state grants to support immersion. Despite these enduring challenges, LILA is an indisputable success and serves as a model for others. This example illustrates that it is the passion, commitment and sense of mission of some indefatigable individuals who know how to use existing mechanisms and create new ones that has been the driving force in the establishment of many US immersion programmes.

INTRODUCTION

In many ways, the US is a country of paradoxes, many of which are driven by conflicts between personal freedom and societal order – fierce independence and governmental supervision. This is also the case with bilingual education. For example, on the one hand, the US government has recognised the critical need for US citizens to speak languages other than English for well over 50 years (Jackson and Malone 2009); on the other hand, it consistently institutes policies that squander existing linguistic resources amongst heritage speakers/immigrant students. Another paradox is that despite persistent anti-immigrant sentiments and English-only agendas, the US is experiencing unprecedented growth in bilingual/immersion programmes (e.g. Eaton 2014; Maxwell 2012; Mellon 2014). Forces such as the belief in the importance of bilingualism and mechanisms such as state-level support for immersion programming serve as effective counterweights to anti-immigrant rhetoric and advocates of English-only policies.

The remainder of this chapter first discusses terminology associated with US immersion programmes. It then describes bilingual education for majority-language learners, minority-language learners and Indigenous minorities by briefly summarising their unique historical contexts and identifying current programme types. Throughout these discussions, the forces, mechanisms and counterweights that have influenced bilingual programming are examined. The chapter concludes with a call for a new paradigm that brings together advocates for all types of bilingual education in the quest to promote bi/multilingualism for all.

A NOTE ON TERMINOLOGY

The use of the term 'bilingual education' as an umbrella term for programmes that use at least two languages as media of school-based instruction has become highly politicised in the US. Historically, 'bilingual education' in the US was used to refer only to programmes developed for minority-language students. As anti-bilingual education initiatives took hold in some states in the late 1990s and early 2000s, the label 'dual-language education' emerged as an alternative and more inclusive term to refer to a range of bilingual programmes serving minority- and/or majority-language students. At the same time, it is also a more restrictive term in that it refers only to additive (strong) bilingual programmes, while the term 'bilingual education', as used internationally, encompasses both weak and strong forms (Baker and Jones 1998). Additive (strong) bilingual programmes are designed to allow students to acquire a new language at no expense to their first, native language, whereas subtractive (weak) bilingual programmes do not provide for continued development and maintenance of students' first languages (Lambert 1984).

In the US, dual-language programmes aim to develop additive bilingualism and biliteracy in at least two languages, grade-level academic achievement, and inter-, cross- or multicultural competence (Christian 2011). They are subject-matter driven programmes in which a foreign, second, heritage or Indigenous language is used as the vehicle to teach academic content for 50% or more of instructional time during the Pre-K–5/6 school years and, ideally, into secondary education. They also provide for the continued development of the majority language, English.

These programmes may serve student populations that are linguistically homogeneous (e.g. students who speak English as a home language), or linguistically heterogeneous (e.g. a combination of English speakers and Spanish speakers). Howard, Olague and Rogers (2003) included four distinct additive bilingual programme models under the 'dual-language umbrella': 'developmental bilingual education' (DBE) – serving minority-language students; 'one-way' foreign language immersion (OWI) – targeting majority-language speakers; 'two-way' immersion (TWI) – enrolling a linguistically heterogeneous student population; and 'heritage' or Indigenous Language Immersion (ILI) – which seeks to revitalise endangered Indigenous languages and cultures, and typically serves children with Indigenous ancestry. ILI programmes may be one-way or two-way, depending upon their student composition (with most being one-way). They have a set of challenges that differs from programmes focused on modern languages and thus should be in a category of their own (Fortune and Tedick 2008).

A challenge with terminology in the US is that often 'dual-language education' is used as a synonym for TWI education. Despite concerted efforts to promote 'dual-language education' as an inclusive, umbrella term, its use as an equivalent for TWI persists. Complicating matters further, 'dual immersion' is used to describe 'two-way' programmes, and 'one-way dual-language' to describe DBE (Thomas and Collier 2012). Moreover, in its state-level initiative, Utah chose 'dual-language immersion' as an umbrella term to represent both OWI and TWI (Leite and Cook, this volume). This terminological challenge inevitably causes confusion, particularly among the American public and often the media.

Because this chapter describes some weak (subtractive) forms of bilingual education and because of the confusion that surrounds 'dual-language education' as an umbrella term, the term 'bilingual education' will be utilised throughout the chapter to refer to programmes that use a minimum of two languages as media of school-based instruction for at least some of K–12 education. The different programme models described in this chapter are summarised in Table 1 (see below).

Table 1: US Bilingual programme models

	Programme	Student population	Goals and description
Subtractive (weak)	Structured English Immersion (SEI)	Minority-language students	English language acquisition and academic achievement – they intensively teach students English to prepare them as quickly as possible to be mainstreamed into regular English-medium education.
	Transitional Bilingual Education (TBE)	Minority-language students	English language acquisition and academic achievement – they use the minority language for instruction as a temporary bridge while students learn English so that they can be mainstreamed into regular English-medium education as quickly as possible.
Additive (strong)	Developmental Bilingual Education (DBE)	Minority-language students	Bilingualism, academic achievement and cross-cultural competence – they maintain and develop students' L1 while they acquire English and use both languages for instruction until at least Grade 5 or 6 (ages 11–12).
	One-Way Foreign Language Immersion (OWI)	Majority-language students (primarily)	Bilingualism, academic achievement and cross-cultural competence – they teach students through the medium of a foreign language and English until at least Grade 5 or 6 (ages 11–12).
	Two-Way Immersion (TWI)	Minority-language and majority-language students	Bilingualism, academic achievement and intercultural competence – they integrate 2 learner groups and provide instruction through the minority language and English until at least Grade 5 or 6 (ages 11–12).
	Indigenous Language Immersion (ILI)	Majority-language students with Native American/ Indigenous ancestry (primarily)	Revitalisation of endangered Indigenous languages and cultures and academic achievement – they use the Indigenous language and English for subject-matter instruction, but programmes vary in terms of the instructional time devoted to both languages. They also emphasise Indigenous cultural values and traditions.

BILINGUAL/IMMERSION EDUCATION FOR MAJORITY-LANGUAGE STUDENTS

Historical context:

In the late 1960s, Professor Russ Campbell of the University of California Los Angeles was disillusioned by the abysmal results of traditional foreign language instruction in the US. He became intrigued by the Canadian French immersion experiment in St. Lambert (see Genesee, this volume), and during visits to St. Lambert he consulted extensively with students, parents, teachers, their McGill University partners and school officials (Campbell 1984). He later convinced Culver City Unified School District in California to adopt the Canadian model and launch in 1971 the first US foreign-language (Spanish) immersion programme for majority-language students (Campbell 1984). Thus, Canada's St. Lambert programme served as a powerful example or mechanism facilitating the establishment of OWI in the US.

As positive research results from programme evaluation studies emerged in California (e.g. Campbell 1984), paralleling those reported in Canada, interest in the programme grew. By 1977, 12 US schools offered OWI and, two years later, that number nearly doubled, according to a directory maintained by the Center for Applied Linguistics (CAL).[6] By 1999, the number of schools offering OWI gradually increased to 280. In the 1980s, federal desegregation monies for public schools served as a mechanism to support OWI programmes. These programmes could attract students from across school districts and in that way were seen as contributing to the desegregation of highly segregated neighbourhood schools. Parents like Shannon Peterson, who believed in the power of bilingualism and its importance for their children, were another important mechanism that served to promote these programmes. Parents lobbied school district officials to offer OWI, and some moved to districts that offered this programme choice.

During the early to mid-2000s, CAL reported a nationwide drop in the number of programmes offering foreign language immersion (see n. 6). At the same time, a large-scale study also reported a significant drop in the number of US elementary schools offering foreign-language instruction from 1997 to 2008 (Pufahl and Rhodes 2011); lack of funding and teachers were two of several reasons cited for this drop. However, by the end of that decade, the tide turned.

The immersion landscape changed dramatically in 2009 when Utah passed unprecedented legislation and provided funding for immersion (see Mehisto, Introduction, and Leite and Cook, Chapter 5). This marked a shift in how programmes were established in some parts of the country – from their grassroots origins to top-down, state-level mandates. States such as Arizona, Delaware, Georgia and Wyoming have since followed Utah's lead, implementing immersion programmes with state level support (G. Roberts, personal communication, 19 March 2014). A powerful networking mechanism that has led several states to follow Utah's example is the National Council of State Supervisors of Foreign Languages (NCSSFL; www.ncssfl.org).

State-based initiatives like Utah's have received considerable positive media attention. This attention has been a strong mechanism spurring the development of immersion elsewhere and its continued growth in areas with a long history of successful immersion programming (e.g. Minnesota, Oregon). Although the actual number is quite likely much higher, the 2014 CAL Directory (see n. 6), which is based on school districts self-reporting, includes nearly 600 foreign-language immersion programmes.

Types of immersion programmes for majority-language students:

The US offers immersion programmes in multiple modern languages (see CAL Directories). Spanish remains the most prevalent for OWI and TWI programmes, but French and Mandarin Chinese are also prominent. Chinese in particular has grown in popularity, not only because of China's expanded role in the global economy, but also because US federal funding for 'critical languages' (like Mandarin, Korean, Arabic) and monies from the Chinese government have served as strong mechanisms to support programme development.

Two main bilingual education programme types – OWI and TWI – are offered for majority-language students; the latter combines majority-language with minority-language students in the same classrooms and offers instruction in English and the minority partner language (e.g. Spanish). Each of these models has variations. The US only offers programmes of the 'early' variety – those that begin in pre-school, kindergarten, or Grade 1 – unlike Canada and other countries that also offer 'delayed' (Grade 4 start), and 'late' immersion (Grade 7 start).

One-way 'partial' immersion education: Partial immersion programmes offer 50% of subject-matter instruction in the second or new language (L2) and 50% in the majority language, English, from the beginning and throughout the duration of the elementary school years. Utah adopted this model (see Leite and Cook this volume) and called it '50:50' rather than 'partial' immersion because it was believed that the term 'partial' would not be interpreted favourably by parents and legislators. Since Utah's adoption of the '50:50' descriptor, it has become increasingly common to see these programmes described as '50:50' rather than partial, although '50:50' was initially used exclusively to describe a TWI variety.

One-way 'total' immersion education: Total OWI programmes begin with 100% of subject-matter instruction in the L2 for the first few years. Then, about 30–45 minutes of English (L1) language arts instruction is formally introduced into the curriculum as early as Grade 2 and as late as Grade 4. More instructional time in English is gradually added each year so that by the end of elementary school (Grade 5 or 6, ages 11–12), students have about 50% of instructional time in each language.

Two-way immersion education: There are two main varieties of TWI programmes: the 50:50 and 90:10 model. The 50:50 model is parallel to partial OWI. In 90:10 programmes, 90% of instruction occurs in the minority language and 10% in English for the first years of the programme, with a gradual increase in English and decrease in the minority language as students advance in grade, until a balance is reached by upper elementary. There are also other variations such as 80:20 or 70:30. The Alicia Chacón International School in El Paso, Texas, is considered an 80:10:10 model, because all students study a third language (Chinese, German, Japanese or Russian) for 10% of the time throughout the programme; it transitions to 45:45:10 for Grades 5–8 (Calderón and Minaya-Rowe 2003). CAL lists in its self-reported TWI directory approximately 450 TWI programmes although, again, the actual number is likely much higher.[7] The TWI model is discussed in more detail in the next section.

As in Canada, studies in the US have shown that majority-language students in OWI and TWI perform at or above grade-level norms on standardised tests of academic achievement administered in English (e.g., Downs-Reid 2000; Essama 2007; Lindholm-Leary 2001). Overall, majority-language students in immersion programmes display fluency and confidence when using the L2, are skilled at using communication strategies and develop high levels of comprehension in the L2 (see Genesee 2004, and Genesee and Lindholm-Leary 2013, for reviews). However, when it comes to production skills, immersion students' language lacks complexity, sociolinguistic appropriateness, grammatical accuracy and lexical precision (see Lyster 2007, for a review).

BILINGUAL/IMMERSION EDUCATION FOR MINORITY-LANGUAGE STUDENTS

Historical context:

The historical context of bilingual education for minority-language students is much more complicated than that for majority-language students, and space limitations do not allow comprehensive coverage of it within this chapter. In a brief history of US bilingual education, Baker and Jones (1998) identify four overlapping periods – permissive, restrictive, opportunistic and dismissive. The 'permissive period' took place during the eighteenth and nineteenth centuries as European immigrants arrived. At this time, linguistic diversity was widely accepted in the US, and many bilingual and even some monolingual German, Dutch and Norwegian schools existed. This permissive attitude toward languages, a force in and of itself, was shaped by other forces, such as competition for students between private and public schools during the second half of the nineteenth century, ethnic homogeneity in many areas and desires to learn English (and by extension to belong to the majority group), while simultaneously maintaining and continuing to develop mother tongues. Despite the overall positive attitudes toward languages besides English that characterised this era, Ovando (2003) stresses that this period did not actively foster bilingualism; 'rather, a policy of linguistic assimilation without coercion seemed to prevail'.

At the beginning of the twentieth century, the permissive period evolved into the 'restrictive period' as attitudes toward bilingualism and bilingual education shifted dramatically. The restrictive period continued through to the 1960s and, arguably, many of its underlying forces persist today. An influx of immigrants at the turn of the century contributed to fear of foreigners and 'the call for integration, harmonization and assimilation of immigrants, whose lack of English language and English literacy was seen as a source of social, political and economic concern' (Baker and Jones 1998). 'Americanisation' emerged as a force. This was reflected in the Nationality Act of 1906, a mechanism that made English a prerequisite to naturalised citizenship. US participation in World War I led to anti-German sentiment, and the English language was perceived as a unifying force, with other languages seen as threats to Americanisation.

The launch of Sputnik by Russia in 1957 sparked concern about the quality of US education and foreign-language instruction. Such concerns were rooted in forces such as the fear of falling behind Russia and the desire for the US to be the lead nation globally. The National Defense Education Act (1958) led to increased foreign language learning for *majority*-language students in K–12 settings and universities and, in turn, promoted a somewhat more tolerant attitude toward languages other than English (Baker and Jones 1998). Ovando (2003) notes, however, that while

> the country was encouraging the study of foreign languages for English monolinguals, at great cost and with great inefficiency, ... it was destroying through monolingual English instruction the linguistic gifts that children from non-English-language backgrounds bring to our schools.

The Civil Rights Movement of the 1960s and the 1964 Civil Rights Act, which prohibited discrimination on the basis of race, colour or creed, symbolised the start of a shift to less negative attitudes toward ethnic groups and more positive attitudes toward linguistic diversity. These mechanisms and forces heralded in a 'period of opportunity' that lasted for two decades. The Coral Way Elementary School established by Cuban exiles in Miami-Dade County, Florida, in 1963 is often associated with the resurgence of bilingual education during this period. Assuming that their stay in the US was temporary, these parents wanted school support in developing their children's native Spanish, but also in acquiring English. The school brought together Spanish-speaking learners of English and English-speaking learners of Spanish, and is credited with being the nation's first TWI programme, though it was not labelled as such (Christian 2011; Fortune and Tedick 2008).

The 'period of opportunity' was marked by significant legislation and a number of lawsuits. These mechanisms were used to further develop bilingual programming. The Bilingual Education Act of 1968 authorised the use of languages other than English in education, but still only allocated funds to support native-language instruction for minority-language students temporarily, with the aim of transitioning them to English rather than supporting ongoing development of their mother tongues. A landmark 1974 US Supreme Court decision known as 'Lau v. Nichols' prohibited English 'submersion' programmes for minority-language children and led to 'Lau remedies', designed to eliminate past educational practices that had been ruled unlawful under Lau v. Nichols. Lau remedies included English as a Second Language (ESL) programmes, English tutoring and some forms of bilingual education. The emphasis remained on transitional use of students' first language (L1) for instruction rather than long-term L1 development. Nevertheless, the Lau v. Nichols decision '... had an enormous impact on the development of bilingual education in the [US]' (Ovando 2003).

The 1980s marked the beginning of the 'dismissive period'. This period gave rise to the 'English Only' movement, which has since been sponsored by various organisations, such as US English, a powerful, conservative, multi-million dollar organisation that strives to make English the official language of the nation. It has successfully lobbied for passage of English-as-an-official-language legislation in many states. May (2012) identifies a number of negative features that characterise the 'English Only' movement, including historical inaccuracy, an over-emphasis on English proficiency as a barometer of educational success, a misrepresentation of bilingual education, and two additional factors, namely:

> ... the inherent nativism of much English Only rhetoric; language is used, in effect, as a convenient proxy for maintaining racialized distinctions in the USA [and] ... the assumption that speaking English is a unifying force, while multilingualism is by definition destructive of national unity. (May 2012)

A counterweight to the 'English Only' movement is 'English Plus', a group that promotes cultural, linguistic and democratic pluralism.

The dismissive period has included additional legislative changes and initiatives, all mechanisms that work primarily against bilingual education. For example, in 1978, the US Congress re-authorised Transitional Bilingual Education legislation, which established that federal funds could not be used for DBE programmes. Later amendments provided for an increase in funds for programmes that did not allow use of students' native languages, although at the same time there was some funding for the development of TWI programmes. State-level legislation outlawing bilingual education has also been prevalent during this period. Proposition 227 (passed in California in 1998) was initiated by millionaire Ron Unz, who claimed that bilingual programmes were failing to teach children English (Ovando 2003). Unz's claims were based in part on some studies showing that bilingual programmes were ineffective (e.g. Gersten 1985; Rossell and Baker 1996); however, such studies have been criticised as methodologically flawed (e.g. Krashen 2000). Proposition 227 requires that minority-language learners be taught primarily in English through sheltered or 'structured English immersion' (SEI) programmes before being transferred to mainstream English-medium classrooms. Two other states soon followed California's lead, passing similar legislation in 2000 (Arizona) and 2002 (Massachusetts), although attempts in Oregon and Colorado failed. The SEI programme label represents a misappropriation of the term 'immersion', since immersion programmes are intended to be additive in nature. California's SEI programmes are clearly subtractive in their intent: 'to place [minority-language] children in an initially all-English instructional program [is] to misapply the immersion process in a harmful, subtractive way' (Lambert 1984).

As Baker and Jones (1998) aptly point out, the history of bilingual education in the US 'shows that there is constant change, a constant movement in ideas, ideology and impetus. There is action and reaction, movement and contra-movement, assertion and response.' Underlying and driving this constant change are the many forces, mechanisms and counterweights that intersect and come into play. Convincing the American public and policy-makers that bilingual education is effective for minority-language learners and that bilingualism for all (regardless of language background) would be an asset for the nation continue to be challenges, yet they must be overcome if the US is to progress beyond this dismissive era (Ovando 2003).

Bilingual/immersion programmes for minority-language students

The nation offers both 'weak' and 'strong' forms of bilingual education for minority-language students (Baker and Jones 1998). The description of programmes presented here is restricted to those that employ the use of two languages for instruction for at least some minimum period of time. Unfortunately, most minority-language students are schooled in English-only programmes in the US.

Transitional Bilingual Education: As a weak form of bilingual education, TBE programmes are designed for linguistically homogeneous groups of minority-language students (typically Spanish speakers). Their primary goal is not for students to become bilingual and biliterate, but rather for students to function in mainstream, English-medium classes; thus they utilise students' L1 only as a temporary bridge to classes taught in English only. These subtractive programmes persist despite the wealth of research evidence that demonstrates the superiority of additive models when it comes to overall academic achievement in English in the long term (e.g. Lindholm-Leary 2001; Lindholm-Leary and Genesee 2010; Thomas and Collier 2012; Valentino and Reardon 2014). Forces influencing the persistence of TBE are unfounded beliefs that bilingual education is ineffective in teaching English and that programmes fostering additive bilingualism will slow linguistic assimilation as they maintain student loyalty to minority languages (Crawford 2004).

Developmental Bilingual Education: DBE programmes represent a strong form of bilingual education serving minority-language learners (typically Spanish speakers) that strives to produce bilingual, biliterate and bicultural students. At least 50% of instruction is provided in the minority language, along with English, through at least the elementary school years; stronger DBE programmes continue through the secondary grades. Research on DBE programme outcomes has generally shown that minority-language learn-ers in DBE academically do as well as or better than peers schooled only in English in the long term (see Genesee and Lindholm-Leary 2013, for a review).

Two-Way Immersion Education (TWI): TWI programmes represent an amalgam of DBE and OWI programmes in that they serve both minority-language and majority-language students, ideally 50% from each language group. They also represent a strong and additive form of bilingual education.

A considerable body of research indicates that the TWI model is highly effective for minority-language learners (Lindholm-Leary 2001; Lindholm-Leary and Genesee 2010; Thomas and Collier 2012; Valentino and Reardon 2014). Studies have consistently shown that both minority-language and majority-language learners in these programmes do as well as or better than peers schooled only in English on standardised tests of achievement in-cluding in English (Lindholm-Leary 2001; see Genesee and Lindholm-Leary 2013, Thomas and Collier 2012, for reviews). Interestingly, however, research on the academic outcomes of minority-language learners, or English learn-ers (ELs), in TWI, TBE and DBE programmes in comparison to structured English immersion (SEI) programmes has been rather inconclusive, in part because of the measures used, the short-term nature of studies and challenges with data sets provided by states such as California (American Institutes for Research 2006). Even meta-analyses have yielded different conclusions be-cause of the different study inclusion criteria they adopt. However, a very recent study provides a quasi-experimental analysis of the relationship be-tween instructional programme type and EL students' longitudinal academic outcomes in English Language Arts and Maths in California. Valentino and Reardon (2014) found that at the Grade 2 level, TWI ELs score significantly lower than their EL counterparts attending TBE, DBE and SEI programmes; however, in the long-term (by Grade 7), they score 'substantially above their peers in other programmes' in English Language Arts and Maths (Valentino and Reardon 2014). Valentino and Reardon (2014) conclude that:

> … provided our longer-term findings, these short-term results highlight the po-tential problems with relying on short-term outcomes (as much of the existing research does) to determine program effectiveness. (Valentino and Reardon 2014)

Lindholm-Leary and Genesee (2010) have reported similar results. When it comes to language proficiency, minority-language students have been found to achieve much higher levels of bilingualism than majority-language stu-dents in TWI programmes, who tend to develop 'functional' proficiency in the minority language that can be characterised as grammatically inaccurate and lexically limited (e.g. Lindholm-Leary 2001; Potowski 2007). At the same time, even heritage minority-language learners often develop grammatical inaccuracies in the minority language (Potowski 2007; Tedick and Young 2014), and students at secondary levels report that they do not have sufficient opportunity in school or support to develop higher levels of language proficiency (de Jong and Bearse 2011).

A number of forces and mechanisms foster the continued growth of the TWI model. These programmes are driven by the belief that bilingualism for all is positive and will benefit the country. They are also influenced by beliefs that peer models of the languages will lead to better language learning and more positive intergroup relationships between the two linguistic groups (de Jong and Howard 2009). They also serve to allay frequent criticisms about the segregation of minority-language students in other forms of bilingual education (Christian 2011). A myriad of mechanisms support the establishment and implementation of TWI programmes, such as significant and robust research findings, as well as state and national organisations like CAL (www. cal.org/twi/index.htm), Dual Language of New Mexico (www.dlenm.org), the Association of Two-Way and Dual Language Education (www.atdle.org), the CARLA Immersion Projects (www.carla.umn.edu/immersion/index. html), and the National Dual Language Consortium (www.dual-language. org). Like TBE and DBE, TWI programmes also benefit from federal funding mechanisms.

BILINGUAL/IMMERSION EDUCATION FOR INDIGENOUS-LANGUAGE STUDENTS

Historical context:

It is beyond the scope of this chapter to discuss the discriminatory policies and practices that US Indigenous communities have faced over the centuries. Of the possibly more than 2000 native languages spoken historically in what is today North America, approximately 139 remain in use and all are endangered. Among US states, Hawaii was the first to establish state-level Indigenous language and culture revitalisation efforts.

In the late 1970s, William ('Pila') Wilson and his wife Kauanoe Kamanā had been hired at the University of Hawaii-Hilo to establish a Bachelor of Arts degree in Hawaiian Studies. They sought to create a programme that would be delivered, in part, through the medium of Hawaiian. Upon the birth of their first child in 1981, they also decided to become a 'Hawaiian-medium family' (Wilson and Kamanā 2001). Wilson's and Kamanā's personal investment in the future of the Hawaiian language and their fear that Hawaiian would be lost were potent forces that propelled them to work with others to build a strong future for Hawaiian-medium education in Hawaii.

In 1983, following the lead of New Zealand's Kōhanga Reo ('language nest' in Māori), Wilson and colleagues established the 'Aha Pūnana Leo ('language nest gathering'), a pre-school focused on developing Hawaiian native speakers, which was populated initially by children being raised in Hawaiian by L2 speakers, namely those leading the movement. In this case, as would later be repeated in other cases, parental commitment was such a powerful force that parents themselves, rather than educators or school systems, began offering pre-school programmes. Later in 1983 the parents received approval from Hawaii's Board of Education to allow Hawaiian-medium education on Niʻihau, an isolated, privately owned island where a small number (100+) of Hawaiian native speakers resided. A three-year battle was required to repeal a ban in place since the early 1900s on teaching through the medium of Hawaiian. New legislation was a mechanism for furthering the movement – the 'Aha Pūnana Leo was legal and plans ensued to open more sites. Yet the needs of their children for continued Hawaiian-medium education after pre-school were initially ignored. Wilson and colleagues then established a 'boycott kindergarten', which they called Ke Kula Kaiapuni Hawaiʻi ('The Hawaiian Surrounding Environment School'), so that their children could attend Hawaiian-medium primary education. Wilson and Kamanā (2001, 150) wrote: 'We were prepared to be arrested for our children's non-attendance at a public or private school if public Hawaiian-medium education was not provided for our children.' In the summer of 1987, the Board of Education approved their action and named the programme the Hawaiian Language Immersion Programme. Other sites were soon established.

Today, Hawaii boasts 20 immersion programmes serving Grades K–12, six of which are charter schools (Hawaiian Department of Education 2014). As a counterweight to the status and ubiquitous nature of English in the community, in one school, Ke Kula ʻO Nāwahīokalaniʻōpuʻu (Nāwahī), the entire K–12 programme is offered through Hawaiian, with the exception of English language classes beginning in Grade 5. Nāwahī's student population is considered to be 'at-risk' with 70% receiving free or reduced price lunches. Nevertheless, since 1999, the school has maintained 100% graduation and 80% college attendance rates (Wilson and Kamanā 2011), much higher than those reported for Native Hawaiians in public schools.

Hawaiian-medium education also continues at the post-secondary level, with, for example, a bachelor's degree in Hawaiian Studies, a post-baccalaureate certificate in Indigenous teacher education, and a PhD in Hawaiian and Indigenous Language and Culture Revitalisation at the University of Hawaii-Hilo. In just 31 years, what Wilson, Kamanā and colleagues have accomplished is nothing short of remarkable. Additional legislation has established Hawaiian (along with English) as an official state language; Hawaiian television and radio stations have been developed; and, most importantly, many more families are using Hawaiian for daily communication within their families, schools and communities. Hawaiian remains endangered, but significant strides have been made in its revitalisation.

Bilingual/immersion programmes for Indigenous minorities

Hawaiian revitalisation efforts have prompted other Indigenous-language communities in the US to use immersion education as a vehicle to revive their native languages. The exact number of Indigenous-language immersion (ILI) programmes nationwide and the exact number of Indigenous languages being revitalised through immersion are unknown. In addition to Hawaiian, CAL's directory for OWI programmes reports ILI programmes in seven other Indigenous languages – Diné (Navajo), Chinook, Dakota, Inupiaq, Ojibwe, Salish and Yup'ik. But, based as it is on self-reports, the directory is incomplete; programmes also exist in Cherokee, for example. Currently Navajo is the only language for which TWI programmes are officially offered – two exist in the state of Arizona.

ILI programmes differ from immersion programmes in modern languages in a number of significant ways. Because their priority is language and culture survival, they are strictly Indigenous-language medium and often withhold the introduction of English in the curriculum until later (Grades 3–5). They emphasise traditional cultural values and practices within the curriculum. They also experience tensions not experienced by programmes focused on modern languages. For example, there is tension between the requirement that ILI programmes administer standardised achievement tests in English and the Indigenous perspective that assessment should represent the Indigenous language and traditional cultural values and practises that permeate the ILI curriculum (Wilson and Kamanā 2011). To date, in comparison to Hawaiian, no other Indigenous-language community in the US has built such an extensive programme covering all levels of the education system; in fact some ILI programmes do not continue beyond pre-school or the primary grades.

CONCLUSION AND CALL FOR A NEW PARADIGM

This chapter began with the story of LILA, which illustrated many of the forces, mechanisms and counterweights underlying bilingual education initiatives that have been further examined throughout this chapter. The complete list is summarised in the table at the end of the chapter. Key here are a number of paradoxes arising from diametrically opposed forces that have a major impact on bilingual education in the US. In particular, in this era of globalisation, a belief in the value of bilingualism is leading to unparalleled growth in immersion programmes for all students – majority-language, minority-language, and Indigenous-language – in some states and communities, while the persistence of a monolingual view of American identity and fear of immigration are contributing to anti-bilingual education agendas in other states. The growth in immersion programmes, the positive media attention surrounding them (e.g. Eaton 2014; Maxwell 2012; Mellon 2014), and recent discussions regarding the repeal of anti-bilingual legislation (e.g. Morrison 2014), perhaps signal that there is hope on the horizon and that the nation may be, broadly speaking, on the verge of a shift towards embracing bi/multilingualism for all.

To give impetus to such a shift, a new paradigm is needed. It is imperative that scholars and educators channel their beliefs and aspirations regarding bilingual education in a united and systematic manner through jointly created mechanisms to advocate for bilingualism for all. All too often forces (e.g. passions and commitments) arise distinctly and therefore align separately with each group – minority-language students, majority-language students and Indigenous-language students. These different 'camps' reflect the fact that bilingual/immersion education programmes have emerged in very different ways and for very different reasons for the three groups, as evidenced in the historical account presented earlier. The divide among these three 'camps' is reinforced by federal funding streams that serve each community separately, and by other distinct mechanisms that support immersion education for the three student groups, such as different professional organisations and conferences, and legislative initiatives (both pro- and anti-bilingual education).

Yet, as the US continues to diversify linguistically and culturally, the distinctions among the three groups and the programmes that serve them are becoming less clear. Spanish-speaking children are enrolling in Spanish OWI programmes designed for native English speakers; children without Hawaiian ancestry are attending Hawaiian immersion schools; a greater number of 'third language' students (whose home language is neither English nor the minority language of the programme) are populating immersion programmes; some TWI programmes are having difficulty enrolling at least one-third English speakers (the recommended minimum guideline for TWI being at least one-third of each linguistic group); and all programme types are serving more 'at-risk' youth – socioeconomically disadvantaged, ethnic minority and special needs students (Fortune and Tedick 2008). Given the range of linguistically and culturally diverse students enrolled in many immersion programmes, there are benefits to joining together as professional colleagues. Ultimately, there is much to be gained from coming together with a unified voice in support of bilingual and immersion education, as opposed to just working in separate 'camps' and pursuing isolated advocacy efforts.

There are also benefits from joining forces to tackle the persistent challenges that are common across all types of immersion programmes in the US. This could be accomplished by jointly building some of the following mechanisms: (1) effective immersion teacher preparation and professional development programmes; (2) incentives to draw more highly qualified people into immersion teaching; (3) strong secondary programmes and higher education bilingual continuation programme options; (4) pedagogical guidelines to support teachers in helping students develop strong enough levels of proficiency to handle the literacy and other cognitive demands in higher grades (especially with the proliferation of 50:50 models); (5) valid and reliable assessment instruments that can be used to communicate language development targets to students and teachers, track language development, compare programme models and establish grade-level benchmarks to guide programme development; (6) well-developed curricula and classroom-based assessments that integrate language, subject matter and culture, and that make visible specific targets, including assessment criteria, and provide students and teachers with strategies for achieving those targets; (7) well-funded research efforts to address the myriad questions facing the field,[8] and (8) centralised support at the federal level to foster the expansion of immersion and other bilingual programming into the future.

As the number of US immersion programmes grows, as research continues to demonstrate the positive impact of bilingual schooling for all learners, and as the need for language skills increases in an ever-more complicated and integrated world, the US just may be on the threshold of significant change regarding bilingual education. Synergy created through the concerted and co-ordinated efforts of scholars, educators, parents, community representatives and other stakeholders could be a force for change. Our challenge is to find ways of uniting to build that synergy, and to find the right mechanisms to allow us together to tap into the forces and other resources that will help deliver on the promise of bi/multilingual education.

ACKNOWLEDGEMENTS

Sincere thanks to Peeter Mehisto, Donna Christian, Fred Genesee and an anonymous Cambridge reviewer for helpful suggestions and insightful comments on earlier drafts of this chapter.

NOTES

1 Shannon Peterson is assistant director of Lakes International Language Academy (LILA). I am indebted to her for telling the LILA story and for her meticulous review thereof.

2 Charter schools operate independently while receiving public funding. There are over 5,000 such schools across the US (www.charterschoolcenter.org).

3 The Minnesota Department of Education (MDE) sponsored approximately 10 schools within a one or two-year period. In 2011, however, they gave each of the schools they authorised one year to find new sponsors.

4 MAIN (www.mnimmersion.org) is now a non-profit member-supported organisation that advocates for immersion programmes in the state, provides annual professional development for immersion teachers, maintains a list of the state's 90+ immersion programmes and posts job openings.

5 CARLA (www.carla.umn.edu) is one of 15 National Language Resource Centers that are funded by US Department of Education Title VI.

6 The link to CAL's Directory of Foreign Language Immersion programmes is: webapp. cal.org/Immersion/.

7 The link to CAL's Directory of TWI programmes is: www.cal.org/twi/directory/.

8 Readers are encouraged to review the Fall 2014 special issue of the *Journal of Immersion and Content-Based Language Education,* an international compilation of articles titled 'Language Immersion Education: A Research Agenda for 2015 and Beyond'.

REFERENCES

American Institutes for Research (AIR). (2006). *Effects of the Implementation of Proposition 227 on the Education of English Learners, K–12.* Washington, DC: Author. Retrieved from www.air.org/resource/effects-implementation-proposition-227-education-english-learners-k-12.

Baker, C. and Jones, S. P. (1998). *Encyclopedia of Bilingualism and Bilingual Education.* Clevedon: Multilingual Matters.

Calderón, M. and Minaya-Rowe, L. (2003). *Designing and Implementing Two-Way Bilingual Programs: A Step by Step Guide for Administrators, Teachers, and Parents.* Thousand Oaks, CA: Corwin Press.

Campbell, R. N. (1984). 'The Immersion Education Approach to Foreign Language Teaching'. In *Studies on Immersion Education: A Collection for United States Educators.* Sacramento, CA: California State Department of Education.

Christian, D. (2011). 'Dual Language Education'. In E. Hinkel (ed.), *Handbook of Research in Second Language Teaching and Learning*, II. NY: Routledge, 3–20.

Crawford, J. (2004). *Educating English Learners: Language Diversity in the Classroom*. Los Angeles: Bilingual Education Services, Inc.

de Jong, E. and Bearse, C. (2011). 'The Same Outcomes for All? High-School Students Reflect on Their Two-Way Immersion Program Experiences'. In D. J. Tedick, D. Christian, and T. W. Fortune (eds), *Immersion Education: Practices, Policies, Possibilities*. Bristol: Multilingual Matters, 104–22.

de Jong, E. and Howard, E. (2009). 'Integration in Two-Way Immersion Education: Equalising Linguistic Benefits for All Students'. *International Journal of Bilingual Education and Bilingualism*, 12: 1, 81–99.

Downs-Reid, D. (2000). 'Using English Achievement Data to Promote Immersion Education'. *The ACIE Newsletter*, 3: 2, Bridge insert, 1–4.

Eaton, S. (2014, March). *Utah's Bilingual Boon: A Red State Embraces Linguistic Diversity*. Retrieved from www.onenationindivisible.org/our-story/utah.

Essama. L. (2007). 'Total Immersion Programs: Assessment Data Demonstrate Achievement in Reading and Math'. *The ACIE Newsletter*, 11: 1, Bridge insert, 1–8.

Fortune, T. and Tedick, D. (2008). 'One-Way, Two-Way and Indigenous Immersion: A Call for Cross-Fertilization'. In T. Fortune and D. Tedick (eds), *Pathways to Multilingualism: Evolving Perspectives on Immersion Education*. Clevedon: Multilingual Matters, 3–21.

Genesee, F. (2004). 'What Do We Know About Bilingual Education for Majority Language Students?' In T. K. Bhatia and W. Ritchie (eds), *Handbook of Bilingualism and Multilingualism*. Malden, MA: Blackwell, 543–76.

Genesee, F. and Lindholm-Leary, K. (2013). 'Two Case Studies of Content-Based Language Education'. *Journal of Immersion and Content-Based Language Education*, 1:1, 3–33.

Gersten, R. (1985). 'Structured Immersion for Language Minority Students: Results of a Longitudinal Evaluation'. *Educational Evaluation and Policy Analysis*, 7, 187–96.

Hawaiian Department of Education. (2014). *Hawaiian Language Immersion Schools*. Retrieved from www.hawaiipublicschools.org/TeachingAndLearning/StudentLearning/HawaiianEducation/Pages/Hawaiian-language-immersion-schools.aspx.

Howard, E. R., Olague, N. and Rogers, D. (2003). *The Dual Language Program Planner: A Guide for Designing and Implementing Dual Language Programs*. Santa Cruz, CA and Washington, DC: Center for Research on Education, Diversity and Excellence.

Jackson, F. H. and Malone, M. E. (2009). *Building the Foreign Language Capacity We Need: Toward a Comprehensive Strategy for a National Language Framework*. College Park, Maryland: National Foreign Language Center. Retrieved from www.cal.org/resources/languageframework.pdf.

Krashen, S. (2000). 'Bilingual Education, the Acquisition of English, and the Retention and Loss of Spanish'. In A. Roca (ed.), *Research on Spanish in the US: Linguistic Issues and Challenges*. Somerville, MA: Cascadilla Press. Retrieved from www.languagepolicy.net/archives/Krashen7.htm.

Lambert, W. E. (1984). 'An Overview of Issues in Immersion Education'. In R. Campbell (ed.), *Studies on Immersion Education: A Collection for United States Educators*. Sacramento, CA: California State Department of Education, 8–30.

Lindholm-Leary, K. (2001). *Dual Language Education*. Clevedon: Multilingual Matters.

Lindholm-Leary, K. and Genesee, F. (2010). 'Alternative Educational Programs for English Language Learners'. In California Department of Education (eds), *Improving Education for English Learners: Research-Based Approaches*. Sacramento: CDE Press. 323–82.

Lyster, R. (2007). *Learning and Teaching Languages Through Content: A Counterbalanced Approach*. Amsterdam: John Benjamins.

Maxwell, L. A. (2012). 'Momentum Builds for Dual Language Learning'. *Education Week*, 21: 26, 1, 16–17.

May, S. (2012). *Language and Minority Rights: Ethnicity, Nationalism and the Politics of Language* (2nd ed). NY: Routledge.

Mellon, E. (2014, 31 March). 'Dual-Language Programs in Schools Gain Following'. *Houston Chronicle*. Retrieved from www.chron.com/news/texas/article/Dual-language-programs-in-schools-gain-following-5364025.php.

Morrison, P. (2014, 28 February). 'Should California Reinstate Bilingual Education?' *Los Angeles Times*. Retrieved from www.latimes.com/opinion/opinion-la/la-ol-california-reinstate-bilingual-education-proposition-227-20140228,0,6600482.story#ixzz2uf2ONLVN.

Ovando, C. (2003). 'Bilingual Education in the United States: Historical Development and Current Issues'. *Bilingual Research Journal*, 27: 1, 1–24. DOI: 10.1080/15235882.2003.10162589.

Potowski, K. (2007). *Language and Identity in a Dual Immersion School*. Clevedon: Multilingual Matters.

Pufahl, I. and Rhodes, N. C. (2011). 'Foreign Language Instruction in US Schools: Results of a National Survey of Elementary and Secondary Schools'. *Foreign Language Annals*, 44: 2, 258–88.

Rossell, C. and Baker, K. (1996). 'The Educational Effectiveness of Bilingual Education'. *Research in the Teaching of English*, 30, 7–74.

Tedick, D. J. and Young, A. I. (2014). 'Fifth Grade Two-Way Immersion Students' Responses to Form-Focused Instruction'. *Applied Linguistics*. DOI: 10.1093/applin/amu066

Thomas, W. P. and Collier, V. P. (2012). *Dual Language Education for a Transformed World*. Albuquerque, NM: Dual Language of New Mexico and Fuente Press.

Valentino, R. A. and Reardon, S. F. (2014). *Effectiveness of Four Instructional Programs Designed to Serve English Language Learners: Variation by Ethnicity and Initial English Proficiency*. Stanford, CA: Stanford University Center for Education Policy Analysis. Retrieved from www.cepa.stanford.edu/content/effectiveness-four-instructional-programs-designed-serve-english-language-learners.

Wilson, W. H. and Kamanā, K. (2001). '"Mai loko mai o ka ʻiʻini: Proceeding from a Dream." The Aha Pūnana Leo Connection in Hawaiian Language Revitalization'. In L. Hinton and K. Hale (eds), *The Green Book of Language Revitalization in Practice*. San Diego, CA: Academic Press, 147–76.

Wilson, W. H. and Kamanā, K. (2011). 'Insights from Indigenous Language Immersion in Hawaii'. In D. J. Tedick, D. Christian, and T. W. Fortune (eds), *Immersion Education: Practices, Policies, Possibilities*. Bristol: Multilingual Matters, 36–57.

FORCES	MECHANISMS
Key values in human relations	**People**
Trust	Committed parents
Respect	Networks (e.g. MAIN)
Competitiveness	Local expertise/expert consultants
Goals	**Structures**
Commitment to a vision that guides programme development	CARLA Immersion Projects
Americanisation	CAL
Indigenous-language revitalisation	NCSSFL
	Dual Language of New Mexico
	Association of Two-Way and Dual Language Education
Beliefs and attitudes	National Dual Language Consortium
	Media
Belief in immersion/bilingual education	
Belief in the power of bilingualism and its importance for children	**Laws and lawsuits (selected examples)**
Importance of Chinese in global economy	The Nationality Act (1906)
permissive attitude towards languages	The National Defense Education Act (1958)
Fear (of negative impact on English language acquisition, teacher job losses, of falling behind Russia)	The Civil Rights Act (1964)
Desire to belong to majority group	Lau v. Nichols (1974)
Xenophobia (ethnolinguistic minorities seen as 'foreigners')	Anti-bilingual education legislation
	Multiple legislative initiatives in Hawaii
Belief that bilingual education is ineffective	**Events**
Barriers	First World War (US involvement 1917–1918)
	Sputnik 1957
Ignorance	Civil Rights Movement
Tensions between western standards and Indigenous-language revitalisation efforts	French immersion – St. Lambert, Canada
	The Utah Model
Emotions	**Vehicles**
Fear	Grassroots initiatives
Anti-immigrant sentiments	Charter schools
Anti-German sentiments	Amity Institute
Fear that endangered Indigenous languages would be lost	Parent/teacher organisations
	Local fund-raising efforts
Contexts	Research findings
	Federal grants
Ethnic homogeneity (19th century)	Parent language classes
Competition for students between public and private schools	Summer language camps

COUNTERWEIGHTS

Fear	Information and public meetings
Negative forces, obstacles	Tenacity, stamina of parents
English-only movement	English Plus movement
Anti-immigrant sentiments	Belief in importance of bilingualism
Status of English in Hawaii	Establishment of pre-K-12 programme almost entirely in Hawaiian

2   EUROPE:
Supra-national Interventions Promoting Bilingual Education

Hugo Baetens Beardsmore (Vrije Universiteit Brussel, Université Libre de Bruxelles)

CHAPTER NAVIGATOR

A real-life example	→	Introduction	→	The Council of Europe	→	The European Commission

The world level	→	Conclusion	→	Tabular summary		

A REAL-LIFE EXAMPLE

In Belgium, one of the 28 member states of the European Union, bilingual education in any form was long considered taboo because in the past it had led to massive language shift from Dutch to French, particularly in the bilingual capital of Brussels. Political opposition to bilingual education was strongly entrenched, despite the fact that surveys consistently revealed that approximately 70% of respondents were in favour of its introduction, irrespective of whether they came from the Flemish north, the French-speaking south or the bilingual capital. To break through the legal impediment to any form of bilingual education, a photogenic and dynamic *comtesse* who had connections with politicians, the captains of industry, journalists, union leaders, influential public figures and academics, founded a movement in 1989 called 'Prolingua' to lobby for immersion-type education in kindergarten and primary schools. Her tactic was to organise public debates where people such as the heads of the major banks and industries, famous sporting figures, a popular Belgian cosmonaut, the leader of the largest teaching union and the odd academic would promote bilingual education and respond to queries. Media reaction was consistently positive and often headlined under photos of the campaigning *comtesse*. After persistent and steady lobbying, legal obstacles to bilingual education were finally removed and there are now more than 250 schools offering different bilingual programmes in French-speaking Belgium, while in Flemish Belgium, where political resistance was much stronger, a limited number of bilingual secondary programmes started in 2014. The *comtesse* had achieved what many academics who had long argued for such programmes never managed to achieve.

INTRODUCTION

Bilingual education has been strongly promoted by European supra-national institutions as a fundamental part of harmonising European integration, based on the principle of 'unity with diversity' as a core ideology. This chapter concentrates on interventions at the supra-national level in the area of bilingual education and does not cover other areas of language policy that may fall under the purview of European institutions. Given that to date there are 24 official working languages covering the 28 member states of the European Union and approximately 60 Indigenous regional or minority languages (*cf.* European Bureau for Lesser-Used Languages), excluding the numerous immigrant languages highly prevalent across the continent, some form of language in education planning is needed in the construction of this highly disparate political entity.

As there are no models on which to base the harmonisation of such a complex linguistic landscape, interventions within the field of language education policy are the result of pragmatic experimentation, ongoing evaluation and the stimulation of good practice, as well as an appreciation of politico-linguistic sensitivities. This all leads to relatively discrete leadership grounded in synthesising best practice and proposing 'models' rather than by supra-national directives or other top-down interventions.

Two supra-national institutions play a role in language education policy debates in Europe: The Council of Europe, based in Strasbourg, which has an officially recognised language policy division, and the European Commission, based in Brussels, which has no official language policy mandate but has Commissioners for Education, Culture, and Youth (as well as for Multilingualism until November 2014) and can intervene in educational matters through its other mandates, for example regional development. Unlike legal or economic affairs, the European Commission cannot impose language or education policy on member states. The same is true for the Council of

Europe. Interventions by these two supra-national institutions are fuelled by 'forces' as defined in the introduction to this volume, such as valuing pluri-lingualism, that are channelled into the development of language education policy (a 'mechanism', as described in Mehisto, Introduction). The additional mechanisms created as a result of this policy often operate indirectly.

THE COUNCIL OF EUROPE

This supra-national organisation, founded in 1949, unites 47 member states with an official mandate to promote human rights, democratic development, the rule of law and cultural co-operation. This mandate has resulted in a unit specifically designed to promote language rights and linguistic aspects of cultural co-operation through the promotion of language learning. Over the years, it has gained considerable influence in defining pan-European cri-teria for promoting language learning and language assessment. The most well-known mechanism is the Common European Framework of Reference for Languages (CEFR), based in part on sets of teaching and learning cri-teria for different levels of achievement, such as the *Threshold Level*, (van Ek and Trim 1998), with equivalent versions in different languages. This chapter will not address the policies produced under the auspices of the Council of Europe since they are generally well known, are aimed more towards foreign language learning and are only indirectly connected with bilingual educa-tion. This section will instead focus on those mechanisms such as charters and policies that have an impact on bilingual education.

The *European Charter for Regional or Minority Languages* (Council of Europe 1992) plays a significant role in fostering bilingual education, among other areas of language policy, in that it encourages governments that have ratified the Charter to guarantee a minimum provision of language contact, if not bilingual education, in order to support the survival and development of a given regional or (Indigenous) minority language. This document em-bodies potential forces, such as respect for minority languages, fairness and justice, and represents a clear mechanism in that, once ratified, it has a legal status that can support (or restrict) access to some form of bilingual educa-tion. This is in addition to other fields that deal with language rights, such as judicial services, media provision. The European Charter (a mechanism) consists of a series of articles that are divided into sub-sections in which a set of alternative dispositions is presented that allows signatories to provide a range of services, from minimal to maximum provision; at least one third of all the articles in each sub-section must be selected for ratification. If the Charter has been ratified, lack of adherence to the articles that have been accepted can lead to the government authorities in question being called to task by the Council of Europe and requested to implement the clauses they have ratified but not implemented. For example, the British government has ratified the Charter and thereby recognises the obligation to provide minimal support for schooling through the medium of Cornish, Manx, Gaelic, Irish and Welsh, if requested, alongside teaching in English. Since education in the United Kingdom is not centralised, the Welsh and Scottish regional assemblies provide ample support and innovative incentives to encourage the acquisition of either Welsh or Gaelic through different forms of bilingual education. They have put a number of mechanisms in place to ensure provision and monitoring of outcomes. However, support for Cornish and Manx language education has been less successfully promoted, and this has led the Council of Europe to intervene. This interventionist stance, based on legal arguments, could be considered a 'counterweight' (see Mehisto, Introduction) in cases where the obligation for minimal bilingual provision is not being provided.

It may seem strange that certain countries with a long history of Indigenous linguistic minorities, or even a bilingual status, have refused to ratify the Charter, whereas others that have long considered themselves monolingual have done so without hesitation. This refusal can be seen as a negative force rooted in fear or distrust that impedes the development of even minimal provision of bilingual education. Belgium has refused to entertain the idea of ratifying the Charter, in spite of its reputation for linguistic tensions, under the claim that the three language communities in the country have satisfactory mechanisms for providing monolingual education in their respective regions, that the German linguistic minority in eastern Belgium, comprising 1% of the population, has probably the most generous linguistic autonomy in the world, and that knowledge of a second and third language is amply present among all sections of the population. Hence, it is claimed (and contested) that there is no need for special bilingual provisions to protect an Indigenous linguistic minority. Bilingual education is present in different regions of Belgium, but in Flanders is severely restricted in scope, primarily due to fear that it incites French-speaking recipients not to learn the language of the region or to integrate linguistically.

Ireland has resisted ratifying the Charter on similar grounds, claiming that as the Irish language is the official national language, with English as a second official language, there is no need to apply the Council of Europe's recommendations. However, although the small native Irish-speaking community in the *Gaeltacht*, or Irish-speaking homeland, receives bilingual education, the vast majority of English-speaking students only receive Irish as a compulsory language subject and, as a result, do not achieve bilingual fluency (Council of Europe 2005–2007).

France is a further example of a country with historical Indigenous minorities (speaking languages such as Breton, Creole, Dutch, Occitan or Provençal) that has not ratified the Charter. This is because an article in its constitution clearly states that 'French is the language of the Republic', thereby excluding all official provision of bilingual education through the medium of a regional language and French (Offord 1996). Alsace-Lorraine has a special status within France whereby the provision of bilingual education in Alsatian/German and French is possible, due to the chequered history of the region which saw the territory oscillate over the centuries between Germany and France. At the time of going to press, the French parliament is again attempting to overcome the barriers to ratifying the Charter that would require some way of either changing the constitution or circumventing it.

These examples illustrate how a political and a moral force, as embedded in the *European Charter for Regional or Minority Languages,* can be thwarted by the counterweight of constitutional restrictions and political ill will.

An illustration of how the Council of Europe operates once the *European Charter for Regional or Minority Languages* has been ratified can be found in a review process for a country from central Europe with a large Roma minority whose linguistic educational rights have not been respected. During a hearing with the Language Policy Division of the Council of Europe on 5 October 2005, a committee of legal experts was established to supervise the implementation of those items from the Charter to which the country in question had subscribed. Three independent specialists were invited to provide information on the specificity of the Roma language and the nature of bilingual education in general. This operation could be considered one of the mechanisms designed as a counterweight to a neglected force. Particular attention was paid to the implementation of Article 8 which states that: (a) education should be made available *in* the relevant regional or minority language; (b) *a substantial part* of education should be made available in the regional or minority language, and (c) these require the teaching of the language as an *integral part* of education. Advice was requested on the difficulties involved in providing education in Roma, given that there is: (a) a severe lack of trained teachers in the language and the culture; (b) a severe lack of teacher training possibilities; (c) a severe lack of appropriate teaching materials; (d) a very high dropout rate amongst Roma pupils, and (d) segregation and discrimination in some schools, as well as the lack of a standardised language with many dialectal varieties. Hence the provision of some form of bilingual education for these populations is not merely a question of political will (i.e. of a force), but is also dependent on mechanisms, or basic tools such as implementation strategies and learning resources within the linguistic community in question, in order to counteract centuries of neglect and stigmatisation of the language and population concerned.

Another supra-national role in language education in general, including bilingual education provision offered by the Council of Europe (Council of Europe 2003), is reflected in the *Language Education Policy* profiles it produces at the request of individual states or regions on their provision of language education within the territory concerned. The official website of the Council of Europe (www.coe.int/lang) can be consulted for reports produced to date.[1] Not all regions have requested the Council of Europe's help in producing a policy profile specifically on bilingual education, but those that implement one serve as interesting examples of how forces, mechanisms and counterweights can operate.

The Council of Europe's *Guide for the Development of Language Education Policies in Europe* illustrates a mechanism intended to help evaluate and realign educational policy with respect to languages in different countries, regions or cities in Europe. The *Guide* is intended to provide the

> ... basis of a coherent approach: clarifying principles and defining goals, analysing situations, identifying resources, expectations and needs, and the implementation and evaluation of these measures. (Council of Europe 2007)

This document offers guidance for drawing up an individual policy profile to be produced by the country or region in question, together with a small team of foreign experts, accompanied by a member of the staff from the language policy division of the Council of Europe. The Council of Europe team visits the country or region for a week after receiving a series of reports drawn up by different stakeholders involved in language education issues. During the week's visit, the team receives a briefing by: representatives of those who contributed to the policy profile, other stakeholders such as representatives of examination boards, teachers' unions, cultural institutions, universities, chambers of commerce and political representatives. The team also usually visits a few schools. The team then draws up a collective report and makes recommendations, which are in turn presented to those involved in producing the report, together with other stakeholders, at a meeting a few months later. This step represents a counterweight and is intended to enable the people from the country concerned to provide corrections to, or criticism of, the report. The final report is then delivered to the country, region or city that requested intervention by the Council of Europe for it to apply any action it deems appropriate. In certain cases the report is acted upon by the responsible authorities; in other cases, it may be used for fine-tuning certain aspects of language education policy, or it may be completely ignored.

How the Council of Europe's guidelines for the development of language education policies are put into practice is to be found in the Country Report for Luxembourg (Conseil de l'Europe and Le Gouvernement du Grand Duché de Luxemburg 2005–6). This particular report is a rare case of an appraisal of a trilingual education system that has been in place for an entire school population since its implementation in 1913. It examines the political dimension of language-policy questions within the Grand Duchy of Luxembourg, the social and economic role of trilingualism, and the obvious role of the national language (Luxembourgish), that is, the forces that lie behind the provision of a trilingual programme. An appraisal is given of the strengths and weaknesses of language education in the Grand Duchy, including an examination of timetables, the role of languages as a vehicle for teaching non-language disciplines, and major successes, along with the influence of language as a factor in under-performance at school. The report highlights both the mechanisms and counterweights in operation in the country, illustrating the fact that trilingualism is an ambitious but ill-defined objective, that the teaching profession in the country has many strong assets but that there is poor coordination between language teaching and content-matter teaching, and that many initiatives are taken, but they have little influence on the education system. The report ends with suggestions for improvements in the specific trilingual model of education in operation, both on the management level and on research requirements.

As a result of the policy profile, the Luxembourg authorities produced a follow-up action plan (Berg and Weis 2007). This represented the reaction of the Luxembourg government to the policy profile and included an adaptation of its language teaching programmes in light of the notion that 'plurilingualism is the real mother-tongue of Luxembourg citizens'. The plans included four domains: communication, curriculum, practice and reflection. Under 'communication', the plan calls for improved communication from the ministry to teachers, between teachers and with parents. The curriculum section deals with the competences, the CEFR, the role of language learning in non-linguistic subjects, the levers for action, bilingual materials, and implications for evaluation. The 'practice' section refers to projects in favour of particular languages, including the Luxembourgish national language, Portuguese as the language of the largest number of immigrants to the country, actions in favour of English and Latin, access to written language skills and projects to stimulate inter-disciplinarity, among others. The final section provides a reflection on general matters to render the system coherent. In brief, this action plan serves as a counterweight to current challenges insofar as it is designed to guide improvements in the trilingual education system in the country.

Another concrete example of a supra-national mechanism that served to adjust plurilingual education is the *Language Education Policy Profile* produced for the Val d'Aosta Region of Italy (Conseil de l'Europe 2007), where the specific programme followed by all schools was accompanied by extensive research. The education system in operation in the Val d'Aosta devotes equal time in all schools to learning Italian and French, with certain subjects approved by the authorities taught through the medium of French. The central authority in Rome has also imposed English lessons throughout the country, including the Val d'Aosta region, from the age of five onwards.

It is left to individual schools to decide how they organise the distribution of the languages, depending on the specificities of their local environment, where Franco-Provençal or a German dialect may also be present. Aspects of both the language and culture conveyed through Franco-Provençal, the German dialects and standard German are also introduced into different levels of the education system, thereby expanding appreciation for the multilingual nature of the region. In primary school, teachers are encouraged to ensure that the dialects, traditions and customs of their regions are not perceived as inadequate and in contradiction with the development of bilingualism in school. Teachers are trained to be aware of the individual and social dimensions of bilingualism and not to apply monolingual norms and ideologies in their teaching. Each school and each teacher is free to adapt the activities and language distribution based on their experience and perceived needs.

Hence the precise mechanisms and strategies for carrying out the avowed multilingual goal is left to the appreciation of those in the local teaching community. This flexibility and the trust placed in local educators are forces that are expected to drive teaching and learning. These act as a positive counterweight to any potential problems embedded in the regional education legislation.

The introduction of English as a subject (starting with 1 hour per week in Primary 1) has proved beneficial to the acquisition of French as a second language (L2). Learners have become more aware of the closer proximity between Italian and French (since both are of Romance origin) than between Italian and English, and they have felt more confident in French as they have noted how much more competent they are in the L2 than in English as a third language (L3). For English as an L3, the goal is to achieve level A1 on the CEFR by the end of primary school. One could interpret the role of English here as a positive counterweight against concerns expressed by some members of the public about the difficulties of acquiring French.

Considerable research into the education system in the Val d'Aosta has been conducted and this research is a mechanism for strengthening confidence in the education system. The knowledge arising from the research is a force that has helped sustain the bilingual policy of the region. The research investigated the following issues:

- the amount of time allocated to each language not only in terms of hours but also in terms of types of activity – for example, teaching each language and teaching through two languages
- strategies employed to develop bilingualism
- specifications regarding the use of the language of instruction
- integration of the language curriculum as a coherent whole
- specification of outcome profiles
- types of evaluation
- measures to integrate learners from outside the region of the Val d'Aosta.

Research was conducted by teams made up of members of the (now defunct) regional centre for research into education (Institut de Recherche de l'Éducation de la Vallée d'Aoste; IRRE-VDA), in collaboration with researchers from Italy, France and Switzerland. Assuied and Ragot (1999; 2005; Cavalli 2005) used 14 tests in the two school languages applied to all nine-year olds in the fifth year of primary school in the region. The goal was to evaluate not the language component but the cognitive skills acquired through the use of parallel texts for the stronger language (Italian), and the weaker school-inculcated language (French).

The research has served as a mechanism to evaluate the imposition of a bilingual system on an entire school population and the results were a positive counterweight to some of the apprehensions held both by administrators and the general public. Interesting results were produced, depending on the language of the parallel measurements. Certain cognitive operations, such as those requiring the identification of the most significant elements in each of the parallel texts, revealed no relevant differences between the two languages. However, in the most difficult set of tests, where it proved impossible to rapidly grasp the nature of the task required – that is, those that called on the most complex set of cognitive skills – the results were better in the second language, French, than the stronger language, Italian. It would appear that in the more demanding tasks the children relied on global comprehension skills when the Italian measures were used. As a consequence they provided more superficial reactions and less precise responses. On the other hand, in the parallel tests using the weaker school language, French, the youngsters concentrated more on the details of the text and provided more precise and accurate responses to the questions (Assuied and Ragot 1999).

In general, the fact of working through L2 French has no negative effects on cognitive skills, and at times it has certain cognitive advantages. The alternation between two languages has no inhibitive effects on cognitive skills. Research findings of many sorts are discussed in the *Language Education Policy Profile*, highlighting the positive results as well as proposing remedial action to be taken where there were weaknesses

To examine the education system in the Val d'Aosta within its sociological and sociolinguistic context, research has also been carried out to measure the integration of the different languages present, the perceptions the inhabitants have of the languages for their identity and in their school system, and different aspects of teaching and learning in the complex programmes used throughout the region (Cavalli et al. 2003). If acted upon, this type of research represents a significant positive counterweight to apprehension with regard to universal bi/trilingual education.

The *Language Education Policy Profile* for the Val d'Aosta concludes with a series of recommendations to improve the plurilingual approach of the education system, a discussion of several options for doing that, and the contributions that different stakeholders might be able to offer in order to make improvements. The document also highlights a whole series of challenges to be met, including reinforcement of the regional languages or dialects, ways of improving teacher training, cross-frontier collaboration, internationalisation, harmonisation of national certification with international diplomas and many others. What this report brings to light is the many mechanisms that have been used in this particular region to reinforce the policy that distinguishes it from the rest of Italy.

Mechanisms and initiatives by the Council of Europe continue to evolve, as the Council of Europe's actions are defined by conventions that are dependent on interpretation. Moreover, the Council of Europe's priorities are set by its steering committees, which are based on requests and needs formulated by national authorities or emanate directly from the field. Projects are developed accordingly by experts and co-ordinated by the Secretariat. The Committee of Ministers draws on the results of such projects to develop language policies further through recommendations to the member states.

THE EUROPEAN COMMISSION

Since education is not part of the mandate of the European Union but falls under the principle of subsidiarity, where the member states are free to organise their education policy as they deem fit, there is no supra-national authority that can direct developments relating to the provision of bilingual education directly. The European Commission can, however, issue recommendations and provide guidelines for the promotion of bilingual education under the terms of the Barcelona Agreement of 2002.

In Barcelona, the heads of state and governments of the then 25 Member States of the European Union requested that the European Commission produce an Action Plan on education intended to help Europe '… become the most competitive and dynamic knowledge based economy in the world' by 2010 (Council of the European Union 2004). The Action Plan encourages language learning among all citizens. The overarching language policy recommendation states that:

> Each country should have a set of carefully formulated and clearly stated objectives for language teaching at the various stages of the education system, going from the stimulation of mutual respect and language awareness to acquisition of specific languages skills. The starting age for learning languages and the methodologies to be adopted should be decided in the light of these objectives. (Council of the European Union 2004)

Primary emphasis is placed on:

- the promotion of the mother tongue and two other languages for all citizens (MT + 2)
- the promotion of linguistic diversity across Europe
- the extension of different forms of bilingual education for a wide-ranging public.

In order to implement the Action Plan, a working group of experts designated by the ministries of education of the then 25 Member States, together with experts from the pre-accession and associated states, met regularly throughout 2004–5 to exchange information from their countries in five major areas:

- early language learning
- languages in secondary education
- linguistic diversity in the education system
- lifelong language learning
- the initial and in-service training of language teachers.

In early meetings, examples of good practice were exchanged, followed by the elaboration of a consensus on priority interventions. The first evaluation of progress on the implementation of the recommendations of the Action Plan took place in June 2004 by means of a questionnaire addressed to each country's ministerial representatives. In order to avoid misunderstandings about European policy, there is no attempt in any policy document to promote a single *lingua franca* to the detriment of any Indigenous European language, whatever impressionistic views, distorted interpretations or unofficial lobbies to the contrary might convey. The following quote expresses this view clearly:

> Learning one *lingua franca* alone is not enough. Every European citizen should have meaningful communicative competence in at least two other languages in addition to his or her mother tongue. This is an ambitious goal, but the progress already made by several Member States shows that this is perfectly attainable. (Commission of the European Communities 2003)

To this end, it is important that policy distinguish between *laissez faire* and *vouloir faire*, as encapsulated in the warning given by Robert Phillipson that 'it would be dangerous for Europe to allow language policy to be left to *laissez faire* market forces' (Phillipson 2003). *Laissez faire* refers to the neglect of awareness-raising on the advantages of multilingual skills, the lack of promotion of diversity in language learning and the effects of lobby-groups in favour of a single language, i.e. English. *Vouloir faire*, on the other hand, refers to the institutional willingness to promote varied languages in education, to promote efficient bilingual education, and to provide incentives to improve language teaching and language learning.

In fact, highly varied initiatives in bilingual education have been and are being implemented in the European Union. The European Union has coined two acronyms intended to clearly demarcate European models from other similar programmes elsewhere. This is a deliberate political decision since it was found, after meetings with specialists and official delegates from the Ministries of Education of the Member States, that 32 different terms were in use across Europe to designate some form of bilingual education. The term 'bilingual education' tends to be avoided at the European level, given that in certain countries it has negative connotations due to past experience with stigmatisation, language shift or inadequate outcomes. (For example, a so-called 'transmutation system', the predecessor of what was later known as 'transitional bilingual education' and 'two-way immersion programmes', was introduced in Brussels in 1881 to enable Dutch- and French-speaking children to receive reciprocal but not parallel bilingual education. The classes failed to achieve their objectives and were abandoned in 1914; Van Velthoven 1987). The term 'immersion' was not selected either, given that it was vigorously rejected by certain delegates from some countries. The term also tends to be associated with Canadian models, whereas many of the European programmes either pre-dated the immersion phenomenon or were developed independently.

Luxembourg does not define trilingual schooling under any specific language label but simply refers to 'education', even though a trilingual programme has been in place since 1913 for the entire population (Berg 1993; Davis 1994). In Bulgaria, bilingual education began in the 1960s, with five secondary schools running a Bulgarian-French bilingual programme which later grew to 53 schools, while in Poland two schools began to introduce French in content-matter subjects in 1962, and others followed (Tschumi and Zajac 2008). Interestingly, given the ideological current in Eastern Europe at the time, the bilingual programmes in these countries selected the exact sciences as content-matter subjects taught through a foreign language to avoid potential political indoctrination (Tschumi and Zajac 2008). The first German-French bilingual school in Germany was the Hegau-Gymnasium in Singen (Baden-Württemberg), founded in 1969. It originated in the Franco-German friendship treaty between General de Gaulle and Chancellor Adenauer, signed in 1963 (Müller-Schneck 2007). The Val d'Aosta region of Italy had some form of bilingual education for centuries and after 1882 both Italian and French were used in schools; this was interrupted by the Mussolini regime between 1925 and 1945 and reintroduced after the fall of fascism (Titone 1974). Similarly, the regions of Trentino-Alto Adige in Italy have offered bilingual education in German and Italian since 1919 (Egger 1978) and the *Scholae Europeae*, or European Schools, which were founded in 1953, have always taught part of the curriculum through two or more languages (Baetens Beardsmore 1993; Housen 2002; 2003; 2008; Swan 1996).

The European initiatives are grouped under the acronyms CLIL/EMILE, or Content and Language Integrated Learning (*Enseignement d'une matière intégrée à une langue étrangère*), and take on varied forms (Marsh et al. 2002). CLIL/EMILE embraces any type of programme where a second language is used to teach non-linguistic content matter including those that may be called immersion. It does not, however, cover language programmes for minority or lesser-used languages where almost the entire curriculum is delivered through these languages. This is similar to what happens in monolingual programmes, such as Welsh language schools in Wales for children where Welsh is the home language. Although non-native speaking children may be present in such schools and thereby undergo an early total immersion experience, the programme itself is not considered a CLIL/EMILE initiative. Nor would children of immigrant language backgrounds undergoing a monolingual submersion experience in a mainstream language be considered as participating in a CLIL/EMILE curriculum.

The majority, but by no means all, of CLIL/EMILE initiatives occur in secondary education as optional choices and may be based on selection via screening tests in the mother tongue and mathematics (as in Bulgaria), or extra preparatory tuition in the second target language (as in Germany). Some are compulsory for the entire school population (as in Luxembourg and the Val d'Aosta in Italy), or are voluntary at the primary level (as in the Basque country); while others are voluntary at the primary level and obligatory at the secondary level (as in Estonia's Russian-medium schools). Certain programmes operate on a modular basis, where different content-matter subjects may be offered in a second language for a maximum of two or three years (as in Germany or England), whereas others increase the curriculum load of content-matter subjects in the foreign language as the pupils progress, as in Luxembourg (Lebrun and Baetens Beardsmore 1993), and in European Schools (Baetens Beardsmore 1993). In most cases, the intention is to enable students to master specific content matter in both the L1 and L2, hence the restrictions in some countries on the amount of contact with a non-linguistic subject via the L2. In short, diverse programmes have adopted the term 'CLIL'.[2]

The ideological stance under which the European Union attempts to promote bilingual education is reflected in an official document under the cumbersome title *The Communication from the Commission to the Council, the European Parliament, the Economic and Social Committee and the Committee of the Regions of 24 July 2003 (COM (2003) 449 final) Promoting Language Learning and Linguistic Diversity: An Action Plan 2004–2006*. This document states that 'Content and Language Integrated Learning (CLIL), in which pupils learn a subject through the medium of a foreign language, has a major contribution to make to the Union's language learning goals. To support the promotion of bilingual programmes, the European Commission has implemented awareness-raising measures among the general public by producing two films for free distribution under the titles *Intertalk: Plurilingual Education Across Europe* and *CLIL for the Knowledge Society: Using Languages to Learn/ EMILE pour une sociéte de la connaissance: Apprendre par les langues*.

Other instruments produced under the auspices of the European Union, although not directly addressing bilingual education, do in fact have some effect on its provision. Comparative studies (European Commission 2012) on how well languages are known, how they are perceived and statistical information on language learning within the member states are favoured mechanisms used by the European Commission to stimulate the promotion of plurilingual skills. Statistical information on language teaching in schools across Europe is regularly produced as a form of encouragement to increase knowledge and use of languages. The most recent publication (Eurydice – Eurostat 2012) reveals that CLIL programmes are part of mainstream education in most countries, although they are not necessarily as widespread as might be desired. In fact, such publications reveal that promotion of 'best practice', or 'leadership from behind' (or even 'name and shame'), are useful techniques used by the European Commission as a counterweight to the reticence towards bilingual education in some countries.

European Commission policies, plans and other mechanisms continue to evolve. Some initiatives originate directly from the staff of the institutions (e.g. Erasmus programmes for student mobility), or from members of the European Parliament (e.g. in convening support for minority languages), while others are the result of lobbying from varied groups (e.g. the promotion of Esperanto as a *lingua franca*, an example of unsuccessful lobbying). It is estimated that there are approximately 15 000 lobbyists active in Brussels, so it is no surprise to find parties interested in language, or to note that bilingual education in Europe operates on some level in a dynamic pan-European context.

THE WORLD LEVEL

Other supra-national institutions also play an indirect role in promoting bilingual education in Europe, although less as political forces than as secondary facilitators. The United Nations Educational, Scientific and Cultural Organization (UNESCO) has often stimulated language teaching and different types of bilingual education, with particular reference to endangered languages; such initiatives often take the form of conferences or research reports (e.g. UNESCO 2003; 2010). The North Atlantic Treaty Organization (NATO) has, in the past, been known to subsidise conferences dealing with translation, interpretation and bilingualism, while the World Bank has also subsidised education programmes in developing countries that have operated on bilingual schooling models. Such interventions, however, are not part of concerted ideological forces that stimulate bilingual education but are more akin to incidental 'sponsoring' of worthy causes.

One supra-national instance that can be considered a significant indirect, yet growing, force in debates on bilingual provision is that of the importance or status accorded to PISA (Programme for International Student Assessment) scores. As of 2000, the Organisation for Economic Co-operation and Development (OECD) tests 15-year old students in OECD and partner countries every three years (OECD PISA 2012 Results). The perceived value of the hierarchical ratings of test results on literacy, mathematics and science represent a powerful force to incite countries to modify their education systems. Although the PISA scores make no statements about bilingual education, it is revealing to note that most of the countries or regions that have generalised bilingual education for all school-goers tend to score higher than the OECD average, and some significantly higher. The detailed national analyses produced by those concerned that follow the PISA results clearly show the effect these comparisons have as counterweights to apprehensions about the provision of bilingual education.

CONCLUSION

If we examine the role of the two European supra-national instances in promoting bilingual education, as briefly illustrated above under the concept of 'forces', we can see that the high status of the organisations involved accord high status to initiatives promoting bi/trilingual education. More specifically, the prestige of the Council of Europe, together with its expertise in promoting language learning, are clearly forces that support more provision of different forms of bilingual education. This is reflected in the number of *Language Education Policy* country profiles produced at the request of individual countries and regions. The legal constraints imposed on those countries that ratified the Charter for Regional and Minority Languages represent a 'mechanism' that can be used as a 'counterweight' to encourage change, at least within the framework of the constraining articles selected by the country in question.

When one looks at the mechanisms available on the European supra-national level, the picture is a mitigated one. Neither of the two bodies referred to here (the Council of Europe and the European Commission) have the political force to impose bilingual education. The *Language Education Policy* profiles reveal the different mechanisms that are applied in different countries to promote plurilingual education. The principle of subsidiarity for educational matters within individual European member states reflects some of the counterweights that can operate, depending on whether a country restricts or promotes different forms of bilingual education.

NOTES

1   To date the following countries or regions have requested the Council of Europe's intervention and their policy profiles produced are all available on the Council of Europe's website: Armenia, Austria, Cyprus, Estonia, Hungary, Ireland, Lithuania, Lombardy (Italy), Luxembourg, Norway, Poland, Sheffield (UK), the Slovak Republic, Slovenia, Ukraine and the Val d'Aosta (Italy).
2   For further information on CLIL in Europe, see Eurydice 2006.

REFERENCES

Assuied, R. and Ragot, A-M. (1999). *Évaluation des compétences cognitives des élèves en situation d'apprentissage bilingue – Classes de troisième année de l'école moyenne – Les épreuves en italien et en français et les consignes de passation, a.s. 1998–9*, Aoste: Assessorat de l'Éducation et de la Culture.

Assuied, R. and Ragot, A-M. (2005). *Enquête sur les compétences cognitives des élèves de dernière année de l'école primaire en situation d'apprentissage bilingue – Rapport de recherche*, Aoste, IRRE-VDA.

Baetens Beardsmore, H. (1993). 'The European School Model'. In Baetens Beardsmore, H. (ed.), *European Models of Bilingual Education*. Clevedon: Multilingual Matters, 121–4.

Berg, G. (1993). '*Mir wëlle bleiwe, wat mir sin*' – *Soziolinguistische und sprachtypologische Betrachtungen zur luxemburgischen Mehrsprachigkeit*. Tübingen: Niemeyer.

Berg, C. and Weis, C. (2007). *Réajustement de l'enseignement des langues – Plan d'Action 2007–2009: Contribuer au changement durable du système éducatif par la mise en œuvre d'une politique linguistique éducative*. Luxembourg : Éditions du CESIJE.

Cavalli, M. (2005). *Éducation bilingue et plurilinguisme – Le cas du Val d'Aoste*. Paris: LAL, Didier.

Cavalli, M., Coletta, D., Gajo, L., Matthey, M. and Serra, C. (2003). *Langues, bilinguisme et représentations sociales au Val d'Aoste – Rapport de recherche*. Aosta: IRRE-VDA.

Commission of the European Communities (2003). *Communication from the Commission to the Council, the European Parliament, the Economic and Social Committee and the Committee of the Regions Promoting Language Learning and Linguistic Diversity: an Action Plan 2004–2006*. Brussels: (COM 2003) 449 final.

Conseil de l'Europe (2007). *Profil de la politique linguistique éducative: Vallée d'Aoste*. www.coe.int/lang.

Conseil de L'Europe, Le Gouvernement du Grand Duché de Luxemburg (2005–6). *Language Education Policy Profile: Grand Duchy of Luxembourg*. www.coe.int/lang.

Council of Europe (2003). *Bilingual Education: Some Policy Issues*. www.coe.int/lang.

Council of Europe (1992). *European Charter on Regional and Minority Languages*. www.coe.int/t/dg4/education/minlang/default_en.asp.

Council of Europe (2005–7). *Language Education Policy Profile: Ireland*. www.coe.int/lang.

Council of Europe (2007). *From Linguistic Diversity to Plurilingual Education: Guide for the Development of Language Education Policies in Europe – Main Version.* Strasbourg: Council of Europe. www.coe.int/lang.

Council of the European Union (2004). *Education and Training 2010.* Brussels: No 6236/04 Educ 32.

Davis, K. (1994). *Language Planning in Multilingual Contexts: Policies, Communities, and Schools in Luxembourg.* Amsterdam/Philadelphia: John Benjamins.

Egger, K. (1978). *Bilinguismo in Alto Edige.* Bolzano: Casa Editrice Athesia.

European Bureau for Lesser-Used Languages. http://eblul.eurolang.net.

European Commission (2012). *Special Eurobarometer 386, Europeans and their Languages.* http://ec.europa.eu/public_opinion/index_en.htm.

European Council (2002). *Presidency Conclusions – Barcelona European Council – 15 and 16 March 2002.*

Eurydice (2006). *Content and Language Integrated Learning (CLIL) at School in Europe,* Brussels, Directorate-General for Education and Culture, http://www.eurydice.org

Eurydice – Eurostat (2012). *Key Data on Teaching Languages at School in Europe: 2012 Edition.* http://aecea.ec.europa.eu/education/eurydice.

Housen, A. (2002). 'Second language achievement in the European School system of multilingual education'. In So, D. and Jones, G. (eds), *Education and Society in Plurilingual Contexts.* Brussels: VUB Academic Press, 96–128.

Housen, A. (2003). 'Processes and Outcomes in the European Schools Model of Multilingual Education'. *Bilingual Research Journal.* 26: 1, 43–62.

Housen, A. (2008). 'Multilingual Development in the European Schools. In De Groof, R. (ed.), *Brussels and Europe – Bruxelles et l'Europe.* Brussels: Academic and Scientific Publishers, 455–70.

Lebrun, N., Baetens Beardsmore, H. (1993). 'Trilingual Education in the Grand Duchy of Luxembourg. In Baetens Beardsmore, H. (ed.), *European Models of Bilingual Education.* Clevedon: Multilingual Matters, 101–20.

Marsh, D. et al. (2002). *CLIL/EMILE – The European Dimension.* Jyväskylä: Unicom.

Müller-Schneck, E. (2007). *Bilingualer Geschichtsunterricht - Theorie, Praxis, Perspektiven.* Frankfurt: Peter Lang.

OECD PISA (2012). Results. www.oecd.org/pisa/keyfindings/pisa-2012-results.htm.

Offord, M. (1996). *French Sociolinguistics.* Clevedon: Multilingual Matters.

Phillipson, R. (2003). *English-Only Europe? Challenging Language Policy.* London and New York: Routledge.

Swan, D. (1996). *A Singular Pluralism: The European Schools 1984–1994.* Dublin: Institute of Public Administration.

Titone, R. (1974). *Le bilinguisme précoce.* Bruxelles : Charles Dessart.

Tschumi, J-A., Marek Z. (2008). 'La spectaculaire avancée des politiques d'éducation linguistiques en Europe'. In *Parler européen aujourd'hui!* Genève: Scala Trans-Europe, www.aede.org.

UNESCO (2003). *Education in a Multilingual World.* Paris: United Nations.

UNESCO (2010). *Educational Equity for Children from Diverse Backgrounds: Mother Tongue-Based Bilingual or Multilingual Education in the Early Years: Literature Review.* www.unesco.org/en/languages-in-education/publications/.

Van Ek, J., Trim, J. (1998). *Threshold Level.* Cambridge: Cambridge University Press.

Van Velthoven, H. (1987). 'The Process of Language Shift in Brussels: Historical Background and Mechanisms'. In Witte, E. and Baetens Beardsmore, H. (eds). *The Interdisciplinary Study of Urban Bilingualism in Brussels.* Clevedon: Multilingual Matters, 15–46.

FORCES	MECHANISMS
Key values in human relations	**Structures**
Trust	Council of Europe
Respect	European Commission
Fairness	Language Policy Unit of the Council of Europe
Justice	
Emotions	**Knowledge building**
Fear	Research
Distrust	Public information initiatives/campaigns
Apprehensions	
Principles for cooperation	**Agreements and benchmarks**
Stakeholder inclusion	European Commission's Action Plan 2003
Power sharing with educators	Language education policy
Flexibility	European Charter for Regional or Minority Languages
Rooting decisions in knowledge arising from research	Common European Framework of Reference for Languages
Ideology	Harmonisation of national certification with international
Goals	diplomas allowing teacher mobility
A vision of minority rights and trilingualism for Europe	
Beliefs	**Vehicles**
Status	Language Education Policy profiles
Prestige	Special Eurobarometer
A belief in the value of plurilingualism	Guide for the Development of Language Education Policies in Europe
A belief in the value of bilingual/plurilingual education	Teacher training
	Teaching materials

COUNTERWEIGHTS

Vouloire faire	Laissez faire
Stigmatisation/no access, or restricted access, to bilingual education	European Charter
Potential negative effect of legislation/central control	Trust/local initiative
Fear of negative impact on L1	Learning L3
Reticence regarding bilingual education	Information sharing

PART TWO:
Getting Started

3   CANADA:
Factors that Shaped the Creation and Development of Immersion Education

Fred Genessee (McGill University)

CHAPTER NAVIGATOR

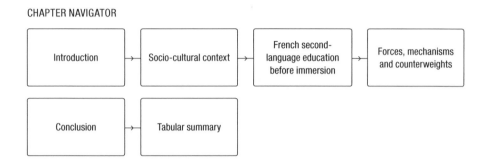

INTRODUCTION

This chapter presents a portrait of Canadian French immersion programmes and the factors that shaped their creation, development and evolution.[1] Many publications on Canadian immersion programmes focus on programme models, student outcomes and pedagogical issues (e.g. Lambert and Tucker 1965; Genesee 2004; Lyster 2007; Swain and Lapkin 1982). Thus there is ample evidence of the strengths and weaknesses of these programmes with respect to these topics, and especially student outcomes. Very briefly, and taken together, this extensive body of research attests to the overall effectiveness of immersion – specifically, research has shown quite consistently that students in these programmes, even those who often underperform in school, attain advanced levels of functional proficiency in French, their second language (L2), and at the same time attain the same levels of competence in English, their first language (L1), and in academic domains, such as mathematics and science, when compared to similar students in English-only programmes. No further discussion of these general results will be undertaken here. Instead, this chapter will focus on the socio-cultural, political, community and educational factors that shaped the initial creation of these programmes, their implementation in the early years and their subsequent development. The factors that shaped Canadian immersion programmes are not necessarily the same factors that are important in the development of programmes in other communities. However, although the focus here is on Canadian-specific aspects of immersion, the goal is to identify factors that educators in other settings might consider as they seek to implement new programmes and/or evaluate existing ones. This perspective is intended to extend discussions of factors that are important in planning and implementing immersion, factors that go beyond the school and immersion classrooms.

The following section describes the socio-cultural-political context that gave rise to the first Canadian immersion programme, and this is followed by a description of St. Lambert Elementary School in Quebec, the school that was home to this programme. The focus is on the emergence, inauguration and early years of the programme in St. Lambert, because this provides insight into how and why decisions were made during these early stages of the programme. These early decisions had important implications for both short-term and long-term programme development.

SOCIO-CULTURAL CONTEXT

The Canadian immersion programmes, like similar programmes around the world – whether they are called immersion, bilingual, CLIL, or something else – are deeply embedded in the socio-cultural-political context of the community where they reside. A description of the context in which Canadian immersion was created is useful for identifying and understanding the forces that shaped it, for better or worse, and for considering how similar forces might operate in the creation of programmes in other communities. Taking account of such forces is especially important in communities that are beginning to plan or implement a new programme because forces outside the school setting itself can derail implementation plans or result in the creation of programmes that are not optimally effective, are unstable, or are unresponsive to community needs, aspirations and expectations. Viewed differently, taking into account local socio-cultural-political realities can lead to the development of stronger and more effective programmes. The fact that community context is so important in the creation of immersion programmes in any community is not surprising since bilingual forms of education can have a far-reaching impact, leading to fundamental alterations in the way education is usually delivered in most schools. This is so for many reasons.

For example, bilingual programmes call for instruction through two or more languages instead of one. This requires teachers and other educators who have competence in two or more languages, or teachers who speak each language fluently, depending on who teaches each school subject. Furthermore, they are likely to have cultural backgrounds and beliefs that differ from the mainstream. Often this also means that educational professionals who are members of minority groups in the community at large must be recruited. This, in turn, might call for the development of programmes that can train professionals to work in a bilingual context. All of these additional requirements call for change and doing things differently.

Like other parts of the new world originally populated by Indigenous peoples, Canada was later settled and governed by different European groups – French and English in this case. While populations of French-speakers can now be found in diverse regions of this very large country, the majority of French speakers live in eastern Canada and primarily in the province of Quebec. When Canada was legally constituted as a confederation of several provinces with designated powers and responsibilities by an act of the British government in 1867, linguistic duality in English and French was recognised only in Quebec; English was the *de facto* language of government and the courts in the other provinces that comprised Canada at that time. It was not until 1969 that both French and English were granted status as official languages across the country by an act of the Parliament of Canada. The Official Languages Act (a mechanism) required that certain federal government services in certain areas of the country (where there are sufficient numbers of speakers of both languages) be provided in both French and English. Contrary to popular understanding both in and outside Canada, the bilingualism policy of the federal government of Canada does not require all individuals to be bilingual, rather only those who dispense designated federal government services – a form of institutional bilingualism. The thrust of this legislation was to recognise the value of both English and French across the nation. The Official Languages Act led to increased interest in bilingualism among Canadians at large and to initiatives designed to increase opportunities for Canadians – both adults and children – to become bilingual. In most cases, this entailed enhancing opportunities for English-speaking Canadians to learn French because, until that time, 'anglophone' Canadians usually had limited competence in the language. In contrast, French-speaking (francophone) Canadians were much more likely to be competent in English and French because English enjoyed higher prestige and status, and more commercial and political utility, in Canada than French. The important point here is that, although the Official Languages Act did not directly require in-dividual bilingualism among Canadians, its recognition of the importance of French as well as English was a force that enhanced the value of bilin-gualism, especially among young English-speaking Canadians.

At the same time that the Canadian federal government was enacting le-gislation to recognise the status of French and English as official languages across the country, events were unfolding in Quebec, the home prov-ince of the largest group of francophones, that would have an even more direct impact on the creation of immersion. Until the passing of the Official Languages Act, French had a secondary role and lower status than English, even in Quebec. This was evident in multiple ways. As already noted, French had no official status outside Quebec until 1969. Also, even in Quebec, dur-ing encounters between English- and French-speaking individuals, the use of English was often favoured over the use of French (Gendron 1972), resulting in asymmetrical rates of bilingualism, with a tendency for bilingualism to be more commonplace among francophones than anglophones. This consti-tuted a significant and real threat to the viability of French to the extent that English could become the common language for all Canadians. Social con-tact and interactions between anglophones and francophones, overall, were very limited and were aptly characterised in the title of a popular novel called *Two Solitudes* (MacLennan 1945).

The minority status of French was also reflected in people's attitudes to-wards each language, as revealed in research by Wallace Lambert and his col-leagues at McGill University (Lambert, Hodgson, Gardner and Fillenbaum 1960). In their innovative study, Lambert and his colleagues asked English- and French-speaking Quebecers to listen to and give their impressions of people speaking either English or French. Unknown to the participants in these studies, they were actually listening to the same perfectly bilingual people on separate occasions, sometimes speaking English and sometimes speaking French. Analyses of the participants' reactions indicated that both groups expressed more positive attitudes towards people when they spoke English than when they spoke French. That English-speaking Canadians expressed more favourable attitudes to speaking English was perhaps under-standable as a form of in-group favouritism. More surprising perhaps was the finding that even native French-speaking respondents expressed more favourable attitudes to people when they spoke English – a form of in-group denigration.

Growing awareness and discontent with the second class status of French, especially in Quebec, led to frustration and desire for change among

French-speaking Canadians. This state of affairs gave way to popular demonstrations and political activism in Quebec that called for changes that would better reflect the status of French as an official language in Canada and as the majority language in Quebec. The social unrest during this period came to be called 'The Quiet Revolution'. Interestingly, the Quiet Revolution in Quebec during the 1960s and early 1970s coincided with similar calls for change on a number of different social fronts (including women's rights, racial discrimination and access to higher education) across North America and in Europe. The social unrest in Quebec at that time led to the election of a provincial government that called for the separation of Quebec from the rest of Canada and the creation of a unilingual French-speaking country. While this initiative has failed, important legislation was enacted by this and subsequent Quebec governments that made French the only official language in Quebec, except in jurisdictions controlled by the federal governments (e.g. the courts), and sought to enhance the status and usage of French in day-to-day contexts. Among other consequences, this legislation (called The Charter of the French Language, also known as 'Bill 101') required that all immigrant children be educated in French only; individuals practicing certain professions in the province were required to pass French language exams, and private businesses were required to give priority to the use of French over English in the workplace and in public advertising. In short, political events in Quebec served to reverse the trend in favour of English to favour the use of, and thus also the learning of, French by anglophones living in the province.

FRENCH SECOND-LANGUAGE EDUCATION BEFORE IMMERSION

During this time, the vast majority of English-speaking children in Quebec were educated in schools where English was the predominant medium of instruction. French was taught as a second language, beginning in primary school, for relatively short periods of time (around 20–30 minutes per day). Instruction was dominated by methods that were current at the time; namely, direct instruction of vocabulary, grammar and certain communication patterns, with lots of practice and feedback to minimise errors. Although instruction in French began in primary school, graduating students reported anecdotally that they lacked the communicative competence they needed to actually use French outside school in encounters with francophones – in stores, on the bus or during leisure activities. In short, the then current method of French instruction was not working. Faced with the evolving importance of French both within the province of Quebec and with evident weaknesses in the current methods of teaching French, a concerned group of English-speaking parents in the small suburban community of St. Lambert near Montreal began meeting to discuss alternative approaches. In their search for alternatives, the St. Lambert Bilingual School Study Group, as they called themselves, sought the assistance and advice of experts in the community. In particular, they consulted with Professors Wallace Lambert and Richard Tucker in the Psychology Department at McGill University; Lambert had conducted pioneering research, discussed earlier, on the social, psychological and cognitive aspects of bilingualism. They also met with Dr Wilder Penfield of the Montreal Neurological Institute who had conducted groundbreaking research on language and the brain. Inclusion of these experts was critical for a number of reasons. First, they gave their full support to the St. Lambert parents and, thus, legitimised their initiative to explore alternative methods of teaching French. Second, the St. Lambert experiment, as it came to be called, was able to call on the scientific expertise of these university-based colleagues, ensuring that their initiative was consistent with current empirical evidence. Third and perhaps most important, Lambert and Tucker agreed to undertake a longitudinal evaluation of the new programme as it evolved. This turned out to be instrumental in ensuring the programme's success and survival and in garnering support from parents across the country.

In contrast, the Study Group's efforts to recruit the support and resources of local and provincial education authorities met with little success and, indeed, opposition. For example, the Ministry of Education of Quebec failed to acknowledge the efforts of the St. Lambert Study Group. Ministry officials did not respond to the proposal prepared by the Study Group and they gave no evidence that they had read it when questioned by parents at a public meeting some years later. The Quebec Ministry of Education had not officially recognised French immersion even in the 1990s, some 30 years after it was inaugurated. Even closer to home, the local School Board that had jurisdiction over St. Lambert Elementary School was initially resistant to this initiative. For example, they were unwilling to commit to continuing the 'experiment' beyond kindergarten, and School Board members expressed so many objections and concerns during the first year that it was not clear that the programme could continue. Moreover, the Study Group itself was obliged to find teachers to work in the programme, to choose suitable textbooks and to develop the programme without the direct support of the school authorities (see Appendix A in Lambert and Tucker 1972, for more details).

Chief among the concerns of school officials was whether the participating students would succeed in the new programme to the same level as in the traditional English-only programme. This is where collaboration with McGill researchers proved invaluable since studies undertaken by Lambert and Tucker provided empirical evidence of the programme's effectiveness (Lambert and Tucker 1972). It is important to point out that, once evidence of the programme's success emerged, the Board enthusiastically supported it. These historical details are noteworthy because they attest to a challenge that is faced by many communities that seek to institute bilingual forms of education – namely, resistance and opposition to change. Many, although not all, school authorities are often resistant initially to institute bilingual forms of education. This is understandable in part because of the considerable changes that are entailed by these programmes. In any case, the reaction of local education authorities and decision makers connected to St. Lambert was a negative counterweight to the positive forces elsewhere in the community that favoured bilingual education.

The first class of immersion students began school in St. Lambert in September 1965. Numerous detailed descriptions of this first immersion programme and of immersion programmes in other communities in Canada are available in other publications (e.g. Genesee 1987, 2004, in Montreal; Swain and Lapkin 1982, in Toronto) and, therefore, no description is provided here. However, what is important to note here about the St. Lambert programme is that it emerged as a result of extensive discussion by key stakeholders, including parents and university-based researchers, despite limited support from and indeed resistance on the part of local and provincial education authorities, as noted earlier. The start of the immersion programme in St. Lambert was also the start of a rigorous and comprehensive longitudinal evaluation undertaken by Lambert and his colleagues to monitor the effects of the programme on student achievement. A second cohort of students began the following year and this cohort was also evaluated on an annual basis in order to examine the generalisability of the results obtained from the pilot class (a complete summary of the first four years of results is presented in Lambert and Tucker 1972). As results from the St. Lambert evaluation became public, interest in initiating immersion programmes in communities across the country increased. At present, there are over 300 000 students in alternative forms of immersion in every Canadian province and territory.

Mounting evidence of the success of the programme and its growing popularity across the country led to the creation of a professional association of immersion teachers in Canada in 1976, known as *L'Association canadienne des professeurs d'immersion* (ACPI; The Canadian Association of Immersion Teachers).[2] ACPI is committed to supporting and providing professional development opportunities to immersion teachers across Canada through annual conferences, the development of educational resources and the dissemination of professional publications. Parents have also been key stakeholders in immersion, as already noted. In recognition of their critical ongoing role, Canadian Parents for French (CPF) was created in 1977, with initial support from the Office of the Commissioner of Official Languages of Canada. CPF is a national network of volunteers who value French as an integral part of Canada. CPF is dedicated to the promotion and creation of French second-language learning opportunities for young Canadians.[3]

Before proceeding, it is important to note here that similar initiatives on the part of French-speaking parents to promote the learning of English as a second language did not emerge for a number of reasons. First, French-speaking parents were concerned about the survival of French in the face of domination by the English language. Thus, francophone parents generally speaking were not seeking more or better instruction in English as a second language in school. Second, in the province of Quebec, efforts to buttress French in the face of threats from English resulted in laws that prevented francophone parents from sending their children to English language schools and schools from offering early instruction through languages other than French.

FORCES, MECHANISMS AND COUNTERWEIGHTS

This brief portrait of the St. Lambert immersion programme illustrates the importance of specific forces, mechanisms and counterweights that shaped it in the beginning and continued to shape it as it evolved. Examples of each source of influence are discussed in this section. They are discussed in an integrated fashion since they were often inter-related, so, for example, a specific force gave rise to a mechanism to support immersion, or a mechanism or strategy was devised as a positive counterweight to offset a negative one; a summary of key forces, mechanisms and counterweights discussed in this section is presented in the table at the end of the chapter.

To begin, it is evident from the preceding portrait that there were a number of significant forces in Canada and in the communities of St. Lambert and Montreal that favoured the creation and implementation of this radical change in public schools. Some of these forces, such as the desire of francophones in Quebec to protect their language, were expressed through political and legislative events; some were more subjective or abstract in nature. Among national-level, political-legislative events that led to and, in fact, favoured the creation of immersion was the recognition of both French and English as official languages by the Official Languages Act. This legislation not only recognised the importance of both languages for all Canadians, but also indicated that federal government resources would be committed to supporting and promoting competence in both languages. Virtually simultaneously, the Quiet Revolution and, in particular, public demonstrations in Quebec in support of French, heightened awareness among anglophones and others (e.g. immigrants who spoke only English or French, or neither) in the province of the value of French. As noted earlier, English was the predominant language learned by immigrants in Quebec, and anglophones generally speaking acquired relatively limited proficiency in French. Similarly, the passage of Bill 101, legislation in Quebec that required the use of French in the workplace and in certain professions, signalled the importance of French for employment and life in general in Quebec. Federal and provincial legislation both signalled to parents that there were clear and real incentives and rewards associated with competence in both English and French.

These forces and mechanisms were significant in mobilising parents to seek alternative forms of education so that their children would be better able to face the challenges and reap the rewards associated with bilingualism. The creation of the St. Lambert Bilingual Study Group was a seminal mechanism that served to harness and focus the efforts of parents and to realise their goals of improved second-language education. The creation of this group originated in the powerful forces of both their positive attitudes toward bilingualism in general and their belief in the value of bilingualism in the future of their children. Without such positive forces, the initiative undertaken by the St. Lambert parents would not have taken place. Pessimistic expectations about bilingualism and its consequences might prevail in other communities and serve as counterweights to parental desires for bilingual education. In these cases, dissemination of research findings and meetings with parents whose children are already in an immersion programme can act as positive counterweights, helping to change attitudes and mitigating fear and scepticism.

The very public visibility of the work of the Study Group served to attract community-wide attention to its initiative. Garnering broad support from the community at large was an important goal of the group and an essential force for promoting their goals. Of particular importance was the Study

Group's success in soliciting the active involvement of university-based professionals, who were able to provide valuable assistance and input in the design of the programme at the beginning and, in addition, offered to monitor its effectiveness over the years. Evidence from research both during the planning stages when alternative models of bilingual education were being explored and subsequently, as the programme grew, served to offset the effect of negative counterweights that prevailed in the beginning – namely, resistance by local school officials, indifference from provincial authorities and doubts from the public at large that such a radical departure from traditional forms of education could succeed. The long-term evaluations spearheaded by Lambert and his colleagues in Montreal and by Swain and her colleagues in Toronto were critical mechanisms for ensuring the sustainability of the programme since they provided empirical evidence of the effectiveness of immersion. Positive coverage of the new programme in the media, including newspapers, radio and television, were also important mechanisms for garnering broad support for immersion. The media were able to 'get the news out' that immersion was effective. Involvement of researchers and the media were critical mechanisms for ensuring expansion of the programme into higher grades in St. Lambert and into other communities.

The results from evaluations of the first two cohorts of students in St. Lambert were published and widely disseminated in highly respected journals. As a result, the St Lambert 'experiment' became widely known around the world and, most importantly, the positive results that came out of these evaluations encouraged other communities – in Wales, the Basque Country and Finland for example – to embark on their own immersion 'experiments'. The evaluation results also reassured communities around the world that these programmes were effective and provided them with the scientific evidence they needed to convince policymakers and politicians in their regions to move ahead with their own programmes. In short, St. Lambert changed the way in which educators thought about promoting bilingualism in school.

Beyond the initial phase of immersion, after it was first introduced in St. Lambert and as it was adopted in other regions of the country, these same forces and mechanisms continued to play important supportive roles. New mechanisms for supporting the programme emerged or were created as it expanded into the higher grades and other communities. For example, and as already noted, some ten years after the first immersion programme in St. Lambert, the ACPI was formed by the efforts of a few dedicated immersion teachers and, in particular, André Obadia, an immersion teacher from one of the first programmes, with the goal of supporting all teachers working in immersion programmes across the country. One year later, Canadian Parents for French (CPF) was created to give a voice to parents who wanted to ensure that their children had enhanced opportunities to learn French. The work of ACPI and CPF, along with positive evidence from research that immersion was a success, became major forces that reinforced interest and enthusiasm for immersion among the population at large. International dissemination of research findings documenting the success of the St. Lambert experiment led to an increased understanding of immersion and a belief that it was a viable option. This increased belief in immersion was an important force that contributed to the launch of similar programmes in several countries. The power of Canadian research findings also led authorities in other countries to put in place mechanisms to research their programmes in order to ensure that immersion worked in their contexts.

In the 1980s and beyond, as the programme matured, immersion continued to grow in Canada. However, a number of counterweights arguably have served to slow the evolution of immersion in Canada from pedagogical perspectives. For example, there is a shortage of qualified immersion teachers, especially in provinces where English predominates. In addition, graduates of immersion face a lack of or limited access to follow-up instruction and exposure to French at the post-secondary level. To be more specific, immersion students who graduate from immersion in secondary school have few ways of pursuing their immersion experience in community college or university. While they are able to take French language courses of a conventional sort, they are generally unable to take non-language courses in university or community college, such as Psychology or Mathematics, taught through the medium of French. In addition, few school systems in Canada that offer immersion provide official recognition that students have completed secondary school requirements in English and French. These are disincentives for students to pursue immersion at the secondary level with the same level of commitment that is found at the elementary level, another example of a negative counterweight that needs attention if the slump in enrolment that many secondary level immersion programmes experience is to be overcome.

Another negative counterweight is evident in the very nature of the educational system in Canada. Control of education is strictly under the jurisdiction of each province and territory. As a result, there is no federal authority or leadership with respect to education across the country. In practical terms, this means that there is no federal ministry of education and no elected politicians who oversee education in all regions of Canada. This has resulted in a lack of federal leadership with respect to immersion, with several important consequences. In this regard, French immersion emerged in response to socio-political circumstances in Canada at the time, as described earlier. These national preoccupations continue to dominate thinking about immersion to this day. However, globalisation and cross-national interdependence have become increasingly important forces in the twenty-first century, and yet conceptualisations of immersion have not evolved to reflect these changes in the world. Arguably, the challenges and rewards of globalisation could be addressed by expanding immersion to incorporate more languages and to support students from immigrant backgrounds to further develop content and language skills through courses taught in their home languages. These initiatives could foster not just bilingualism but multilingualism. There are almost no signs of this happening in the current leadership vacuum. A more concrete example of the consequences of the lack of national leadership is the lack of resource allocation or development by federal government agencies in support of immersion. National initiatives to develop instructional materials, assessment tools, and teacher training possibilities and standards would support all immersion schools and teachers efficiently by coordinating efforts across the country. At present, and for the foreseeable future, each province is responsible for providing its own resources. As a result, there is wide variation in the amount and quality of support provided by each province. As a consequence of the lack of ongoing collaboration among provinces, there may be unnecessary duplication of resource development and little sharing of expertise and experience beyond that which can be provided by ACPI or CPF. It is even difficult to obtain a thorough national overview of immersion programmes, their learning resources and their leadership/management practices because of the lack of a national agency responsible for overseeing immersion. In short, the lack of national leadership is a negative counterweight to the evolution of alternative conceptualisations of immersion, the development of instructional resources and assessment tools, and the provision of professional training opportunities for teachers.

CONCLUSION

This chapter has gone beyond other reports on the St. Lambert French immersion programme to describe the forces, mechanisms and counterweights that were important in its creation, early implementation and long-term evolution. All educational innovations are complex and their success ultimately depends on how effective programme creators are at identifying and managing the forces, mechanisms and counterweights that favour or dis-favour their efforts. The story of the St. Lambert project is noteworthy with respect to specific forces and mechanisms that favoured it. Among these, the most noteworthy were the socio-political climate and events in the imme-diate community and across the country. These gave value to bilingualism and garnered strong commitment among a dedicated group of parents who undertook to change the system. On a related note, the story of St. Lambert illustrates the power of grassroots stakeholders – especially parents – in the face of educational authorities who were ambivalent and, arguably, opposed to change. Indeed, the St Lambert parents' perseverance, clear sense of mis-sion and indefatigable spirit were critical forces underpinning the creation of the programme; less committed and focused parents would have given in to the resistance they faced.

The St. Lambert community counteracted resistant forces by creating two mechanisms that were critical for getting the programme going and pre-serving it – the St. Lambert Bilingual Study Group and a collaboration with McGill researchers who committed to undertaking a long-term evaluation of the programme. The history of St. Lambert illustrates that, in addition to devoting attention to strictly educational matters, such as the development of curriculum and materials, the hiring and training of teachers and administra-tors, and parent-school relationships, efforts must be focused on identifying forces and counterweights outside the school itself that could undermine or destabilise a new programme. It is important that this be done with the view to both short-term and long-term development of a programme. In the case of the Canadian immersion programmes, Canadian Parents for French and the Canadian Association of Immersion Teachers were created to serve the long-term needs of immersion as it expanded and matured. Noticeably lack-ing in the Canadian case are federally coordinated mechanisms, although there are varying levels of support from each of the ten provincial and three territorial governments in Canada. Coordinating provincial support has proven difficult. Creating mechanisms to attract and sustain support from national or central authorities is important for the long-term evolution of bilingual programmes since often it is only these kinds of agencies that have the resources and the authority that are needed to encourage growth and evolution in the long run and on a large scale.

REFERENCES

Gendron, J.D. (1972). *Commission of Inquiry on the Position of the French Language and on Language Rights in Quebec: Language of Work*. Quebec City, Quebec: L'Éditeur officiel du Québec.

Genesee, F. (1987). *Learning Through Two Languages: Studies of Immersion and Bilingual Education*. Cambridge, Mass.: Newbury House.

Genesee, F. (2004). 'What Do We Know about Bilingual Education for Majority Language Students?' In T.K. Bhatia and W. Ritchie (eds), *Handbook of Bilingualism and Multiculturalism*. Malden, Mass.: Blackwell, 547–76.

Lambert, W.E., Hodgson, R., Gardner, R. C. and Fillenbaum, S. (1960). 'Evaluational Reactions to Spoken Languages'. *Journal of Abnormal and Social Psychology* 60, 44–51.

Lambert, W.E. and Tucker, G. R. (1972). *The Bilingual Education of Children: The St. Lambert Experiment*. Rowley, Mass.: Newbury House.

MacLennan, H. (1945). *Two Solitudes*. Montreal: Duell, Sloan, & Pearce.

Swain, M. and Lapkin, S. (1982). *Evaluating Bilingual Education: A Canadian Case Study*. Clevedon: Multilingual Matters.

NOTES

1 This chapter focuses on immersion in French as a second language because French is the most common variety of immersion. However, there are immersion programmes in other languages in Canada, including Hebrew, Mohawk, Inuktitut, Ukrainian, Spanish, German and Chinese. They are much less common and the forces that shaped the development of these programmes are not necessarily the same as those that shaped French immersion.

2 www.acpi.ca.

3 www.cpf.ca/en/about-us/what-is-cpf/ (retrieved September 2013).

FORCES	MECHANISMS
Societal	**People**
The Quiet Revolution in Quebec asserting the importance of French	St. Lambert Bilingual Study Group to consolidate support for innovation
Globalisation and the value of bilingual/bicultural competence	Canadian Parents for French
	Association canadienne des professeurs d'immersion
Considerable local autonomy and decision-making at school level	Strong community leaders committed to change
Principles for cooperation	**Knowledge building**
Trust and respect for university researchers and the value of research	Evaluation of pilot programme by university researchers
	Publications in local, national and international magazines, newspapers and specialised journals
Goals	National conferences on bilingualism and bilingual education
A wish to bridge the two solitudes through bilingualism	
A desire to prepare students to live and thrive in a bilingual environment	
Beliefs	**Legislation**
A belief that all children can learn more than one language	Canada's Official Languages Act
A belief in instrumental and personal benefits of bilingualism	Quebec's Charter of the French Language
Recognition of the legitimacy and status of both French and English both locally and internationally	

COUNTERWEIGHTS

Resistance to change by provincial authorities	Positive and enthusiastic parent support
Scepticism from school authorities	Strong support from researchers and research evidence
Lack of national educational goals to support bilingualism	National non-political parent and teacher support organisations
Lack of follow-up and recognition of bilingual competence by universities	A belief and interest among parents in the value of bilingualism in work and personal life
Decentralised control of education and no national resources	Strong government support for immersion in some provinces and territories

4 ESTONIA:
Laying the Groundwork for Bilingual Education

Peeter Mehisto (Institute of Education, University College London)

CHAPTER NAVIGATOR

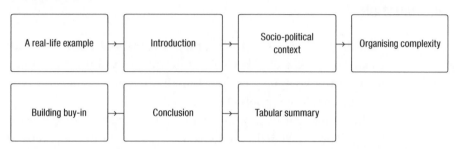

A REAL-LIFE EXAMPLE

In Tallinn, Estonia, on 2 October 2000, reporters from three television stations, two newspapers and one radio station came to witness the Estonian Minister of Education and the Minister for Population Affairs open the Estonian Language Immersion Centre. The Centre was charged with co-ordinating the development of a national language immersion programme. All speakers stressed their support for the immersion centre. They also expressed the community's high expectations for the voluntary early Estonian-language immersion programme that had just been launched in four out of the country's 102 schools that offered Russian-medium education. Over 70 representatives of the diplomatic corps and other national and international immersion programme stakeholders[1] attended the opening.

For an educational programme with a student population of only 137 to receive such high level attention is exceptional. This broad-based local and international support was systematically constructed through a shared knowledge-building and power-sharing exercise. Stakeholder inclusion was a major force in developing and expanding the programme, and the creation of an immersion centre was a key mechanism in helping to realise the stakeholders' vision of bilingual education. Three years after this event, the immersion centre was able to co-ordinate the launch of a new late immersion programme and rapidly expand both the early and late programmes. Fourteen years later, the programme would include 55 kindergartens, 36 schools and approximately 7 000 students (Immersion Programme 2014). This chapter tells the story of how the early immersion programme was launched.

INTRODUCTION

This chapter focuses on **forces, mechanisms and counterweights** that were consciously used or otherwise came into play during the initial development of the voluntary early Estonian language immersion programme in Russian-medium schools. The rationale for focusing on this very early stage is the conviction of key Estonian decision-makers that it was this initial stage, which included a systematic approach to development, the engagement of stakeholders and shared decision-making, that was central to the programme's long-term success. The chapter first explains the desired impact of the Estonian immersion programme, the intended outcomes and the outputs or investments needed to achieve these outcomes. It is this level of detail that was required for key stakeholders to understand the implications of programme development and to agree on how to move forward. Second, the chapter explains how that agreement was achieved.

The chapter is based on personal recollection, as I played a key role in identifying the immersion option and drawing stakeholders in education together to plan and establish the programme. I eventually co-managed the programme and, in particular, helped organise delivery of Canadian assistance to support Estonia's efforts to establish it. My recollections have been triangulated with a review of programme-related documents and interviews with key stakeholders.

SOCIO-POLITICAL CONTEXT

In 1939, Soviet Russia began a process that would lead to the occupation of Estonia in 1940 and again in 1944 after the intervening 1941–44 German occupation. The first years of Soviet occupation were characterised by a process of 'centralized denationalization' that included 'systematic deportations, executions, and population transfers' (Kello 2009), and destruction of existing social and democratic institutions. The remainder of the occupation would see extensive immigration into the country primarily from Russia, 'russification', as well as continued restrictions on freedom of speech, assembly and travel (Raun 2001; Zetterberg 2009). Language, culture, nationhood, democracy and national values were all under threat.

After the re-establishment of Estonian independence in August 1991, a threat to Estonia's security from Russia remained omnipresent. In fact, Russian troops did not fully withdraw from Estonia until August 1993. Henry Kissinger (1994) viewed Russian peace-keeping proposals in what Russian authorities referred to as its 'near abroad', which included Estonia, as 'indistinguishable from an attempt to re-establish Moscow's domination'. Moscow's tone towards Estonia was characterised as 'negative, unhelpful, and bullying' (Blank 1998).

When Estonian independence was re-established in 1991, the majority of Russian speakers and other ethnic groups from the former Soviet Union who remained in Estonia did not speak the official language – Estonian (Vihalem 2008). With rare exception, Estonian was the native and strongest language of Estonians. Russian speakers had the option of placing their children in Estonian-medium or Russian-medium schools. The overwhelming majority chose Russian-medium schools. These schools were unsuccessful, generally speaking, in supporting graduates in achieving sufficient fluency in Estonian to allow for further study through that language or entry into a full range of professions available in the labour market (Pavelson 1998). State-sponsored university education was primarily offered through Estonian, and a language law required some degree of fluency in Estonian in numerous professions.

The large number of people who did not speak Estonian was seen by the government as a barrier to social cohesion and a risk to national stability (Government of Estonia 2000). Moreover, as successive Estonian governments perceived the Russian Federation as a potential threat to national security, the country sought additional security guarantees through entry into the European Union (EU) and the North Atlantic Treaty Organization (NATO).[2] This required that Estonia embrace the values of those organisations and, in particular, that they make changes in language and electoral legislation in order to meet standards set by the Organisation for Security and Co-operation in Europe (OSCE) (NATO 2004). The desire for national stability, cohesion and security guarantees were major forces contributing to the many decisions that would allow for the launch of the immersion programme.

ORGANISED COMPLEXITY: A VISION

The process of developing bilingual education programmes is complex (Baker 2011; Cummins 2000; Hornberger 2008; Howard et al. 2007; Mackey 1976; Mehisto 2011). Many mechanisms are required, including quality learning materials, professional development for teachers and leaders, public information materials and research to inform programme development. Furthermore, the creation of each of these mechanisms is a complex process in its own right.

Adding to this complexity are the many potentially positive and negative forces that need to be harnessed and managed. These include a belief in the value of bilingualism, stakeholder inclusion in programme development and a high level of trust or distrust among stakeholders. A further level of complexity resides in the fact that the understandings and actions of stakeholders (such as students, parents, teachers, administrators and politicians) always have the potential of interacting in unique ways to create their own constraints and opportunities.

These complexities of bilingual education invite, particularly during the initial planning stages, two fundamental questions:

- how can stakeholders organise and manage these complexities, and
- how can stakeholders keep so many complexities in mind during programme development?

These questions are all the more pertinent as the limits of human cognition are such that 'people tend to assess the relative importance of issues by the ease with which they are retrieved from memory', and this can lead to poor decisions (Kahneman 2011). Of equal importance is the fact that information not retrieved from memory cannot be harnessed in programme development.

A results-based management (RBM) framework developed by the Canadian International Development Agency was used by the Estonian Ministry of Education to organise these complexities and plan for the development of the bilingual programme. The RBM framework was also the primary vehicle for synthesising previous knowledge about bilingual education in Estonia with new learning obtained from Canada, Finland and other nations that had developed bilingual education. The RBM framework was nicknamed by Estonian stakeholders as the 'tablecloth'. This was an indication of their buy-in to the framework. The 'tablecloth' or RBM framework became a focal point for stakeholder dialogue and for guiding programme development (see Table 1).

Table 1: A results-based management framework

Results-Based Management Framework (RBM)				
Primary goal:				
ACTIVITIES	**OUTPUTS**	**OUTREACH**	**OUTCOMES**	**IMPACT**
		Main Beneficiaries: Delivery Agents National Stakeholders International Stakeholders	**To be achieved by ?**	**To be achieved by ?**
	PERFORMANCE INDICATORS			
	Output indicators	**Outreach indicators**	**Outcome indicators**	**Impact indicators**

Risks and risk reduction strategies
Risk:
Risk Reduction Strategy:
Risk:
. . .

A results-based management (RBM) framework begins with one central goal. As a next step, the impact that project or programme stakeholders wish to have on society is analysed. An impact is the very long-term influence one hopes to have on society. Next, decisions are made about how those impacts will be assessed using quantitative and qualitative measures of success (impact indicators). Programme stakeholders then continue to build the framework, moving from the right side of the framework toward the left, as follows:

- outcomes (long-term results to be achieved in e.g. 4–5 years) and outcome indicators
- outreach (stakeholders who will benefit from the programme and deliver it) and outreach indicators
- outputs (short-term results needed to achieve intended outcomes) and output indicators
- activities (some major actions for achieving outputs)

- risks (possible dangers to achievement of results) and risk reduction strategies.

The overall **goal** was to establish a national immersion programme. The long-term intended **impact** of the future Estonian immersion programme was agreed upon first by a broad cross-section of stakeholders that included educators, local and national government officials, academics and school leaders. These intended impacts were:

1) With the support of society, through a network of immersion schools, participation of [ethnic] non-Estonians in Estonia's economic, political and social life will have increased and this increased participation will have created a wider avenue of opportunities for integration and stability.

2) Non-Estonians will feel more secure living in Estonia and will consider themselves equal members of society.

3) By allowing for an increased diversity of choice and competition, immersion schools will have contributed to the overall improvement of the quality of education.

4) The project will have helped to guarantee the stability and the development of Estonian-language schools in those areas where Estonians are in a minority (see Tool 5).

The first two intended impacts were associated with security and stability in society that could be achieved through integration. They echoed Estonia's concerns about security based on fears that the alienation or separateness of ethnic non-Estonians was a threat and that greater security could be achieved through integration of non-Estonian speaking minorities. The fourth desired impact was motivated by a concern among members of the delegation that Estonian-language schools in areas where Russians were in a majority could become immersion schools for Russian-speakers, thereby marginalising native speakers of Estonian. In essence, these impacts expressed the 'moral purpose' of the immersion initiative, a key force to be harnessed in any education reform project (Fullan 2001). Guided by that moral purpose and the vision embodied in the intended impacts, the Estonian stakeholders agreed on four **outcomes** to describe a future state of affairs, four years into the programme:

1) A well-functioning immersion centre with the appropriate know-how and empowerment is established. This centre co-ordinates research in immersion education, provides service in methodology, disseminates

information, and organises public relations and co-operation among all interest groups.

2) Curricula and teaching materials specific to immersion exist and conditions for their further development are guaranteed.

3) Working model(s) of language immersion programs which can be implemented in different types of schools in Estonia is/are defined.

4) Immersion schools are an integral part of the Estonian educational system operating without foreign [financial] assistance [e.g. from the Canadian International Development Agency].

The first intended outcome, the establishment of an immersion centre, was motivated by a desire to avoid what Canadians had reported, during a study visit by Estonians to Toronto, as a major weakness in Canadian immersion programmes – a lack of thorough central planning in the development stage and a lack of coordination among stakeholders and regions as the programme matured. The fourth outcome was intended to help Estonia plan for sustainability and to reassure potential international bodies who might help finance the project that Estonia was serious about assuming responsibility for its immersion programme.

In terms of **outreach** (stakeholders including beneficiaries and delivery agents), a systematic process was undertaken to identify the individuals, groups and organisations that could affect or be affected by the immersion programme. This helped us to discover several stakeholders that were not immediately apparent. This stakeholder analysis fostered an understanding of the need to create value for stakeholders on the assumption that an organisation that does not create value for its stakeholders is not likely to survive (Näsi 2002). Nine primary groups of stakeholders were identified in the RBM framework:

- the Estonian Ministry of Education
- county governments
- local governments
- schools
- kindergartens
- Estonian institutions of higher learning
- foundations/alternative funders
- media and foreign partners.

Within several of these broad stakeholder categories, a further breakdown of internal stakeholders was carried out. For example, schools as a stakeholder group included school advisory boards, management, teachers, parents and students. This additional breakdown reflected an understanding of the interconnectedness of stakeholders and the need to plan for the building of relationships with stakeholders. Later we would learn that a further breakdown of stakeholder categories was required. For example, teachers included some of the following groups: experienced, inexperienced, experienced in teaching yet inexperienced in bilingual education, monolingual, bilingual, supportive of immersion and unsupportive of immersion.

The RBM framework also identified nine secondary stakeholders, and in the case of foreign partners, subcategories of stakeholders: universities; embassies; Canadian Parents for French (CPF);[3] the European Immersion Institute; the United Nations Development Program (UNDP); the OSCE, and the European Commission. These stakeholders were seen as potential sources of knowledge and support. It was thought that foreign universities and Canadian Parents for French could advise us and that the European Commission and the UNDP could provide additional financing. In addition, the immersion programme held the potential for improving Estonia's status in the eyes of international organisations concerned with issues of ethnic integration such as the OSCE. This could potentially create additional value for the Estonian government – a key immersion programme stakeholder – and in turn could create value for the Estonian immersion centre.

The identification of primary and secondary stakeholders brought with it, at the very least, an understanding that to be successful, the immersion programme needed to involve these groups and reach agreements with them. One RBM framework performance indicator was 'memoranda, minutes …, agreements' from stakeholder meetings. The large number of stakeholders attending the opening of the immersion centre discussed in the real-life example above is an indication of the success of this approach.

In addition to the already identified impacts, outcomes and stakeholders, the RBM framework identified **outputs**. The outputs were those results that needed to be achieved in order to accomplish the planned outcomes stated above. These outputs focused on immersion programme management, professional development of stakeholders, curriculum development, development of learning materials, building a research base, creating support structures, providing parent information and managing public relations. For example, under the heading of 'management', the outputs included the establishment of an immersion centre (including office space, staff, equipment, resource centre), a project management structure and a system for reporting on progress (see Table 2). These were central to the achievement of the first intended outcome of establishing a well-functioning immersion centre.

Table 2: Intended outputs from the results-based management framework

OUTPUTS

The following points are not presented in order of priority or in sequence of implementation:

Management

Have established:
- a project management structure (1, 2 – see indicators listed below)
- a process for determining priorities and a system for reporting on progress (1, 2, 3, 35)
- an Immersion Centre (space, staff, equipment, resource centre) (1, 2, 3, 11, 38, 40, 41)
- work groups (11)

Have in place:
- immersion schools and teachers (7, 8)
- a plan for the creation of the material and intellectual learning environment required in the schools (1, 2, 3, 35)
- a public relations strategy and work plan (1, 11, 12)
- a pre- and in-service training strategy and work plan (1, 3)
- a work plan for the development of resource materials (1, 3)
- a research strategy and work plan (1, 3)
- the project evaluation criteria, strategy, and work plan (1, 3)
- strategies and a work plan to support students with special needs (1, 3)
- a strategy and work plan for the introduction of immersion into kindergarten (1, 3, 9, 37)
- an extra-curricular activities strategy and work plan (1, 3)
- recommendations for the expansion of the immersion model (1, 10, 37)

Training

Training for the following takes place based on evaluation results and training plans:
- project team (13, 14, 20)
- authors of teaching materials (13, 14, 20)
- officials (min. of ed., local govt., county govt., education dept.) (13, 14, 20)
- immersion teachers (classroom and subject area and kindergarten) (13, 14, 15)
- support staff (13, 14, 20)
- school teams (13, 14)
- future trainers (13, 14, 15, 20)
- mentors and methodologists (13, 14, 15, 20)
- evaluators and monitors (13, 14, 20)

An agreement with Estonian and foreign universities allowing 4 MA students and 1 PhD to study immersion (16)

Curriculum

Have in place:
- school-level general curriculum guidelines from kindergarten to the end of Grade 9 and a timetable from kindergarten to the end of Grade 6 to include the immersion programme (17–21, 51, 52)
- grade-by-grade curriculum and courses of study by subject field from kindergarten to Grade 4 (17–21)

Have created a system for honing and developing a common school-level curriculum (17, 18, 21)

Teaching materials

An inventory of Estonian- and Russian-language teaching materials used from kindergarten to the end of Grade 4 (13)

A determination of what teaching materials are required for kindergarten to the end of Grade 4 (1, 14)

Written guidelines (principles/criteria) for materials development (21, 29)

Draft textbooks and other teaching materials for kindergarten to the end of Grade 4 (27, 28)

A teachers' handbook on immersion methodology and didactics (26, 27)

Research

An ongoing exchange/dialogue with research scientists (1, 2, 32, 33, 36)

Teaching materials are tested (31, 34)

Various programmes for Estonian language teaching are analysed and their effectiveness determined (31, 34, 36)

An ongoing programme of research in related fields (31, 36)

Support structures

Have in place:
- one technically equipped Immersion Centre, and immersion classrooms in participating schools (38)
- a system for exchanging information among partners in education (28, 39, 40–43)
- an electronic immersion chat room (42)
- an Immersion Centre Home Page (28, 40)
- a databank including teaching materials, information on immersion and a resource materials catalogue and resource materials (28,40,41)
- an association of immersion teachers (incl. kindergarten) (44, 51)
- an association of parents who support immersion (45, 51)

Parent information and public relations

The regular publication of:
- an annual report (46, 47, 51)
- a newsletter (47, 51)

The systematic occurrence of:
- information days/open houses (48, 12, 50)
- conferences (48, 12, 50)
- annual contests or language days for immersion students (public speaking, written and oral language skills) (12, 49–51)
- exchange of information with schools with intensive language programmes (i.e. French or German) (49)

The existence of Estonian- and Russian-language brochures, pamphlets and other "popular-science-type" literature on immersion (8, 49)

A promotional video for prospective immersion parents (8, 49)

The outputs section of the RBM framework reflects an understanding by those involved in creating it that the framework was just the beginning of the planning process and that more plans would need to be created. These included plans for developing pre- and in-service training and learning materials, and plans for programme expansion and public relations (see Table 2). 'A system for reporting on progress' indicated an understanding of the need to be transparent and to keep stakeholders informed of progress.

Central to reporting was the use of both quantitative and qualitative **indicators** (see Table 3). Each desired output, outcome and impact was aligned with at least one numbered indicator that could be used to determine whether or not these had been achieved. The development of such indicators was meant to act as a counterweight to an overemphasis on short-term student achievement. Moreover, by agreeing on a broad range of indicators, it was possible to celebrate many 'short-term wins', not just student achievement, and to maintain momentum during the programme development phase (Kotter 1996). Importantly, deciding on success indicators from the outset allowed programme developers and stakeholders to collectively take control of how the programme would be judged, and to disempower opponents who were likely to overemphasise one specific measure or point of view.

We aimed to create SMART indicators (Doran 1981) that were 'Specific', 'Measurable', 'Achievable', and 'Relevant'. However, indicators were not 'Time-bound', as timelines would be decided in work plans. The process of creating indicators required particular care to ensure they would be useful and not become a financial burden and involve unrealistic amounts of work. As a counterweight to quantitative indicators such as the number of people undertaking professional development, qualitative indicators were also created such as the extent to which learning from training sessions was being applied in actual classroom practice and the extent to which teaching materials reflected curriculum goals. These represented high expectations. High expectations would be a major force in programme development, and are a major force in successful bilingual education in general (Baker 2006; Cloud et al. 2000; Lyster 2007).

Table 3: Indicators for programme management outputs in the RBM framework

- Board of Director's approval of centre statutes, organisational chart, reports, strategies and/or work plans
- a signed Memorandum of Understanding (TDSB-EME)
- the size and focus of the project's budget and donor investments
- adopted job descriptions, policies and procedures
- the immersion centre is the moral and professional authority in the field
- the extent to which the teaching materials reflect the curriculum goals and guidelines
- Ministry of Education approval of an immersion-inclusive curriculum
- the number of students at the end of each school year who have achieved the established academic standards
- the extent to which skills obtained through training are applied.

Activities were the penultimate part of the RBM framework to be completed. This part included some major planned activities to inform stakeholders of what actions needed to take place. However, as different types of completed work plans were listed in the output column, there was an understanding that many other activities still needed to be planned and agreed upon.

Risk analysis took place last. Those working on the framework were concerned that the immersion programme would be underfinanced and that staff turnover at the immersion centre might be high if salaries were not competitive with those in the private sector. Identification of the risk paved the way for the development of a counterweight. Negotiations eventually led to higher-than-average salaries of future immersion centre employees. Finally, to maintain sufficient financing, the ongoing involvement of key stakeholders, including potential donors, was planned for.

In summary, the results-based management framework and its component parts served as a 'group decisions support' system/mechanism (Huxham 1996) for Estonian immersion programme stakeholders. It helped bring order to our understanding of immersion, to new learning, to hopes and to plans. In addition, it reduced potential risks to programme development. It helped us avoid cognitive overload or complexity collapse. Thus, the RBM constituted a form of 'organised complexity', for it synthesised 'simultaneously a sizable number of factors which are interrelated into an organic whole' (Weaver 1948). The RBM fostered 'cognitive fluency' (Unkelbach 2006) – the relatively rapid and easy cognitive processing of what was required to create an immersion programme. As many stakeholders were involved in its development, the

RBM framework can be considered a public and transparent agreement, thus increasing the likelihood that goals would be achieved (Thaler and Sunstein 2008).

Importantly, the RBM framework also sought to take into consideration the consequences of planned actions. It was thus an effects-based approach which addressed 'complexities by concentrating on their most nonlinear aspects: humans, their institutions, and their actions' (Smith 2006). The framework detailed stakeholder 'institutions' and emphasised the need for coordinated action by articulating required agreements among, and planned 'actions' by, stakeholders. By building in a research component where student achievement and learning materials, among others, would be evaluated and the immersion programme analysed for its effectiveness, the framework called for the assessment of the impact of programme investments and the application of learning from the assessment process. The RBM framework also reflected a desire to influence people's perceptions and behaviour. It included a substantial parent information and public relations component whose ultimate goal was to support parents in establishing an association of parents for immersion. The RBM framework sought to reduce the risk of staff turnover by 'including participants in development processes' in order to 'increase their ownership and develop a reluctance to leave behind [their] own brainchild'.

It was less important that the RBM framework be perfect than that it be an exercise in knowledge building and that stakeholders agree amongst themselves that this was the vision of what needed to be accomplished, who would be involved and what needed to be invested into creating the programme. It was also a principal means for communicating that vision. On the one hand, the RBM framework offered a certain stable vision of how to move forward; on the other hand, it included a research component and several other elements that would foster reflection and discussion during programme implementation so that corrective measures could be undertaken when necessary – an iterative approach. The RBM would remain a living document, returned to and reported on regularly. Furthermore, enough time and effort had to be invested in building the RBM framework to ensure people understood and supported it. Estonian Ministry of Education (EME) senior official Epp Rebane (2009) said that she began to wonder initially why organisers kept refining planned outcomes, outputs and indicators and seeking Ministry approval for changes, but with hindsight 'this approach was justified as project development had been problem free/immaculate'. However, this also suggests that there are limits to how much time officials can dedicate to an initiative such as this and that we had come close to reaching that limit.

BUILDING BELIEF AND AGREEMENTS

Over one year of stakeholder cooperation and more than 100 000 euros (at the time a considerable sum for Estonia) were invested into learning about the immersion option before the RBM framework was fully developed and agreed upon. One of the first mechanisms that was used to begin to build a case for immersion was a letter from the Estonian Minister for European Integration to the Canadian Ambassador that identified the need to improve language-learning opportunities for Russian speakers and that invited Canadian input in this area. Local government officials and educators were interviewed to gauge their interest in immersion. All interviewees expressed a strong interest in learning more about Canadian immersion programmes. This provided a sufficient case for the Canadian Embassy to invite Estonian officials and potential donors to an initial meeting on immersion. For Canada, a nation that had fought in two major wars in Europe during the twentieth century, supporting regional stability in Europe was a foreign policy priority (Asari 2009).[4]

Several representatives of the Estonian Ministry of Education (EME) were invited to the initial meeting at the Canadian Embassy Office in order to increase the likelihood that a critical mass of the Ministry's senior leadership would work together to build a common understanding of immersion and its possible application in Estonia. Those invited could be considered a high-status group capable of influencing public as well as government opinion, policy and financing decisions. By June 1998, an 11-member steering committee consisting of these same stakeholders began to meet on a monthly basis at the Canadian Embassy Office in order to explore the immersion option. I was a member of that committee.

One member, Kai Võlli (2009),[5] who in 1998 was an adviser in the EME's General Education department, indicated that when the committee began its work she was 'more curious about the idea than a convinced supporter of immersion'. In the Estonian context, she considered immersion programmes as isolated, special cases that 'could not be replicated on a national level, and which would not necessarily be sustainable'. Auli Udde (2010),[6] Principal Estonian Language Adviser in the same Ministry department, affirmed that the first meeting in 1998 'did not convince her in the slightest' of the merits of immersion. Epp Rebane (2009),[7] then Head of the EME's General Education department, remarked that her 'initial stance was sceptical and cautious', as a cursory description of immersion programmes and their results did not seem 'possible or credible'. Their beliefs were common among many Estonian stakeholders.

In short, beliefs were a major force in preventing the adoption of an immersion programme, and it would take more than information-sharing to help people change their beliefs (*cf.* Kegan and Laskow Lahey 2009). Nevertheless, despite these beliefs, these officials were prepared to learn more about immersion. The committee approved an Estonian, Canadian and Finnish collaboration project that started a process of knowledge- and partnership-building that would allow participants to decide whether immersion was appropriate for Estonia or not. Finland had its own successful immersion programmes, and its education system enjoyed a high status in the eyes of Estonian officials.

Committed individuals, drawing on personal and professional relationships and networks, were key mechanisms for moving the project forward. An important counterweight to the risk inherent in this proposed knowledge-building project was trust arising from past cooperation and the knowledge that all the partners had a reputation of delivering on their commitments. It was the 'soft' forces of trust and respect for diverse opinions that would help people keep an open mind regarding immersion and would allow them to seek and quickly obtain financing from the Canadian International Development Agency (CIDA), the EME and the Finnish Ministry of Foreign Affairs. Finland, like Canada, was interested in promoting regional stability. Each donor's willingness to support the project made the other donors feel more secure in their decision to support the project. The speed at which financing was provided helped to ensure that momentum was maintained and stakeholder attention was not drawn to other pressing needs. Moreover, government officials were given a safe opportunity to learn about immersion education as one option for addressing what was perceived as a pressing national priority. Immersion was not being pushed on anyone; instead, people were being drawn toward it.

With CIDA financing, an international seminar on immersion was prepared in close cooperation with the EME. The EME first surveyed 31 schools in order to map the current context. At least 13 schools were already providing some form of additional Estonian language teaching above and beyond that required by the national curriculum (Vare 1999a). In general, the attitudes of respondents towards immersion were positive, yet they raised some concerns and described needed investments. Respondents proposed financing the development of immersion-specific learning materials, teacher training and extra-curricular language camps (Eskor-Kiviloo 1999). They cautioned that learning Estonian should start in kindergarten and that the amount of content learned should not decrease due to a change in the language of instruction (ibid.).

A three-day international seminar was held in November, 1998. This seminar is described in detail because it was a seminal moment in the development of the programme. It helped create a context favourable to the immersion option, build important relationships and begin a systematic planning process. Forces that would continue to play a role in programme development were identified and, to the extent to which it was possible, managed. In addition, key mechanisms for programme development were discussed. The seminar included 15 representatives from schools serving Russian-language students; 10 from local or national governments; 7 from Estonian institutions of higher learning (one of whom also worked in a school); 6 from NGOs; 5 from potential foreign partner institutions; 4 from foreign universities; 3 from foreign embassies and the UNDP; and 1 politician and 1 teacher trainer. Although more stakeholders, such as parents and students, could have been included, it was still a substantial gathering of stakeholders. In order to exclude people who could potentially undermine progress in the immersion initiative, representatives from schools considered to be antagonistic to the idea of immersion were not invited for there were enough challenges to be faced among those who were simply uncertain about the idea. The local and international officials attending the seminar accorded the event high status. Moreover, these same people could potentially help launch a national immersion initiative.

Key stakeholders made opening remarks that expressed, on record, their support for and/or their concerns regarding the idea. These presentations were followed by others that built the case for immersion. The goal of some of these presentations was to provide an honest report of measures to be taken for and the practical difficulties of programme implementation in order to counteract the 'too-good-to-be-true' image of immersion among some officials, and to recruit long-term commitments to the initiative. Fred Genesee (1999) described Canadian immersion programme goals and characteristics along with the results typically obtained by Canadian English-speaking immersion students learning French. This provided evidence of the effectiveness of the immersion option. Robert McConnell (1999), a Toronto District School Board (TDSB) coordinator of modern languages, described in detail the practicalities of managing a Canadian immersion programme. Teacher and researcher Nordgren and Bergström (1999) gave an overview of teacher-led activities in Finnish immersion classrooms and stressed the importance of teachers cooperating with researchers. The fact that Finnish and Canadian presenters expressed similar messages about immersion helped to build confidence in the option. Two Estonian educators from Russian-language schools provided evidence that immersion could be successfully implemented in Estonia (Asser 1999, Lille 1999). All of the above speakers touched on the importance of research, the need to be systematic, to have clearly stated goals, to work with parents and to articulate guiding principles – such as the voluntary nature of the programmes and the need to support first language (L1) in addition to second language (L2) development.

Silvi Vare (1999b) summarised research showing that between 1991–8 the level of Estonian language knowledge among non-Estonians had remained static and went on to make the case that immersion was one possible way forward. Further research was presented showing that the vast majority of Russian-speaking parents and graduating high-school students preferred a bilingual (Russian-Estonian) model of education (Vassiltšenko 1999) over a Russian-only or Estonian-only model. In addition, professor Larissa Vassiltšenko (ibid.) reported that teachers in Russian-medium schools were very resistant to educational change, most preferring the status quo. Parental support and student preference would become an important counterweight to the resistance expressed by these teachers.

Estonian academic Mart Rannut (1999) argued that knowledge of Estonian would foster integration of Russian speakers and reduce Russian government influence on them. His intervention reinforced the belief that integration of ethnic Russians would contribute to social cohesion and national security. He also suggested that voluntary immersion programmes could work even in cities such as Narva where native Estonian speakers constituted less than 5% of the population (ibid.).

Power and responsibility were shared with seminar participants as they were invited to assess immersion options and make recommendations to the EME. This fuelled their engagement. Participants analysed four models of immersion: early total, early partial, delayed, and late immersion. They concluded that early total immersion was the most suitable model for Estonia because parents were more ready to accept immersion at the elementary than at the secondary school level (Vare 1999c). They also concluded that more elementary level Estonian-language teachers would be available if such a model were adopted because of declining enrolment at that level. They also argued that it is easier for teachers at the elementary level who traditionally teach all subjects, including language, to teach in immersion than it would be for secondary level teachers who viewed themselves as subject-matter specialists and not as language teachers. In addition, they suggested that Estonia could draw on its own, albeit limited, experience with early immersion (ibid.). They pointed to the need to: define goals/roles; address the possible lack of teacher trainers; avoid over-politicisation of immersion education; ensure the programme is voluntary, and plan for independent research to measure programme success. They reported that there would be opposition to the move; that pilot schools should apply for the privilege of participating; that stakeholders needed to be involved in planning; that people needed training in planning the change, and that parents needed to be involved and helped in forming a group in support of immersion (ibid.). All of these insights were critical in planning for successful start-up and follow-through in programme development. For example, the schools that later made a well-prepared application to join the Estonian immersion programme were experienced planners and were committed to the programme. By being warned about inevitable resistance to the programme, we were able to develop strategies to lessen resistance and to deal with it in an effective manner. Making the programme voluntary reduced opposition to it.

After considerable plenary session discussion and amendments, seminar participants adopted a final communiqué (Vare 1999), which stated that:

- It is sensible to establish language immersion programming, because 30 years of international experience and research have shown that immersion is an effective language learning method, which ensures the learning of the target language without adversely affecting a student's mother tongue, identity or academic achievement;

- successful implementation of language immersion programming in Estonia requires thorough preparation.

The communiqué, a key mechanism for moving forward, itself not only reflected the group's desire to proceed with the immersion initiative, but also served as a counterweight to possible opposition to the initiative by stating that research had shown that immersion would not adversely affect L1 learning or academic performance in general. The communiqué also recognised the complexity of the task and the need for stakeholder cooperation. More specifically, it identified the need for teacher training and recognised the need for education officials to expand their knowledge base.

An understanding of the importance of stakeholder relations is reflected in the fact that the communiqué was sent to 30 major stakeholders, including those in national, regional and local government, in institutions of higher learning, and to foreign embassies and missions. A compendium (Vare 1999e) containing all seminar speeches, group work summaries and the final communiqué was published in Estonian and Russian. This publication, a mechanism for promoting development of the programme, was distributed to all seminar participants, the 30 major stakeholders and to all Russian-language schools. This signalled the importance placed by the EME on building awareness among stakeholders, managing knowledge,[8] drawing conclusions and taking action.

In January 1999, a delegation of Estonians visited Canada for 12 days to learn about immersion programmes. The delegation included teachers, head-teachers, deputy headteachers and researchers, as well as local and national government officials, including the Secretary General of the EME. This demonstrated to the Toronto District School Board (TDSB) the Estonian government's commitment to the proposed immersion project, as well as to stakeholder inclusion. Prior to travelling, the Secretary General of the EME expressed doubt about the widespread applicability of immersion. After the trip, in contrast, he thought that it would be suitable for even 'russified' areas of Estonia. Equally importantly, the trip was a seminal moment for other participants. Ministry official Epp Rebane (2009) stated that 'I only fully began to believe in it when I saw with my own eyes in Canada how effective it was'. Ministry official Auli Udde (2010) concurred that it was the people she met in Toronto and 'the [Canadian] children's language skills' that convinced her that immersion was a viable option.

Meetings took place with an array of senior TDSB officials, school managers, teachers, support staff, parents and students. In addition to the above, the delegation met with an Ontario Ministry of Education official, representatives of Canadian Parents for French, as well as with University of Toronto and York University faculty. Issues covered included programme management, public relations, cooperation with parents, research, in- and pre-service training, financing, the development of learning materials, teacher support mechanisms, the advantages and disadvantages of various types of immersion programmes, network building and curriculum development. Significant effort was invested in building relationships with the TDSB who would become a major partner and stakeholder in the Estonian immersion programme.

The trip was designed to allow the Estonian group to discuss and distil its learning and to plan for programme implementation in Estonia. In addition to daily formal debriefings, an entire day was given to articulating what an immersion programme in Estonia should achieve and how this could be done. The study visit was both a 'pull' and 'push' experience, which according to Fullan and Hargreaves (2012) is an essential dynamic in education reform. More specifically, the opportunity to learn through meetings with immersion stakeholders was a strong pull, and the day-long debriefing at the end of the visit was a push to synthesise learning and make decisions based on that learning. It was the RBM framework that provided the vehicle for synthesising that learning. The Estonian Minister of Education flew to Canada at the end of the study visit to discuss the delegation's conclusions and to lobby for continued Canadian support. This acted as an incentive for the Estonian delegation to work effectively and efficiently, and accorded additional status to the immersion initiative. This, in turn, allowed for high-level meetings with Canadian officials that led to an invitation from CIDA's president for the TDSB and the EME to submit to CIDA a project proposal for the financing of a future Estonian immersion programme.

The study visit to Canada, like all visits of Estonian immersion programme stakeholders to Finland, was followed by a series of letters from the Estonian side to its partners. These letters required skill and teamwork to craft. They were carefully constructed not simply to thank people, but to serve as a mechanism to ensure that collaboration among individuals and groups was reinforced and, indeed, officially established, and to move the project forward. They were part of the project-building architecture, the foundation work that documented past accomplishments and the current state of affairs, explained intentions and expectations, and built a case for the future.

A small group of five individuals – one university researcher, one deputy headteacher, one local and one national government official and myself – were charged with completing the RBM framework which was then circulated to various stakeholders for their feedback. This was central to maintaining the engagement of stakeholders in the initiative. In Canada, an indefatigable Robert McConnell championed the framework and the project with the Toronto District School Board. The framework became the basis for developing the project proposals that would be financed by the EME, CIDA, the Finnish Ministry of Foreign Affairs and numerous other donors.

CONCLUSION

In summary, numerous forces, mechanisms and counterweights were consciously used or otherwise came into play in laying the groundwork for the establishment of the Estonian immersion programme. A major force was a desire to increase national stability, security and social cohesion. NATO and EU membership were seen as counterweights against a perceived threat to Estonian national security emanating from Russia. The immersion initiative came to be considered an important mechanism for achieving that policy goal.

Stakeholder inclusion and relationship building grounded in trust and respect were important forces. They fuelled dialogue and decision-making through mechanisms such as a high-powered steering committee and study visits. During a study visit, the use of additional mechanisms such as debriefings and a full day for planning helped participants manage knowledge. The opportunities to learn strongly pulled or attracted people to the idea of immersion while the debriefings and planning sessions pushed people in a measured manner to synthesise learning, draw conclusions and plan for how to move forward. Having a government minister attend the end of a study visit motivated all participants to achieve and articulate a common result.

A considerable portion of the dialogue leading up to the establishment of the immersion programme was structured using mechanisms such as a communiqué, a results-based management (RBM) framework and letters. These all, and in particular the RBM framework, helped to organise the complexities of establishing a bilingual programme, and facilitated group decision-making and the articulation of intentions/goals and actions to be taken. As they constituted agreements among stakeholders, they were acts of power sharing – a powerful force in stakeholder engagement and in reaching achievable decisions that would be supported. The RBM framework was thus an act of both collective autonomy and responsibility. The RBM helped stakeholders remain grounded in the realities of programme implementation through an iterative approach that included mechanisms such as research and evaluation of the programme. Taken as a whole, the plans for establishing an immersion programme can be seen as a set of mutually agreed upon high expectations – a driving force – for the Estonian Immersion Centre, the immersion programme and for its stakeholders.

NOTES

1   A stakeholder is 'any group or individual who can affect, or is affected by, the achievement of the organization's objectives' (Lépineux 2005, referring to Freeman 1984).
2   NATO is a military alliance founded in 1949 and now comprised of 28 member states.
3   Canadian Parents for French (CPF) was founded in 1977, and is a powerful lobby that is dedicated to the promotion and creation of French second-language learning opportunities for young Canadians.
4   Marina Asari was the Head of the Canadian Embassy Office in Tallinn. This and further references to Asari (2009) refer to interview data. I interviewed 15 decision-makers in 2009 and 2010. In addition to Asari, interviewees included the then Minister of Education and Research, four former Government minsters, a member of parliament, three senior officials at the Ministry of Education and Research, the former and current directors of the immersion centre, key immersion centre managers, and the director of the national Integration Foundation. Ten people were interviewed in person. Those interviews were recorded. Five people preferred to respond in writing.

5   This and further references to Võlli (2009) refer to interview data.
6   This and further references to Udde (2010) refer to interview data.
7   This and further reference to Rebane (2009) refer to interview data.
8   'Knowledge management is the process of capturing, distributing, and effectively using knowledge' (Davenport 1998).

REFERENCES

Asser, H. (1999). 'Keelekümblus kakskeelse õppekava kaudu' ('Language Immersion Through a Bilingual Curriculum'). In S. Vare (ed.), *Keelekümblus kui integratsiooni võti (Immersion – A Key to Integration)*. Tallinn: Haridusministeerium, 29–34.

Baker, C. (2011). *Foundations of Bilingual Education and Bilingualism (fifth edition)*. Bristol: Multilingual Matters.

Baker, C. (2006). *Foundations of Bilingual Education and Bilingualism (fourth edition)*. Clevedon: Multilingual Matters.

Blank, S.J. (1998). 'Russia and the Baltics in the Age of NATO Enlargement'. *Parameters*. Autumn, 50–68.

Cloud, N., Genesee, F. and Hamayan, E. (2000). *Dual Language Instruction: A Handbook for Enriched Education*. Boston, Mass.: Heinle & Heinle.

Cummins, J. (2000). *Language, Power, and Pedagogy: Bilingual Children in the Crossfire*. Clevedon: Multilingual Matters.

Davenport, T. and Prusak, L. (1998). *Working Knowledge: How Organizations Manage What They Know*. Boston, Mass.: Harvard Business School Press.

Doran, G.T. (1981). 'There's a S.M.A.R.T. Way to Write Management's Goals and Objectives'. *Management Review*, 70: 11, 35–36.

Eskor-Kiviloo, H. (1999). 'Koolidele saadetud kusimustiku kokkuvote' ('School Questionnaire Summary'). In S. Vare (ed.), *Keelekümblus kui integratsiooni võti (Immersion – A Key to Integration)*. Tallinn: Haridusministeerium, 81–6.

Fullan, M. (2001). *Leading in a Culture of Change*. San Francisco: Jossey-Bass.

Hargreaves, A. and Fullan, M. (2012). *Professional Capital Transforming Teaching in Every School*. New York: Teachers College Press.

Genesee, F. (1999). 'Teise keele kümblusprogrammid' ('Second Language Immersion Programmes'). In S. Vare (ed.), *Keelekümblus kui integratsiooni võti (Immersion – A Key to Integration)*. Tallinn: Haridusministeerium, 7–16.

Government of Estonia (2000). *Riiklik programm: Integratsioon Eesti ühiskonnas 2000–2007 (State Programme: Integration in Estonian Society 2000–2007)*. Tallinn: Government of Estonia.

Hornberger, N.H. (ed.) (2008a). *Encyclopedia of Language and Education (second edition)*. New York, NY: Springer.

Howard, E.R., Sugarman, J., Christian, D., Lindholm-Leary, K.J. and Rogers, D. (2007). *Guiding Principles for Dual Language Education (second edition)*. Washington, DC: Center for Applied Linguistics.

Huxham, C. (1996). 'Group Decision Support for Collaboration'. In C. Huxham (ed.), *Collaborative Advantage*. London: Sage, 141–51.

Immersion Programme (2014). *15 Years of Language Immersion*. Tallinn: Innove Language Immersion Programme.

Kahneman, D. (2011). *Thinking Fast and Slow*. London:Allen Lane.

Kegan, R. and Laskow Lahey, L. (2009). *Immunity to Change: How to Overcome It and Unlock the Potential in Yourself and Your Organization*. Boston: Harvard Business Press.

Kello, L. (2009). 'The Advantages of Latitude: Estonia's Post-Communist Success Story'. In K. Brockmann, D. Bosold (eds), *Democratization and Security in Central and Eastern Europe and the Post-Soviet States*. Berlin: Deutsche Gesellschaft für Auswärtige Politik e.v., 7–11.

Kissinger, H. (1994). 'Foreign Policy as Psychoanalytic Social Engineering: NATO: If the Administration's Partnership for Peace is designed to propitiate Russia, how can it also serve as a way station into the Atlantic alliance?' *Los Angeles Times*, 23 January 1994.

Kotter, J.P. (1996). *Leading Change*. Boston: Harvard Business School Press.

Lépineux, F. (2005). 'Stakeholder Theory, Society and Social Cohesion. *Corporate Governance*. 5: 2, 99–110.

Lille, V. (1999). 'Keeleõppe nullklass Aseri Keskkoolis' ('Preparatory Class for Language Learning in the Aseri School'). In S. Vare (ed.), *Keelekümblus kui integratsiooni võti (Immersion– A Key to Integration)*. Tallinn: Haridusministeerium, 35–40.

Lyster, R. (2007). *Learning and Teaching Languages Through Content: A Counterbalanced Approach*. Philadelphia, PA: John Benjamins.

Mackey, W.F. (1976). *Bilinguisme et contact des langues*. Paris: Klincksieck.

McConnell, R. (1999). 'Keelekümbluse kogemustest Kanadas' ('The Canadian Language Immersion Experience'). In S. Vare (ed.), *Keelekümblus kui integratsiooni võti (Immersion – A Key to Integration)*. Tallinn: Haridusministeerium, 17–20.

Mehisto, P. (2011). *Navigating Management and Pedagogical Complexities in Bilingual Education: An Estonian case study*. PhD thesis. London: University of London.

Näsi, J. (2002). 'What is Stakeholder Thinking? A Snapshot of a Social Theory of the Firm'. In J. Näsi, S. Näsi (eds), *Management Tensions and Configurations. Papers on Strategic Management Issues in the Stakeholder Society, Reports from the School of Business and Economics, Nr. 30*. Jyväskylä: University of Jyväskylä, 15–29.

NATO (2004). *Enhancing Security and Extending Stability Through NATO Enlargement*. Brussels: NATO.

Nordgren, B., Bergström, M. (1999). 'Mitmekeelsuse kasvatus Soomes' ('Multilingual Education in Finland'). In S. Vare (ed.), *Keelekümblus kui integratsiooni võti (Immersion – A Key to Integration)*. Tallinn: Haridusministeerium, 21–8.

Pavelson, M. (1998). *Mitmekultuuriline Eesti: väljakutse haridusele (A Multicultural Estonia: Challenges for the Education System)*. Põltsamaa: Vali Press.

Raun, T.U. (2001). *Estonia and the Estonians (second edition)*. Stanford, CA: Hoover Institute Press.

Smith, E. (2006). *Complexity, Networking, and Effects-Based Approaches to Operations*. Washington, DC: National Defense University Centre for Advanced Concepts and Technology.

Thaler, R.H., Sunstein, C. R. (2008). *Nudge: Improving Decisions About Health, Wealth, and Happiness*. New Haven, CT: Yale University Press.

Rannut, M. (1999). 'Keelekümblus kui keeleõppepoliitika osa' ('Language Immersion as Reflected in Language Policy'). In S. Vare (ed.), *Keelekümblus kui integratsiooni võti (Immersion – A Key to Integration)*. Tallinn: Haridusministeerium, 61–6.

Unkelbach, C. (2006). 'The Learned Interpretation of Cognitive Fluency'. *Psychological Science*. 17: 4, 339–45.

Vare, S. (1999a). 'Eessõna' (Foreword). In S. Vare (ed.), *Keelekümblus kui integratsiooni võti (Immersion – A Key to Integration)*. Tallinn: Haridusministeerium, 4–6.

— (1999b). 'Eesti keele õpetamine vajab uuendamist' ('Estonian Language Teaching Needs to be Modernised'). In S. Vare (ed.), *Keelekümblus kui integratsiooni võti* (*Immersion – A Key to Integration*). Tallinn: Haridusministeerium, 45–56.

— (ed.) (1999c). 'Ruhmatööde kokkuvõte' ('Group Work Summary'). In S. Vare (ed.), *Keelekümblus kui integratsiooni võti* (*Immersion – A Key to Integration*). Tallinn: Haridusministeerium, 70–78.

— (ed.) (1999d). 'Lõppdokument' ('Final Communiqué'). In S. Vare (ed.), *Keelekümblus kui integratsiooni võti* (*Immersion – A Key to Integration*). Tallinn: Haridusministeerium, 79.

— (ed.) (1999e). *Keelekümblus kui integratsiooni võti* (*Immersion – A Key to Integration*). Tallinn: Haridusministeerium.

Vassiltšenko, L. (1999). 'Vene kogukonna haridusvajadused' ('The Russian Community's Education Needs'). In S. Vare (ed.), *Keelekümblus kui integratsiooni võti* (*Immersion – A Key to Integration*). Tallinn: Haridusministeerium, 57–60.

Vihalem, T. (2008). 'Keeleoskus ja hoiakud' ('Language Skills and Attitudes'). In R. Vettik (ed.), *Eesti Ühiskonna Integratsiooni monitooring 2008* [*Monitoring Report on Estonian Societal Integration 2008*]. Tallinn: Integratsiooni Sihtasutus, 71–80.

Zetterberg, S. (2009). *Eesti ajalugu* (*History of Estonia*). Tallinn: Tänapäev.

FORCES	MECHANISMS
Key values in human relations	**People**
Trust Respect	A high-powered steering committee High status supporters Networks Committed indefatigable individuals Experts in the field (Estonian, Canadian, Finnish)
Principles for cooperation	
Stakeholder inclusion Power sharing Recognition of local expertise Frankness regarding challenges Transparency of plans & of how success will be measured	**Knowledge building**
	A carefully constructed seminar that engaged participants in analysis and decision-making A communiqué (developed with stakeholders) Managed knowledge (e.g. a compendium of seminar presentations and group work) Study visits (including diverse stakeholder representatives from practitioner to Minister)
Goals	
High expectations for all Buy-in to a vision (intended impacts) to guide programme development Relationship building Construction of a coherent narrative common to key stakeholders	**Agreements**
	Letters (constructed in teams) Debriefings & resulting minutes and decisions A results and effects-based management framework
Beliefs	**Vehicles**
A belief in the value of and a desire for greater national stability and social cohesion Fear of Russia A belief in immersion A belief by many teachers in russian-medium schools in the status quo Seeing is believing (seeing immersion students with one's own eyes)	Adequate financing (preferably flexible) An immersion centre to lead & manage change Teacher in- & pre-service training In-service training for government officials Language camps for students Project evaluation criteria & project research Criteria for selecting schools
Founding principles	**Plans**
Time for learning and discussion Learning for all Voluntary nature of programme Additive nature of programme (does not detract from l1 or subject learning) Competition for schools to enter programme Meticulous planning An iterative, results & effects-based approach	Strategies and work plans for the creation of: - student and teacher learning materials - extra-curricular activities - effective learning environments A strategy and work plan for: - project expansion - managing public relations

COUNTERWEIGHTS

Individual learning	Group learning
Strong pull	Measured push
Status quo in monolingual schools	Benefit to students and society
Many indicators of success	Short-term student achievement
Results-based plans	Iterative approach
Challenges of immersion	Benefits of immersion
Risk-taking	Trust/confidence in partnerships

5 UTAH:
Making Immersion Mainstream

Jamie Leite (Utah State Office of Education) and Raquel Cook
(Utah Valley University)

CHAPTER NAVIGATOR

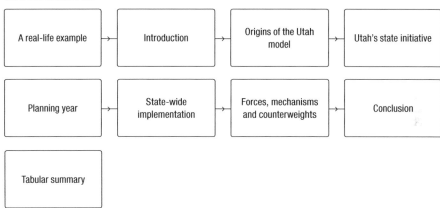

A REAL-LIFE EXAMPLE

In 1979, 11 first graders and 16 second graders, backed by highly supportive parents, entered Utah's first immersion programme at Cherry Hill Elementary School (Howe 1983). One family, whose child had already experienced immersion, helped launch the Spanish programme for English-speaking children by convincing the Alpine School District to provide $2000 for supplies. Over the following 30 years, Alpine would offer similar programmes at eight other elementary schools. However, by 2009, only three programmes remained. State standardised testing, a lack of support in some secondary schools, and the departure of teachers and students contributed to the decline.

In addition to Alpine, other school districts in the state of Utah began creating immersion programmes. In 1999, concern for English language learners at Timpanogos Elementary School in Provo led administrators to establish a 50/50, two-way Spanish immersion programme. In the following years,

Salt Lake School District launched a similar programme at two schools, and Washington County School District started a whole-school Spanish immersion programme. Shortly thereafter, Davis and Granite School Districts also began to develop a Spanish immersion programme for four of their own schools.

For 30 years, between 1979 and 2009, immersion programmes throughout the state of Utah were established as the result of educator and parent groups lobbying their local school boards. The motivations of these groups varied from enrichment opportunities for gifted children, to bilingual support for immigrant children, to preparation for future missionary opportunities. However, these grassroots initiatives often lacked adequate financial resources, and educators did not have systematic access to professional development. Although some collaboration took place, schools, individual teachers and principals had to assume the responsibility for creating curriculum, teaching and advocating for immersion with little external support.

This environment changed in 2008 when mechanisms such as legislation and funding came together in support of a state-sponsored language immersion model. By the autumn of 2014, Utah had made immersion a mainstream option in 118 public schools across the state, with over 25 000 students enrolled in five languages: Chinese, French, German, Portuguese and Spanish. This was the first and largest state-supported immersion initiative in the United States.[1] As a religiously and politically conservative state with fewer than three million inhabitants, Utah is a surprising location for such a rapidly growing state-funded programme. However, despite its conservative nature, Utah is becoming a model for the expansion of dual-language immersion across the country.[2]

INTRODUCTION

This chapter traces the origins of the Utah model of immersion, which grew from a series of separate grassroots programmes into a state-wide language initiative. It discusses how this initiative led to the creation of a state-approved 50/50 immersion model, starting in Grade 1 and continuing throughout high school and into local universities. Finally, the chapter examines the forces, mechanisms and counterweights that are influencing the development of the Utah immersion programme.

ORIGINS OF THE UTAH MODEL

In 2004, at the invitation of Davis School District Assistant Superintendent Craig Poll, Principals Becky Hunt and Ofelia Wade accepted the challenge of integrating Spanish immersion into their schools. They began by contacting renowned immersion academics and were directed to Tara Fortune at the Center for Advanced Research on Language Acquisition (CARLA) at the University of Minnesota. Under Fortune's guidance, Hunt and Wade delved into the literature on language education and began visiting immersion programmes. They developed a proposal outlining a 50/50 immersion model in which students would learn curriculum with an English-speaking teacher for half the day and a Spanish-speaking teacher for the other half of the day. The Davis school board approved the proposal in 2005, pledged $20 000 for programme development and set aside a year for planning.

During this planning year, Gregg Roberts, the world language specialist at Granite School District in Utah, visited the Davis School District. Roberts was inspired by plans to launch an immersion programme in two schools. In 2006, after Davis School District officially launched immersion at Eagle Bay and Sand Springs, Roberts received permission from Granite's school board to implement a pilot programme in two schools patterned after the one that Wade and Hunt had created. In the autumn of 2007, Granite School District began 50/50 Spanish immersion at Vista and William Penn Elementary Schools.

UTAH'S STATE INITIATIVE

While immersion was being developed in Davis and Granite, a small committee composed of world language specialists from Alpine, Davis, Granite and Murray School Districts began meeting with supervisors at the Utah State Office of Education (USOE) to discuss issues in language education. The group, which included Gregg Roberts, eventually became the Utah World Languages Coordinators' Committee. In late 2005, the state supervisor responsible for language education retired from the USOE, leaving the World Language Specialist position vacant. Because there were insufficient funds to hire someone full-time, Roberts initially filled the position on an informal basis and later began officially splitting his contract between Granite and the USOE. As an enthusiastic champion who believed in the value of immersion, Roberts would become a key mechanism in launching a state-wide dual-language immersion programme.

Soon after Roberts transitioned into his new role at the USOE, the state governor's office requested a meeting with him to discuss language education. During that meeting, Governor Jon Huntsman, himself a Chinese speaker, and Senator Howard Stephenson, Chair of the Utah State Senate Education Committee, tasked Roberts with creating a distance-education programme that would introduce Chinese and Arabic into the state's high schools. In March 2007, using future economic growth as a selling point, Senator Stephenson helped pass two bills in the Utah legislature that were critical to the future development of these and other language programmes across the state. Senate Bill 2 provided $100 000 of ongoing funding for a full-time world language specialist, a position that Roberts was soon offered; and Senate Bill 80 provided $230 000 over six years to create the Critical Language Pilot Program for online Chinese and Arabic programmes in 20 secondary schools across Utah.

Once these programmes were functioning successfully, Roberts was able to draw on this political capital to convince Senator Stephenson that if legislators wished to increase the number of Utah citizens proficient in foreign languages, they would need to focus on younger learners and involve more students at a lower cost. Roberts proposed the state-wide replication of the type of Spanish immersion programme being offered by the Granite and Davis districts. Governor Huntsman and Senator Stephenson used their influence to help bring Roberts's vision of an elementary school language immersion programme into being. In 2008, Senate Bill 41 proposed the creation of a state-wide dual-language immersion programme. Several key individuals – State Senator Howard Stephenson, House sponsor Bradley Last and Deputy Superintendent Larry Shumway – played critical roles in convincing state legislators to vote for the bill, which was entitled *The International Education Initiative: Critical Languages Programs*. The law earmarked a total of $750 000, with $480 000 for the existing Critical Language Programme and $270 000 for the dual-language immersion programme. In the 2008 general legislative session, Senate Bill 41 became law with a unanimous vote.

Following the Davis and Granite model, the law stated that the immersion programme would offer 50% of instruction through English and 50% through the target language, beginning in kindergarten or Grade 1, with the intention of adding one grade level each year. Though Huntsman and Stephenson initially intended for the immersion programme to be in Chinese, Roberts lobbied for Spanish and French as well. The legislation foresaw 15 schools with immersion: six with Spanish, six with Chinese, one with Navajo and two with French. However, the Navajo reservation school chose not to participate and, surprisingly, 21 new schools applied for the programme. All were accepted and received grants of $6000 to $18 000 each. In addition to these 21 schools, the four schools piloting immersion in the Davis and Granite School Districts also received state support.

Under the auspices of the governor's office and with the support of key stakeholders from the education and business communities, three summits served as a mechanism for creating a long-term language plan for the state. The first was the Governor's Language Summit, which focused on the link between language education and Utah's capacity to participate in the global economy. Attendees included state K–12 administrators, local university professors and renowned national language experts. Six months later, the Utah International Education Summit brought together influential K–12 and university educators from across the state to discuss the logistics of implementing language immersion in Utah's schools. Finally, the Salt Lake City Language Summit concentrated on the need for language skills among the workforce. This third summit was sponsored by the World Trade Center Utah and included 15 representatives from local businesses who provided their insights and ideas regarding the need for language and cultural skills in navigating a global economy.

The three summits were central mechanisms in driving forward the language education agenda. A major outcome was the Utah Language Roadmap, which established an ambitious language education plan to prepare Utah students to enter a changing global economy for the benefit of Utah's businesses, education system, government agencies and citizens (Roberts and Talbot 2009). Written primarily by Gregg Roberts and Sandra Talbot, the roadmap was endorsed by the Governor, the State Superintendent of Schools and the World Trade Center Utah. Within the roadmap, eight languages were determined to be essential for Utah's economic future: Arabic, Chinese, French, German, Japanese, Portuguese, Russian and Spanish.

PLANNING YEAR

In preparation for the August 2009 launch of programmes, Roberts worked closely with Myriam Met, a consultant Roberts has described as 'the mother of Utah dual-language immersion', and a team including Ann Tollefson,

Sandra Talbot and Kaye Murdock. During the 2008–9 planning year, stakeholders visited immersion programmes throughout the United States. The ultimate goal was to balance established research and practice in language acquisition with the practicality of implementing immersion on a larger scale. Three of the most influential visits took place in Fairfax County Public Schools in Virginia, Montgomery County Public Schools in Maryland and Portland Public Schools in Oregon. After observing these programmes, the team decided to combine what they felt were the strengths of each. From Fairfax, they took the 50/50 model, which split content instruction between two languages. From Montgomery County, they replicated the scheduled time for explicit instruction in target language literacy. From Portland, they formed English and target language teacher teams at each grade level who would share a cohort of students and collaborate to ensure that each achieved academic and linguistic proficiency. The strength of the Utah team was its ability to compromise in an effort to maximise the benefits of immersion while pragmatically alleviating potential threats from those that might oppose the programme.

Roberts wanted the 50/50 model in Utah for several reasons. First, the model had been successfully implemented by Davis and Granite School Districts. Second, allotting 50% of the day for students to develop their English literacy skills with a certified English-speaking teacher acted as a counterweight to parental and administrative fears about any possible negative impact on English language proficiency that might have resulted from a more extended immersion component. Third, the 50/50 model involved two classrooms per grade, allowing twice as many students to be enrolled in immersion while only dedicating one full-time employee per grade to the target language. This practicality made the transition to the programme easy, inexpensive and marketable, with minimal effect on the rest of the school population. The model was also believed to be replicable and sustainable, with the ability to remain consistent across the state.

Highly qualified teachers with proficiency in the target languages were considered essential to the success of the future state-wide immersion programme. Accordingly, immersion programme teachers were, and continue to be, required to obtain at least an Advanced-Mid level score on the Oral Proficiency Interview (OPI), a proficiency test developed by the American Council on the Teaching of Foreign Languages (ACTFL), in the target language. In subsequent years, additional testing requirements have been added to assess reading and writing.

To create the initial candidate pool of Spanish, French and Chinese immersion teachers, administrators looked to the local Utah population to find licensed teachers with native or native-like language proficiency in the target languages. However, the demand outweighed the local supply, and the state needed to bring teachers in from outside the United States. Roberts began Utah's International Guest Teacher Programme by negotiating or renegotiating Memoranda of Understanding (MoU) with agencies in five countries: China, France, Mexico, Spain and Taiwan. Each MoU was signed by the USOE and a foreign state or federal agency that was responsible for creating a candidate pool of experienced and credentialed foreign teachers with English proficiency. Under the leadership of Sydnee Dickson, specialists in the Department of Curriculum and Instruction and staff in the Department of Educator Licensing at the USOE collaborated to facilitate licenses for international teachers to teach in Utah.

Today, guest teachers are granted a work visa for one to three years. USOE or district representatives interview candidates virtually or through in-person recorded sessions, creating a pool from which principals can choose their teachers. At the local level, international guest teachers provide students with an authentic connection to the target culture and language. As a counterweight to their inexperience in the American school system, guest teachers are paired with English partner teachers who have roots in the community and school. Across grade levels in the immersion programme, principals also attempt to balance the numbers of international guest teachers with local speakers of the target language.

STATE-WIDE IMPLEMENTATION

In the autumn of 2009, at the time of the programme's launch, several significant events occurred at the state level. Governor Jon Huntsman became the American Ambassador to China and Lieutenant Governor Gary Herbert, another supporter of immersion, became governor. Larry Shumway, a significant force in the passing of Senate Bill 41, became the State Superintendent of Schools. These three individuals would have an impact on the development of immersion by serving as mechanisms for growth.

Prior to the start of the programme, the first Annual Utah Dual Immersion Institute (AUDII) was held in August 2009. Over 150 teachers and administrators attended the one-day event. Myriam Met and Tara Fortune were keynote speakers. Twenty-five schools in ten districts around the state participated in the event as members of the initiative: the four original Granite and Davis District schools, eight additional schools with Spanish immersion, five schools with French and eight with Chinese.

During this first year, consultant Greg Duncan used the ACTFL proficiency scale to develop state-level language proficiency benchmarks for each language in listening, speaking, reading and writing. The proficiency standards now guide instruction at all levels of dual-language immersion in Utah. Teachers receive training regarding language proficiency and use standardised proficiency reports at parent-teacher conferences to assess and report to parents on the progress of each student. Standardised formative and summative assessments have also been selected by the state team.

FORCES, COUNTERWEIGHTS AND MECHANISMS

Forces:

Since 2009, the initiative has grown to support more than 25 000 students in over 100 schools in five languages. While the original impetus for the initiative was economic, the sustaining force has been the public's favourable attitude towards language learning. Though politically and religiously conservative, one-third of Utah's workforce is bilingual (Sterling 2012). This multilingual and well-educated workforce is arguably the reason the state recovered from the recent economic recessions faster than the rest of the nation.

The Church of Jesus Christ of Latter-day Saints, headquartered in Salt Lake City, contributes to the high number of bilinguals. As part of their missionary efforts, the 'Mormon' church sends young men and women around the globe to learn and then to teach through foreign languages. Utah becomes home to many of these former bilingual missionaries, many of whom believe in the value of language education. Governor Jon Huntsman's former experience as a Chinese-speaking missionary led to his conviction that language learning is of great value.

Counterweights:

The implementation of dual-language immersion in Utah did not happen without opposition. Some parents refused to put their children in Chinese immersion citing ideological differences with China, its history or its political leanings towards communism. When Spanish was introduced in other schools, some criticised it as being supportive of illegal immigration by lowering the standards of English instruction for English language learners. Later, after Spanish and Chinese immersion programmes became more prevalent, some parents opposed the introduction of new immersion languages such as Portuguese. Beyond concerns about the chosen immersion language, many worried that dual-language immersion would have a negative impact on the schools in which programmes were housed. They felt that immersion would harm academic performance, detract attention from English-medium classrooms or act as elitist programmes by drawing academically advanced students. Many teachers saw immersion as a threat to their employment or their school atmosphere.

This sizable number of fears had the potential to act as a negative counterweight to the fledgling immersion programme. To counter concerns and misinformation, state and local administrators made communication a priority by disseminating information through parents' nights, faculty meetings, emails, websites and newsletters. The state team advocated for dual-language immersion as a mainstream and general education option, rather than a gifted programme, that would be appropriate for students of varying backgrounds and all ability levels (Fortune and Menke 2010). They shared research findings regarding the benefit of continued support in a student's native language and emphasised that dual-language immersion could increase academic rigour by closing the achievement gap between English language learners and native English speakers (Thomas and Collier 2012). Principals also worked to assure teachers that they would not lose their jobs because of immersion. Public opinion continues to slowly change as a result of the continued efforts of supportive school administrators, teachers and parents who raise awareness of the programme, its goals and its results.

During the first year, student applications to participate in the immersion programme came in slowly but steadily around the state as principals advertised and invested in public relations efforts. Though some believed that the immersion programme was destined to fail, within a year schools had waiting lists as they could not meet the demand. Most schools give preference to students with a sibling in the programme or to heritage learners whose parents or family members may be native speakers of the language. Beyond these exceptions, students are chosen through a lottery. No students are precluded from participation based on their learning profile. After the first year, students are only admitted to the programme if they have the requisite second language skills.

Mechanisms:

In 2010, Governor Gary Herbert and State Superintendent Larry Shumway's goal was to implement the immersion programme in 100 schools, enrolling

30 000 students by 2015. Table 1 shows the number of schools participating in dual-language immersion across the state from August 2009 to August 2014.

The growth in numbers, in part at least, came from pre-existing immersion programmes that joined the official state model since 2009. As a pioneer of immersion in Alpine School District, Principal Karl Bowman converted his school to the new state model in August 2010. Mechanisms such as financial and political support provided by state-wide infrastructure convinced him and other early developers to join the programme. Growth has also come as schools have expanded their programmes by offering several classes per grade level. Other schools have moved from offering a single strand to implementing a whole-school model in which all students participate in immersion. The number of languages offered by the state has also expanded to include Portuguese in 2012 and German in 2014, with plans for continued expansion.

Table 1: Dual-language immersion programme growth in Utah

School Year	Chinese	French	German	Portuguese	Spanish	Total number of Programmes	Total number of Students
2009–10	8	5	0	0	12 total (6 one-way, 6 two-way)	25	1400
2010–11	14	6	0	0	20 total (10 one-way, 10 two-way)	40	5500
2011–12	17	9	0	0	30 total (16 one-way, 14 two-way)	56	9400
2012–13	25	10	0	2	40 total (20 one-way, 18 two-way, 2 secondary)	77	14 000
2013–14	28	11	0	5	54 total (24 one-way, 24 two-way, 6 secondary)	98	20 000
2014–15	33	14	2	6	63 total (26 one-way, 26 two-way, 11 secondary)	118	25 000

Schools that choose to participate in the state model receive special funds from the legislature – an obvious mechanism motivating schools' participation. In 2010, Utah allocated ongoing financing of immersion totalling

$980 000 each year. Securing this funding has largely been the result of the continued efforts of Senator Howard Stephenson, who has been the mechanism in the state legislature advocating for the dual-language immersion programme. In March 2013, Stephenson successfully secured an increase in funding for the state's 100 immersion schools to approximately two million dollars. From these funds, approximately $10 000 is awarded to each school annually with the remaining money allocated to the state team for curriculum development, professional development, assessments and salaries.

Throughout the growth of the programme, Roberts has developed committees for designing curriculum, preparing materials and offering professional development to teachers. Each language is led by a director who is supported by a number of language coordinators commensurate with the number of schools offering immersion in that language. The directors and coordinators are housed in school districts around the state, acting as counterweights between the state and districts. Consultants Myriam Met, Ann Tollefson, Greg Duncan and numerous university professors have been constant advisors to the development of the initiative. Together, the directors, coordinators and consultants have been responsible for developing and translating curriculum in each of the content areas. A core belief in the value of the programme and trust in each other's contributions has been a driving force that has allowed the team to resolve conflicts and work towards a common goal.

Another important mechanism is the Dual Language Immersion Advisory Council, which is composed of principals and administrators from every school and district involved in dual-language immersion for Grades 1–9. Although schools are required to follow the state model and target language curriculum in order to receive funding and materials, they retain some liberty in implementation. Principals are encouraged to take ownership of programme logistics with the support of their individual school districts.

Utah universities serve as fundamental mechanisms by preparing teachers for a dual-language immersion teaching credential. Local universities have also committed to continued language development by accepting the responsibility to develop and teach hybrid courses for Grades 10–12 of the secondary immersion programmes. They are also preparing to serve these students after high-school graduation through advanced language courses at the university level. These offerings should act as a counterweight to students' early withdrawal from the programme as there is a practical outlet for their immersion studies beyond K–12 education (see Genesee in this volume).

National grants have also helped Utah's dual-language immersion programmes by supplementing state funding. Utah was a recipient of a K–12 Chinese Flagship Grant in 2011 and Foreign Language Assistance Program

(FLAP) grants in 2009 and 2010. As a leader in K–12 Chinese immersion, Utah developed the Flagship – Chinese Acquisition Pipeline (F–CAP) Consortium for collaboration between universities and state and local education agencies across the country. Utah was also awarded national STARTALK grants for Chinese annually from 2009 to 2013, and for Portuguese from 2012 to 2014. These mechanisms have helped support the Chinese and Portuguese programmes by financing summer student camps and teacher training for less commonly taught languages.

In 2012, Delaware became the second state in the United States to implement a state-wide immersion initiative modelled after Utah. Georgia and Wyoming have followed suit by allocating state funds specifically for dual-language immersion programmes. Utah has opened the doors of its classrooms to national and international visitors interested in implementing similar programmes. Focused attention from national media has contributed to interest in Utah dual-language immersion, raising the prestige of the programme and further fuelling programme expansion in Utah and other states.

CONCLUSION: DUAL-LANGUAGE IMMERSION TODAY

This chapter has examined the development of state-wide dual-language immersion in Utah as well as the forces, mechanisms and counterweights that shaped the implementation of the programme. Forces in Utah, including a culture of language learning, interest in the state's economic future, local knowledge of languages and a positive attitude toward language learning, provided fertile ground for a movement that would be simultaneously grass-roots and top-down. Mechanisms in human form have included stakeholders from every sphere: politicians, lawmakers, educators, business people, parents and students. The concerted efforts of these stakeholders have provided counterweights that balance the concerns and challenges threatening future expansion. Moving into the future, Utah's challenge will be to sustain momentum as people in positions of authority are replaced with new leaders who may or may not have passion for dual-language immersion. These leaders will be required to prove that the benefits outweigh the costs of the programme. In particular, they will need to demonstrate that immersion will not adversely affect those students who are not in the programme.

In August 2014, students from Davis School District's original Spanish pilot programme entered Grade 9 and students from the first year of the state model entered Grade 6. As dual-language immersion students around the state continue to progress, Utah remains committed to offering them articulated language instruction from Grade 1 onward, through to university education. Utah plans to sustain the continued expansion of the programme while further institutionalising it at the school, district and state levels. Gregg Roberts has stated that 'monolingualism is the illiteracy of the 21st century', and Utah hopes to stamp out this form of illiteracy by continuing to mainstream immersion in Utah and beyond.

REFERENCES

Christian, D. (2011). 'Dual Language Education'. In E. Hinkel (ed.), *Handbook of Research in Second Language Teaching and Learning* 2. New York, NY: Routledge, 3–20.

Fortune, T.W. and Menke, M. (2010). *Struggling Learners and Language Immersion Education: Research-based, Practitioner-informed Responses to Educators' Top Questions.* Minneapolis, MN: Center for Advanced Research on Language Acquisition (CARLA).

Fortune, T.W. and Tedick, D.J. (2008). 'One-way, Two-way, and Indigenous Immersion: A Call for Cross-Fertilization. *Pathways to Multilingualism: Evolving Perspectives on Immersion Education.* Clevedon: Multilingual Matters.

Howe, E.C. (Dec 1983). 'The Success of the Cherry Hill Spanish Immersion Program in Orem, Utah'. *Hispania,* 66: 4, 592–97.

Roberts, G. and Talbot, S. (2009). *Utah Language Roadmap for the 21st Century.* www.thelanguageflag-ship.org/media/docs/roadmaps/utah%20language%20road%20for%20the%2021st%20century.pdf (retrieved August 2012).

Sterling, T.G. (2012). 'Utah: An Economy Powered by Multilingual Missionaries'. *The Next America.* www.nationaljournal.com/thenextamerica/utah-an-economy-powered-by-multilingual-missionar-ies-20120723 (retrieved August 2012).

Thomas, W.P. and Collier V.P. (2012). *Dual Language Education for a Transformed World.* Albuquerque, NM: Dual Language Education of New Mexico, Fuente Press.

NOTES

1 For a history of immersion programmes in the broader context of the United States, see Tedick in this volume.

2 'Dual-language immersion' is defined here as a language education model dedicated to additive bilingualism and biliteracy with a minimum of 50% of the daily subject matter taught in the target language at the elementary level (Christian 2011; Tedick and Fortune 2008). Utah has chosen to use the term 'dual-language immersion' as an umbrella term to characterise all of its immersion programmes. Within Utah's official state model, two programme types may be found at the elementary level: (1) one-way or foreign language immersion, a model in which native English speakers learn a foreign or world language through immersion; and (2) two-way immersion, a model that pairs balanced numbers of native English speakers with native speakers of the target language, with instructional time divided between the two languages.

FORCES	MECHANISMS
Key values in human relations	**People**
Trust Respect	Committed parents High-status supporters (business, education, government) Networks Dedicated individuals Expert consultants
Principles for cooperation	
Stakeholder inclusion Power sharing Recognition of local expertise	
	Knowledge building and leadership
Goals	Utah World Languages Coordinators' Committee A series of summits under the auspices of the governor
Commitment to a vision that guides programme development Relationship building Construction of a coherent narrative common to key stakeholders	Dual Language Immersion Advisory Council Annual Utah Dual Immersion Institute A public information campaign Study visits to other states Committees for designing curriculum, preparing materials and offering professional development to teachers Directors and coordinators for each language
Beliefs	
A sense of mission A belief in immersion A belief in the value of building a multilingual workforce Fear (of a loss of proficiency in English, job losses) Prestige	**Agreements**
	Legislation Guest teacher programme Memoranda of understanding Language proficiency standards
Founding principles	
Time for learning and discussion Learning for all Voluntary nature of programme Additive nature of programme (does not detract from L1 or subject learning)	**Vehicles**
	State financing Centrally produced curricula Centrally produced learning materials STARTALK grants Teacher pre- and in-service training State-level office to coordinate programme
	Plans
	A one-year planning stage A pilot programme Targets Standardised assessment instruments

COUNTERWEIGHTS

Fear	Information and public meetings
Lack of interest	Initial perceived success
Mormon conservatism	Mormon tradition of seeking converts
Monolingualism as sufficient	Monolingualism as illiteracy
Elitism	Access primarily through lottery
Central control or direction	Encouragement of local initiative
Centrally used funding	Locally used funding
Emphasising one language	Emphasising a wide variety of languages
Programme attrition	Primary through university articulation
Ideological differences	Information campaign

6 BASQUE COUNTRY:
Plurilingual Education

Yolanda Ruiz de Zarobe (University of the Basque Country)

CHAPTER NAVIGATOR

```
┌─────────────────┐   ┌─────────────────┐   ┌─────────────────┐   ┌─────────────────┐
│                 │   │                 │   │ Overview of     │   │ Research in     │
│ A real-life     │ → │ Introduction    │ → │ Basque          │ → │ Basque          │
│ example         │   │                 │   │ education system│   │ Autonomous      │
│                 │   │                 │   │                 │   │ Community       │
└─────────────────┘   └─────────────────┘   └─────────────────┘   └─────────────────┘

┌─────────────────┐   ┌─────────────────┐   ┌─────────────────┐
│ Forces,         │   │                 │   │                 │
│ mechanisms      │ → │ Conclusion      │ → │ Tabular summary │
│ and counter-    │   │                 │   │                 │
│ weights         │   │                 │   │                 │
└─────────────────┘   └─────────────────┘   └─────────────────┘
```

A REAL-LIFE EXAMPLE: A PLURILINGUAL PROGRAMME IN THE COMMUNITY

In 2003, the Department of Education, Universities and Research of the Basque Autonomous Government initiated a 'Plurilingual Experience' in 12 schools of the Basque Autonomous Community (BAC). Six of these schools took part in a case study to analyse the effect of plurilingual education. The aim of this pilot study was to evaluate the effectiveness of the Plurilingual Experience programme in secondary education. Among other issues, the Department of Education sought to:

- confirm if there was an increase in linguistic proficiency in the third language (L3)
- study the impact of the introduction of this Plurilingual Experience at several educational levels on the three languages
- analyse the effect of the Plurilingual Experience on content learning.

The plurilingual programme required that at least seven hours per week be taught in the foreign language – a language other than Basque or Spanish – for four years during compulsory secondary education when students are generally 12–16 years of age. In post-compulsory education, when students are 16–18 years of age, 20–25 per cent of subjects were to be taught in the foreign language.

This longitudinal case study proved to be successful (Basque Institute of Educational Evaluation and Research, Basque Government 2007). Importantly, this study may have acted as one of the key mechanisms to drive the expansion of trilingual education in the Basque Country. In part, it was the experience and knowledge gained from the pilot study and the research into it that gave education officials and the community the assurances they needed to believe that trilingual programmes could be successful. Starting in 2010, a Trilingual Education Framework ((L1 + L2) + L3) was introduced in a significant number of private and public schools of the BAC in the fourth year of primary education (ages 10–11) and in the first year of secondary education (ages 12–13).[1] With regard to the curriculum, this was to be designed by each school depending on the availability of appropriate teaching staff and other educational criteria.[2]

INTRODUCTION

This chapter focuses on the implementation of Content and Language Integrated Learning (CLIL)[3] in the Basque Autonomous Community (BAC), a bilingual community in which both Basque and Spanish are official languages. The chapter first provides an overview of the Basque education system. It then reviews research on plurilingual education in the BAC. Finally forces, mechanisms and counterweights that have influenced the development of plurilingual education are discussed.

OVERVIEW OF THE BASQUE EDUCATION SYSTEM

The BAC is one of seventeen autonomous communities in Spain. The education system in the BAC offers three linguistic models: model A, model B and model D:

- in model A, Spanish is the main language of instruction and Basque is only taught as a subject for approximately four to five hours per week
- in model B, school subjects are taught either in Spanish or in Basque, with differences in intensity in use between the languages (ideally 50/50 in each language but see below)
- in model D, all school subjects are taught in Basque, and Spanish is taught as a subject for three or four hours per week.

These models were implemented after *the Basic Law for the Normalisation of the Use of Basque* was adopted in 1982. Since then, several other laws have been passed to help ensure that those living in the BAC know and use Basque:

- the *Law on Bilingualism* adopted in 1983 to help ensure the use of Basque in and outside the school context
- *Normalizazio Legearen Garapena* (NOLEGA; 'The Development of the Normalisation Law'), adopted in 1984 to implement suitable complementary measures for the development of Basque and the implementation of the three models (A, B, D) in 1993 in all state, semi-private and private schools.

In recent years, there has been a gradual change in the use of these models. More specifically, the prevalence of schools using model A has decreased by 70% in primary education, while model D has increased by 50%, and model B by 18%. The same is the case in secondary education, with an increase in model D and B and a progressive decrease in model A (García Gurrutxaga et al. 2011, 273). On average, model D accounts for 69% of all students in pre-primary, primary and secondary schools. These percentages confirm that far-reaching changes have occured in the status of Basque in the education system (Gorter, Zenotz, Etxagüe and Cenoz 2012, 212).

Nevertheless, as Cenoz (2009) points out, there are variations within each programme model. The following types of differences can be found in the three models:

- A+: with extra Basque or Basque as the language of instruction for one subject
- A+ English: Spanish as the main language of instruction and English as an additional language of instruction for some subjects
- B: this model has always had a great diversity regarding the distribution of the languages
- B+ English: Basque, Spanish and English as languages of instruction
- D+ English: Basque as the main language of instruction and English as an additional language of instruction for some subjects
- Foreign: English, German or French as the main languages of instruction and Spanish (and Basque in some cases) as an additional language of instruction.

Therefore, although schools use Basque and/or Spanish as their primary language(s) of instruction, they may also offer plurilingual education; in other words, different programme alternatives are used to teach through a foreign language, which in the vast majority of schools is English. Other languages, such as French or German, are offered as an optional language at secondary level, except in some international schools where these are the primary medium of instruction. In addition to the types of models already presented, new typologies are being adopted, such as the Trilingual Education Framework mentioned earlier. This further reinforces Cenoz's (2009) conclusion that 'the combination of the three models, the diversity of model B with more or less use of Basque and Spanish, and the increasing use of English as an additional language of instruction make it impossible for the Basque educational system to fit as a single type in a typology'.

Moreover, a review of the various education programmes available in the BAC show that there is an increasing number of programmes with instruction through a foreign language, and most notably English, both in the private and in the public sectors. In the public sector, these programmes include all grades until the end of compulsory secondary education, at the age of 16. These projects are called: *Early Start to English* in pre-primary education, *Ingelesa Edukien Bidez* (INEBI; 'English through Content') in primary, and *Bigarren Hezkuntzan Ingelesa Edukien Bidez* (BHINEBI; 'English through Content in Secondary Education') in secondary (these three programmes are related to the teaching of the English language). The Plurilingual Experience and the recently implemented Trilingual Education Framework are programmes which involve the teaching of any subject in a foreign language. All of these programmes aim to develop continuity across the education system by integrating content and language learning in the curriculum.

At the same time, since 1991, the *ikastolas* (Basque-medium schools that can be public or private) have been involved in the Multilingual *Eleanitz* project, a multilingual project to integrate languages in the curriculum, including the two official languages plus two additional languages, English and French. The objective of the *Eleanitz* project is to promote communicative competence in all the languages studied. Based on the Council of Europe's 2001 Common European Framework of Reference for Languages (CEFR), students are required to reach a B2+ in Basque or Spanish, a B1+ in English, and an A2 in French at the end of compulsory education (Ball and Lindsay 2010, 171).

Normalisation of the use of Basque has been an important component of all these innovative programmes in the BAC. Furthermore, the implementation of bilingualism in the schools of the BAC paved the way to multilingualism. For instance, the *ikastolas* were created in the 1960s to promote the Basque language and culture and to offer students who did not already know Basque the opportunity to learn this language, one of the official languages of the BAC. An Ikastola Network (*Ikastolen Elkartea*) was also established, which is a federation of Basque-medium schools that is 'committed to the development of the Basque language ... [it] supports the schools through the publication of materials, in-service teacher-training programmes, management and administrative services' (Ball and Lindsay 2010). Since then, there have been other programmes to promote Basque; for example, the programme *Euskaraz Bizi* ('To live in Basque') (Gorostidi 1991) which includes extra-curricular activities and motivational campaigns to promote the out-of-school use of Basque. Furthermore, as part of the effort to move from a bilingual to a multilingual education system, since the 1990s, the Ikastola Network has implemented the multilingual *Eleanitz* programme (*Eleanitz Bizi*; 'To live multilingual'). This programme aims to reinforce the teaching of foreign languages through the use of CLIL methodologies, without losing the focus on Basque. To this end, the Ikastola Network has designed a project for integrating the teaching and learning of all languages in the curriculum, as mentioned above. This project involves the early introduction of English as an L3 at the age of four and content-based instruction which, in the case of the *ikastolas*, has been adopted mainly by teaching social sciences through English (Social Science and Language Integrated Curriculum; SSLIC). The social sciences curriculum is the same in English as it is in Basque, as are the number of hours allocated to the subject (Muñoa 2011). The Ikastola Network has also created didactic materials for the integrated curriculum for all levels of compulsory education and for all four languages (Basque, Spanish, English and French). These materials are important for training teachers, as they provide feedback for improvement, as we will see in the next section. Such teacher training is usually obligatory for all the schools in the project and for all teachers at any stage of the project (Ball and Lindsay 2010). Both programmes have been researched in order to determine what has been achieved. In the next section we analyse some of the research results.

RESEARCH IN THE BASQUE AUTONOMOUS COMMUNITY

In the last few years, there has been a growing interest in research on plurilingual education in the BAC. Studies have been undertaken both by the Basque Institute of Educational Evaluation and Research (ISEI-IVEI), which is an agency of the Basque Department of Education, and by the Ikastola Network, among others. For example, the Basque Institute of Educational Evaluation and Research carried out a longitudinal case study from 2004 to 2006 on the secondary education component of the Plurilingual Experience (Alonso et al. 2008), as described in the opening section of this chapter. The evaluation looked at English proficiency (listening and reading comprehension, written and oral production and grammatical knowledge) using Cambridge (ESOL) tests. They also collected qualitative data using interviews and questionnaires.

The quantitative data from language testing indicated that the experimental group, who had been learning several subjects through the medium of English, achieved better results in English than the control group; moreover, these advantages were maintained and even increased over the course of this longitudinal evaluation. Furthermore, the qualitative data gathered through interviews, questionnaires and teachers' blogs suggested that the level of student achievement in content subjects taught through English was similar to that of the control group, who had been learning the same school subjects in Basque or Spanish. Learning through the foreign language did not seem to have any negative effects on achievement in the content subjects, although no specific tests were administered to assess content learning. On a more general level, the programme was evaluated very positively by key stakeholders (school management, teachers, students and their families).

Following on from this case study, the Trilingual Education Framework, which was implemented in two different stages (in 2010–13 in 46 schools and in 2011–14 in a total of 89 schools), has also yielded positive results. In order to be part of the project, 20% of the teaching load had to be undertaken in each of the three languages (Spanish, Basque and English), and some curriculum subjects had to be taught through English. The project also involved some funding for teacher training programmes in the experimental groups. In order to analyse the experience, the following areas were studied: reading in Basque and Spanish, mathematics and scientific competence. English proficiency was measured at the end of the first and the third years.

The results showed that both the control and the experimental groups achieved similar results in Spanish and Basque, as well as in mathematics and scientific competence. However, the experimental group had significantly higher results in English competence than the control group. Interestingly, both in English (the foreign language) and Basque (the minority language), there seems to be a minimum number of hours required in the curriculum in order to obtain better results than in the control group. Nevertheless, this is not necessary in the case of Spanish, which is the majority language of the community (Basque Institute of Educational Evaluation and Research, Basque Government 2014).

Similar positive results were obtained by the Ikastola Network in an experimental project undertaken in 2003 which involved over 400 students in the third year of compulsory secondary education (ages 14 to 15). In this case, in addition to assessing proficiency in English, the researchers also analysed content knowledge in social science using a comprehension and production test, administered in Basque to both the control and the experimental groups. Both groups received three hours of social science instruction per week; for the control group this was in Basque (their L1 or L2), while for the experimental group, English (their L3) was the medium of instruction. Otherwise, both groups had regular English-as-a-foreign-language courses with a difference in the starting age: the control group started learning English at the age of eight, while the experimental group had been introduced to English at the age of four (see Muñoa 2011 for a thorough description of the study).

The results demonstrated that the experimental group performed better in all the English skills and, at the same time, demonstrated that students learning through English achieved the same level of mastery of social sciences content as students studying through Basque. Furthermore, the experimental group was able to explain in Basque the content matter they had learned in the foreign language (Ruiz de Zarobe and Lasagabaster 2010). These very positive outcomes may be explained, in part at least, by the fact that the teachers in the experimental group had received specific in-service training in CLIL and had also received methodological support (Ball and Lindsay 2010). The importance of materials development (both in Basque and in the foreign languages), teacher training courses and other pedagogical support have been further documented by researchers of the Ikastola Network (Elorza and Muñoa 2008).

Research on CLIL carried out, among others, by researchers at the University of the Basque Country (e.g. Ruiz de Zarobe and Jiménez Catalán 2009; Ruiz de Zarobe and Lasagabaster 2010; Ruiz de Zarobe 2011) found different results depending on the language skill being measured, as has been the case in other European studies (Dalton-Puffer 2011). Positive outcomes in favour of CLIL have been reported with respect to some components of writing (overall general competence and lexical and syntactic complexity), oral fluency, reading and receptive vocabulary, for instance, in contrast, the results with respect to morphosyntax and pronunciation are less clear. Further research is called for in order to provide greater insights into the effectiveness of the CLIL approach.

ANALYSIS: FORCES, MECHANISMS AND COUNTERWEIGHTS

One of the most important mechanisms that favours the implementation of plurilingual programmes in the BAC is that the Basque Country has two official languages, Basque and Spanish. Moreover, the high status of English is a driving force, as reflected in the fact that 95% of the schools that have adopted trilingual programmes have chosen English as the third language.

Bilingualism may have a positive effect on third language acquisition, with advantages that range from cognitive benefits (Bialystok 2003, 2005) to metalinguistic awareness (Jessner 2006, 2008). However, as Cenoz (2009) points out, in order to gain maximum benefit from bilingualism when learning an additional language, it is necessary to identify the conditions needed to achieve bilingualism. In other words, it is important to understand the mechanisms and forces that have an impact on learning the second language so they can be harnessed in the learning of an additional language.

A central force that influences plurilingual education in the Basque Country is the value that is placed on foreign language learning. In comparison to other European countries, English is not very often used outside the classroom in everyday life, although the situation is slowly changing. Currently, there is easy access to English on the internet, for instance, but television and films shown in cinemas are dubbed. Original versions are seldom available. In this regard, plurilingual programmes are a useful mechanism for enhancing students' opportunity to expand their exposure to English as a foreign language during the school day without requiring extra time in the curriculum.

Despite the value placed on plurilingualism (a force) and the existence of plurilingual education programmes (mechanisms), the success of plurilingual education programmes is also dependent on some of the following conditions:

A jointly held belief in the value of CLIL can be an important force in programme development. CLIL programmes need to be embraced and promoted by all those involved (school management, teachers, students and parents), not just by individual teachers (Muñoa 2011).

High-quality learning materials are an essential mechanism in programme development. Materials must respond to the needs of students (Muñoa 2011). In the case of the *ikastolas*, the Ikastola Network prepares instructional materials, both in English and in Basque. Teachers use these materials in the classroom and provide feedback to the Network so that it can adapt them further if necessary. A similar process has been applied in Basque state schools. It is a very dynamic process whereby educators create materials and teacher-collaborators pilot them to analyse the outcomes and provide feedback about their effectiveness so that improvements can be made. Thus, the network is an important mechanism for coordinating the development of materials and encouraging teacher engagement (a force). Piloting (a mechanism), which also involves gathering and applying teacher feedback, also acts as a positive counterweight to the risks associated with the creation of new learning materials.

Professional development of teachers is another important mechanism for promoting success since teaching through a foreign language involves much more than changing the language of instruction (Muñoa 2011). As Ball and Lindsay (2010) suggest, training is always more effective when it is grounded in practice so that good practice and areas for improvement can be identified. Equally, teachers should have clear professional standards (a mechanism), not only with respect to their knowledge of the language, but also with respect to their professional development in CLIL. While it is evident that more studies are necessary to assess CLIL and plurilingual education in the Basque Country, research has nevertheless been a critical mechanism for evaluating the results of trilingual programmes in order to determine whether objectives have been achieved.

CONCLUSION

The aim of this chapter has been to present an overview of plurilingual education in the Basque Autonomous Community. It has briefly reviewed the Basque education system and research conducted on plurilingual education in the BAC. On the one hand, it is evident that belief in the value of plurilingualism has been a driving force in programme development. On the other hand, fears about the impact that learning an L3 could have on proficiency in Basque have partially been reduced by an extensive research programme – a mechanism acting as a counterweight. Other mechanisms supporting the realisation of plurilingual education include government financing, which has helped to generate numerous essential mechanisms. These forces, mechanisms and counterweights are summarised in the table found after the references to identify some of the factors that come into play as regards to plurilingual education in the BAC.

Finally, we cannot overlook the fact that plurilingual education is highly contextualised. Different forces, mechanisms and counterweights have important consequences for the development of the programmes in each community. Further research, drawing on previous outcomes, will help to ensure continuity in programmes, research and theoretical frameworks.

ACKNOWLEDGEMENTS

Funding from research grants FFI 2012-31811 by the Spanish Ministry of Economy and Competitiveness and IT311-10 (UFI 11/06) by the Basque Department of Education, Research and Universities is gratefully acknowledged. The author is also grateful to the reviewers who have been so helpful in the process of writing this chapter. Special thanks go to Colin Baker for his insightful comments.

NOTES

1   There have been two major Trilingual Education initiatives: in 2010–13 in 46 schools (1600 students), and in 2011–14 in 89 schools (3100 students) in the BAC.
2   Sincere thanks to Esmeralda Alonso from the Department of Education, Universities and Research of the Basque Autonomous Government, for her insightful comments on the various projects undertaken by the Basque Government.
3   As plurilingual education involves the concurrent teaching and learning of content and language, the term CLIL is sometimes used interchangeably with the term plurilingual education. When it is not, any distinction in use is explained.

REFERENCES

Alonso, E., Grisaleña, J. and Campo, A., (2008). 'Plurilingual Education in Secondary Schools: Analysis of Results'. *International CLIL Research Journal*, 1: 1, 36–49.

Ball, P. and Lindsay, D. (2010). 'Teacher Training for CLIL in the Basque Country: The Case of the Ikastolas – An Experience Model'. In D. Lasagabaster and Y. Ruiz de Zarobe (eds), *CLIL in Spain: Implementation, Results and Teacher Training*. Newcastle-upon-Tyne: Cambridge Scholars Publishing.

Basque Institute of Educational Evaluation and Research, Basque Government (2007). www.isei-ivei. net/eng/pubeng/Trilingual-students.pdf (retrieved May 2014).

— (2014). www.iseiivei.net/eusk/argital/HMH/HMH_2014_txosten_exekutiboa.pdf (Basque); www. isei-ivei.net/cast/pub/MET/MET_2014_informe_ejecutivo.pdf (Spanish) (retrieved May 2014).

Bialystok, E. (2003). 'Bilingualism, Aging and Cognitive Control: Evidence from the Simon Task'. *Psychology and Aging*, 19, 290–303.

— (2005). 'Consequences of Bilingualism for Cognitive Development'. Oxford: Oxford University Press.

Cenoz, J. (2009). *Towards Multilingual Education: Basque Educational Research from an International Perspective*. Bristol: Multilingual Matters.

Dalton-Puffer, C. (2011). 'Content and Language-Integrated Learning: From Practice to Principles'. *Annual Review of Applied Linguistics*,31, 182–204.

Elorza, I. and Muñoa, I. (2008). 'Promoting the Minority Language through Integrated Plurilingual Language Planning: The Case of the Ikastolas'. *Language, Culture and Curriculum,* 21: 1, 85–101.

García Gurrutxaga, M-L., Nozal, M., Villa, M. and Aliaga, R. (2011). 'Teaching Learning Foreign Languages in the Basque State Schools'. In Y. Ruiz de Zarobe, J.M. Sierra and F. Gallardo (eds), *Content and Foreign Language Integrated Learning: Contributions to Multilingualism in European Contexts*. Frankfurt am Main: Peter Lang.

Gorter, D., Zenotz, V., Etxagüe, X. and Cenoz, J. (2014). 'Multilingualism and European Minority Languages: The Case of Basque'. In D. Gorter, V. Zenotz and J. Cenoz (eds), *Minority Languages and Multilingual Education: Bridging the Local and the Global*. Berlin: Springer.

Gorostidi, J.L. (1991). *Euskaraz Bizi*. Lizarra-Estella: Euskal Herriko Ikastolen Elkartea.

Jessner, U. (2006). *Linguistic Awareness in Multilinguals*. Edinburgh: Edinburgh University Press.

— (2008). 'A DTS Model of Multilingualism and the Role of Metalinguistic Awareness'. *Modern Language Journal*, 92, 270–83.

Muñoa, I. (2011). 'Key Factors to be Considered by CLIL Teachers'. In Y. Ruiz de Zarobe, J.M Sierra and F. Gallardo (eds), *Content and Foreign Language Integrated Learning: Contributions to Multilingualism in European Contexts*. Frankfurt am Main: Peter Lang.

Ruiz de Zarobe, Y. and Jiménez Catalán, R.M. (eds) (2009). *Content and Language Integrated Learning: Evidence from Research in Europe*. Bristol: Multilingual Matters.

Ruiz de Zarobe, Y. and Lasagabaster. D. (2010). 'CLIL in a Bilingual Community: The Basque Autonomous Community. In D. Lasagabaster and Y. Ruiz de Zarobe (eds), *CLIL in Spain: Implementation, Results and Teacher Training*. Newcastle-upon-Tyne: Cambridge Scholars Publishing.

Ruiz de Zarobe, Y. (2011). 'Which Language Competencies benefit from CLIL? An Insight into Applied Linguistics Research'. In Y. Ruiz de Zarobe, J.M. Sierra and F. Gallardo (eds), *Content and Foreign Language Integrated Learning: Contributions to Multilingualism in European Contexts*. Frankfurt am Main: Peter Lang.

Ruiz de Zarobe, Y., Sierra, J.M. and Gallardo del Puerto, F. (eds) (2011). *Content and Foreign Language Integrated Learning: Contributions to Multilingualism in European Contexts*. Frankfurt am Main: Peter Lang.

FORCES	MECHANISMS
Key values in human relations	**People**
Collaboration Teacher input into learning materials	Engaged and committed teachers and other stakeholders
Principles for cooperation	
Stakeholder inclusion	**Knowledge building and leadership**
	Piloting Research
Beliefs	
A belief in the value of plurilingual education	
	Agreements
	Legislation Professional standards
Founding principles	
An iterative approach (learning as you go)	
	Vehicles
	Government financing Teacher professional development A management body to run programmes

COUNTERWEIGHTS

Risk	Piloting of programmes and materials
Lack of time for language teaching	Plurilingual education
Out-of-school language environment	School language environment
Fear of possible negative effect of plurilingual education	Additive nature of the programme

7   KAZAKHSTAN:
From Twenty Trilingual Schools to Thousands?

Peeter Mehisto (Institute of Education, University College London)

CHAPTER NAVIGATOR

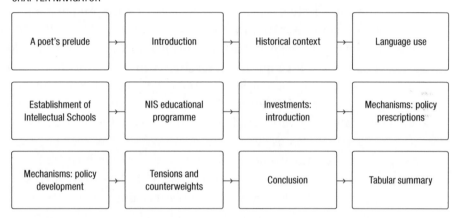

A POET'S PRELUDE

By studying the language and culture of other nations, a person becomes their equal and will not need to make humble requests ... We ought to educate ourselves, learn what other people know so as to ... be a shield and a pillar for our people.

(Kazakh poet Abai Kunanbayev, written in the 1800s,
published in English in 2005)

INTRODUCTION

The President of Kazakhstan, Nursultan Nazarbayev, initiated the establishment of a national network of 20 maths and science-oriented trilingual schools in 2008. Various content subjects in these schools are to be taught through Kazakh, others through Russian, and still others through English. By 2014, 16 purpose-built Nazarbayev Intellectual Schools were already operational throughout Kazakhstan – the ninth largest country in the world. The remaining four schools are scheduled to open in 2015. President Nazarbayev declared that these schools should 'enhance the intellectual potential of the nation'. The Intellectual Schools are also to serve as a platform for innovation in education, and are expected to support the nation's reform of pre-school, primary and secondary education, and the development of widespread proficiency in Kazakh, Russian and English.

The Intellectual Schools are managed by the Autonomous Educational Organisation Nazarbayev Intellectual Schools (AEO NIS). AEO NIS is developing its own curricula, learning materials and educator training programmes. It cooperates extensively with the Ministry of Education and Science and its sub-agencies, and with other government and non-governmental stakeholders, to accomplish its goals. In addition, it cooperates internationally with Cambridge University, Johns Hopkins University, the University of Pennsylvania and the University College London's Institute of Education, among others. AEO NIS is now also working with partner schools in Kazakhstan to share its experience with them so that these schools can offer trilingual education and improve teaching and learning in general. This chapter tells the story of how the Intellectual Schools' trilingual education programme is being developed.

The chapter first describes the language environment in Kazakhstan as this has major implications for trilingual education. It discusses how AEO NIS was created and outlines how AEO NIS is managed. This is followed by a portrait of the Intellectual Schools and their trilingual programme. The chapter also details investments made by the state through AEO NIS into building the Intellectual Schools' trilingual programme, and how the entire education system is expected to benefit from those investments. Challenges faced during these processes are outlined. Forces, mechanisms and counterweights are discussed in an integrated fashion alongside a discussion of investments and challenges. Finally, tensions and counterweights will be discussed in a separate section.

It should be noted that I have strong ties with AEO NIS. I have been working with AEO NIS as a consultant for several years and, therefore, this chapter in part reflects my first-hand experiences.

LANGUAGE ENVIRONMENT

The policies of the Government of Kazakhstan with reference to language are focused on social cohesion and an acceptance of linguistic diversity. For example, in 1995, the Russian language was accorded co-official status with Kazakh, the state language. President Nazarbayev (1996) has stressed the importance of 'equality, brotherhood, friendship and unity of people of all nationalities' and the importance for Kazakhs to retain fluency in Russian while learning other languages. In his 'Kazakhstan 2050 Strategy' address to the nation, Nazarbayev (2012) counterbalanced a target for Kazakh to take on a 'lead role in all spheres of life' in Kazakhstan with the ambitious goal for young people to learn 'Russian and English equally well as Kazakh'. There is a Presidential decree on the *Development and Functioning of Languages in the Republic of Kazakhstan for 2011–2020* that supports the learning of those three languages and others. There are also action plans to implement the decree. Over 19.1 billion tenge (19.2 million EUR) were allocated for the implementation of the *Action Plan for Languages for 2011–2013*.

The percentage of ethnic Kazakhs in the population has grown steadily, as has the status of the Kazakh language, since the establishment of independence from the Soviet Union in 1991. Kazakhs have shifted from being a minority to being the majority so that, by 2009, ethnic Kazakhs constituted 63.1% of the population (see Table 1). In most major urban environments, Kazakhs remain a minority, whereas ethnic Russians remain a minority in most rural areas. Nationally, the demographic shift in favour of ethnic Kazakhs was primarily due to the departure of ethnic Russians, Ukrainians, Germans and other nationalities to their ancestral homelands and, to a lesser extent, to the repatriation of approximately one million Kazakhs from countries such as China, Mongolia, Russia, Turkmenistan and Uzbekistan (Commission on Human Rights 2012; Tazhibayeva 2010; Usupova 2012). There are still some three million ethnic Kazakhs living abroad and, although fewer are now returning to Kazakhstan than in the past (*cf.* Buri and Finke 2013), this group represents a potential source of further demographic change. Furthermore, the ethnic Kazakh birth rate remains positive. It is about twice as high as the birth rate among ethnic Russians, who are experiencing a negative birth rate (see Table 2). If this trend is maintained, the percentage of ethnic Kazakhs in Kazakhstan will continue to rise.

Table 1: Percentage of total population of Kazakhstan by ethnicity (Zimovina 2003; CIA 2013)

Ethnicity	1959	1970	1979	1989	1999	2009
Kazakhs	30.0	32.4	36.0	39.7	53.5	63.1
Russians	42.7	42.8	40.8	37.8	29.9	23.7
Ukrainians	8.2	7.2	6.1	5.4	3.7	2.1
Germans	7.1	6.5	6.1	5.8	2.4	1.1
Tatars	2.1	2.2	2.1	2.0	1.7	1.3
Uzbeks	1.5	1.6	1.8	2.0	2.5	2.9
Others	8.4	7.3	7.1	7.3	6.3	5.8

Table 2: Birth rates and natural increase among ethnic Kazakhs and Russians (Agency of Statistics of the Republic of Kazakhstan 2013a)

	Per 1000 people								
	Index of birth rate			Index of death			Natural increase		
	2009	2010	2011	2009	2010	2011	2009	2010	2011
Kazakhs	25.4	25.7	25.6	5.9	5.8	5.7	19.5	19.9	19.9
Russians	12.9	12.8	12.8	14.4	14.9	14.6	-1.5	-2.1	-1.9

LANGUAGE USE

Despite the fact that ethnic Kazakhs are now the majority, and their numbers as a percentage of the total population are on the increase, Kazakh is not necessarily the first or strongest language of substantial numbers of Kazakhs. During the 2009 national census, 94.4% of all respondents reported that they understood spoken Russian and 84.8% indicated being able to read and write the language. With respect to proficiency in Kazakh, these figures were 74% and 62% respectively. These statistics should be accepted with some caution since language proficiency was not defined by the census and respondents may have overestimated their proficiency. According to a survey conducted in 17 cities, there appears to be a preference for the use of Russian, whether for media consumption, communication at work, with friends or in the home (Association of Sociologists and Political Analysts of Kazakhstan 2007, as referred to by Aminov et al. 2010). Generally speaking, urban areas in the north are primarily Russian-speaking, and urban and rural areas in the south and the west of the country are primarily Kazakh-speaking. Nonetheless, in more recent years, a small but noticeable shift towards the increased use of Kazakh is being experienced in the primarily Russian-speaking northern areas. This is driven by a movement of Kazakh-speakers to cities such as Astana, which has seen a three-fold increase in population over the last 16 years (Tasmaganbetov 2014), and by various government policies and programmes that have resulted in an increase in the number of jobs requiring knowledge of Kazakh and in the use of Kazakh in diverse media (Fierman 2010). At the same time, there is a growing concern that ethnic Kazakhs in the Kazakh-dominant regions of southern and western Kazakhstan are no longer regularly using Russian in the public sphere, leading to a possible decline in fluency in Russian among the population at large. As a case in point, the Intellectual Schools in these regions are finding that fewer teachers are available who can teach through the medium of Russian. Considering Kazakhstan's geopolitical position and the fact that it entered the Eurasian Customs Union in 2010 with Russia and Belarus, the demand for Russian skills in Kazakhstan is likely to remain strong.

Similarly, when one examines language use in educational settings, numerous complexities become apparent. Various languages are used as media of instruction. In the mid-1990s, just under 60% of Kazakh parents were choosing Kazakh-medium education whilst almost all ethnic Russians were choosing Russian-medium education (Kolstø and Malkova 1997). In 2013, the Agency of Statistics of the Republic of Kazakhstan (2013b) reported, without a breakdown by ethnicity, that the percentage of students studying in Kazakh-medium classes was 64.2%, the percentage in Russian-medium classes was 32% and that the remaining 3.8% of students were studying through other languages such as Uzbek, Uyghur or Tajik. The latter languages are used as the main medium of instruction in 76 schools, and to teach some content subjects in a further 74 schools (Ministry of Education and Science 2013a). The move to Kazakh-medium education is taking place in a context where Russian-medium education is still perceived as being of better quality. This popular perception is reinforced by the results of the *Programme for International Student Assessment (PISA)* (OECD 2013), which show that 66% of Kazakh-language versus 27% of Russian-language 15-year-old students are reading below Level 2.[1] Furthermore, according to the National Centre for Education Statistics and Assessment, in general, students in Russian-medium classes are outperforming students in Kazakh-medium classes on the national scholastic achievement test, the Unified National Test (UNT); the UNT serves as a gate-keeping mechanism for higher education (Ayubayeva et al. 2013).

It is noteworthy that Kazakh is also gaining ground in higher education in contrast to Soviet times, when the majority of higher education was delivered through Russian. In 2014, 57.9% of all students enrolled in universities were studying primarily through Kazakh and 40% primarily through Russian (National Center of Educational Statistics and Evaluation 2014). During the 2012–13 academic year, 54.8% of technical and vocational college students were studying primarily through Kazakh, and 45.1% through Russian (Agency of Statistics of the Republic of Kazakhstan 2013d). The increased use of Kazakh in the post-secondary education sector is likely to accord it greater status and act as a motivational force for learning the language in primary and secondary schools (see Genesee in this volume). If the still limited shift to using English at the tertiary level continues, this may have a similar effect.

ESTABLISHMENT OF THE INTELLECTUAL SCHOOLS

The Nazarbayev Intellectual Schools (NIS) were initiated in 2008 as a mechanism to achieve three primary goals: (1) to create a network of schools that would act as experimental sites offering innovative educational programmes from pre-school to high school (Shamshidinova et al. 2014); (2) to raise 'a new generation of intellectual elite' who can compete globally whilst maintaining traditional Kazakhstani values (Nazarbayev 2009), and (3) to cultivate fluency in Kazakh, Russian and English. This in turn would foster social cohesion and national stability, help to build a common Kazakh sense of identity and integrate the nation further with the rest of the world. Collectively, these multiple aspirations became a force driving the development of NIS and the reform of the secondary education system at large. These are an exceptionally high set of expectations to place on one organisation. As a counterweight to the risks associated with these expectations, AEO NIS, which operates with 100% of its financing coming from the state budget, benefits from high levels of support from government (decree of the Government of the Republic of Kazakhstan 45213 May 2008).

The primary mechanism for developing the Intellectual Schools was a newly created joint stock company named Orken ('sprout' or 'shoot' in Kazakh). Another powerful mechanism was Orken's Board of Directors. The Deputy Prime Minister of Kazakhstan was its chair. Other members included senior representatives of the Office of the President of Kazakhstan, the Ministry of Education and Science, the Ministry of the Economy and Budget Planning, the Ministry of Finance, and the Orken CEO. The President's support of the initiative accorded it high status. This was a powerful force that facilitated access to mechanisms such as various national and local government agencies, extensive cooperation with several of the top ranked universities in the world, and budgetary resources. It also facilitated the use of forces such as stakeholder inclusion and cooperation.

Despite being able to rely on such powerful forces and mechanisms, a series of negative counterweights hindered the establishment of a truly innovative educational programme. These included requirements to follow the existing national curriculum, to use national assessment instruments and to take into account regulations related to teacher remuneration. In response, Orken's board arranged for new legislation according full 'academic' autonomy to Orken's successor organisation, AEO NIS. The legal status of AEO NIS allows it to build schools, hire teachers and other staff, set pay scales, provide professional development, select students, adopt its own curricula, develop learning materials, monitor progress in programme development, use its own school-leaving assessment instruments, and issue students interim and final certificates (Law of the RK No. 394-IV 2011). AEO NIS is a central mechanism for developing the Intellectual Schools; however, it also includes several sub-agencies that serve as important mechanisms in their own right:

- **The Centre of Excellence**. The primary function of this centre is to share AEO NIS experience with state schools (henceforth referred to as comprehensive schools). It provides professional development to comprehensive schools' teachers, vice-principals and principals, as well as to the staff of the Intellectual Schools. The centre has developed its professional development programmes in cooperation with Cambridge University's Faculty of Education. In order to deliver professional development and to build capacity within the existing national in-service teacher training system, the centre is working in close cooperation with Orleu (the National Centre for Professional Development) and Kazakh universities. Over 120 000 educators are to be trained during its first five years of operation.

- **The Centre for Educational Programmes**. This centre develops curriculum documents that aim to synthesise best Kazakhstani and international educational practice. It is also responsible for guiding the implementation of trilingual education. In addition, the centre facilitates the implementation of curriculum through training and programme monitoring and evaluation. The Centre co-operates with the National Academy of Education to develop new national education standards and subject programmes in order to support the current national shift from an 11-year to a 12-year education system. The Centre also co-operates with Cambridge International Examinations to develop and implement curricula.

- **The Educational Resource Centre**. This centre develops hard copy and electronic learning materials for K–12. Among others, it cooperates with Kazakh authors, editors and illustrators, and with Cambridge University Press and University College London's Institute of Education.

- **The Centre for Pedagogical Measurement**. This centre develops systems for assessing the quality of primary and secondary education and for programme evaluation. It cooperates with Cito, The Netherlands' National *Institute for Educational* Measurement, as well as with Johns Hopkins University's Center for Talented Youth, and with Cambridge International Examinations.

EDUCATIONAL PROGRAMME

In the area of trilingual education the Intellectual Schools aim to support students in developing:

- Grade- and age-appropriate levels of L1 (Kazakh/Russian) competence in reading, writing, listening and speaking
- Grade- and age-appropriate levels of advanced proficiency in L2 (Russian/Kazakh) reading, writing, listening and speaking
- Grade- and age-appropriate levels of advanced proficiency in L3 (English) reading, writing, listening and speaking
- an understanding and appreciation of Kazakh culture and values
- a respect for other cultures
- knowledge, skills, attitudes and habits that foster intercultural communication.

In addition, AEO NIS's trilingual programme is expected to support students in developing:

- Grade- and age-appropriate levels of academic achievement in non-language school subjects in the sciences or the humanities, such as Mathematics, History and Geography, taught primarily through the L1, the L2 or the L3
- the cognitive and social skills and habits required for success in an ever-changing world.

The Intellectual Schools offer kindergarten (ages 3–5), pre-school (ages 5–6), and primary (ages 6–11, Grades 1–5) education at two schools, and secondary-school (ages 11–16, Grades 5–10) and high-school (age 16–18, Grades 11–12) programmes at all of its schools.

At primary level, two schools (which include a kindergarten, pre-school and primary programme) offer three streams: in the first two streams, all students are taught either Russian or Kazakh as a second language and English as a third language, beginning in Grade 1.

- Stream 1: for students with Kazakh as an L1 with Kazakh as a medium of instruction for most subjects

- Stream 2: for students with Russian as an L1 with Russian as a medium of instruction for most subjects

- Stream 3 is for non-Kazakh speakers with Kazakh as a primary medium of instruction (language immersion).

In stream 3, Russian is taught in language classes beginning in the second term of Grade 2. All other Grade 1 and 2 classes in Stream 3 are taught in Kazakh. English is introduced as a third language in Grade 3. The first cohort of Stream 3 students is currently (2014) in Grade 3, where Information and Communications Technologies will be taught through Russian. A decision as to what will be taught in which language in Grades 4–5 is yet to be made.

Parents of children living in the catchment areas of the primary level Intellectual Schools are eligible to apply to their city education department for placement in NIS. Places are allocated on a first come, first served basis. AEO NIS is provided with a list of accepted students.

At the secondary-school and high-school levels, two options are available. The **first option** is an International Baccalaureate (IB) programme offered at one combined AEO NIS secondary and high school. The IB programme begins in Grade 7. Admission to the programme is based on centrally administered testing. Testing instruments and procedures have been developed in cooperation with Johns Hopkins University and Cito. The IB model is trilingual, with a heavy emphasis on English in Grades 10–12. The **second option** applies to all other AEO NIS schools. They offer Grades 7–12 trilingual, maths and science-oriented programmes leading to dual national and international certification (in collaboration with Cambridge International Examinations). As with the IB programme, admission to these remaining schools is based on centrally-administered testing. The testing is conducted by AEO NIS's Centre for Pedagogical Measurements and is intended to act as a positive counterweight to any possible attempts at dishonesty on high-stakes tests (Winter et al. 2014).

The current 16 combined secondary and high-school level Intellectual Schools offer two streams:

- Stream 1: for students with Kazakh as a medium of instruction for most subjects

- Stream 2: for students with Russian as a medium of instruction for most subjects.

In both streams, some content subjects are taught through Kazakh and some subjects through Russian, while others are taught through English. The History of Kazakhstan, Geography and the Basics of Law are taught through Kazakh. World History and Computer Science are taught through Russian. Bilingual team-teaching (L1 + L3) is used for teaching Mathematics (Grade 8), Physics, Chemistry, Biology and Computer Science (Grade 9). This involves having two teachers (a native speaker of students' L1 and an L3 (English) speaker) present in the same classroom. In high school (Grades 11–12), Kazakhstan in the Modern World and Geography are taught through Kazakh. A combined literature course is offered where Kazakh literature is taught through Kazakh, and Russian and World Literature are taught through Russian. Mathematics, Physics, Chemistry, Biology, Computer Science, Economics, Global Perspectives and Project Work are taught through English. Most teachers are native speakers of their primary language of instruction.

The emphasis on English in the last years of high school is intended to help students achieve sufficient fluency in English for studying in English-medium higher education programmes. Yet there is concern that this emphasis on English may have an unintended impact on students' L1 and L2 fluency (Baetens Beardsmore 2014) at the high-school level and beyond. As a counterweight to this concern some of the following strategies are being explored: using L1 to teach Mathematics; translanguaging; the balanced use of three languages in extra-curricular activities; summer and winter Maths and Science camps in the L1 and/or L2, and having school development plans include strategies 'for ensuring that students learn and use the terminology and concepts taught through English in their L1' (AEO NIS 2013a). Examples of extra-curricular activities undertaken across NIS include an initiative to read 100 books (60 in Kazakh, 20 in Russian, 20 in English), and events entitled 'Ten Days in the Parents' Workplace', and 'Two Weeks in a Village'. Through a Wikipedia club project, NIS students have written and posted about 5000 articles in Kazakh, Russian and English (AEO NIS 2013b). Annually, the highest achieving *Shanyrak* (students' community) from each school from the Kazakh and Russian streams travel to a given region of the country to research together a topic of interest to them. Finally, AEO NIS intends to commission independent research on the teaching practices and student learning of and through the three languages.

INVESTMENTS: INTRODUCTION

With a leadership and management body (AEO NIS) in place, with a trilingual education model defined and with sufficient government support, the question is: how has AEO NIS started to build a trilingual education system? AEO NIS's challenge is to give systematic and simultaneous attention to multiple co-evolving issues and to do this in a context that insists on rapid and large-scale implementation of numerous concurrent reforms. In addition, as AEO NIS and its stakeholders try to institute innovative practices in education, aimed at going beyond where they have gone before, they need to learn as they go forward.

At its core, AEO NIS is creating mechanisms to provide structure and direction to its schools. In the next three sections, mechanisms (plans, policy prescriptions and professional development) will be discussed. To a lesser extent, a discussion of forces and counterweights will be incorporated into these three sections. Finally, tensions and counterweights will be discussed in a separate section. It is noteworthy that investments made into developing the Intellectual Schools and sharing their experience with other schools are numerous and, therefore, this chapter can only discuss key initiatives.

MECHANISMS: PLANS

If constructing a trilingual education system is seen as a journey, planning instruments identify where one wants to go and how one would get there. One of the major challenges to planning and implementation is that new understandings need to be agreed upon and expressed with clarity of thought. Not only does this need to be done within a given planning document but across diverse plans, guidelines, learning resources and other policy prescriptions. This would be a challenge for any system as complex as AEO NIS. In 2012, as a result of considerable internal discussions across AEO NIS, its staff articulated the following major long-term intended outcomes for achievement:

1) AEO NIS has a management system in place and professional staff to efficiently fulfil its mission.

2) Stakeholders support AEO NIS initiatives and contribute resources to their development and implementation.

3) Curricula and learning materials have been created and conditions for their further improvement are in place.

4) A comprehensive system for the professional development of teachers, school managers and other stakeholder groups (e.g. principals, vice-principals, trainers of teachers, parents, developers, Ministry of Education staff) has been created and conditions for its further expansion and development are in place.

5) A pre-service programme for pre-school and school personnel is adjusted in accordance with NIS needs.

6) A transparent quality assurance system is fully functional and informs further development.

7) AEO NIS network of fully equipped educational facilities is in place.

8) Projects are developed with international partners and are integrated with AEO NIS strategic and work plans.

9) Trilingual education is an integral part of the educational system.

10) A pilot project has been prepared for launching the eventual spread of the NIS educational model in comprehensive schools in Kazakhstan (from 2016 to 2028).

These outcomes reflect both mechanisms and forces, some of which are expected to act as counterweights to each other. Mechanisms for the development of the Intellectual Schools included management systems for delivering pre- and in-service professional development, for the ongoing development of learning materials and curricula, and for quality assurance. AEO NIS was itself positioned as a central mechanism. Other mechanisms included educational facilities (the construction of which AEO NIS manages), pilot projects, strategic plans and work plans. Significantly, several of the above intended outcomes demonstrate an understanding of the importance of forces such as transparency, stakeholder inclusion and external evaluation, and a belief in the value of capacity-building and quality for ensuring the effective operation of mechanisms. This is further reinforced by some of the indicators proposed for measuring the achievement of the outcomes. For example, in relation to learning materials development, not only did AEO NIS decide that the number of learning materials and an expert analysis of the quality of learning materials were important success indicators, but that the level of student/teacher/parent satisfaction with materials was also to be measured. This reflects an understanding that AEO NIS must meet stakeholder expectations and that the Intellectual Schools' future is dependent on forces such as stakeholder satisfaction. Most of these outcomes were integrated in one form or another into the AEO NIS 2020 Strategy, adopted in 2013.

AEO NIS also planned for additional outcomes in its 2020 Strategy. For example, as its responsibilities grew, AEO NIS decided that the 'Intellectual Schools gain considerable autonomy and work in cooperation as a professional learning community …' (AEO NIS 2013c). This not only aligned with key AEO NIS values – autonomy and autonomous learning, but would in principle allow AEO NIS to concentrate on high-level goals and avoid micromanagement of schools. At the same time, quality assurance mechanisms such as student assessment instruments, networking options and public reports, and a conference focusing on distributed leadership, are being instituted as these have the potential to act as constructive counterweights to any possible abuse of authority in schools and ensure that autonomy goes hand-in-hand with accountability and cooperation. Furthermore, the 2020 Strategy seeks to ensure that the goal of achieving high degrees of proficiency in Kazakh, Russian and English was reflected throughout the Intellectual Schools system, be that in libraries, extra-curricular activities, electronic platforms or in student career guidance. In other words, trilingualism has become on the ideational level a force – a value that helps to guide change. Trilingualism is beginning to be used consistently as a reference point to review AEO NIS plans and activities. The 2020 Strategy also reflects a belief in the value of building long-term relationships with highly respected partner institutions, networking, piloting, quality and transparency.

Finally, new counterweights were developed to address emergent challenges. For example, obtaining high-quality translations on the open market proved to be so difficult, in particular in Kazakh, that the 2020 Strategy foresaw the development of a translation unit. The unit is to use best practices in the field of translation, such as translation memory and terminology database software, and agreed upon translation and revision processes.

MECHANISMS: POLICY PRESCRIPTIONS

In order to achieve its planned outcomes, AEO NIS has created numerous mechanisms. There is a Curriculum and Assessment Model that describes which subjects are taught and assessed through which languages and in which grades. In the area of curriculum development, two sets of documents are primary drivers of innovation in teaching and learning: (1) subject programmes (primary curriculum documents), and (2) course plans (suggestions for ways of implementing subject programmes). There are separate programmes and course plans for each subject and grade. Both sets of documents include expectations regarding the integration of content and language. All subject programmes stress the need to teach academic language and to set language objectives for content lessons. The course plans provide general guidance on how to integrate language learning into content classes. Positive counterweights such as professional development and mentoring have had to be found against a tendency for some teachers and even textbook authors to use the suggested course plans as a prescription to be followed to the letter, as opposed to as suggestions to be used with professional judgement.

Subject programmes and course plans are also part of a larger ecology of interconnected mechanisms. The **External Assessment Model** and the **Integrated Criteria-based Assessment Model** are two such mechanisms. A recent review of language learning and teaching plans commended AEO NIS for its assessment policy (Baetens Beardsmore et al 2014). Concomitantly, the reviewers suggested the assessment models be better aligned with best practice in trilingual education by articulating those aspects of assessment that are unique to trilingual education.

Other mechanisms providing direction to stakeholders are:

- the **Trilingual Education Policy for Nazarbayev Intellectual Schools**. This articulates aims and values of trilingual education, roles and responsibilities of stakeholders, and major pedagogical principles, and makes connections with other key documents.
- the **Trilingual Implementation Guidelines for Nazarbayev Intellectual Schools**. The guidelines provide practical advice to schools on how to implement trilingual education.
- **Core NIS Pedagogical Principles and Values**. This mechanism draws out core pedagogical principles. It also suggests ways that these principles can be implemented by teachers, principals and students (see Tool 10).
- **Integration of Content and Language: Guidance for Teachers**. It discusses key concepts related to content- and language-integrated learning and offers practical strategies for teaching and learning.
- **Team Teaching: Overview**. This suggests team teaching strategies in bilingual contexts.

- **Criteria for Producing Learning Resources**. These are under development. They propose generic criteria for learning resources development, but also suggest some 30 criteria that are specific to language learning and developing intercultural dispositions, skills and knowledge. They are intended to guide the authors, editors and international partners and foster alignment with curricular and other policy goals.
- New textbooks for all subjects from Grades 1–12. These are being accompanied by teacher guides.

The rapid speed at which AEO NIS is expected to deliver on a wide range of stakeholder expectations suggests that this is a major force influencing programme development. It also represents a risk for AEO NIS and its staff (Shamshidinova et al. 2014). Moreover, understandings and needs evolve. To respond to changing needs and to mitigate risks AEO NIS uses counterweights such as audits, consultations with local and international experts, professional development, programme reviews, built-in revision cycles for the subject programmes and course plans, transparency in plans, and the existence of its highly knowledgeable and well-placed Board of Trustees. For example, a language learning review (a mechanism) was undertaken in 2013–2014 suggesting numerous ways of enhancing language learning (Baetens Beardsmore et al. 2014).

MECHANISMS: PROFESSIONAL DEVELOPMENT

Both the creation and effective use of the above mechanisms are in part dependent on the ongoing professional development of AEO NIS managers, school principals and vice-principals, teachers, trainers and government officials. Study tours have taken place in Canada, Estonia, Singapore and Switzerland, and elsewhere. Intellectual Schools' conferences focus on a broad range of topics including best practices in education, education reform, distributed leadership, change management, programme evaluation and trilingual education.

Intellectual Schools' teachers have been provided with short-term courses in Content and Language Integrated Learning (CLIL), team teaching, assessment, language immersion and lesson study. Teachers are encouraged and supported in conducting action research and lesson study using a critical-friend approach. This is meant to facilitate cross-curricular collaboration, including with content and language teachers. The action research initiative is being supported by Cambridge University's Faculty of Education's partner schools.

Other professional development mechanisms include a database of model lesson videos, conferences, conference materials and internet forums that include expert advice. Several of these aim to create learning environments for teachers, and concomitantly to foster their autonomous learning. In addition, through the national Bolashak Programme teachers can apply for 6–18-month internships abroad. Teachers are supported in undertaking Masters degrees at Nazarbayev University. Teachers have access to a UK-based Post Graduate Certificate of Education (PGCE) course.

The primary and most systematic mechanism for teacher and principal professional development is a three-level course. AEO NIS's Centre of Excellence delivers the courses to NIS and comprehensive school staff. For each level of the three-level courses, participants have a one-month face-to-face course (160 hours), followed by one month (80 hours) for applying learning in the classroom, with support from trainers who visit schools and who are available online. This is followed by another one-month face-to-face course (160 hours), followed by six months (240 hours) of post-course implementation of tasks in schools. During this six-month phase, educators receive in-school and online support from trainers. Finally, teachers receive post-course support consisting of seminars, roundtables, and online consultations and forums. The three-level courses have been developed in co-operation with Cambridge University's Faculty of Education and cover a broad range of best practices in education. Teachers receiving a passing grade on the completion of each of the three-level courses then receive a salary increase ranging from 30% for the successful completion of Level Three (Basic level) to a 100% salary increase for the completion of Level One (Advanced level). However, in their review of the three-level professional development programme, Baetens Beardsmore et al. (2014) stressed the need to include aspects relevant to trilingual education. Maintaining an in-depth focus on trilingual education in all relevant mechanisms is proving to be a challenge.

TENSIONS AND COUNTERWEIGHTS

Clearly the Intellectual Schools are well resourced. This has facilitated the development of the Intellectual Schools and their trilingual programme. All language classes are split in two to allow students to get more practice speaking. In addition, in 2013, 260 teachers from abroad were hired to teach through English. This number is expected to exceed 400 in 2015, although AEO NIS is also seeking, through professional development initiatives, to increase the number of Kazakh staff who can teach through English. In many classes, a native speaker of Kazakh or Russian is present in the classroom at the same time as a native speaker of English. It is hoped that as the number of Kazakh teachers capable of teaching in two languages increases, the need for team teaching and for hiring international teachers will decrease.

However, tensions may arise. For example, the Intellectual Schools are drawing teachers away from existing comprehensive schools by offering substantially higher salaries, as well as better professional development opportunities and working conditions than are available in the nation's comprehensive schools. Moreover, teachers in comprehensive schools who earn considerably less than Intellectual Schools teachers, and who work in poorer facilities and with fewer learning resources, could resist the Ministry's proposed education reforms emanating from AEO NIS. To counter potential resentment that might undermine the planned reforms and the Intellectual Schools, numerous mechanisms have been created. AEO NIS has, in concert with Ministry officials, instituted a public information campaign to explain ways in which the entire education system can benefit from the Intellectual Schools initiative. It is also sharing the Intellectual Schools' knowledge base with comprehensive schools through mechanisms such as online platforms, the sharing of its learning materials and professional development. The government is also providing complementary incentives. For example, comprehensive schools' teachers completing each of the three levels of the Centre of Excellence courses developed by AEO NIS for comprehensive schools receive a salary increase ranging from 30% for completing one level to 100% for completing all three levels. Finally, demonstrating respect (a force) for and understanding of the comprehensive schools' best practices, needs and challenges would likely also lessen resistance.

Furthermore, AEO NIS's success may be seen as a positive force and AEO NIS itself as the mechanism to be used to facilitate further reforms. This view may invite the Kazakh government to ask yet more of AEO NIS. For example, AEO NIS has been tasked with undertaking a step-by-step programme to spearhead the reform of education throughout Kazakhstan's entire Grades 1–12 education system across over 7000 schools – an exciting, but formidable task. This 'translation' of the Intellectual Schools' experience by the state comprehensive system will likely take well over a decade. It will need to be resourced effectively and efficiently, and be flexible enough to take into account local needs. The task of spearheading education reform at a national level constitutes a very high expectation. Expectations need to be managed and kept realistic in order to ensure that they do not act as negative counterweights. Currently, AEO NIS is using a step-by-step approach by first piloting planned reforms in 30 schools. It is also co-constructing new curricula with the National Academy of Education and 100 teachers from comprehensive schools. It is planning a gradual implementation of the new curriculum in stages over twelve years, beginning in Grade 1, but with ways of allowing other grades to benefit immediately from curricular enhancement. It is also delivering two to four weeks of professional development to approximately 200 000 teachers over the next two years in addition to the existing previously discussed Centre of Excellence three-level courses. Among these 200 000 educators are language teachers (Kazakh, Russian, English), who will receive one month of training in contemporary approaches to language teaching.

All of the above forces, mechanisms and counterweights need to be managed by AEO NIS staff, and this process is dependent on their knowledge and skills and the development of a workplace culture that encourages innovation, and accepts and learns from the inevitable occasional failures and problems. Counterweights to any knowledge and skills gap in the area of management and leadership can be found in ongoing professional development opportunities and by involving external expert advice. Furthermore, any organisation taking on substantial new targets also needs to ensure workload is well managed and that staffing levels are sufficient to meet increased demands. Government needs to be kept well informed and engaged to ensure expectations regarding AEO NIS remain realistic, and financial support remains sufficient.

CONCLUSION

The Autonomous Education Organisation Nazarbayev Intellectuals Schools are seen by the government as a means to address several pressing needs – a desire to promote widespread trilingualism and social cohesion, a desire to raise competency in, and use of, the Kazakh language, a wish to improve the quality of education across the country and a need for highly qualified people to meet the demands of a rapidly expanding economy. These are very high expectations. For the time being, these government desires, wishes and needs ensure that AEO NIS enjoys substantial moral and financial support. As a counterweight to the dangers inherent in potentially unrealistic stakeholder expectations, AEO NIS will need to guide stakeholders in understanding what they are currently delivering, and what can be realistically accomplished in which timeframe.

The current imperative to deliver quickly on multiple targets, many of which are massive in scope (e.g. rewriting all student textbooks for all grades, training 120 000 teachers in a five-year timeframe), may have an impact on quality. The rapid pace of work may not always allow for deep-order reflection and stakeholder dialogue, or for fine-tuning products in the short term. This reality invites an iterative approach, where learning from the process of developing these trilingual schools can be identified, captured and applied as the schools are further developed, and as lessons learnt are translated to the school system as a whole. A full-fledged research programme into student achievement and how that correlates with teaching, learning and programme management practices could make an important contribution to knowledge capture and development. In other words, AEO NIS staff must continue to lead a major and complicated education reform while simultaneously learning about best practices in leadership, management and pedagogy, including about trilingual education, and how to scale up those reforms to the nation at large. At the same time, it will be essential to take into account that the Nazarbayev Intellectual Schools operate in a very different context to that of the comprehensive schools. Moreover, government and AEO NIS need to make sure that AEO NIS manages to retain its staff and keep them engaged and motivated.

Finally, it is thus particularly important that AEO NIS continue to focus on creating value for the entire education system, in order to ensure that it meets its mission and that the trilingual programme flourishes. This will be central to maintaining government and other stakeholder support.

NOTES

1   Level 2 means that students can at best 'only handle the simplest and most obvious tasks, most can be expected not to continue with education beyond compulsory schooling, and therefore risk facing difficulties in reading … throughout their lives' (OECD 2014).

REFERENCES

Abdakimov, A. (1994). *History of Kazakhstan (From Ancient Times to the Present Day)*. Almaty: Almaty.

AEO NIS (Autonomous Educational Organisation Nazarbayev Intellectual Schools) (2013a). *The Trilingual Implementation Guidelines for the Nazarbayev Intellectual Schools*. Astana: AEO NIS.

— (2013b) *Nazarbayev Intellectual Schools Annual Report – 2013*. Astana: AEO NIS.

— (2013c) *Autonomous Educational Organisation 'Nazarbayev Intellectual Schools' 2020 Development Strategy*. Astana: AEO NIS.

— (2013d) Integrated Programme of Development: Biology Grade 11 Course Plan: July 2013. Astana: AEO NIS.

Agency of Statistics of the Republic of Kazakhstan (2013a). *Demographic Indexes for the Period 2007– 2013*. Astana: Republic of Kazakhstan.

— (2013b). *Number of the Pupils in General Education Schools by Kind of Studying Language*. www.kaz. stat.kz/digital/naselsenie_kz/Pages/default.aspxminside (retrieved November 2013).

Aminov, K., Jensen, V., Juraev, S., Overland, I. Tyan, D. and Uulu, Y. (2010). 'Language Use and Language Policy in Central Asia'. *Central Asia Regional Data Review*, 2:1.

Ayubayeva, N., Bridges, D., Drummond, M.J., Fimyar, O., Kishkentayeva, M., Kulakh- metova, A., McLaughlin, C., Mehisto, P., Orazbaeyv, S. and Shinkarenko, V. (2013). *Development of Strategic Directions for Education Reforms in Kazakhstan for 2015– 2020: Final Report of the Early Years and Secondary School Working Group*. Astana: Nazarbayev University.

Baetens Beardsmore, H., Baker, B., Crawford, A., Genesee, F., Hamayan, F. and Mehisto, P. (2014). *Review of Language Learning and Teaching Plans at the Nazarbayev Intellectual Schools*. Report.

Buri, T., Finke, P. (2013). 'The Kazak Oralman: Comparing Migratory Decisions, Integration Patterns and Transnational Ties in Three Different Settings'. In P. Finke, G. Schlee (eds), *CASA – Centre for Anthropological Studies on Central Asia: Framing the Research, Initial Projects*. Halle: Max Planck Institute for Social Anthropology.

CIA (Central Intelligence Agency) (2013). *CIA Factbook: Kazakhstan*. Washington: CIA. www.cia.gov/library/publications/the-world-factbook/geos/kz.html (retrieved November 2013).

Commission on Human Rights under the President of the Republic of Kazakhstan (2012). *Special Report on the Situation concerning the Rights of Oralmans, Stateless Persons and Refugees in the Republic of Kazakhstan*. Astana: President's Office.

Fierman, W. (2006). 'Language and Education in Post-Soviet Kazakhstan: Kazakh-Medium Instruction in Urban Schools'. *The Russian Review* 65, 98–116.

Kolstø, P. and Malkova, I. (1997). 'Is Kazakhstan Being Kazakified?' *Analysis of Current Events* 9:11, 1 and 3–4.

Kunanbayev, A. (2005). *Abai: Book of Words*. Semey: MKA (Abai International Club).

Law of the Republic of Kazakhstan No. 394–IV. (2011, 19 January). *On the Status of Nazarbayev University, Nazarbayev Intellectual Schools and Nazarbayev Fund*. Astana.

Mehisto, P., Kambatyrova, A. and Nurseitova, K. (2014). 'Three in one? Trilingualism in Educational Policy and Practice'. In D. Bridges, (ed.), *Educational Reform and Internationalisation: The Case of School Reform in Kazakhstan*. Cambridge: Cambridge University Press.

Ministry of Education and Science (2013a). Personal email communication.

National Center of Educational Statistics and Evaluation (2014). *Statistics of Education System of the Republic of Kazakhstan*. Astana: National Collection.

Nazarbayev, N. (2009). 'Kazakhstan in the Post-Crisis World: Intellectual Breakthrough to the Future'. Lecture at Kazakhstan National University after Al-Farabi, Almaty, October 2009.

— (2012). 'Kazakhstan 2050 Strategy: New Political Course of the Established State'. Annual State of the Nation Address. www.kazakhstan.org.sg/content/intro.php?act=menu&c_id=43 (retrieved November 2013).

OECD (Organisation for Economic Cooperation and Development) (2013). *Kazakhstan*. Paris: OECD.

Shamshidinova, K., Ayubayeva, N. and Bridges, D. (2014). 'Implementing Radical Change: Nazarba-yev Intellectual Schools as Agents of Change'. In D. Bridges, (ed.), *Educational Reform and Internationalisation: The Case of School Reform in Kazakhstan*. Cambridge: Cambridge University Press.

Tasmaganbetov, I. (2004). Speech of the Mayor of the Astana city Imangali Tasmaganbetov at Astana Economic Forum, Astana.

Tazhibayeva, M. (2010). 'The Long Migration Home for Oralmans'. *Central Asia Online*. www.centrala-siaonline.com/en_gB/articles/caii/tures/ main/2010/01/12/feature-02 (retrieved February 2012).

Usupova, A. (2012). 'V kasachstane projivaet okolo milliona oralmanov'. *Tengri News*. www.tengrinews.kz/kazakhstan_news/v-kazastane-projivaet-okolo-milliona-oralmanov- 216240/ (retrieved March 2012).

Winter, L., Rimini, C., Soltanbekova, A. and Tynybayeva. M. (2014). 'The Culture and Practice of Assessment in Kazakhstan'. In D. Bridges, (ed.), *Educational Reform and Internationalisation: The Case of School Reform in Kazakhstan*. Cambridge: Cambridge University Press.

Zimovina, E.P. (2003). 'Population Dynamics and Ethnic Composition of Kazakhstan in the Second Half of the 20th Century'. *Demoscope Weekly*, 3–16 March, 103–4.

KAZAKHSTAN: SUMMARY OF FORCES, MECHANISMS AND COUNTERWEIGHTS

FORCES	MECHANISMS
Beliefs and desires	**Legislation**
A belief in the value of Kazakh, Russian and English A desire for social cohesion and stability A belief in the value of quality education A desire to achieve internationally	Law according AEO NIS special status
	People
Economic growth	The President of the Republic of Kazakhstan A high-powered board of trustees High-status supporters Networks Committed indefatigable individuals National and international experts Highly qualified local and foreign teachers
A need for improved language skills	
National aspirations	
To raise 'a new generation of the intellectual elite' To have all schools benefit from NIS project To foster national cohesion and stability To compete globally while maintaining Kazakh traditions and values	**Professional development**
	Study visits to high-performing education systems A core 3-level extensive professional development programme Short-term courses (e.g. CLIL, team teaching, assessment, lesson study) Action research Conferences Online platform Bolashak scholarships for teacher internships abroad UK-based PGCE course
Government expectations	
High expectations regarding trilngualism, and programmes for talented youth High expectations regarding NIS's capacity to support education reform in comprehensive schools High speed of delivery	

Continued over page

FORCES	MECHANISMS
Founding principle	**Vehicles**
Autonomy	AEO NIS to manage and lead the initiative
	AEO NIS Centres such as:
Organisational values	a) the Centre of Excellence to deliver training
	b) the Educational Resources Centre to create
Transparency	learning materials
Quality	c) the Centre for Pedagogical Measurement to
	assess student achievement
Principles for cooperation	d) the Centre for Educational Programmes to
	develop curricula
Stakeholder inclusion	New schools
Greater autonomy for each Intellectual School	Translation unit
Working with high status, highly qualified international	Trilingual extra-curricular programmes
partners	
Higher education	**Finance**
Value placed on the use of Kazakh and English	Substantial budget
	Salary incentives
	Teaching and learning resources
	Course plans
	New textbooks, student workbooks and teacher guides
	Trilingual libraries
	Policies
	Subject programmes
	Integrated Criteria-based Assessment Model
	Trilingual Policy
	Trilingual Implementation Guidelines
	Core NIS Pedagogical Principles and Values
	Plans and reports
	2020 Strategy
	Work plans
	Public reports
	External audits and reviews

COUNTERWEIGHTS

High expectations	High level of government support
Existing legislation restricting AEO NIS	New legislation giving AEO NIS autonomy
Possible cheating on high-stakes tests	Testing by Centre for Pedagogical Measurement
Concern about L1 in high school	L1 supported through translanguaging / extra-curricular
Difficulty in obtaining high-quality translations	Developing own translation unit
Risks	Audits, experts, professional development, programme reviews, reports
Potential resentment from other schools	Sharing NIS experience with other schools
Speed of programme development	Built-in cycles for revision and improvement

VOICES FROM THE FIELD:
England

Silke Fernandes and Penny Roberts are part of a core team who have applied to English authorities for the right to open a bilingual primary school in England. Silke Fernandes is a Public Health researcher and a mother who wishes to provide her children with access to bilingual education. Penny Roberts is a teacher and an educational psychologist who has spent the last four years developing and opening new schools for the London Diocese.

The initiative to establish Harrow Bilingual Primary School, which has been renamed St. Jérôme Church of England Bilingual School, started with a team of five multilingual parents who all attended the same local church in London, England. We all have a passion for languages, which most of us have been able to share with our own children by raising them bilingually. We have seen in our own children the benefits of growing up speaking two languages and we believe that this should be available to all children. There is a growing need, due to parental demand and in the context of globalisation, to give young people in the UK opportunities to develop language skills. We decided, therefore, to use the English Free Schools initiative to create a bilingual primary school with a Christian ethos. This government initiative aims to provide local communities with greater control over education and to create opportunities for innovation and diversity in the school system. Frankly speaking, we were at the onset greatly unaware of the magnitude of this project and probably slightly naïve; however, we were to embark on an invaluable learning journey.

The Free Schools initiative application process is rigorous and lengthy, which should not be surprising given the amount of public money that has been invested in the programme. The application process requires successful bidders to demonstrate, among other things, a coherent vision that fits with the priorities of the Free Schools initiative. It also requires that bidders provide evidence that their proposed school will raise educational standards and that they have the experience, skills and time to set up and run a successful school.

A key priority for the Free Schools programme is to provide schools that meet the local needs of the communities they will serve. In our case, the founder parents live in Harrow, which is one of the most multicultural communities in London and beyond. It is a place where birth rates and immigration have led to a chronic shortage of school places. Over half of children entering state schools in our community speak a first language other than English. There is no one dominant language and it is not unusual to find more than 50 languages spoken in a single school. Consequently, we needed to devote time and energy to ensuring our bid and approach took into account and served the interests of children who speak neither English nor French upon arrival.

A first milestone was achieved when we were accepted onto the New School Network Development Programme, a charity that helps groups to prepare a strong application and provides applicants with funds predominantly to cover marketing expenses. Due to considerable critical media coverage of the Free School initiative we were aware that our application had to be very robust and that the core team had to prove it had the skills required for the opening of a school. These skills include finance, project management, marketing, teaching and, most importantly, senior leadership experience in a school. Since the latter was our main shortcoming, we approached the London Diocesan Board for Schools (LDBS) for support. The LDBS is the educational arm of the London Diocese, running over 150 Anglican schools in and around London. They have been fully involved in the application process and supported us throughout. Through their vast network of contacts a highly experienced French-speaking head teacher from a local school and a project manager with valuable experience in opening a number of free schools joined our team. This support will extend beyond the opening of the school because the LDBS provides ongoing support for its schools. We hope that the headteacher will become our executive teacher, continuing to run his own school and ours.

The LDBS was very interested in our proposal for a number of reasons. They have been heavily involved in opening new schools to help meet the unprecedented population growth in London. Furthermore, from September 2014 it is compulsory for English schools to teach a modern foreign language from Key Stage 2 (age 7+), but currently few primary schools have appropriately skilled staff. The LDBS is keen to equip its 136 primary schools to meet this requirement to a very high standard. They recognise the difference between modern foreign language teaching and the bilingual approach, but they see the potential for our new school to serve the wider school community by supporting the training of primary school teachers in best practice in bilingual education and providing a hub for training, research, and school-to-school support across the whole Diocese.

Although the Free School programme is supposed to increase innovation and diversity, all state-funded English schools are still measured against a handful of benchmarks that do not necessarily fit with non-standard school approaches such as bilingual education. These standard benchmarks include: a phonics test in English at the end of Y1 (age 6), an English and Maths test at the end of Year 2 (age 7) as well as at the end of Year 6 (age 11), and measuring the amount of progress that children make in English and Maths between ages 7 and 11. The government's first priority is for any new school to be successful against these benchmarks. Funding can be removed or management replaced if benchmark standards are not met. This affected the preparation of our bid and the presentation of the bid at the interview stage – we need St. Jérôme Bilingual School (previously called Harrow Bilingual Primary School) not only to provide pupils with a bilingual experience wherever possible but to succeed amongst its peers as a conventional primary school.

It is likely that we will not have the complete freedom to deliver a truly bilingual environment within the Free School programme when the school first opens. For example, all core subjects must be taught in English. However, as the school shows it is successful, the head and governors will have freedom to develop the bilingual approach over time. To put the school in the best position, we hope to work with experts in the field to research the impact of the bilingual environment on children from the diversity of backgrounds that we expect to serve. We also plan to offer an extended (optional) enrichment programme based around the core curriculum areas. This will be delivered in French to children in Key Stage 1. We hope and expect that early successes will allow the school to teach some core subjects in French once children reach Key Stage 2. Those who have followed the enrichment programme will have the language knowledge and skills to study some subjects through French. This means that even within the (understandable) constraints of the programme we see the potential for children to leave this primary school able to speak, read and write in both English and French.

We are aware that to fully realise our vision over time we require the full commitment of the head teacher to the bilingual curriculum, consultation with experts in the field, a supportive governing body and the commitment of parents to the likely additional effort involved in exposing their children to English and French. We have worked with the different stakeholders throughout the process and have been able to overcome a number of obstacles. We were able to recruit a French-English bilingual governor for our governing body, who is fully supportive of our vision and is strongly lobbying for bilingual education. We have engaged with the local authority and gained support from our local Member of Parliament who has raised our case in Parliament and written of his support. We have consulted experts in the field and published literature to inform our curriculum plan. It has unquestionably been helpful to counteract any concerns over the suitability of bilingual education to the multicultural context in London by citing research-based evidence of the benefits of bilingual education in similar settings. To be able to reach a large proportion of the local population we have had two articles published in the local paper, distributed leaflets in our borough, and carried out marketing at local events and in the town centre. We also wanted to engage local parents in a more intimate way, to be able to hear about their views, hopes and fears, and persuade them to send their children to our new school. For that reason, we started to conduct focus group discussions with parents willing to participate; these enabled us to gain great insights, which we are using to adapt our plans and clarify our vision. This has also helped us to understand common fears that surround a bilingual education approach among parents.

A small number of bilingual schools have already opened under the Free School programme and we have been fortunate to learn from their experiences. We quickly recognised the importance of building a network of bilingual schools in the UK that can support each other and build upon each other's experiences. To formalise such a network will be another priority for our group once our school is approved.

Despite the many obstacles behind us and certainly still lying ahead of us, we hope for our application to be approved for opening in September 2015.[1] We are convinced that many doors will open for young people coming to our school and are determined to provide them with an excellent education in two languages.

NOTES

1   On 30 September 2014 the United Kingdom Department of Education approved the Harrow Bilingual Primary School application.

VOICES FROM THE FIELD:
Canada

Robert McConnell is a former Coordinator of Modern Languages for the Scarborough Board of Education and the Toronto District School Board. He was responsible for early and late French immersion programmes, from kindergarten to Grade 12. Robert McConnell is a past President of both the Ontario Modern Language Teachers Association and of the Canadian Association of Second Language Teachers. He is the author of more than 300 books in the field of modern languages.

IF ONLY I HAD KNOWN THEN WHAT I KNOW NOW ... Monolingualism can be cured

It is my intent in the following few pages to alert immersion programme implementers/managers to a few core principles and key issues to which particular attention should be paid. They will be immediately recognisable as either a force, a mechanism or a counterweight.

The greatest and most powerful force in convincing a school board to embark and set sail on the good ship immersion is a convinced, committed and vocal group of insistent parents. In the Canadian context, it was English-speaking parents rather than elected or appointed senior educational officials who rallied around the above slogan. It was parents who decided that enough was enough. They simply were not going to accept that their children were never going to become bilingual in French and English.

Politicians and school board senior officials listen when taxpayers and voters speak with one voice. If one can generalise, these parents are, in the Canadian context at least, usually ambitious for their children and are, themselves, well-educated and well-travelled. They realise the growing importance of foreign language skills and their value in the global village. Ranged against them, however, are darker forces. These are forces, overt or covert, that can present a formidable obstacle to the planting of the seed of immersion, or act to poison the flower as it tries to take root. These forces may range from people feeling threatened by 'the other', to unilingual teachers fearing they might be made redundant to make room for bilingual teachers. They might also include principals not wanting the hassle of a new, strange programme in their school, especially one that requires teachers with skills that they themselves do not possess. These principals pose themselves the question, 'Why would one want or need to learn a foreign language anyway?' They never learned to speak French, and that never stood in the way of their becoming the perfect, well-rounded, totally fulfilled people that they are.

There will be other, less negative forces, also working to undermine the incipient immersion programme. For example, these are concerns emanating from parents of goodwill who hesitate to place their child in immersion because they are afraid that he or she will suffer language confusion. They fear the child's progress in English will be impeded, that their English-speaking child may even turn, (oh horrors!) into a little French child before their very eyes.

However, once parents on the 'yes' side of the equation have convinced the school board to commit the substantial resources required to the immersion programme, careful long-range planning is the order of the day for central board staff responsible for implementation.

In the broadest sense, and being aware of the forces, mechanisms and counterweights involved, one must be very clear and specific regarding:

- the outcomes; i.e. the end results one is attempting to achieve
- the factors that will promote or hinder the realisation of these outcomes
- the methods that will be used to evaluate the outcomes
- the commitment to the programme on the part of educational officials and parents.

More specifically, particular attention must be paid to:

- a clarification of the roles of Ministry of Education personnel, school board superintendents, consultants, school principals and teachers
- the development and refinement of Ministry of Education and school board policy regarding immersion
- the articulation of reasonable and achievable outcomes
- the quality and knowledge base of the consultative staff
- the selection of principals and teachers
- the adequacy and security of long-range funding for the programme
- the provision of teacher pre-service courses and in-service staff development
- the availability of appropriate curriculum guidelines, texts and support materials
- the procedures for ongoing programme monitoring and evaluation

- the appropriate selection of immersion schools to ensure a solid client base and room to expand
- a commitment to support the continuity of the programme from grade to grade, and from elementary to secondary school
- the selection of the grade at which formal native-language learning will commence
- a decision regarding what, and at what grade level, subjects will be taught in the target language and which in the native language
- the provision of remedial and special education support
- the creation of immersion teacher professional organisations and networks to facilitate the sharing of expertise and resources and to maintain morale (in Toronto, to foster a sense of common purpose, I also initiated monthly meetings of immersion principals so they could share experiences, challenges and solutions).
- co-curricular activities, i.e. the facilitation of students' contact and interaction with a wide range of speakers of the target language
- publicity, public relations and open communication among all stakeholders; most people are reasonable if one takes the time to listen to them, understand what they are saying and, as much as possible, act on their concerns. They often become one's greatest allies.

By way of confession, the above comments have the advantage of hindsight. In actual fact, immersion expanded so rapidly in Canada that initially, we flew by the seat of our pants. Nonetheless we were forced to learn quickly.

The forces, mechanisms and counterweights observable in an effective immersion school and programme display a number of discernible key features:

- the school principal is knowledgeable about both the theory and practice of immersion, and is clearly supportive of both immersion and the regular programme
- as much as possible, there should be a balance in numbers in any given school between the regular programme and the immersion programme, so that neither feels undervalued or isolated. It is imperative that teachers in the regular programme not feel their job is threatened
- to foster mutual respect, understanding and communication it is advantageous if some of the regular programme staff are also fluent in the new target language
- both the staff and the parents' advisory group must operate as one unit for the common welfare of all students in the school. This requires strong leadership skills on the part of the principal. To facilitate communication,

it is also essential that teachers in the immersion programme be able to speak with parents in the parents' own language
- a bilingual librarian is essential, and a bilingual principal is highly desirable
- should the principal not be bilingual, it is important that he or she communicate to students the value of the target language by learning and using with them at least a basic vocabulary
- both programmes must feel they are being treated equitably and that they have their fair share of the school's resources
- both programmes are respected and honoured: announcements are given in both languages, artwork displays in the halls celebrate both programmes, the signs in the school are bilingual
- enrichment activities are provided equally to both programmes
- extra-curricular activities are open to all students and conducted in the common language.

COMMON PROBLEMS AND PRACTICAL SOLUTIONS

Despite the undeniable success of immersion, there are certain challenges specific to this programme which must be addressed.

Staffing

The success of the programme will be a direct reflection of the skill and commitment of the teachers. However, teachers who display both excellent language skills and appropriate pedagogical qualifications are at a premium. In order to ensure that teachers possess the requisite language skills, formal oral and written tests should be administered by a central office team. Principals can then interview and choose from this pool the teachers who would be best suited to fulfil the needs of the school.

In order to attract and identify top quality teachers, school boards are usually required to advertise nationally. This is particularly true for the secondary level in specialised subjects such as Mathematics. Due to a dearth of teachers in Toronto and its environs with the required French language skills, the Toronto District School Board has for years actively recruited in Quebec. When these teachers, typically young single women, arrive in Toronto, they very often experience culture shock. The school board can do much to alleviate this by pairing them with another francophone teacher who has gone through the same experience.

To ensure an adequate supply of teachers, school boards must also work closely with Faculties of Education. The latter are usually quite receptive to designing suitable programmes if this helps enhance the employment prospects of their graduates.

Funding

The immersion programme requires an initial and ongoing investment to establish and maintain a suitable library in each school. Before embarking on programme implementation, administrators must insist upon a long-term commitment on the part of the school board to provide these funds.

Materials

Particularly in the early grades, teaching materials written for native speakers are usually not suitable for immersion classes due to the advanced level of language. In Canada, in the initial years of the programme, this was a very severe problem. Over the course of the years, however, school boards have developed networks to exchange materials. In addition to this sharing, central money must also be provided to ensure that appropriate curriculum resources can be developed locally as required.

Enrichment/Special education

Parents of gifted students enrolled in immersion are sometimes concerned that their child might not receive the enrichment opportunities available in the English programme. Immersion administration and teachers must reassure parents that immersion is enrichment in itself, and that other opportunities are offered through programme modification. In addition, enrichment opportunities can be provided centrally by means of special reading and cultural programmes.

In the area of special education for students with learning disabilities, it is generally not financially possible for school boards to offer central assistance in the new target language. A full range of services is, however, available in English. At the school level, remediation is always available from the classroom teacher. Some schools may also have the staff available to provide certain special education services in both languages.

TRANSPORTATION

Although most school boards provide bus transportation to their immersion schools, some do not. This can lead to charges of elitism, as only wealthier parents can afford to arrange privately to have their child transported to school.

In school boards where no transportation is provided, car pools are an obvious alternative. The best solution, of course, is political, and parents are advised to lobby for the provision of such services.

ATTRITION

Students transferring out of immersion can be of serious concern, since they are rarely replaced by students moving in from another jurisdiction. Students may leave for a variety of reasons, ranging from a parental job relocation to the belief that they will fare better academically in an all-English programme.

In the former instance, of course, the child will be lost to the programme unless one exists in the location to which the parents are moving. In the case of voluntary transfers, however, a number of strategies are available to encourage students to remain in the programme. These include:

- ensuring that immersion classes are of the highest quality
- facilitating bilingual exchanges, establishing week-long 'immersion camps', and providing other opportunities where the students can spend an extended period of time in a 'French-only' milieu. In Toronto, for example, we initiated a five-week French credit course in Switzerland for secondary students. That programme is now in its 45th year.
- inviting visits to class by students in higher grades, as well as by immersion graduates
- increasing, in secondary school, the diversity of programme options
- granting a 'Certificate of Bilingualism' at the completion of the programme.

CONCLUSION

Initiating, implementing and maintaining an effective immersion programme requires an intimate knowledge of the various forces, mechanisms and counterweights that are in constant flux and bear directly on its success. We who are 'true believers' and know the value of language learning must temper our idealism with the cold eye of practicality if we wish to ensure that our students are provided the opportunity to experience the joy and thrill of being able to communicate in another 'tongue' and live comfortably in another culture.

VOICES FROM THE FIELD:
Spain

Until recently, Pilar Medrano managed the 'MEC/British Council Bilingual Project'. She was in the post for 17 years. She was responsible for developing the Project's integrated curriculum and a teacher training programme, as well as promoting contacts between Spanish and British schools.

As the result of an agreement between the Ministry of Education and Science and the British Council in Spain, a Bilingual Project was launched in 1996. It aimed to offer students in state schools an enriched model of education through a bilingual and bicultural curriculum.

Children from all socio-economic and academic backgrounds were given access to the programme. It was launched, on a volunteer basis, in 44 infant and primary state schools in 10 regions of Spain, and in the two autonomous cities of Ceuta and Melilla, with 1800 pupils aged 3 and 4. This was a completely new experience for these schools. Eighteen years later, 84 primary and 44 secondary schools participate in what is now a well-established programme, with a total of 38 000 pupils aged between 3 and 16, taught by about 1400 teachers.

The programme is managed by the Spanish Ministry of Education, Culture and Sport in partnership with the British Council, and in close cooperation with the regional authorities, who in the year 2000 assumed primary responsibility for education. All the regions participating in this bilingual programme except one are primarily monolingual.

The bilingual programme uses an Integrated Curriculum that is based on the Spanish Core Curriculum and the English National Curriculum and combines content and methodological approaches from both educational systems. The curriculum is delivered through early partial immersion in English. By the end of compulsory schooling, the aim is for students to not only be fluent in both Spanish and English, but to be better prepared to meet the demands of the marketplace and to engage in intercultural action.

English is used as a medium of instruction for 40% of contact time. The Integrated Curriculum document states both the content and learning targets for each subject at the pre-primary, primary and secondary levels. In pre-primary, two teachers – one who speaks Spanish and the other who speaks English with the children – teach basic skills and content through a holistic approach. In primary, there is a strong focus on English language and literacy, and in particular reading and writing. Synthetic phonics is proving particularly suitable to teach pupils to read and write in English from the age of 4 or 5. Geography, History, Science and Art are also taught in English and a strong emphasis is placed on a cross-curricular and hands-on approach. At the secondary level, students take English Language and Literacy, Social Sciences and Natural Sciences in English, and have the opportunity to take – at the age of 16 – UK-based externally marked exams in order to obtain their Cambridge IGCSE. Students also take Spanish national exams in order to obtain their national Secondary Certificate.

MECHANISMS

Three main mechanisms support the achievement of programme goals: an integrated Spanish-English curriculum, experienced teachers and an on-going teacher training programme.

An internal study in 2000 recommended the writing of a special curriculum in order to establish clear learning targets for content and language, which would help to achieve and maintain common standards across all schools. A group of Spanish and English teachers from project schools was commissioned to write a curriculum document that would draw on classroom experience and observation, and include suggestions for teaching and learning strategies.

In 1996, it was not simply possible to hire a sufficient number of qualified teachers. Most Spanish state schools did not have teachers who were prepared to implement a bilingual programme. As a consequence, it was decided that it was necessary to hire supernumerary teachers who would be able to start such a programme with young children. These teachers were either UK primary-school trained or Spanish bilingual teachers, and brought with them many of the teaching skills and much of the cultural knowledge needed to deliver an integrated curriculum. They have also contributed to creating an international culture in the schools.

However, the programme would not have been sustainable if it had depended largely on the contribution of supernumerary teachers. Therefore, it was clear for stakeholders, from the beginning, that Spanish teachers had to undergo professional development and become bilingual so that they could take over the programme and lead it. In addition to language learning, the ongoing teacher training programme focuses on the need for a different methodological approach in the bilingual classroom and takes into account the specific needs of the programme. It covers areas such as the teaching of Literacy, Phonics, Science, Geography, History, Art and assessment for learning.

FORCES

Some of the major forces driving the programme are:

- The high social status of languages, particularly of English, and the need to use these languages in education and the workplace. Parents are convinced that learning languages is critical for the success of their children in school and the job market.
- The political will to change the approach to the teaching of foreign languages.
- The deep conviction that bilingual education should be offered to children from all social and economic backgrounds, while maintaining high expectations.
- Long-term commitment and support from key stakeholders – the Spanish Ministry of Education, Culture and Sport, the Local Education Authorities, the British Council, the schools, parents – have also moved the programme forward. This commitment has been channeled through mechanisms such as a clear definition of roles, duties and expected outcomes, and realistic timelines.

COUNTERWEIGHTS

Some negative forces have had to be countered in order to reinforce the programme.

Societal support has always been one of the decisive forces driving programme development; however, parents and school managers initially feared that the learning of content and proficiency in Spanish might suffer. The previously discussed curriculum helped to assuage that fear. The key counterweight to fear, however, was a three-year external independent evaluation that was commissioned from a joint UK-Spanish team. The research demonstrated that students were achieving curriculum outcomes in all subjects tested. Proficiency in Spanish was at least as high as in monolingual programmes. This was an endorsement for the bilingual programme and its pedagogical approach.

The ongoing support that Spanish teachers received, as well as an ongoing training programme, acted as a counterweight to teachers' initial fears that they would not be able to achieve what was expected of them. Spanish teachers are now demonstrating that they can support students in meeting high curricular expectations in two languages.

CHALLENGES

Challenges could be considered another force in the development of any project. They focus attention and energy. As they are overcome, they generate new goals and new challenges.

Currently, the programme looks both outside, towards European recognition, and inside, to improve results. Though for a great majority of pupils the aim of an enriched model of education is being achieved, 10% of children – as it was pointed out in the findings of the evaluation study – are not achieving curriculum expectations. This is quite a complex challenge that must be addressed from different angles: ongoing curriculum renewal, differentiated learning, professional development and internal research.

PART THREE:
Looking at the Long-Term

8   Wales:
Towards a National Strategy

W. Gwyn Lewis (Bangor University)

CHAPTER NAVIGATOR

A real-life example	→ Introduction	→ Socio-political context	→ Welsh in education
Growth and expansion	→ The power of politics	→ Strategic aims	→ Co-ordinated national strategy
Conclusion	→ Tabular summary		

A REAL-LIFE EXAMPLE

In Ysgol Gymraeg Trelyn, Y Coed Duon (Blackwood), Caerphilly, Wales, on 18 November 2013, the Welsh Government's First Minister, Carwyn Jones, launched a three-year Welsh-medium education information campaign called *Live in Wales: Learn in Welsh*. The aim was to raise awareness of Welsh-medium and bilingual education among expectant parents and parents with children aged 0–3 about the advantages of sending their children to a Welsh-medium school. The campaign was launched in a predominantly English-speaking area of southeast Wales to counter the current situation where 'parents are not always aware, or do not have easy access to information about Welsh-medium schools' (Welsh Government 2013c).

The First Minister was accompanied by the Welsh Government's Minister for Education and Skills, Huw Lewis, who was eager to emphasise the advantages of Welsh-medium education:

> Our ... campaign aims to dispel some of the myths around Welsh-medium education, such as that non-Welsh-speaking parents are unable to help their children with homework and their development. Welsh-medium education can offer children new skills and can be a very enriching experience. (Welsh Government 2013c)

This Welsh Government campaign came nearly four years after the publication of the first-ever *Welsh-medium Education Strategy* (2010), a historic milestone in 75 years of Welsh-medium education in Wales. This strategy arose from the Welsh Government's commitment in 2007 to 'create a national Welsh-medium Education Strategy to develop effective [education] provision from nursery through to further and higher education, backed up by an implementation programme' (Welsh Assembly Government 2007).

During stakeholder consultations leading to the publication of the *Welsh-medium Education Strategy,* the government reported on the international recognition Wales has received for its success in delivering Welsh-medium education for 75 years – originally by responding to the wishes and demands of Welsh-speaking parents (Welsh Assembly Government 2009). Many children from non-Welsh speaking homes were also taking advantage of Welsh-medium education, and it was claimed that the aim of the Strategy was 'to build on the notable successes and good practice of the past and present' by focusing specifically on developing the Welsh-medium education and training infrastructure (Welsh Assembly Government 2009, Ministerial Foreword). The Government's *Welsh-medium Education Strategy* set out the following vision:

> To have an education and training system that responds in a planned way to the growing demand for Welsh-medium education, reaches out to and reflects our diverse communities and enables an increase in the number of people of all ages and backgrounds who are fluent in Welsh and able to use the language with their families, in their communities and in the workplace. (Welsh Assembly Government 2010)

This chapter tells the story of how the Welsh arrived at securing such a Strategy.

INTRODUCTION

Ever since the first 'designated' Welsh-medium primary school was opened in Aberystwyth in 1939, Welsh-medium and bilingual education has developed and flourished across Wales to meet the demands of Welsh-speaking – and non-Welsh-speaking – parents. The history of the development of Welsh-medium education in Wales is one of continuing struggle by grass-roots movements. This chapter focuses on those forces, mechanisms and counter-weights that have come into play during this 75-year struggle to ensure that Welsh-medium and bilingual education has an increasingly high profile and that Wales is an international leader of bilingual education policies and practices (Lewis 2008).

SOCIO-POLITICAL CONTEXT

Wales, with a population of 3.1 million, is a relatively small country of about 20 779 km². It is one of the three constituent nations that comprise the United Kingdom. The Welsh language has a rich cultural and literary tradition dating back to sixth-century heroic verse in Old Welsh. Welsh evolved from the Celtic branch of what linguists term 'Indo-European' and, of the languages now spoken in Britain, Welsh has by far the oldest roots, going back at least 2500 years and perhaps as much as 4000 years (Davies 1993). Both Welsh and English have co-existed in Wales for over six centuries, ever since the country was 'colonised' by England in the fourteenth and fifteenth centuries, a force which led to increasing Anglicisation and ultimately to Welsh becoming a minority language in terms of numbers, power and status (May 2000).

At the beginning of the twentieth century there were almost a million (977 000) Welsh speakers (aged 3+) in Wales. This decreased over the last century, reaching a low of 504 000 in 1981. However, because of the influence of Welsh-medium schools and the core status given to Welsh in the National Curriculum in Welsh-medium schools under the Education Reform Act of 1988, this figure increased between 1981 and 2001. Unfortunately, the 2011 Census results (Welsh Government 2012a) show that the number of Welsh speakers has decreased by around 20 000 from 582 000 in 2001 to 562 000 (19% of Welsh residents) in 2011. Although the overall decline is not large, the fall in numbers in traditionally stronghold areas in the north and west is a cause for concern, especially since the counties of Ceredigion and Carmarthenshire have less than 50% of Welsh speakers for the first time ever (see Figures 1 and 2 below).

Figure 1: Number of people aged 3+ able to speak Welsh, 1911–2011

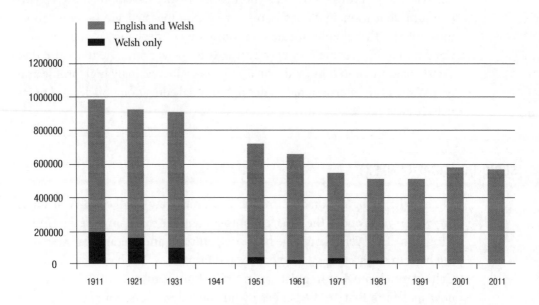

2011 Census: First Results on the Welsh Language, SB 118/2012,
Welsh Government (Welsh Government 2012a).

Today, there are over half a million Welsh speakers in Wales and Figure 2 illustrates their distribution and concentration across the country. The most western areas – which have more than 40% of the population able to speak Welsh – constitute what is referred to as the 'Welsh-speaking heartland'. Preserving the Welsh language in its traditional heartlands and revitalising it in the more Anglicised areas – together with the conviction and belief in the many advantages of becoming bilingual – are two of the major forces behind Welsh-medium and bilingual education.

WELSH IN EDUCATION

Until the late nineteenth century, the language of formal education in Wales was predominantly English. The exception was a network of Sunday schools developed by Welsh non-conformist religious movements in the eighteenth century, which resulted in Wales becoming a literate nation long before the establishment of a national education system (Lewis 2008). The passage of the 'Act of Union' by the English parliament in 1536, incorporating Wales into England, deemed that no person should hold public office if he could

Figure 2: Proportion of people (aged 3 and over) able to speak Welsh, by local authority, 2011

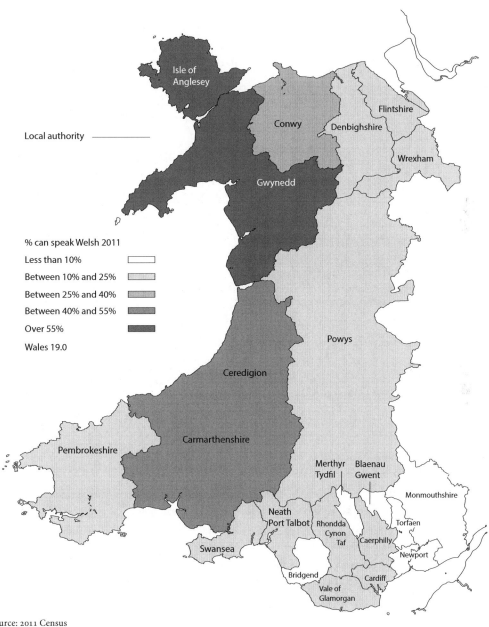

Local authority

% can speak Welsh 2011

Less than 10%

Between 10% and 25%

Between 25% and 40%

Between 40% and 55%

Over 55%

Wales 19.0

Isle of Anglesey

Conwy

Flintshire

Denbighshire

Wrexham

Gwynedd

Powys

Ceredigion

Carmarthenshire

Pembrokeshire

Merthyr Tydfil

Blaenau Gwent

Monmouthshire

Neath Port Talbot

Rhondda Cynon Taf

Torfaen

Caerphilly

Swansea

Newport

Bridgend

Cardiff

Vale of Glamorgan

Source: 2011 Census
173b. 12-13
Geography and Technology
© Crown Copyright and database right 2012. All rights reserved.
Welsh Government. Licence number 100021874.

not speak English, and it was not until the late nineteenth century that the Welsh language received recognition in the field of formal education. The infamous report of the Committee of Enquiry into the role of education in Wales, published in 1847 and referred to as *Brad y Llyfrau Gleision* ('The Treachery of the Blue Books'), insisted that the moral and material condition of Wales could only be improved by the introduction of English (Roberts 1998). This, together with the controversial and cruel tradition of the 'Welsh Not' (a piece of wood hung around the necks of children heard speaking Welsh in some schools, leading to corporal punishment at the end of the day), and the Education Act of 1870, which established a complete network of English-medium schools, contributed to the exclusion of Welsh from the formal education system (Davies 1993; May 2000; Lewis 2008).

A seminal moment for Welsh-medium education was the appointment of O.M. Edwards as Chief Inspector for Wales of the new Board of Education in 1907. Edwards was instrumental in promoting positive attitudes towards the Welsh language in schools. The Board's highly influential report *Welsh in Education and Life* in 1927 called for an inquiry 'into the position occupied by Welsh in the educational system in Wales and to advise how its study may be promoted' (Williams 2003, 22). Edwards and his office lent their considerable status to the expansion of Welsh in the education system. Thanks to Edwards' efforts, many rural schools used Welsh as their medium of instruction and administration but, with rare exception, Welsh-medium education was almost unheard of in Anglicised areas (Williams 2003). However, by 1939, a most significant date (and arguably, a turning-point) in the history of Welsh-medium education, the tide was beginning to turn. After Edwards' death in 1920, his son Ifan ab Owen Edwards established *Urdd Gobaith Cymru* (The Welsh League of Youth – also known simply as the *Urdd*) in 1922. Equally importantly, *Plaid Genedlaethol Cymru* (The National Party of Wales) was established in 1925, and *Undeb Cenedlaethol Athrawon Cymru* (UCAC) – The National Union of Teachers of Wales – in 1940. These mechanisms created a firm foundation for the development of Welsh-medium education. Importantly, they also channelled the powerful forces of love and respect for the Welsh language, thereby giving considerable impetus to the language and those lobbying for more Welsh-medium education provision.

The growth of Welsh-medium and bilingual education is considered to be one of the most remarkable developments in the Welsh education system during the second half of the twentieth century (Williams 2003; Welsh Assembly Government 2010). But it also depicts a historic struggle by both Welsh and English-speaking parents, often against public opinion (even by Welsh speakers in Welsh-speaking communities), and against sceptical and negative education officers, councillors and politicians (Williams 2003). The development of Welsh-medium education has been fragile, patchy and inconsistent, with different areas of Wales following their own patterns rather than a unified national direction; more specifically, some local authorities have been more proactive than others in increasing opportunities for pupils to access Welsh-medium education. Consequently, up until 2010, it can be said that Welsh-medium education was characterised by a lack of policy and coherent direction, with pressure from parents being the main driver in lobbying education policy-makers to plan ahead to meet the increasing demand (Williams 2003).

ABERYSTWYTH 1939: VISION AND VENTURE

The first Welsh-medium school of 'modern' times was a private initiative set up by a small number of professional Welsh-speaking parents in Aberystwyth in September 1939. It was created in response to the influx into the town of evacuees from England as the Second World War broke out. Williams (2003) advocates that this came about as a result of a series of coincidences acting as both forces and mechanisms. At the time, Ifan ab Owen Edwards (O.M. Edwards' son) was a lecturer at Aberystwyth University, and his son (also called Owen) was a pupil in the Welsh-medium stream at the local primary school. The *Urdd* headquarters was also located in Aberystwyth, and a young teacher, Norah Isaac, was about to lose her job with the *Urdd*.

When it was understood that evacuees from Liverpool were being sent to Aberystwyth, these parents (led by Ifan ab Owen Edwards) decided that the only way to safeguard their children's Welsh language and identity would be to establish a private, fee-paying Welsh-medium school. Williams (2003) sums up the significance of this venture:

> The Urdd Company lent its support; Norah Isaac was employed as a teacher; and the school opened on September 25th 1939, with 7 pupils. Rarely had such a crucial experiment been planned and executed in such a short space of time and in such a highly-charged atmosphere. If there had been no war, and if Owen had not been 5 years old, one wonders what would have become of Welsh-medium education. (Williams 2003)

The story of this 'first' modern Welsh-medium school is that of success. As word spread, the number of pupils attending the school grew steadily: 17 in 1940, 32 in 1942, 56 in 1944, and 71 in 1945. In 1948, the school received a very satisfactory report by His Majesty's Inspectors, which stated that it merited inclusion 'in the Ministry's list of efficient schools' (Welsh Department, Ministry of Education 1948). This built trust in Welsh-medium education, acting as a counterweight against fears that Welsh-medium schools could not provide high quality education. By 1952, Cardiganshire Local Education Authority (LEA) opened a new Welsh-medium school in Aberystwyth and the numbers rose immediately to 160 (Williams 2003).

GROWTH AND EXPANSION

Since 1939, a series of accelerating and progressive forces and mechanisms have come into play in support of Welsh-medium education. In 1942, R. A. Butler (President of the UK Board of Education) encouraged Welsh LEAs to set up mechanisms for more effective teaching of the Welsh language in school. In response to a letter from UCAC, his encouragement was formalised in Circular 182, 'The Teaching of Welsh' (October 1942). This circular meant that LEAs were obliged to open discussions on how to raise the status of Welsh and to draft plans to promote Welsh language teaching in their schools, at exactly the same time as the UK Government was drafting the 1944 Education Act.

The 1944 Education Act has special significance in the development of Welsh-medium education. Many educationalists interpreted Section 76 of the Act as a 'parents' charter' – a mechanism giving Welsh-speaking parents the right to insist upon Welsh-medium education. Iorwerth Morgan, who served as Secretary of UCAC, summed up the significance of the 1944 Education Act as a prime mechanism that opened the door:

There were three clauses in the 1944 Education Act that were valuable for the Welsh language:

- The Act contained one whole, concise section (Section 76) concerning the rights of parents to choose the kind of education that their children should receive and the responsibility of Education Authorities to give consideration to their wishes.
- The Welsh Joint Education Committee was set up (in 1948).
- The Central Advisory Council for Education (Wales) was also set up.
(Morgan 2003)

Much importance is given to this act, but Morgan goes on to emphasise that the Welsh-medium schools opened after 1944 were not established *solely* on the basis of the act, which stated that 'pupils are to be educated in accordance with the wishes of their parents'. It is true that enthusiastic parents seized upon this clause; but, it is important to also acknowledge the role played by Local Education Authority (LEA) officials and councillors alongside parents as a driving force.

The first Welsh-medium 'state' school established as a result of the 1944 Education Act was in Llanelli. The campaign began in 1945 and, following a series of public meetings, a petition was circulated (supported and endorsed by the Welsh chapels in the town) and sent to the LEA and the Ministry of Education's Welsh Department. Consequently, on 1 March 1947 (St. David's Day), Ysgol Gymraeg Llanelli opened its doors with 34 children.

This gave hope to supporters of Welsh across Wales and, in the following two years (1948–1949), a number of campaigns for Welsh-medium schools were co-ordinated throughout Wales. The counties of Flintshire, Caernarfonshire and Glamorgan followed suit by opening eight Welsh-medium schools in 1949 alone (Williams 2003). Flintshire, with its visionary Director of Education Dr Haydn Williams, led the way and 'set a new marker for Education Authorities in Wales' (Morgan 2003), by opening three Welsh-medium primary schools in 1949; Glamorgan opened four primary schools in the same year and eight others by 1956. That year would be historic as it saw Flintshire leading the way yet again by opening the first Welsh-medium secondary school, Ysgol Glan Clwyd. The first Welsh-medium secondary school in south Wales (Ysgol Rhydfelen) was founded in 1962. Flintshire in north Wales and Glamorgan in south Wales became synonymous with the pioneering spirit of Welsh-medium education protagonists in the 1950s and 1960s:

> the guiding force in north Wales was the determination of the Director of Education, Dr Haydn Williams, but it was the parents/councillors who were the trail-blazers in the south. (Humphreys 2003)

Between May 1947 and September 1956, 30 Welsh-medium schools were established in north and south Wales, a decade described as the one 'that saved the Welsh language from sinking into utter insignificance, if not oblivion and [in which] solid foundations were laid for the development of Welsh-medium education for the remainder of the century' (Morgan 2003).

As Welsh-medium schools grew in number, parents' associations within them gathered momentum, culminating in the establishment of a new movement called *Undeb Rhieni Ysgolion Cymraeg* (The Union of Welsh-medium School Parents) in 1952 (see Genesee and Mehisto in this volume, who discuss the establishment of similar organisations in Canada and Estonia). The movement's aims were as follows:

- to organise meetings at a local and national level to support applications by parents for Welsh-medium schools
- to draw up memoranda on parents' viewpoints to be presented to the Ministry of Education, Welsh Joint Education Committee (WJEC), LEAs and professional bodies
- to facilitate and aid parents' applications for nursery or primary schools and help those already in existence. (Undeb Rhieni Ysgolion Cymraeg, minutes, 1952, in Morgan 2003)

A belief in the value of Welsh-medium education was the force that drove this movement. This has become one of the strongest forces behind campaigns to open Welsh-medium schools and the Union was instrumental in influencing central UK Government policy during the 1950s and 1960s. Renamed *Rhieni Dros Addysg Gymraeg* (RhAG) (Parents for Welsh-medium Education) in 1983, this movement continues to play a crucial role in lobbying politicians, education officers and councillors.

Campaigns for Welsh-medium education are characterised by a number of common problems and hurdles: the necessity to lobby the authorities about the need and demand for Welsh-medium provision; lack of suitable and adequate school premises; lack of resources, both human and material; the need to ensure progression from one phase of the education system to the next; and lack of strategic planning to provide for the increase in the numbers of pupils opting for Welsh-medium education (Williams 2003). With no prior experience of planning in response to parental demand, some LEAs adopted the principle that a minimum of 30 children were needed before they would consider setting up a Welsh-medium school – although Dr Haydn Williams had been happy to open a school for between five and ten children. The lack of suitable premises was initially addressed by parents – when the numbers were quite small, chapels or church vestries were used, but as the numbers increased, LEAs had to find suitable buildings. Often, Welsh-medium schools had to manage with renovated old school buildings that were empty because of deteriorating conditions. However, the enthusiasm, dedication and sense of mission of parents, teachers and supporters of Welsh-medium education were important forces that led to a great deal of effort directed to overcome such problems.

As non-Welsh-speaking parents began to appreciate the advantages of Welsh-medium education, the 1960s, '70s, '80s and onward have seen a steady increase in the number of non-Welsh-speaking parents taking advantage of immersion education in Welsh for their children. Today, in many areas across Wales, the majority of children attending Welsh-medium schools come from non-Welsh-speaking families who do not speak Welsh at home. Consequently, Welsh-medium education today is a combination of heritage/maintenance language education and immersion education (Lewis 2008). It is the belief in the value of Welsh-medium education amongst non-Welsh speakers (as well as amongst Welsh-speaking parents) that has become a major force in the Welsh-medium education system – this is 'a major plank in language revitalisation and language reversal' in Wales (Baker 2004).

Although Welsh-medium schools were initially established to provide education through the medium of Welsh to Welsh-speaking children, they have always developed the English language skills of all their pupils by using both Welsh and English for teaching and learning, and therefore can be categorised as 'bilingual schools' (Lewis 2008; Baker 2010). This gives rise to wide variations in bilingual teaching methodologies, especially in terms of the amount ot teaching through Welsh and English, and in the distribution and allocation of languages across the curriculum (Lewis, Jones and Baker 2013; Jones and Lewis 2014) – with growing experimentation in the concurrent use of both languages in the same lesson period in the name of *trawsieithu* ('translanguaging') (Lewis, Jones and Baker 2012a; 2012b). Further, the General Certificate of Secondary Education (GCSE) examinations system in Wales (WJEC) accommodates bilingual pupils in a way that reflects bilingual teaching and learning, and acknowledges translanguaging as a feature of classroom practice by providing both English and Welsh versions of examinations in all subjects offered and requested by Welsh-medium schools and by allowing pupils to answer questions in either language on the examination paper.

Today, patterns of Welsh-medium and bilingual provision across Wales are complex (Welsh Assembly Government 2009; 2010), with the terms 'Welsh-medium' and 'bilingual' ambiguously used to refer to the 'kaleidoscopic variety' (Baker 1993) of settings. This ambiguity led the Welsh Government in 2007 to refine its definition of Welsh-medium schools in a way that reflects how much curricular time is allocated and assigned to Welsh and English on a sliding-scale across primary and secondary schools (Welsh Assembly Government 2007b).

Welsh-medium nursery and pre-school provision has also played a crucial role in ensuring a firm foundation in Welsh for generations of pupils. Welsh-medium playgroups (*cylchoedd meithrin*) seek to promote the education and development of children under five through the medium of the Welsh language. The body which organises these pre-schools is *Mudiad Meithrin*, a voluntary organisation established in 1971, that aims 'to give every young child in Wales the opportunity to benefit from early years services and experiences through the medium of Welsh' (www.meithrin.co.uk/home/). *Mudiad Meithrin* currently has 981 units throughout Wales, including 578 *cylchoedd meithrin* pre-school groups and 403 *Ti a Fi* parent-and-toddler groups (Hickey, Lewis and Baker 2014).

According to the School Census Results of 2013, 33% (452) of primary schools and 25% (53) of secondary schools were classified as Welsh-medium/bilingual, attended by 63 192 (24%) pupils and 37 692 (20%) pupils, respectively (Welsh Government 2013a).

THE POWER OF POLITICS

On the political front, the 1960s saw the beginning of a number of campaigns to rekindle Welsh awareness and identity (as distinct from a 'British' identity and separation from being 'English') and, specifically, the Welsh language itself. In 1962, *Cymdeithas yr Iaith Gymraeg* (The Welsh Language Society) was formed, partly as a result of the annual BBC Wales Radio Lecture given on 13 February 1962 by Saunders Lewis, *Tynged yr Iaith* ('The Fate of the Language'). This grass-roots pressure group has been proactive for over 50 years, acting as a counterweight against resistance to the normalisation of Welsh. It has campaigned on a number of issues relating to the status of the Welsh language, including Welsh/bilingual road signs (1960s); S4C, the Welsh television channel (1970s/1980s); the Welsh Language Act (1990s/2000s); the Welsh Language Measure (2010); and *Coleg Cymraeg Cenedlaethol* (the Welsh National College) (2011). The 1960s and 1970s witnessed the first *Plaid Cymru* (National Party of Wales) candidates being elected to Westminster as Members of Parliament for Welsh constituencies – Gwynfor Evans in 1966, who was joined by Dafydd Elis Thomas and Dafydd Wigley in 1974. Following a referendum in 1997, the devolved National Assembly for Wales was created by the Government of Wales Act, 1998. Since 2011, the Assembly is able to legislate in the 20 areas that are devolved without having to consult the UK parliament in London; 'Education and Training' is one of these devolved areas.

In December 2010, with approval of the Welsh Government-proposed Welsh Language Measure (Wales), came a new Welsh Language Strategy (as well as the aforementioned *Welsh-medium Education Strategy*). This Measure gave the Welsh Language official status in Wales and created an entirely new environment for the use of Welsh by those responsible for delivering public services. The Welsh Language Board (set up by the UK Government under the Welsh Language Act 1993) was abolished and the Office of the Welsh Language Commissioner (*Comisiynydd y Gymraeg*) was established in its place (www.comisiynyddygymraeg.org/english/Pages/Home.aspx).

A CO-ORDINATED NATIONAL STRATEGY AND DIRECTION

Over the past 75 years, two primary mechanisms have been responsible for significant growth in the provision of Welsh-medium education – enthusiastic parents and LEAs with their strategic plans (Jones 2008). However, recognition must also be given to a third mechanism, namely Her Majesty's Inspectors of Schools. They reported Welsh-medium education as offering a similar quality of education to that in English-medium schools, and thereby promoted Welsh-medium education. It is noteworthy that up to 2010, all this growth had been achieved by grass-roots mechanisms and forces, without a unified and co-ordinated national policy and direction from central government.

In the absence of a national policy and strategy, a number of 'voices' started to call on the devolved Welsh Government to take the lead in formulating and implementing a vision for developing Welsh-medium education for the twenty-first century. In 2008, Meirion Prys Jones, the then Chief Executive of the now defunct Welsh Language Board, expressed concern about a lack of national level leadership in education. Jones (2008) posited that:

> It is time for the Welsh Assembly Government to adopt the role of a body responsible for planning the development of Welsh-medium education and training. The elected government of Wales needs to ensure that it has the capacity to plan the future of education in Wales in its entirety, not only the English-medium element. The sad truth of the matter is that that is all that has been done so far. However, there are encouraging signs in the *One Wales* document …

Jones was drawing on the Welsh Assembly Government's (2007a) policy document *One Wales: A Progressive Agenda for the Government of Wales* (An agreement between the Labour and *Plaid Cymru* groups in the National Assembly) published on 27 June 2007, which had issued an encouraging commitment to 'create a national Welsh-medium Education Strategy to develop effective provision from nursery through to further and higher education, backed up by an implementation programme' (Welsh Assembly Government 2007a). This document, which also proposed a training programme for educators, built on previous policy documents of the Welsh Assembly Government contributing towards revitalising Welsh – and in particular, *Iaith Pawb: A*

National Action Plan for a Bilingual Wales (Welsh Assembly Government 2003).

In the 2009 Ministerial Foreword to the consultation document for the proposed Welsh-medium Education Strategy, the Government acknowledged existing weaknesses by announcing that a stronger framework and policy infrastructure needed to be established and developed in order to sustain the system:

> We wish to see a Welsh-medium system that is based on forward planning across all phases of education and training through the medium of Welsh. Accurate assessment of demand, and the commitment and capacity to respond to that demand, are key principles of the process, at all stages from the early years through to higher education and lifelong learning. (Welsh Assembly Government 2009)

The aspirations of 75 years of ad-hoc development of Welsh-medium education were encapsulated in the vision statement in the Government's first-ever national Welsh-medium Education Strategy:

> To have an education and training system that responds in a planned way to the growing demand for Welsh-medium education, reaches out to and reflects our diverse communities and enables an increase in the number of people of all ages and backgrounds who are fluent in Welsh and able to use the language with their families, in their communities and in the workplace. (Welsh Assembly Government 2010)

In order to realise this ambition of creating a Wales where Welsh-medium education and training form an integral part of the education infrastructure, six strategic aims encompassing a variety of forces and mechanisms were identified:

STRATEGIC AIMS

1) **To improve the planning of Welsh-medium provision in the pre-statutory and statutory phases of education, on the basis of proactive response to informed parental demand.**

   Mechanisms such as strategic plans and systematic analyses of demand, and forces such as a commitment to act on the evidence of demand and effective stakeholder collaboration can help drive the delivery of Welsh-medium education in a more systematic manner.

2) **To improve the planning of Welsh-medium provision in the post-14 phases of education and training, to take account of linguistic progression and continued development of skills.**

The disposition to view Welsh-medium provision at all levels of the education system as an integrated whole is a force that needs to lead to stakeholder collaboration and planning. In particular it is important to improve the quality and increase the provision of the post-14 phases of Welsh-medium education. Otherwise, a lack of Welsh-medium provision in the post-14 phases could act as a negative counterweight to the delivery of Welsh-medium education at the pre-school and primary levels.

3) **To ensure that all learners develop their Welsh-language skills to their full potential and encourage sound linguistic progression from one phase of education and training to the next.**

Welsh-medium education from the early years, with robust linguistic progression through every phase of education, offers the best current option for developing a broad range of language skills in Welsh. Schools, local authorities and other providers need to plan strategically to facilitate continuity in linguistic development.

4) **To ensure a planned Welsh-medium education workforce that provides sufficient numbers of practitioners for all phases of education and training, with high-quality Welsh-language skills and competence in teaching methodologies.**

Mechanisms ensuring a sufficiently qualified workforce for Welsh-medium education are fundamental to the success of this Education Strategy. The needs of Welsh-medium provision in all sectors require increased numbers of staffing. Training in language and methodological skills are key.

5) **To improve central support mechanisms for Welsh-medium education and training.**

Mechanisms are required to support Welsh-medium learners and provision in general. This would include improved access to a sufficient range of Welsh-medium qualifications, along with assessment through the medium of Welsh. More Welsh-medium electronic and hard-copy teaching and learning resources are required for general and vocational education.

6) **To contribute to the acquisition and reinforcement of Welsh-language skills in families and in the community.**

Education and training alone cannot guarantee that speakers become fluent in Welsh or choose to use the language in their everyday lives. Informal learning opportunities such as youth organisations, sports and arts programmes (mechansims) are required to support and complement the formal process of developing Welsh-language skills. This calls for collaboration across Welsh Assembly Government Departments and other agencies.

(Welsh Assembly Government 2010)

In 2012, the Welsh Government published a new five-year Welsh Language Strategy for 2012–17, *Iaith Fyw: Iaith Byw / A Living Language: A Language for Living* (Welsh Government 2012b). Although education is not analysed in detail in this strategy, it does emphasise the importance of the Government's Welsh-medium Education Strategy as an essential mechanism in producing the Welsh speakers of the future, alongside encouraging the use of the language in families and increasing their awareness of the value of the language in modern-day Wales.

As the demand for Welsh-medium education continues to increase, with parents continuously campaigning for further provision at every level of the education system, tensions are apparent in many areas as LEAs are accused of failing to respond adequately to meet growing demand (RhAG 2014). As we move forward to evaluate the effectiveness of the Welsh-medium Education Strategy, it is imperative that consideration is given to understanding which forces need to be managed and what mechanisms are required to address the needs of Welsh-medium education in Wales in the twenty-first century – not only in schools, but also in order to ensure 'effective progression into, and further development of, Welsh-medium course options in higher education' (Welsh Assembly Government 2010). To address the latter, Coleg Cymraeg Cenedlaethol was established in 2011 by the Welsh Government as a national body which plays a key role in planning, supporting and developing Welsh-medium education and scholarship at universities in Wales (www.colegcymraeg.ac.uk/en/).

CONCLUSION

The Implementation Programme that accompanied the Welsh-medium Education Strategy details the work expected of the Welsh Government and its stakeholders in all phases of education and training. In order to monitor progress made with implementing the Strategy, fixed five-year and indicative ten-year targets based on intended outcomes were established. Progress made against the targets is being analysed and reported on annually by the Welsh Government.

In its 2012–13 *Welsh-medium Education Strategy Annual Report*, the Minister for Education and Skills (Welsh Government, 2013b) outlined successes and failures in meeting the targets of the Strategy. Among the main achievements he listed:

- just over one in every five learners aged seven is in Welsh-medium education
- progress has been made against 63 of the 74 actions (85%) in the implementation programme, with work on the remaining 11 actions commencing during 2013–14
- the School Standards and Organisation Act (Wales) 2013, places Welsh in Education Strategic Plans (WESPs) on a statutory basis, further challenging LEAs to plan for Welsh-medium education, with some authorities being required to proactively assess the demand for Welsh-medium education
- 160 new titles to expand the range of teaching and learning resources available to schools and colleges who teach through the medium of Welsh or teach Welsh as a second language were published.

However, despite the successes, little progress has been made against a number of the Strategy's targets. For example, 25% of seven-year olds are unlikely to be taught through the medium of Welsh by 2015. The Minister also specified that better planning and Government pressure is needed to stimulate growth in Welsh-medium education in some areas. This is substantiated by the Committee of Experts of the European Charter for Regional or Minority Languages (Council of Europe, 2014), who concluded that there is still evidence of substantial unmet demand in parts of Wales for Welsh-medium primary and secondary education and that the gap between demand for and provision of Welsh-medium education remains large in many counties (Welsh Government 2013b).

The Minister concluded the 2012–13 Annual Report by reiterating the Government's continued commitment to Welsh-medium education:

we are serious about ensuring that all interested parties can view the progress made and comment on the actions undertaken. It is clear that this Welsh Government takes Welsh-medium education seriously and has introduced specific measures to improve the planning, delivery and outcomes of this distinct provision. (Welsh Government 2013b)

Despite the Education Strategy, much remains to be done to ensure that Welsh-medium education becomes an integral part of the education infrastructure in Wales. There is an ongoing need – even in 2015 – to further manage the forces, mechanisms and counterweights that interact with each other and that continue to either undermine or support efforts to meet the targets of the Strategy and that help ensure that the aspirations of those parents and children who have chosen or wish to choose Welsh-medium education at any level of the system are met. There is no room for complacency – as emphasised by RhAG (2014), 'The opportunity to turn national political consensus into actual developments on the ground must be grasped with both hands.' This is the challenge that faces all stakeholders in favour of Welsh-medium education and training in all phases in the first half of the twenty-first century.

REFERENCES

Baker, C. (1993). 'Bilingual Education in Wales'. In H. Baetens Beardsmore (ed.), *European Models of Bilingual Education*, 7–29. Clevedon: Multilingual Matters.

— (2004). Editorial. *The Welsh Journal of Education*. 13: 1, 1–7.

— (2010). 'Increasing Bilingualism in Bilingual Education'. In D. Morris (ed.), *Welsh in the Twenty-First Century*, 61–79. Cardiff: University of Wales Press.

Council of Europe (2014). *European Charter for Regional or Minority Languages: Fourth Report of the Committee of Experts in respect of the United Kingdom*. Strasbourg: Council of Europe

Davies, J. (1993). *The Welsh Language*. Cardiff: University of Wales Press.

Hickey, T.M., Lewis, G. and Baker, C. (2014). 'How Deep is your Immersion? Policy and Practice in Welsh-medium Preschools with Children from Different Language Backgrounds'. *International Journal of Bilingual Education and Bilingualism*, 17: 2, 215–34.

Humphreys, G.E. (2003). 'Ysgol Rhydfelen 1962–1974'. In I.W. Williams (ed.), *Our Children's Language: The Welsh-medium Schools of Wales 1939–2000*, 99–111. Talybont: Y Lolfa.

Jones, M.P. (2008). 'The Way Forward for Welsh-medium Education'. In *Creating a Bilingual Wales/Creu Cymru Ddwyieithog: The Role of Welsh in Education*, 3–6. Cardiff: Institute of Welsh Affairs.

Jones, B. and Lewis, W.G. (2014). 'Language Arrangements within Bilingual Education'. In E.M. Thomas and I. Mennen (eds), *Advances in the Study of Bilingualism*, 141–70. Bristol: Multilingual Matters.

Lewis, W.G. (2008). 'Current Challenges in Bilingual Education in Wales'. In J. Cenoz and D. Gorter, (eds), *AILA Review 21. Multilingualism and Minority Languages: Achievements and Challenges in Education*, 69–86. Amsterdam/Philadelphia, PA: John Benjamins.

Lewis, G., Jones, B. and Baker, C. (2012a). 'Translanguaging: Origins and Development from School to Street and Beyond'. *Educational Research and Evaluation: An International Journal on Theory and Practice,* 18: 7, 641–54.

Lewis, G., Jones, B. and Baker, C. (2012b). 'Translanguaging: Developing its Conceptualisation and Contextualisation'. *Educational Research and Evaluation: An International Journal on Theory and Practice,* 18: 7, 655–70.

— (2013). '100 Bilingual Lessons: Distributing Two Languages in Classrooms'. In C. Abello-Contesse, P.M. Chandler, M.D. López-Jiménez and R. Chacón-Beltrán (eds), *Bilingual and Multilingual Education in the 21st Century: Building on Experience,* 107–35. Bristol: Multilingual Matters.

May, S. (2000). 'Accommodating and Resisting Minority Language Policy: The Case of Wales'. *International Journal of Bilingual Education and Bilingualism,* 3: 2, 101–28.

Morgan, I. (2003). 'The Early Days of Welsh-medium Schools'. In I.W. Williams, (ed.), *Our Children's Language: The Welsh-medium Schools of Wales 1939–2000,* 21–44. Talybont: Y Lolfa.

RhAG (2014). Website of RhAG/Parents for Welsh-medium education. www.rhag.net/?iaith=eng&id= (retrieved March 2014).

Roberts, D.T. (1998). *The Language of the Blue Books.* Cardiff: University of Wales Press.

Welsh Assembly Government (2003). *Iaith Pawb: A National Action Plan for a Bilingual Wales.* Cardiff: Welsh Assembly Government.

— (2007a). *One Wales: A Progressive Agenda for the Government of Wales* (An agreement between the Labour and Plaid Cymru Groups in the National Assembly). www.wales.gov.uk/strategy/strategies/onewales/onewalese.pdf?lang=en (retrieved March 2014).

— (2007b). *Defining Schools According to Welsh-medium Provision.* Information document No: 023/2007. Cardiff: Welsh Assembly Government.

— (2009). *Welsh-medium Education Strategy: Consultation.* Consultation document No: 067/2009. Cardiff: Welsh Assembly Government.

— (2010). *Welsh-medium Education Strategy.* Information document No: 083/2010. Cardiff: Welsh Assembly Government.

Welsh Government (2012a). *2011 Census: First Results on the Welsh Language.* SB 118/2012. Cardiff: Welsh Government. www.wales.gov.uk/statistics (retrieved March 2014).

— (2012b). *A Living Language: A Language for Living. Welsh Language Strategy 2014–2017.* Cardiff: Welsh Government.

— (2013a). *School Census Results, 2013.* SDR 109/2013. www.wales.gov.uk/statistics (retrieved March 2014).

— (2013b). *Welsh-medium Education Strategy Annual Report 2012–2013.* Cardiff: Welsh Government.

— (2013c). Welsh Government Press Release. www.wales.gov.uk/newsroom/welshlanguage/2013/13111 8welshlang/?lang=en (retrieved March 2014).

Williams, I.W. (ed.) (2003). *Our Children's Language: The Welsh-medium Schools of Wales 1939–2000.* Talybont: Y Lolfa.

www.colegcymraeg.ac.uk/en/ (retrieved March 2014).

www.comisiynyddygymraeg.org/english/Pages/Home.aspx (retrieved March 2014).

www.wales.gov.uk/topics/educationandskills/publications/guidance/welshmededstrat/?lang=en (retrieved March 2014).

www.wjec.co.uk (retireved March 2014).

FORCES	MECHANISMS
Key values in human relations	**Organisations**
Trust (among stakeholders) Fairness Justice for the minority-language speakers	Undeb Rhieni Ysgolion Cymraeg (The Union of Welsh-medium School Parents) Rhieni dros Addysg Gymraeg (Parents for Welsh-medium Education) Cymdeithas yr Iaith Gymraeg (The Welsh Language Society) Mudiad Meithrin (Welsh-medium Pre-school provision) Her Majesty's Inspectors of Schools (HMI) Welsh Language Board Coleg Cymraeg Cenedlaethol (Welsh National College) High-powered steering committees Teachers' association that supports bilingual education
Principles for cooperation	
Political devolution (welsh government) Stakeholder inclusion Recognition of local concerns – parents Disposition to viewing all levels and phases of education as an integrated whole	
Individuals	**Legislation and plans**
Stamina and enthusiasm of key individuals A sense of mission and commitment Status of supporters	1944 Education Act 1988 Education Reform Act Welsh Language Act Welsh Language Measure *Iaith Pawb: A National Action Plan for a Bilingual Wales* *One Wales: A Progressive Agenda for the Government of Wales* Welsh-medium Education Strategy A living language: a language for living School Standards and Organisation Act *Live in Wales: Learn in Welsh* Welsh in Education Strategic Plans (WESPs)
Goals	
High expectations for all Meticuluous planning	
Beliefs	
Desire to maintain minority language and culture A belief in bilingual education (by parents of diverse socio-economic and linguistic backgrounds) Fear of the negative effects of a powerful high status language (English) Fear of language shift (decrease in the number of Welsh speakers)	**Key individuals**
	Committed indefatigable individuals High-status supporters such as Her Majesty's Inspectors, Welsh Government
Founding principles	**Instruments**
Voluntary nature of programme Buy-in to a vision to guide programme development (national government-led strategy) Frankness regarding challenges	Initial teacher education/training and in-service training Welsh-medium/bilingual education programme Evaluation and annual reports

COUNTERWEIGHTS

Politicians (local and central government)	Grass-roots movements
Status quo of English-medium education	Benefit to students and society of immersion
Challenges of immersion	Benefits of immersion
Risk taking	Trust/confidence
Public (majority) opinion	Minority idealism

9 THE NETHERLANDS:
Quality Control as a Driving Force in Bilingual Education

Rick de Graaff (Utrecht University) and Onno van Wilgenburg
(European Platform, Internationalising Education)

CHAPTER NAVIGATOR

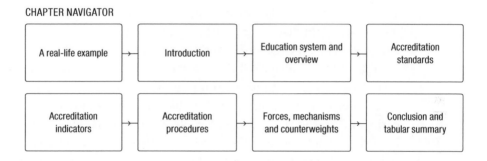

A REAL-LIFE EXAMPLE: A DAY IN THE LIFE OF THE CLIL ACCREDITATION COMMITTEE

Jan Steen College is a rural secondary school with a long-standing bilingual programme. Students in the programme are taught at least 50% of their subjects through English and the remainder through Dutch. This state school is expecting an accreditation visit from the European Platform, which coordinates bilingual education in the Netherlands. Prior to the accreditation committee visit, the school reported that it had a strong internationalisation programme that was undertaking exchange projects with schools in Italy and Mexico. European and International Orientation (EIO) is a key accreditation criterion. Also, the school detailed how the content of its curriculum was supporting internationalisation.

All bilingual programme teachers have passed the Cambridge Proficiency Exam, having achieved at least the required Common European Framework of Reference (CEFR) level B2 (Council of Europe 2001). Although the school's bilingual programme is nearly 14 years old, the previous Content and Language Integrated Learning (CLIL) training was provided six years ago, and in fact some new teachers might not have had any CLIL training at all. The accreditation standards require teachers to demonstrate CLIL skills, such as the ability to create rich learning environments where students are actively engaged in communication and where the learning and use of academic English language is fostered. The school has not provided evidence that pre-university students have achieved a CEFR B2 level in the third form (i.e. 15-year olds), which is another accreditation criterion.

The accreditation visit lasts one day and this time, as always, is conducted by a committee of three individuals – an experienced CLIL teacher trainer from a university, an employee of the European Platform, and a principal of a bilingual school. For the first hour of the visit, the committee discusses the school's bilingual policy with the principal, the vice-principal and the bilingual department coordinator. During this meeting, it is confirmed that there has been no formal CLIL training for the past six years, but apparently there has been much informal training in the form of visits to CLIL conferences, peer-to-peer learning and the sharing of good practices at teacher-led national workshops. Each member of the committee observes half of four English-medium lessons; their visit is comprised of 12 observations, each lasting 25 minutes. Subjects taught through English include the sciences, humanities, the arts and Physical Education. On the whole, lessons are exemplary. Language support and development go hand-in-hand with subject teaching. An active learning approach is applied, with students communicating actively in English. Some lessons are largely teacher-centred, with students getting little or no chance to speak, and there is no explicit focus on the learning of subject-related language.

The rest of the day involves interviews with the CLIL coordinator, European and International Orientation coordinator, subject teachers, English teachers, students and parents. The focus is on their experiences and beliefs, in order to help the committee check and further refine their understanding of the bilingual programme. In addition, the school provides additional proof of pre-university students' English language proficiency – recent speaking, reading, writing and listening test results.

The committee evaluates the school by giving it a score on each of the 45 accreditation indicators. The scores are presented and a discussion proceeds with the school management team that looks at strengths and weaknesses. The principal acknowledges that CLIL training is long overdue. There is general relief that students appear to be reaching the B2 level. At the next national meeting of bilingual schools, Jan Steen College's success is publically recognised and it is awarded the European Platform's five-year accreditation certificate.

INTRODUCTION

This chapter describes the accreditation process for the 120 schools in the Dutch national Network of Bilingual Schools. The chapter first discusses the context of bilingual secondary education in the Netherlands. In addition, it details the rationale for the accreditation process and its role as an internal mechanism initiated by the national Network aimed at assuring the provision of quality bilingual education. Furthermore, the chapter traces the forces, mechanisms and counterweights acting on and originating from current educational practice.

BILINGUAL EDUCATION OVERVIEW

In the Netherlands, students enter one of three possible streams of secondary education at the age of twelve: *vmbo* (junior pre-vocational education, 4 years), *havo* (general secondary education, 5 years), or *vwo* (pre-university education, 6 years) (*cf.* www.government.nl/ issues/education 2014). English, French and German are the most frequently taught foreign languages (see Van Els and Tuin 2010; Moonen et al. 2012, for further background information on the teaching and learning of foreign languages in the Dutch educational system). However, English is also a compulsory subject in the upper two years of primary and throughout secondary education. Final examinations for upper secondary consist of two parts: a state-controlled reading examination and internal school examinations which test the other language skills (speaking, writing, listening, as well as understanding of literature). Targets based on the Common European Framework of Reference for Languages (Council of Europe 2001) have been established that range from A2 (Basic User), for junior pre-vocational, to B2 (Independent User) for pre-university education.

Schools are relatively autonomous with respect to curriculum content and teaching methodology. The Dutch government does not directly mandate educational innovation at the school level. This applies to bilingual education as well, which has been a bottom-up development initiated by school boards, teachers and parents since the early 1990s. Currently, approximately 120 (of 700) secondary schools offer a bilingual stream at the secondary level, usually in parallel with a 'regular' non-bilingual stream. In bilingual schools, at least 50% of the curriculum is taught through a second language. Virtually all bilingual schools offer Dutch-English bilingual education; only a few offer a Dutch-German programme. Bilingual education was first introduced in the pre-university *vwo* stream, but is now being increasingly offered in the *vmbo* and the *havo* streams as well (*cf.* www.ikkiestto.nl).

Research conducted in the Netherlands has demonstrated that students in bilingual streams reach higher levels of English proficiency than students in regular streams (Huibregtse 2001, Admiraal et al. 2006, Verspoor et al. 2010, 2012). On national examinations, bilingual programme students also achieve results in Dutch and content-matter subjects that are at least on par with those of students in regular programmes. In addition, De Graaff et al. (2007) and Schuitemaker-King (2012), in their studies of 80 lessons and 15 subject teachers in the Netherlands, found that subject teachers teaching through English were able to facilitate CLIL by applying effective language teaching strategies in subject classes.

It is noteworthy that the bilingual programme is coordinated by the European Platform, a central mechanism in programme development. The mission of this government-financed agency is the development of internationalisation in Dutch education. The schools that operate under the European Platform are grouped under the national Network for Bilingual Schools.

ACCREDITATION STANDARDS

The Dutch *Standards for Bilingual Education in English* resulted from a lengthy, multi-year discussion through the national Network for Bilingual Schools beginning in the mid-1990s. It was agreed that the standards should be compatible with the Dutch curriculum, should support students in preparing for compulsory national examinations in Dutch and should be aligned with the programmes of international and non-international schools. After several years of discussion, the standards were adopted in 2002 by all Dutch bilingual schools. Stakeholder inclusion was an important force in helping to ensure that schools accepted and used the standards – a key mechanism in programme development. The standards serve as a guide for new as well as experienced bilingual schools. Key criteria from the standards include (see Tool 8 on this book's website for full version):

- in the lower grade levels (ages 12–15), a minimum 50% of lessons should be taught through English
- in the upper grades (ages 15–18), 25% of teaching and study time should be in English

- students reach level B2 in Year Three (age 15)
- teachers are well-versed in CLIL methodology
- students engage in project-based collaboration with students abroad at least once
- teachers have at least a B2 level of language proficiency
- students' proficiency in Dutch may not be negatively influenced
- national exam results for the subjects taught in English may not be negatively influenced
- authentic teaching resources and learning materials in English are used, covering the Dutch curriculum as well as an international orientation
- schools offering a bilingual programme in the upper grades must offer the International Baccalaureate *English Language and Literature* course.

ACCREDITATION INDICATORS

The standards are presented in an accreditation framework that contains 45 indicators in the following categories: learning results; programme quantity; programme quality; international orientation; CLIL pedagogy; quality control; organisational preconditions, and individual and team-based professional development (see Tool 9). Every five years, accreditation committees appointed by the European Platform ascertain whether a school conforms to each individual indicator and, by extension, to the standards. Indicators are scored on a binary scale (+/-). Twenty-three of the indicators are norm-indicators, meaning that each one must be met for the school to merit certification. Failure to meet any one single norm criterion results in non-accreditation. These norm indicators outline the minimum quality level that is required of all schools – for example, that at least 50% of subjects should be taught through English and that there should be international collaboration. The non-norm indicators form part of an ideal CLIL learning environment as agreed upon by all the schools in the network; for example, schools should have at least three native speakers of English on staff: one in the English Language Department and two in the other subject departments. This indicator is motivated by a desire to give learners additional opportunities to hear native English (of whichever variety) in diverse subject areas. Native speakers are also likely to bring different teaching methods and an international perspective. However, since schools face many staffing challenges, this is not a minimum requirement, but a goal. During accreditation visits, schools are invited to elaborate on their efforts to expose students to native-speakers of English, preferably through direct contact with qualified teachers, but also by other means, such as guest speakers, exchange programmes and online collaboration with peers abroad.

ACCREDITATION PROCEDURES

All 120 schools that form the national Network for Bilingual Schools in the Netherlands subscribe to the standards and the accreditation framework. These documents are the basis for accreditation. Schools generally take one to two years to prepare for the launch of their bilingual programme. Students enter the programme in the first year of lower secondary school (age 12). When the first cohort of students is in its second year, a mock accreditation visit takes place. Two years later, the lower secondary programme (for students of age 12–15) undergoes accreditation. Should a school extend the bilingual programme into upper secondary, another accreditation takes place three years later. From thereon, schools must renew their accreditation every five years (see Table 1 for an overview of the accreditation process).

Table 1: Bilingual secondary school development and the accreditation process

Year	Stages	Type of visit	Committee
1	school joins the network; prepares for one year (sometimes for two years)	none	
2	school starts bilingual classes; first students are in Year One	none	
3	first cohort of students is in Year Two	advisory visit and mock accreditation leading to a progress report	an experienced principal and a European Platform staff member
4	first cohort of students is in Year Three; B2 level achieved	none	
5	fully operational bilingual stream in the three lower forms; first cohort is in Year Four.	lower secondary programme accreditation visit possibly resulting in accreditation	a CLIL expert, an internationalisation specialist and an employee of the European Platform
6, 7	schools wishing to do so extend the bilingual stream to upper secondary	none	
8	first cohort takes final exams and graduates from school	senior programme accreditation visit possibly resulting in accreditation	a CLIL expert, an internationalisation specialist and an employee of the European Platform
12, 17, 22 …	the school has been accredited for five years	re-accreditation visit possibly resulting in re-accreditation	a CLIL expert, a principal from a different bilingual school and an employee of the European Platform

If a school does not pass an accreditation round, a further visit with a different committee will take place within two years. Should a school fail two consecutive accreditations, the Network regulations stipulate that the school lose its membership in the Network and its accreditation. To date, no school has failed the accreditation more than once. This underlines the purpose and effectiveness of the accreditation process; it is a model for focused educational redesign. If the model is implemented with insight and sufficient effort, and supported by professional development, it provides a powerful mechanism for the creation of a sustainable bilingual programme.

The accreditation procedure itself is evaluated on a yearly basis by the committee members, the European Platform and the steering group of the Network. The standards are discussed and evaluated regularly by the members of the Network for Bilingual Schools, and adapted if necessary.

FORCES

Trust is a major driving force in school-based programme development. This includes trusting the Network to make decisions which, by extension, leads to trust in the mechanisms created by the Network. Trust is a precondition for effective collaboration among schools, coordinators and teachers. Trust combines with another force, the autonomy that arises from a fundamental human desire to have a degree of control over one's own life. Network schools and teachers enjoy a degree of autonomy as they are left with the responsibility of deciding how best to apply the standards.

A strong sense of commitment to the standards and the bilingual programme is another substantial force encouraging quality bilingual education. The commitment arises from the sense of ownership that is created as the schools themselves develop the standards. Furthermore, the primary stakeholders (school principals and bilingual department coordinators) are responsible for their implementation. In addition, many principals, programme leaders and teachers report feeling a strong sense of responsibility not only for their own school's bilingual programme, but for the Network as a whole. This is exemplified by how they advocate for bilingual education in the community. Moreover, during the bilingual programme accreditation visits an external principal of a bilingual school from the Network always participates. He or she usually provides valuable feedback to the principal of the school being accredited, and also learns from the accreditation procedure. This sharing of responsibility for accreditation intensifies the principals' commitment to the bilingual programme in general and to its standards.

The standards and the accreditation process aim to create a shared vision that guides the development of a programme to foster additive bilingualism and a European and international orientation among students. As such, the accreditation standards and procedures support and enhance teachers' and other stakeholders' belief in the value of CLIL as an effective pedagogical approach for subject and language learning. The standards also constitute high expectations. High expectations are a powerful force for both students and teachers in the development of rich learning environments that use internationalisation and bilingual education as an authentic setting for content and language learning. Furthermore, these high expectations act as a powerful stimulus for deeper learning by both teachers and students. Moreover, the accreditation system personifies a belief in the need for quality control and peer evaluation as an instrument for improving professional development and programme quality.

MECHANISMS

In its commitment to quality, the Network of Bilingual Schools' main vehicles for programme implementation are committed pupils, parents, teachers, principals and school boards, as well as a stimulating teachers' network. The belief in and commitment to the bilingual programme amongst these people are the primary forces fuelling the mechanisms that contribute to successful teaching and learning. In addition, three sets of mechanisms have played a central role in the development of the Network of Bilingual Schools and the accreditation of the bilingual programmes in these schools.

First, the national Network of Bilingual Schools, the European Platform as the national coordinating organisation and the quality control committees are all central mechanisms that create structures and opportunities through which quality and cooperation can be developed. Tangible examples of such opportunities are regular symposia for teacher professional development in CLIL, a professorship for research on bilingual education supported financially by the Network, pre-service and in-service CLIL teacher-training programmes, regular national meetings of bilingual school co-ordinators and participation in European networks for bilingual education development. Opportunities for cooperation and discussion have led to the creation of standards for bilingual programmes, teacher competences and accreditation indicators. These are important mechanisms for enhancing programme development and management. They also constitute a coherent discourse that is held in common by key stakeholders, both from participating schools, from candidate schools, and from local, regional and national educational policy makers.

Second, within this organisational framework, all participants and stakeholders agree on clear benchmarks; namely, standards for bilingual schools and a quality control process, both of which are compulsory for membership in the Network. Furthermore, all schools adhere to the Common European Framework of Reference for Languages, as well as to the Common Framework for European Competence. These instruments provide a shared point or reference for discussions about quality bilingual education.

Finally, logos, certificates and other branding instruments are valuable mechanisms that can contribute to a sense of belonging, uniqueness and pride that further reinforce commitment to the programme. Only accredited schools may use these branding instruments. Therefore, they play a substantial role in schools' public relations and communication campaigns. Other mechanisms that promote high quality bilingual education are exclusive 'members only' training programmes for bilingual schools' coordinators, and national activities for bilingual students, ranging from mathematics to cricket contests, as well as annual debating, drama and junior speaking contests.

COUNTERWEIGHTS

Counterweights can consist of either forces or mechanisms or a combination of these that play an active part in the dynamics of programme implementation and development. This section will not only discuss existing counterweights, but argue that counterweights need to be used consciously to counter potentially negative mechanisms or forces.

Expansion of the bilingual programme is dependent on an ongoing push-and-pull phenomenon. Parental pressure and student interest in bilingual education act as counterweights to the hesitation of school boards to take on additional responsibilities. Thus, raising parent and student awareness of the benefits of bilingual education can contribute to programme expansion insofar as better-informed parents and students are likely to actively demand more high-quality bilingual programmes.

Although the standards are owned by the national Network of Bilingual Schools and each member school is therefore co-responsible for the standards and the accreditation procedure, the schools may see the standards and in particular the 'norm' criteria as undermining their autonomy. As a counterweight, schools have a certain freedom to apply the quality criteria in terms of their local context; for example, they can decide which subjects from the sciences or the humanities they want to offer in English, or if they prefer to organise face-to-face or virtual school exchange projects. Schools can also choose to take international English-medium formative and summative exams from awarding bodies such as Cambridge International Examinations.

Bilingual education is characterised by a strong focus on second language development in subject learning. However, as compulsory final examinations in the Dutch secondary education system are administered in Dutch only, this acts to some extent as a counterweight to English-medium programming because most bilingual schools switch back to using Dutch in the upper grades for teaching the science and social science subjects. This invites teachers to adopt strategies (counterweights) to ensure that students who switch back to using Dutch as a medium of instruction in those subjects continue also to develop academic language proficiency in these domains in English.

As a counterweight to potential negative backwash effects of focusing on assessing student achievement using high-stakes tests, it would in the future also be important to identify and assess less-discussed potential benefits of bilingual education programmes. These might include positive student attitudes regarding language learning and use, their satisfaction with the programme and the extent to which they acquire intercultural competence and a global orientation. Equally importantly, it would be helpful to assess the effects of the bilingual programme on innovative teaching practices, such as increased cross-curricular and international student collaboration.

As a counterweight to elitism, the Dutch-English bilingual programme is now being offered in all three streams of Dutch secondary education, including the pre-vocational stream. Although relatively few schools are participating so far, there is a growing belief that bilingual education is a positive challenge that is suitable for students in all streams. Schools are still discovering ways to better implement bilingual programmes in junior vocational education. An adapted version of the standards has been adopted recently for this stream.

Most bilingual schools demand a fee from students for participation. This money is used for extra-curricular activities and professional development programmes. As a counterweight to the elitism that this policy could create, schools waive the fee for students from economically disadvantaged backgrounds. To ensure that the additional fees are spent as designated, schools must show during the accreditation procedure how the additional fees have been used.

Schools are under increased pressure to meet student needs. Not only bilingual education, but other types of programmes, such as Science ('Technasium'), Entrepreneurship ('Entreprenasium'), Culture and Sports are gaining popularity as well. Bilingual schools, therefore, may face competition from schools offering such challenging programmes. A clear counterweight to the potential pressure from other schools is the well-established nature of the bilingual programme along with its well-developed standards and accreditation procedures. These can help build the quality of the bilingual programme and stakeholder confidence in it.

CONCLUSION

The Network of Bilingual Schools, the standards and the accreditation procedures discussed in this chapter have proven their relevance over the past 15 years. These central mechanisms have created structures and opportunities through which forces for quality bilingual education can be facilitated and supported: trust, commitment, cooperation, a shared vision, belief in the educational power of CLIL, and European and international orientation. On the one hand, the strength of the forces and mechanisms in the Dutch context have proven to operate as effective counterweights to criticism, scepticism and competition from other promising curriculum innovations. On the other hand, they have intensified our own evaluation of bilingual education, raised awareness of our own gaps in knowledge and guided programme improvement.[1]

NOTES

1   On 1 January 2015, the European Platform merged with the Nuffic, the Dutch organisation for internationalisation in higher education. The name of the new organisation is EP-Nuffic (www.epnuffic.nl). The European Platform is open to international dialogue about its standards and accredication procedures.

REFERENCES

Admiraal, W., Westhoff, G. and De Bot, K. (2006). 'Evaluation of Bilingual Secondary Education in the Netherlands: Students' language proficiency in English'. *Educational Research and Evaluation*, 12: 1, 75–93.

Council of Europe (2001). *Common European Framework of Reference for Languages: Learning, Teaching, Assessment*. Cambridge: Cambridge University Press.

De Graaff, R., Koopman, G.J., Anikina, Y. and Westhoff, G. (2007). 'An Observation Tool for Effective L2 Pedagogy in Content and Language Integrated Learning'. *International Journal of Bilingual Education and Bilingualism*, 10: 5, 603–24.

Huibregtse, I. (2001). *Effecten en didactiek van tweetalig voortgezet onderwijs in Nederland* ('Effects and pedagogy of bilingual secondary education in the Netherlands'). Unpublished PhD thesis. Utrecht: Universiteit Utrecht.

Moonen, M., Stoutjesdijk, E., De Graaff, R. and Corda, A. (2013). 'Implementing CEFR in Secondary Education: Impact on FL Teachers' Educational and Assessment Practice'. *International Journal of Applied Linguistics*, 23: 2, 226–46.

Schuitemaker-King, J. (2012). *Teachers' Strategies in Providing Opportunities for Second Language Development*. Unpublished PhD thesis. Groningen: Rijksuniversiteit Groningen. www.irs.ub.rug.nl/ppn/341337757.

Verspoor, M., Schuitemaker-King, J. Van Rein, E., De Bot, K. and Edelenbos, P. (2010). *Tweetalig onderwijs: vormgeving en prestaties. Onderzoeksrapport* ('Bilingual Education: Formats and Outcomes'). Groningen: Rijksuniversiteit Groningen.

Van Els, T. and D. Tuin (2010). 'Foreign Languages in Dutch Secondary Education'. In U. Ammon, J. Darqueness, and S. Wright (eds), *Sociolinguistica Jahrbuch*. Berlin/New York: De Gruyter, 101–19.

FORCES	MECHANISMS
Key values in human relations	**People**
Trust in the qualities and competencies of colleagues from other bilingual schools in the network Respect for differences in pedagogical vision between schools	Committed parents Committed teachers Committed principals and school boards A stimulating teachers' network
Principles for cooperation	**Structures**
Stakeholder inclusion High expectation for all stakeholders Shared responsibilities for educational development Commitment to goals and standards criteria	National Network of Bilingual Schools National coordinating organisation (European Platform) Quality control committees
Goals	**Knowledge building**
A desire for bilingualism An interest in intercultural competence and internationalism	Regular symposia for professional teacher development on CLIL Professorship for research on bilingual education supported financially by Network of Bilingual Schools Pre-service and in-service CLIL teacher training programmes
Beliefs	Regular national meetings of bilingual school coordinators
A belief in the power of content and language integrated learning A belief in the power of European and international education A belief in value of challenging students and teachers leading to better learning and teaching A belief in the value of peer evaluation	Participation in European networks for bilingual education development
	Agreements and benchmarks
Processes	Standards for bilingual schools, compulsory for network participation
An iterative approach to programme improvement	Quality control procedure Common European Framework of Reference for Languages International Baccalaureate
Founding principles	
Construction of a shared educational vision common to key stakeholders Buy-in to a vision of programme development Encouragement of individual initiative Dhared responsibility for ensuring a quality programme	**Vehicles**
	Additional fee for extra-curricular activities, professional development and bilingual schools network participation Logos and other branding Strategy and work plan for public relations Training programme for bilingual schools coordinators National activities for bilingual students

COUNTERWEIGHTS	
School board hesitation	Parental demand
High-stakes test results	Other less tangible benefits
Challenges of bilingual education	Benefits of bilingual education
National network coordination	School autonomy
Instruction through L2	National subject examinations in L1
Risk of elitism	Widening access
Additional fee	Fee waiver
New school profiles with different focus, such as science, pulling students away	Attractive and proven potential of bilingual schools

VOICES FROM THE FIELD:
Aotearoa/New Zealand

Toni Waho is principal of Palmerton North's Mana Tamariki total immersion school and a Trustee of the National Te Kōhanga Reo Trust. He is also the Chair of Te Runanga Nui o ngā Kura Kaupapa Māori o Aotearoa the national association of Māori-language schools.

MANA TAMARIKI – A total immersion environment growing Māori-language families

The context

Indigenous peoples colonised and overcome by a more powerful socio-ethnic-linguistic group have in many cases shifted from speaking their own Indigenous language to speaking the language of the coloniser. The linguistic shift for Māori occurred over 100 years after contact with their mainly *Pākeha* (English) and therefore English-language colonisers. The Māori community's rapid language shift paralleled its geographical shift from subsistence agriculture and rural dwellings to the post-World War II urban environments. The policy of 'pepper potting' dark-skinned Māori amongst white working-class communities in state-provided housing did not accommodate the Māori language. Where once Māori was the language of the rural community, neighbourhood and home with English as the language of the school (often enforced by corporal punishment – strapping, caning and detentions if the Māori language was used), urbanised Māori tribal kinship communities dissolved into individual households, dotted amongst 'foreigners'. The Māori home was no longer a sufficiently strong force to sustain the language against the pressure of the English-language neighbourhood, community, school and society.

By the late 1960s a group of urban-raised Māori youth emulated the Black Panther movement of the USA and formed a national Māori youth movement in opposition to the English language and European-dominated institutional

181

racism impacting on Māori. The Māori were, and still are, over-represented in prisons, in menial employment and among the unemployed. The Māori generally speaking have poorer health, education and housing than the 'English'. Māori youth (*Ngā Tama Toa*; 'The Young Warriors') drew on the traditional force of *Mana Māori Motuhake* (Māori Independence and Autonomy). This force is a strong feature of traditional Māori culture. Māori leaders of the time were the grandchildren of those who fought against colonisation. They carried with them the depths of the Māori culture they had experienced growing up. *Ngā Tama Toa* articulated their demands to the New Zealand state. These included the upholding of the 1840 Treaty of Waitangi, which gave England the right to govern the New Zealand islands, but also guaranteed that the Māori would be protected and remain in control of all that they valued. The Treaty was a central mechanism used to access basic rights being denied to the Māori community. A general belief in the values and principles embedded in the Treaty would be a major force for change for the Māori in New Zealand society and for interethnic relations.

Te Reo Māori Society (The Māori Language Society) emerged in 1970. The Māori Language Society had as its sole focus the protection and revitalisation of the Māori language. It organised a petition calling for the Māori language to be made an official language of New Zealand and for it to be taught in schools. While this was not realised until 1987, the Society successfully first won some recognition for the language through the designation of Māori Language Day, which grew to become Māori Language Week (a mechanism). The Society's activities paved the way for the first national research project on the Māori language led by Dr Richard Benton. The 1979 results, showing that only 8% of Māori spoke the language fluently, shocked Māori and the country at large. The shock was a positive force for change.

The Māori Affairs Department of the New Zealand Government investigated bilingualism around the globe. Dr Tamati Reedy reported to Māori elders about the work done in Palestine in the 1890s to teach Hebrew through total immersion through kindergartens and schools. In 1982, Māori leaders and elders, who had been raised in pre-World War II Māori-speaking communities, adopted *Te Kōhanga Reo* – 'the language nest' – as the means by which they could transfer their native language to the youngest members of Māori society. Māori parents were encouraged to take their 0–5 year-old children to engage with their elders in a total immersion Māori-language environment. The core of the concept is that the *mokopuna* (grandchildren) are immersed with their Māori elders who are native speakers of the language. The elders are in the main *kuia* and *whaea* (grandmothers and mothers/

aunties). Over time, training programmes and a specific curriculum called *Te Whāriki for Te Kōhanga Reo* was developed by Dr Reddy and his wife Tilly. *Te Kōhanga Reo* ignited the imagination of the Māori. Imagination was a powerful force and the language nests were the mechanism for moving from the ideational realm to the tangible realisation of the idea. By 1993, 800 *Te Kōhanga Reo* were operating with 14 000 children. Today, the use of language nests have plateaued and stabilised at around 470, with 9 000 children under the guardianship of the National Te Kōhanga Reo Trust Board. The almost halving in the number of *Te Kōhanga Reo* is commensurate with the natural passing of the elders and the gap left by the absence of native speakers in the following generation. In addition, the movement was not fully supported by the government. The National Te Kōhanga Reo Trust Board submitted a claim to the Waitangi Tribunal which is responsible for determining whether or not the government has breached the Treaty of Waitangi. The Tribunal supported the Trust Board's claim that the government had undermined and weakened *Te Kōhanga Reo* as well as failed to support it sufficiently.

Kura Kaupapa Māori schools emerged in 1985. They are promoted by their leaders as the best option for graduates of *Te Kōhanga Reo*. *Kura Kaupapa* Māori (KKM) began as primary schools then grew from 1991 to include Wharekura (secondary school departments). In 1989, leaders of *Kura Kaupapa* Māori wrote *Te Aho Matua o ngā Kura Kaupapa* Māori (*Te Aho Matua* – loosely translated as 'The Principles of Enlightenment'). This important mechanism consists of six sections that guide the community to uphold the holiness and wholeness of the child, nurtured within their essential social fabric – their *whānau* (extended family including their teachers) – in an environment underpinned by Māori spirituality, curriculum and pedagogy. In 2014, there are 72 KKM established under the Education Act. Of these schools, 42 enrol children aged 5–12 years and 30 retain their students until the end of their secondary education. Approximately 6000 students are enrolled in the primary and 1500 in the secondary programmes. There are teacher-training programmes targeted at *Kura Kaupapa* Māori and in 2015 the specific curriculum for the network of KKM based on *Te Aho Matua* will be launched.

Recent first-time data shows that students who are totally immersed in the Māori language throughout their schooling, with the introduction of English as a language of learning after at least eight years of learning in Māori, equal or surpass mainstream English language students in achieving secondary school qualifications. This confirms that a Māori-medium education within a Māori spiritual and cultural framework is working for these students, overturning the mainstream experience for Māori children in English-language education programmes, where failure and discontentment are too high.

This context introduces the reader to the *Mana Tamariki* community. It shows that the historical forces have been at play in relation to the Māori language since the 1970s. *Mana* Māori *Motuhake* ('Māori Independence and Autonomy') has for centuries been at the core of Māori tribal structures and culture. In the post-colonial era the Māori tribes united around the force of *Mana* Māori *Motuhake*. This has also been represented in the Treaty of Waitangi as *Tino Rangatiratanga* ('Supreme Chieftainship'). The concept is a force against colonisation and this is tied to the retention of the Māori language. The essence of Mana Māori Motuhake goes hand in hand with the Māori-language revitalisation effort.

THE MANA TAMARIKI REAL-LIFE EXAMPLE

Mana Tamariki opened as a *Kōhanga Reo* in 1990 in the city of Palmerston North. Māori people make up about 15% of a total population of 85 000 people. The city's ethnic-cultural mix is reflective of Aotearoa as a whole. In 1990, there were only three families in Palmerston North raising their children (four children as a combined total from the three families) using Māori as the language of the home and where both parents spoke only Māori to them. Two of those families (three children) established a *Te Kōhanga Reo o Mana Tamariki* with nine other children from English language homes. *Te Kōhanga Reo o Mana Tamariki* opened at a time and in a city where there were very few elder native speakers. Three of the parents from the two establishment families were highly fluent second-language speakers of Māori. They worked with the children on a daily basis and grew the organisation to what it is today. A *Kura Kaupapa* Māori also opened in the city in 1990. Like all *Kōhanga Reo* communities at the time, *Mana Tamariki* was confident that they could take a child from an English-speaking home, immerse the child in *Kōhanga Reo* and help that child to develop a level of proficiency in Māori that would allow him/her to continue to study entirely through Māori at a *Kura Kaupapa* Māori.

From 1990–94 the parents of the *Kōhanga* children sent them to the only *Kura Kaupapa* Māori in the city. The children had enough language proficiency to progress to a full school curriculum provided at the *Kura* in a total Māori-medium immersion setting. The *Kura* they sent their children to quickly grew in size, fed from the six *Kōhanga Reo* in the city. It became clear that another *Kura* would be needed. *Te Kura Kaupapa* Māori o *Mana Tamariki* became the second *Kura*.

By 1995, the leaders of *Mana Tamariki* had raised their own consciousness about language revitalisation, embracing the theories of Joshua Fishman and Bernard Spolsky. While the efforts in *Kōhanga Reo* and *Kura Kaupapa* Māori across Aotearoa were laudible, very little attention was being given by policy makers and Māori-language leaders, including leaders of *Kōhanga Reo* and *Kura Kaupapa* Māori, to the language of the home. In establishing *Te Kura Kaupapa* Māori o *Mana Tamariki* in 1995, the leaders decided to require that at least one parent would speak only Māori, and never English, to the children of the KKM at all times. They also decided to phase the implementation of the policy in the *Kōhanga* over a two-year period so that that the families enrolled at the time remained in the *Kōhanga* as welcomed, loved and valuable members of the community. All families were encouraged to adopt the 'at least one Māori-language parent' rule, and those who chose not to do so understood that they would still be able to enrol their child at the first *Kura Kaupapa* Māori where that policy was not in place. The focus of the new policy was growing Māori-language families to achieve the core element of critical stage 6 of Fishman's Graded Intergenerational Disruption Scale (GIDS) – that is to say to create a situation where Māori was spoken in the home, neighbourhood and community.

Since 1995, *Te Kōhanga Reo o Mana Tamariki* and *Te KKM o Mana Tamariki* have nurtured over 200 children, creating 60 Māori-speaking families largely as a result of the 'at least one Māori-language parent' rule. Children enrol from as early as possible (below one year of age in most cases) and can remain in the programme until the age of 18. Just prior to secondary school (Year 8), students begin formal instruction in the English language for one morning a week, having already been heavily immersed in Māori for 9–11 years, and raised in a family where at least one parent speaks only Māori to them at all times. In junior secondary school (ages 12–14, Years 9–10), 80% of the programme is delivered through Māori and 20% through English. In senior secondary school (ages 15–18, Years 11–13), at least 51% of the programme is delivered through Māori. This is a unique community in the national Māori-language landscape. The families are highly committed to the language goals and outcomes for their children and their families. By no means has it been an easy journey, especially for those families where there is only one parent upholding the 'at least one Māori-language parent' rule and where there are older siblings of the *Mana Tamariki* children in the family who do not have a Māori-language relationship with the Māori-speaking parent. Twenty years after the implementation of the 'at least one Māori-language parent' rule, the organisation is beginning to consider if a 'two Māori-language parents' rule is desirable, possible and achievable. Evidence from student achievement outcomes shows that children raised in families with two Māori-language parents – half of the *Mana Tamariki* community – do better in both languages in terms of language achievement outcomes.

The outcomes for all the students are immensely positive and there is no doubt in the minds of the leadership of this community that it is the partnership forged between families, their children and the educators that is the primary contributing factor. If one party is not on board with the programme, the child will not thrive. Teachers cannot dictate and must work in partnership to build a learning programme and learning environment that is relevant, valued and desired by the recipients and their families. Parents must make the language commitment, turn their lives around to reorient to a Māori-language journey for their descendants, and engage with educators as partners. Students must have a voice, even from the earliest years, about what they learn and how they learn.

Through *Te Whāriki* and *Te Aho Matua*, the commitment of *Mana Tamariki* to the holiness – the Indigenous spiritualism – of the child and their wholeness (not just one narrow aspect of their development but their total development) in partnership with the family and school is what works for *Mana Tamariki*. Along the path travelled by *Mana Tamariki*, they have met with other educational philosophies and approaches to working with children. The New Zealand Early Childhood sector is world-renowned for its child-centred, child-initiated play approach to learning, which *Mana Tamariki* has found conducive to their Indigenous Māori approach. The Italian *Reggio Emilia* infant-and-toddler nurseries and 'the 100 languages of children' approach has also been embraced by *Mana Tamariki*, and they are working on how to integrate the approach throughout the children's school learning journey. In terms of assessment for learning, Margaret Carr's 'learning stories' approach – *Paki Ako* within *Mana Tamariki* – forms the basis for the *Kōhanga Reo* to monitor a child's language and learning development within *Mana Tamariki*. The *Kura* is challenged by the *Paki Ako* approach and is considering how to embrace it alongside *Ngā Hua o te Ako*, which aligns with *Te Aho Matua*.

Children graduate from *Mana Tamariki* as highly proficient young bilingual adults, steeped in Māori values and beliefs, attaining the national senior secondary qualifications that will enable them to continue their education at tertiary level, including university if they so choose. They are proudly held up by their community as 'raukura' – 'plumes of adornment' – for their families, tribes and nations as keepers of their Māori ways, which they can then pass on to the next generation through their Indigenous language.

MANA TAMARIKI AS IT RELATES TO THE PARADIGM FOR THIS BOOK

The historical **forces** that paved the way for *Mana Tamariki* to emerge are embedded within the Māori culture. The strong central place of *Mana* Māori *Motuhake* ('Māori Independence and Autonomy') has been passed down from generation to generation. The focus and drive from within the Māori world has changed from generation to generation as well, the most recent generation being the inheritors of the wave of spirit generated by the activities of *Ngā Tama Toa* and *Te Reo Māori Society* in the late 1960s and early 1970s. Also, core to the Māori culture is the innate place of spiritualism and the connectedness that Māori have with the spirit and physical world. The rebuilding of Māori society, even as Māori families are dispersed around New Zealand (and Australia) and often live long distances from their traditional tribal regions, has seen the recollectivisation of Māori through their 'whānau' ('extended family') – the principal Māori social unit. Groups of individuals with no genealogical or familial connections agree to act and function as if they have real familial bonds. Communal decision-making and collective responsibility are the forces that cement ties between the families who have come together in support of common goals about language, their children, their families and the reclamation of a strong Māori identity.

There are multiple internal and external **mechanisms** that have an impact on the *Mana Tamariki* community. *Te Kōhanga Reo* and *Kura Kaupapa* Māori are funded by the New Zealand Government. Despite the findings of the Waitangi Tribunal affirming that the Government must do more for *Kōhanga Reo*, these government-funded programmes are major mechanisms giving thousands of Māori families and their children access to a Māori-medium education. While 21% of Māori children are in *Kōhanga Reo*, only 4% are in *Kura Kaupapa* Māori, 6% are in dual-language education schools (with no period of total immersion), and 2% are in *Wharekura* (secondary school programmes). Government funding generates other mechanisms of support such as training programmes, learning materials, curriculum development, transportation and facilities. Other mechanisms such as monitoring and evaluation to maintain public accountability for the use of government funds provide regular snapshots of the use of funds; however, there are almost no mechanisms to monitor language outcomes. There is a whole discussion currently going on about the veracity and applicability of Māori student curriculum outcomes that are used as the measurement of language outcomes.

From within *Mana Tamariki* key mechanisms are the common goals articulated through the aims, purposes and objectives of the organisation, including the 'at least one Māori-language parent' rule. Commitment to Māori spirituality, despite the dominance of Christianity within the Māori world, is a unique focus of *Mana Tamariki*, as is the commitment to growing Māori-language families. *Te Whāriki* and *Te Aho Matua* extol the total immersion of the child in the target language as early as possible for as long as it takes to grow the proficiency of the child's Māori language before introducing English as a language of learning in Year 8. This occurs in a city where, beyond the family and beyond the *Mana Tamariki* learning environments, English is the dominant language of the neighbourhood and wider community.

Even with internal and external mechanisms serving *Mana Tamariki* and supporting *Te Kōhanga Reo, Te Kura Kaupapa* Māori and the families of *Mana Tamariki* to grow Māori-language families, there is still a negative attitude within the wider community across New Zealand towards languages other than English. This negative force is difficult to counter. *Te Reo Māori* is still swamped by English. There are, however, **counterweights** that Māori-language leaders have fought for and successfully put in place. Prior to 1994, they established a small number of self-funded Māori-medium radio stations and won the support for about half an hour of daily Māori-language television programming on state-funded broadcasters. After Māori leaders appealed to the Privy Council in England, negotiations resulted in the New Zealand Government funding Māori-medium radio stations and a Māori-language television station. Radio is funded to broadcast at least eight hours daily in the language and Māori Television is required to provide 100% Māori-language programming for children. In addition, Government funding has allowed for the establishment a 100% Māori-language television channel. These counterweights are focused mainly on the Māori community. The Māori-language Commission (*Te Taura Whiri i te Reo Māori*), established in 1987 as a result of Māori leaders successful claim to the Waitangi Tribunal arguing that the Government failed to protect the Māori language, is also a principal counterweight. The Commission targets wider New Zealand society in promoting positive attitudes towards the Māori language. After 20 years, the Commission has had a storng influence, with an increase in positive attitudes across New Zealand towards the language, but the overwhelming majority of New Zealanders maintain a pro-English view, favouring English over the Māori language for the Māori.

Within *Mana Tamariki*, a major **counterweight** to the pressure of the English-speaking environment is that all *Mana Tamariki* business is conducted through the Māori language. From the moment that a family requests enrolment, the Māori-speaking parent(s) engage(s) with the organisation through the Māori language. Almost all the Māori-speaking parents learned the language as a second language, a handful of whom are now graduates of *Mana Tamariki* raised in families as a new generation of native speakers. There is a casual monitoring of the adherence to the 'at least one Māori-language parent' rule and in 20 years since its adoption only one family has withdrawn because of a decision by the teenage child to no longer learn through *Te Reo Māori*. The families use and take the Māori language wherever they go. By making the commitment to the 'at least one Māori-language parent' rule, the Māori language has moved beyond the *Kōhanga Reo* and *Kura Kaupapa* Māori has been successfully established in the home, neighbourhood and the community.

National forces, mechanisms and counterweights have brought about a reversal in the shift of the Māori people away from the Māori language, reaching a peak in 2006, when 25% were speaking Māori fluently. There are worries that the 2013 statistics show a drop in fluent speakers to 21%. Within *Mana Tamariki* the forces, mechanisms and counterweights have created families where the Māori language has a prominent role in all families and for 50% of the families it is the principal language of the family. Research conducted in 2006 showed that none of the *Mana Tamariki* families would have developed solely Māori-language relationships between their children and at least one of the parents without the *Mana Tamariki* rule. The partnership forged between *Mana Tamariki* and the families is crucial in building an environment that satisfies the families' needs for the education of their children and that helps to grow Māori-language families.

NOTES

For those interested in learning more about *Mana Tamariki* and *Kaupapa*:

Ministry of Education (2009). *Te Whatu Pokeka, Kaupapa Māori Assessment for Learning, Early Childhood Exemplars.* Wellington: Learning Media Limited.

Whare Māori, Series 1, Episode 11. Māori Television doumentary produced for Māori Television by Scottie Productions (http://www.maoritelevision.com/tv/shows/whare-maori/S01E011/whare-maori-series-1-episode-11). Section on Mana Tamariki starts at 26:13 minutes.

Ministry of Education (2006). *Waho, Toni: Te Reo o te Whanau – intergenerational transmission of the Maori language in Families*; 2006. Wellington: Huia Publishers for the Ministry of Education.

VOICES FROM THE FIELD:
Cymru / Wales

Meirion Prys Jones is a former teacher, LEA Education Adviser, Registered Inspector of Schools and head of the Welsh Language Board. He is currently Chief Executive of the European Network to Promote Linguistic Diversity (NPLD).

A few local education authorities, parental pressure for more provision of Welsh-medium education and practical guidance from Her Majesty's Inspectors of Schools have been, up to the end of the 1980s, the primary drivers of Welsh-medium education in Wales. By that point very little support, apart from some minor financing, had been provided by the UK Government. The inclusion of Welsh (first language) as a core element within the National Curriculum for England and Wales, introduced in 1988, was very much an afterthought. The teaching of the Welsh language and Welsh-medium education for most of its recent history has been a bolt-on, and certainly an afterthought to the mainstream provision. The new Welsh-medium Education Strategy adopted in 2010 signalled a change and the promise of improving the provision of Welsh-medium education, but the early signs are not encouraging.

Following the establishment of the Welsh Language Board (WLB) by the Welsh Language Act (1993), The Welsh Office, which was a division of the UK Government in Wales, decided that the WLB should have a 'strategic overview of Welsh-medium education in Wales'. The Board attempted repeatedly to get a clear definition of what this entailed, but this was never provided. Since the WLB also had the more tangible authority to agree on Welsh Education Schemes with each Local Education Authority (LEA), this opened the door for the WLB to consider the provision of Welsh-medium education across Wales and also to market the provision available. It also provided, for the first time, an opportunity to consider what should be developed in terms of a social and economic context for pupils attending Welsh-medium schools.

I was fortunate enough to be appointed the WLB's Education Officer from the outset in 1994, and then later on the Chief Executive until the WLB was closed down in 2012, when its functions were split between the Welsh Government and the new post of Welsh Language Commissioner. The WLB from the outset was extremely fortunate with regard to its Board members, many of whom brought with them a wealth of experience that greatly informed the work of the Board. Two members in the early days had a great influence on the priorities we agreed on and the way that we operated in the field of education. Dr Gareth Roberts and Professor Colin Baker, both from the University of Bangor, guided the work of the education team for many years. Colin Baker also provided not only a Wales-wide perspective to our work, but he also gave us a world-wide perspective on all the current trends, not only in education but also in all aspects of language planning. His influence on the development of the project on Language Transmission in the Home was instrumental in the process of establishing the flagship WLB project called *TWF* – Raising Children Bilingually. The TWF project provided practical support for parents and guidance for health professionals about the advantages of speaking Welsh with their children, especially in families where one parent spoke Welsh. This project has since been replicated in many communities across Europe.

In Wales, the main area where the demand for provision in Welsh has not been met is within the education sector. In 1994, when the WLB started its work, two of the eight Local Education Authorities in Wales had no strategic plan, and very little knowledge about what they had available within their authority for parents who were looking for a Welsh-medium education for their children. Politicians and education officers in many authorities were very much against the idea of 'giving in' to parents and opening new schools. For example, the Local Authority of West Glamorgan, despite having some of the communities with the highest density of Welsh speakers in South Wales, refused for many years to open Welsh schools. This included letting schools develop to be much larger than their buildings allowed. With changes in the Chair of Education and Director of Education, the whole situation changed and two schools were opened in two years. The reorganisation of Local Government in Wales in 1996 gave the WLB an opportunity to agree on Welsh Education Schemes with each authority. In these schemes, the LEAs had to consider their provision in terms of numbers attending Welsh-medium education and also the location of the provision available. All the LEAs took these plans seriously and schemes were agreed which ensured that a Welsh-medium education was available for any child in Wales whose parent requested that provision at primary level. Later on, some LEAs under the guidance of the WLB started the process of attempting to assess the demand for Welsh-medium education (WME) amongst parents before their children started school. The reasoning behind this process was that this would ensure that there were sufficient places available for new pupils in every LEA, as a lack of places had become a serious problem in some LEAs. This work produced surprising results, with some surveys showing that there was a huge level of interest in WME if the provision could be provided within the communities where the children lived. Wrexham, for example, after undertaking a survey, showed that the demand was in the mid-40% where the current provision only provided places for 10% of the school population. Following the survey, the LEA came under considerable pressure to increase the number of Welsh-medium schools within its area.

Why parents choose a Welsh-medium education for their children is an extremely complicated issue especially in the context of parents who do not speak Welsh. Many choose a WME for their children because they believe that the quality of the education is high and certainly pupils attending Welsh-medium schools well in all the tests used to measure their achievements. Many parents also feel that they have lost out on being able to speak the language. Many will have been brought up in families where one or both grandparents spoke Welsh, but where the language was not transmitted to the following generation. Some will choose WME because the school has a good rugby/football team!

One of the areas where WME has had to work harder over the past decade is ensuring continuity from one education sector to the other. There is a drop-off in numbers between sectors and also in areas where there has traditionally been a higher density of Welsh speakers. The WLB undertook a very successful project funded by the Welsh Assembly Government which provided advice and guidance to parents in a number of schools on the advantages of continuing with a Welsh-medium education. The comments received from parents suggested that more marketing and information was needed as many people were unaware of the social, cognitive and financial benefits of a Welsh-medium education.

An interesting development during the past 20 years was the realisation by one education minister that there needed to be more opportunities for parents in Wales to choose WME for their children and therefore there needed to be more points of entry. Instead of discussion of this idea in Wales and finding out what was already available, the Minister flew to Canada to look at the ideas being developed there. She came back with a range of ideas, some of which were already being implemented in Wales and some of which were new. Several of these were explored further, but interestingly the only ones that survived were the ones which had already been developed in Wales.

Looking back, the lack of understanding of what really is happening within the education sector in Wales and especially in the Welsh-medium schools has been one of the main weaknesses of the Governments in Wales. Linked to this is an inability to build on the sector's strengths. This has been underlined by the succession of civil servants that have come to Wales to take responsibility for education in Wales, without having a prior understanding of the context and the current structures here. By the time they have started to learn something, they leave. By now, things have changed slightly, and time will tell if things will improve. But this issue of consistency, of developing a holistic sustainable strategy and keeping to it are not obvious facets of education in Wales. Compare this to the Basque situation where Mikel Sabithe has been responsible for the development of Basque-medium education since 1983 and where the increase in the number of pupils receiving education through the medium of Basque has grown phenomenally to the extent that around 90% of pupils at the age of 11 are receiving their education partly or wholly through the medium of Basque. This is the challenge Wales should set itself.

There has been a high level of expectation from many of the stakeholders in Wales, especially from parents, regarding the continued development of WME. There is a strong belief that bilingual education is a high quality education. Many key individuals and organisations over the past 50 years have been instrumental in pushing and moving the provision forward in terms of the provision of teaching materials and in terms of strategic development. Some very meticulous planning has taken place in some LEAs, especially in North Wales, where by now all children receive either a Welsh-medium or a bilingual education. But over the years successive governments have turned a blind eye to these developments. The publication of the new all-Wales Welsh-medium Education Strategy in 2010 was a significant event in this context.

This document built up a strategic narrative which gave a common vision to all the stakeholders and clarified the way forward regarding the importance of developing certain aspects of the programme. However, since then there has been little further engagement between the Government, civil servants and key stakeholders. Experts in the field have been closed out of the discussions by the civil servants, who in general have little practical experience of education, schools and the development of bilingual education, and, as a consequence, even basic aspects of the provision (such as ensuring a good high quality supply of well trained teachers) have not been developed.

In a recent poll, 45% of parents stated that they would wish their children to be fluently bilingual by the time they left school in Wales. The Welsh Government, however, has been unwilling to mainstream the provision of WME and has *de facto* decided to keep to the status quo of monolingual schools. The benefits of a bilingual education are understood but not acted upon for political reasons as the Welsh language is still regarded unofficially as an issue for nationalists. Therefore there is no well-ordered discussion about how Wales can build on the success of WME and how it can reap the social, cognitive and financial benefits of bilingualism in a country which by now is the poorest region in Western Europe.

Learning Welsh in school and having the ability to speak the language fluently does not mean of course that a young person will use that language in his or her daily life. The WLB had a very strong vision that the Welsh language, if it is to survive, needs to be spoken by people in all aspects of their lives. The Board invested heavily in a range of innovative projects, with community based groups, with young people, and with all kinds of developments in the field of technology and by promoting the use of Welsh within schools but outside the classroom. These were highly successful, but unfortunately the Government, despite seeing the success of these initiatives, was unwilling to increase levels of funding to develop them further. We, therefore, know the way ahead and know what needs to be done, but are without sufficient transport to get us there.

PART FOUR:
Understanding the
Role of Context

10 UNITED ARAB EMIRATES:
Searching for an Elusive Balance in Bilingual Education

Fatima Badry (American University of Sharjah, UAE)

CHAPTER NAVIGATOR

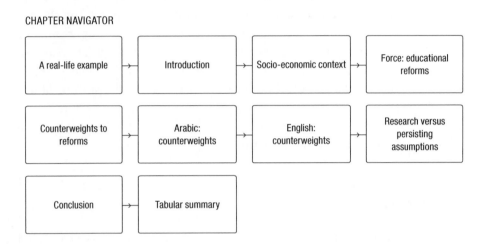

A real-life example → Introduction → Socio-economic context → Force: educational reforms

Counterweights to reforms → Arabic: counterweights → English: counterweights → Research versus persisting assumptions

Conclusion → Tabular summary

A REAL-LIFE EXAMPLE

When the Jamali[1] family moved to the United Arab Emirates (UAE) from Saudi Arabia, they were convinced that their children would continue their schooling in both English and Arabic. The parents were keen on finding a private school to build on the Arabic and English language skills of their two older children. In the UAE, they found this to be no easy task. The children were first placed in a bilingual school where Arabic was the medium of instruction for Literature, Religion, Civic Education and Arabic Language Arts, and English was used for Science, Technology, Engineering and Mathematics subjects (STEM). Yet the school culture seemed to favour English, the status language in the UAE. Teachers who knew English spoke it in the hallways and children generally preferred to interact in English in the playgrounds because it made them 'sound cool'. Dissatisfied with the school's approach to Arabic, the parents moved their children to one with a reputation for better supporting Arabic. But, soon afterwards, they became dissatisfied with that school too because English was not taught well and because the teachers often made fun of the children who spoke Arabic with 'an accent'.

Outside school, English seemed to dominate as well. The children started speaking it at home and in their linguistically diverse and international neighbourhood when they played with other children. The parents then decided to enroll all their children in private schools where English was the language of instruction because, as the mother put it, the choice was either a poor-quality Arabic school or a better quality English-medium school, even though that meant sacrificing Arabic. After a few years in the UAE, the mother observed that while her oldest child was able to 'maintain' some Arabic, the second child (one year younger) had lost most of it. Today, the family is considering leaving the UAE and moving back to Saudi Arabia so their younger children can learn Arabic in school and through interaction with others in the community.

INTRODUCTION

In the UAE, parental complaints such as those illustrated by the example above are centered not only on Arabic curriculum schools' poor record in helping students learn Arabic, but also on their failure to enable students to develop good academic English skills, as demonstrated by their performance on standardised test scores, parental statements often reported in the media (Ahmed 2013; Al Lawati 2008; Al Kaff-Al Hashemi and Underwood 2013), and government inspectors' reports (Knowledge and Human Development Authority 2014). This double dissatisfaction often leads parents with sufficient financial resources to place their children in private schools that follow an American, British, Australian or French curriculum.[2] In these schools, Arabic has recently been introduced as a requirement by the Ministry of Education, but it is generally taught with low expectations as a foreign language. Ultimately, parents who want their children to maintain and further develop their knowledge of Modern Standard Arabic pay for private tutoring.

Many of the forces and mechanisms that are part of the reforms described in this chapter have the potential of leading to successful dual-language education in Arabic and English; but, just as powerfully, there are counterweights that potentially hinder such development. It should be noted that developing successful bilingual education has been challenging across the contemporary Arab World. To varying degrees, literacy in Modern Standard Arabic is impeded by several sociolinguistic counterweights, to be discussed in this chapter. However, the UAE and Qatari contexts are extreme cases in the region, specifically due to their wealth, their rapid socio-economic transformations and their demographics.

This chapter first sketches the socio-economic factors that have shaped the development of the UAE, before discussing the forces and counterweights affecting the success of educational reforms in general. Specific attention will be devoted to their impact on Arabic-English bilingual development. It is argued that the interplay between these factors and persisting assumptions invalidated by research on bilingualism and psycholinguistics have placed Arabic, the national language, in a disadvantaged position and all but relegated it to the status of a heritage language. At the same time, academic language skills in English remain below expected levels despite the considerable resources being allocated to English-medium education.

SOCIO-ECONOMIC CONTEXT

The federation of the seven Emirates that constitute the UAE (Abu Dhabi, Dubai, Sharjah, Ajman, Fujairah, Ras Al Khaimah and Umm Al Qaiwain) was established in 1971. The UAE has the sixth largest oil reserves in the world. Its leaders' resolve (a force) to use the wealth arising from these oil reserves to modernise their nation has helped transform the socio-economic and cultural fabric of the society. The UAE has evolved from a set of tribal communities to first-world global cities with futuristic buildings, a modern infrastructure and strong economic growth that successfully compete with major urban centres across the world.

Demographically, the UAE is a very diverse country. Emiratis are a minority in their own nation, where 80 to 91%[3] of the population are non-nationals (National Bureau of Statistics 2011). More than 50% of UAE residents come from South Asia (mainly from India, Pakistan, Bangladesh and Afghanistan) while the second largest group, around 23%, come from other Arab countries and Iran. The remaining residents are Westerners from the Americas, Australia and Europe, and East Asians from China, the Philippines and Indonesia (UAE Interact 2010). Such diversity has made English the default *lingua franca* for communication among all groups and in most public spaces. In addition, both government and citizens consider English as the essential vehicle for accessing contemporary knowledge and catching up with the advanced world (Balance Arabic 2012). An additional force behind the widespread adoption of English among millenials is its role as the language of technology and pop culture under globalisation forces (Godwin 2006). All these factors have led to English becoming an important language in the UAE educational system. As Farrell and Fenwick (2007) have noted, adopting English in education in many parts of the developing world has the 'dual advantage of making English-language curriculum materials instantly available to help transform education systems and, at the same time, produce an English-literate workforce required for participation in the global economy'.

There are many forces that favour Arabic as well. Arabic is the official language of the UAE. Affectively, it is a symbol of Emirati identity as an Arab nation, linking it to larger Pan Arab nationalism. Arabic is also a source of pride thanks to its rich literary and scientific traditions. Arabs are often nostalgic about their language which, at one point in history, was the language of science and knowledge, and they hope that it can be rejuvenated to play the same role in the future. Equally important is its inextricable ties to Islam. It is also the thread that binds the UAE to its geographic, historical and cultural milieu as part of the Arabian Gulf Cooperation Council (GCC) and the Arab world at large.

FORCES: EDUCATIONAL REFORMS

Three major forces support or undermine the UAE population in developing Arabic-English bilingualism – a belief in the value of education, a belief in the need for English language proficiency, and the assumption that Arabic is not an effective medium for the delivery of high-quality education. Because of its relatively young population, with over a third between 15 and 24 years of age, education is expected to play a key role in transforming the society. Since its establishment, the UAE has attempted to implement a system of bilingual education to help it achieve its two major goals of transforming the country into a knowledge society by encouraging the use of English and preserving its Arab identity by defending the status of Arabic (AlMunajjed and Sabbagh 2011; Badry 2012; Findlow 2006; Mohammed 2008). Prioritisation of education at the federal level began in 1971. The federal Ministry of Education administers schools through 'educational zones' (districts) that oversee all schools in each of the seven Emirates. In addition, in 2005, the Abu Dhabi Educational Council (ADEC) and the Dubai Educational Council (DEC) were set up by the two wealthiest Emirates to implement additional reforms and assessments. They have, in practice, taken over control from the federal bodies in these two Emirates. The educational zones and councils are also in charge of supervising a growing number of private schools which serve expatriate communities and around half of the national student population (48%).

The UAE has made major strides in improving education. Before oil was discovered in 1962, there were about 20 schools serving fewer than 4000 students. By 2012, the number of both public and private schools had increased to 1185 serving a student body of 859 200 (National Bureau of Statistics 2013) and is composed of an approximately equal number of males and females (Al Matuei 2013). Literacy rates are high for both genders – 91% among females, and 89% among males above the age of 15 (Al Amiri 2012). Robust financing of education is foreseen in the UAE's strategic plans, reaching 28% of federal government spending in 2009 (National Qualifications 2013).

The Ministry of Education's 2009–14 five year plan adopted new initiatives stressing the improvement of Arabic and English proficiency (Ministry of Education strategy 2009–14). The K–12 Arabic curriculum defines objectives and outcomes at each level for the four language skills: speaking, listening, reading and writing in Modern Standard Arabic highlighting the need to teach correct usage of Arabic grammar.[4] Reforms dealing with English aim to narrow the persistent gap between high-school graduates' skills and university admission requirements (Ministry of Education strategy 2010–20). According to Hassan (2007), the former Minister of Education, an important objective of the education reforms is to equip students with sufficient proficiency in English to avoid intensive English programmes when they enroll in universities.[5] To accomplish this goal, English was introduced as a subject from Grade 1,[6] and the Common Educational Proficiency Assessment (CEPA), a standardised English test, is administered at the end of high school. Admission into public universities and the awarding of government scholarships are determined by students' CEPA scores. For private universities, minimum scores in the Test of English as a Foreign Language (TOEFL) or the International Language Testing System (IELTS)[7] are prerequisites to admission.

Educational reforms have recently made assessment an integral part of education policies. In 2007, the UAE administered international standardised tests such as Trends in Mathematics and Science Study (TIMSS) and Progress in International Reading Literacy Study (PIRLS) to students in Grades 4 and 8 in selected schools. The 2011 results showed that there have been significant improvements in achievement compared to 2007. However, although UAE 'students came out on top in science and maths compared to other participating Arab countries (Tairab and Al Shannag 2013), they were still short of the international average and placed 40th out of 60 globally' (Salama 2012). PIRLS and the OECD Programme for International Student Assessment (PISA) scores were also lower than average. Analysis of the various standardised test results reveals that 'the majority of Emirati students, especially males, were low or average performers' (Salama 2012). To improve English proficiency and international tests scores, English as a medium of instruction in Science, Mathematics and Information Technology has been piloted since 2007 in 50 'MAG' schools ('Schools of the Future') (Ahmed 2011). MAG schools have stated measurable learner outcomes, have quality assessment systems, emphasise computer skills, and use new textbooks and materials. To familiarise stakeholders with these changes, workshops and seminars for teachers and school leaders are frequently held across the UAE. Foreign experts are regularly invited by the Ministry or the councils to assess progress and make recommendations on how to improve the quality of education and English teaching in particular. This shift to English is based on a pervasive belief among most stakeholders that English promotes learner-centered approaches which, in turn, leads to the development of critical thinking, improved study skills and creativity, skills believed not to be fostered by the old-fashioned teacher-centered methodologies and memorisation associated with Arabic (Al Najami 2007).

COUNTERWEIGHTS TO REFORM

There is, however, a widely shared feeling, frequently reported in local media, that the reforms have overall been unsatisfactory. Negative counterweights consisting of both forces and mechanisms that undermine reforms are multiple. They are also hard to pinpoint, partly because of constant changes that make it difficult to evaluate what may have worked and what may not have in any given reform. The general consensus is that there is a significant 'gap between investment and outcome' in the successive educational reforms that have been carried out in the last two decades, and that performance among schools has been very uneven (Nazzal 2013; Pennington 2014). Some observers attribute this variability to teachers' qualifications (Collins 2011). Some educators blame this, in turn, on a top-down approach, be that at the federal or local level, which does not empower teachers. This may lead to feelings of marginalisation that are likely to result in a lack of commitment. Collins

(2011) reports various reasons why teachers choose to leave the profession. For instance, one teacher stated: 'I had no empowerment or appreciation. It was all orders and demands and no one listens to your worries.' Another national declared that: 'The pressure inside schools with all the changes, the lack of appreciation and the financial demands of life outside is pushing people [teachers] out.' Teachers also report poor working conditions, job insecurity and low pay. The above factors have led many teachers to shun the profession, which is a serious obstacle to achieving Emiratisation,[8] the national goal of increasing the participation of UAE nationals in the labour force. The *National* newspaper reported teacher turnover at around 60% in 2011 among both expatriates, who make up the majority of teachers, and nationals in both public and private schools (Collins 2011). In addition, there are significant inequalities in pay scales between teachers from Western countries and those from other regions, favouring the former; this, in turn, leads to feelings of discrimination among non-Western teachers and contributes to the low prestige of teachers in society. All these factors make the teaching profession unattractive, particularly among male UAE nationals.[9] For example, UAE male teachers are around 1% of the 14% total number of male teachers in Dubai schools for which statistics are available (Dickson and Le Roux 2012). As a further consequence, the UAE has to rely primarily on expatriate teachers, which further feeds feelings of discrimination.

The home is another site of counterweights in the development of Arabic and English. Generally speaking, there is a positive correlation between parents' personal active involvement in raising their children and improved academic performance (Hoff 2006; Rowe 2008; Scheele, Leseman and Mayo 2010). In UAE families, however, child rearing is often carried out by nannies and maids who are generally not trained in childcare, do not speak Arabic and have poor English skills. Poor language input and limited opportunities for rich interaction in either Arabic or English have a negative impact on children's language development. There is also a prevailing attitude that education is mainly the responsibility of the school. Parents have little shared reading time and little active engagement with their children's school experience (Al Sumaiti 2012). Often, private tutors are hired to help with homework and other school activities.

In summary, despite strong motivation on the part of the UAE's leadership and substantial investments of effort and resources, various educational reforms fall short of achieving the government's educational goal of bilingualism. The following sections analyse some of the mechanisms that government is using to foster reform and the counterweights that are obstacles to reform.

ARABIC: COUNTERWEIGHTS

Members of the Federal National Council (UAE assembly) and citizens have frequently reported (Al Baik 2008; Issa 2013a; Youssef 2008) that the status of Arabic as a national language in the UAE is threatened. These fears were strengthened by a report published by the Knowledge and Human Development Authority (KHDA) on improvements of outcomes in Dubai schools. The report pointed out that language skills 'in Arabic, whether as a first or additional language, lagged far behind' skills in English, Mathematics and Science (Malek 2013).

In 2012, the government adopted the Arabic Language Charter – a key mechanism and counterweight – as part of an ambitious project to protect Arabic and promote it as a language of science and the future. The project, described as 'an integrated strategy to establish the UAE as a global '"centre of excellence" for Arabic language', includes several initiatives (Emirates 24/7 News 2012). Among these are 'plans to enhance Arabic content online … poetry, story, calligraphy and reading competitions for school students [that] will … be rolled out under the supervision of the Ministry of Education'. An 'international committee of experts' was appointed to propose ways to modernise Arabic teaching methods in Science. It recommended that teachers using Arabic as a medium of instruction should be retrained, curricula improved, Arabic used as a medium of instruction in a broad range of subjects and a culture of reading be developed (Al Khan 2013). This determination to encourage the use of Arabic was reiterated during the International Forum on the Arabic language, organised by the Arabic Language International Council and UNESCO, held in Dubai (7–10 May 2014). The Prime Minister announced awards for institutions and individuals contributing 'to support the Arabic language in the areas of education, media, Arabisation, technology, preservation and dissemination of the Arab linguistic heritage' (Gulf News 2014).

For its part, the Abu Dhabi Educational Council (ADEC) launched initiatives to promote the learning and teaching of Arabic in its model schools. Mechanisms were created to offer 'direct support for teachers, students, principals and parents through national projects. These projects enhance the role of the Arabic language in the preservation of identity by making it favourable to children from KG to Grade 5' (ADEC website). In 2012, ADEC announced other initiatives which include using a standards-based approach to assessment, providing teaching material resources, supporting professional development and encouraging parental involvement in their children's education (ADEC Key Initiatives, n.d). It is too early to evaluate the effectiveness of these initiatives.

Despite the positive mechanisms and initiatives planned to support the learning of Arabic, Arabic teachers generally complain that they receive no support to develop learning materials and that they have insufficient IT equipment (personal communication with teachers in MAG schools in Dubai in 2012). There seems to be less emphasis on professional development and a greater focus on teachers' knowledge of Arabic and Islam as evidenced by the KHDA's latest announcement that a battery of tests will be used to assess new Arabic teachers' knowledge of grammar and religion before they are licensed to teach in Dubai schools (Issa 2013b). Focusing on religion and grammar in teacher development ignores other equally important weaknesses identified with teaching through Arabic. In its latest inspection report, the KHDA found that '[a]lmost three-quarters of schools had shortcomings in Arabic as a first and additional language. In some, there was a slight improvement in speaking and listening but little improvement in reading and writing. Approaches to teaching and learning in Arabic were too often repetitive and did not motivate or engage students' (Knowledge and Human Development Authority 2014). There are also unconfirmed claims that teachers of Arabic receive lower salaries than those teaching in English. This state of affairs acts as a negative counterweight to the positive aspirations embodied by the charter.

Outside school, Modern Standard Arabic (MSA) faces additional challenges due to its diglossic nature and perceptions about its worth as a language of knowledge production. Two linguistic varieties of Arabic serve socially defined and distinct functions. MSA is the language of literacy and all written and formal communication. Dialectal Arabic[10] is the spoken variety, acquired as a first language and used in daily informal interactions. Additionally, there are intermediate varieties that result in Arabic being a multiglossic continuum as opposed to a diglossic binary distribution. When children begin to read, they are expected to do so in MSA. This presents specific constraints in learning to read as children are unfamiliar with MSA.

Developing proficiency in MSA depends almost exclusively on classroom exposure as there are few socially sanctioned opportunities for its use by children outside the classroom, given its multiglossic characteristic. In addition,

prevalent socio-economic choices and practices carry subtle ideological messages that devalue Arabic and relegate it to a heritage language status in its
own territory. Arabic is generally perceived nostalgically as a 'home' language. Its value is tied to religion, community, family and heritage, which in
a society that aims to be 'modern', subordinates it and confines it within the
boundaries of tradition by denying it its potential function as a language of
contemporary communication and knowledge (Al Ameri 2013; Swan 2013;
Issa 2013c).[11]

ENGLISH: COUNTERWEIGHTS

Despite all the efforts and socio-economic forces in favour of English, around
'95 per cent of public school graduates are so ill-prepared for further education in English and sciences that they need to enroll in remedial courses
for up to two years to improve their English-language and IT skills' (Collins
2011). Some reasons for this failure are tied to the counterweights to educational reforms discussed earlier, but many are tied to misconceptions about
language acquisition. These are addressed next.

RESEARCH VS PERSISTING MISCONCEPTIONS

Research into the question of the optimal age to introduce a second language
(L2) reveals that there are benefits to both early and later exposure, depending
on many other factors (see Cummins 2000; Singleton 2001). However, UAE
language reforms seem to be driven by the assumption of 'the earlier the better'. Very little consideration is given to the impact of such early exposure on
children's first language (L1) development. English immersion from kindergarten, in the absence of other conditions conducive to L1 maintenance and
development, ignores evidence that age is one factor among many that influence language acquisition in school and that a strong foundation in L1 can
facilitate L2 acquisition (Cummins 2000; Genesee 2009; Riches and Genesee
2006).

Research suggests that the success of specific bilingual programmes
depends as much, if not more, on the interaction between contextual, pedagogical and linguistic variables (Baker 2003; Beatens Beardsmore 1996;
Garcia 2009; Swain and Lapkin 2005), as on the specific model that is being
followed. Two of the factors stressed by Swain and Johnson (1997) as essential

for the success of an immersion/bilingual programme are a balance between the two languages in the curriculum and support for the L1 in the community and school culture. The UAE's so-called 'immersion' model lacks these two features. Arabic and English are not used equally 'to educate generally, meaningfully, [and] equitably' (Garcia 2009, 6). English is the medium of instruction in high-status STEM subjects (Science, Technology, Engineering and Mathematics). The community's linguistic perceptions and practices view knowledge of English as a premium commodity in the workplace, despite official declarations that Arabic is the official language. Moreover, even dialectal Arabic varieties are increasingly losing ground in the private spaces of family and friends and in the virtual spaces of social media, particularly among millenials (Al Baik 2008; Al Lawati 2008; Badry 2012; Issa 2013a; Malek 2013; Matthew 2008).

Research stresses the need to consider not only methodological variables but also societal values and attitudes when designing a dual-language programme. In the Arabic sociolinguistic context, language-in-education policies need to take into account the diglossic nature of Arabic and the low status of Arabic as a commodity in the local market compared to English. Such factors act as counterweights to the development of Arabic literacy, which may in turn impact English language development. In a consultancy report on the design of a dual-language Early Childhood Learning Center (ECLC), Badry, Baetens Beardsmore, Frigols-Martin, Mehisto and Wagner (2012) recommended that in the UAE context the L1 should be prioritised 'to help children achieve a generally accepted and communally shared level of competence' before they are immersed in English. They also stressed the importance of adopting innovative teaching methods to help children build on their limited knowledge of Dialectal Arabic and facilitate a gradual transition from Dialectal Arabic to Modern Standard Arabic (see also Badry 2004). However, these recommendations were met with resistance from prospective parents who 'objected to paying money for their children if they are going to learn "just Arabic," and refused to enroll their children if English was not introduced from the beginning'. As a result, English was introduced at the start of the programme; however, of concern is the fact that Arabic input and use appear not to be well thought through. Although bilingualism is greatly appreciated in the UAE, its successful development is undermined by not encouraging the use of both Arabic and English in meaningful ways. The decision to immerse children in English from kindergarten in the absence of opportunities outside school to first develop Arabic, in a context where Arabic is disadvantaged, is more akin to submersion or subtractive models discussed in bilingualism research than to an additive bilingual pro-gramme (e.g. Baker 2001; Garcia 2009; Genesee, 1984; Swain and Johnson 1997). In its latest inspection report, the KHDA warned that '[t]here was no overall improvement in attainment or progress in Arabic as a first language, and there was evidence of decline particularly in the primary phase'. Even those schools classified as outstanding by the KHDA 'had an area of Arabic where a significant improvement was required' (Knowledge and Human Development authority 2014).

As discussed earlier, the majority of teachers are not UAE nationals. In class they tend to speak their native variety of Dialectal Arabic and conduct literacy activities in MSA. As a result, young children are being exposed to several varieties that are different in important ways at all linguistic levels, including differences in phonological and syllabic structures to differences in lexicon and syntax. Consequently, when children are introduced to literacy, they are faced with added layers of unfamiliarity with the oral language that they are expected to map onto the written text. As reading research suggests, some of the difficulties faced by young Arabs in reading are due to the differ-ences between oral and written Arabic varieties (Ibrahim and Aharon-Peretz 2005; Saiegh-Haddad 2005) in addition to the nature of the orthographic system of Arabic, which uses many diacritics and makes processing complex both visually and linguistically (Abu Rabia 2001; Ibrahim 2011; Taha 2013).[12] However, teaching materials continue to ignore diglossic differences and assume that the transition from the vernacular dialectal varieties to MSA, the language of literacy, is automatic; moreover, the particularities of Arabic orthography are not guiding decisions in the development of reading materi-als for young readers.

CONCLUSION

The value placed by the UAE government on education and bilingualism, positive attitudes towards bilingualism among many stakeholders and the UAE's willingness to invest resources into dual-language education all sup-port the nation in achieving its declared goal of Arabic-English bilingualism. A major mechanism such as the Arab Charter also aims to contribute to this goal. At the same time, more powerful negative counterweights, in the form of forces and mechanisms, undermine the goal of bilingualism. Arabic is los-ing ground, both as a spoken variety and as a language of knowledge produc-tion, because it is being undervalued and underused in society and because of an assumption that the higher level goal of global competitiveness can only be achieved through English-medium education. This is reflected in the use of English to teach STEM subjects and in the practice of linking Arabic only to subjects more oriented toward the past and traditions.

The learning of Arabic and English is undermined by a number of factors, including a plethora of top-down and short-lived reforms often designed by foreign consultants, low teacher salaries, very high turnover in teaching staff, a lack of learning resources, inadequate teacher training, and parental detachment from early child rearing and the education process. Much deeper, broad-based analysis is required by the government of the forces, mechanisms and counterweights that are currently interacting in ways that are leading to the unintended consequences of ineffective and inefficient approaches to achieving high degrees of bilingualism. Neither is the government improving performance on international benchmark examinations such as PIRLS and PISA. In addition to teacher training and testing, government plans need to address parental beliefs and behaviours both as forces and counterweights. Effective and efficient long-term plans, which also revisit an appropriate reallocation of resources, are needed to improve the quality of education in general and bilingual education in particular in the long-term.

NOTES

1   This is a fictional name to protect the identity of the family.
2   There are also many Indian, Pakistani and Filipino private schools serving large communities from these backgrounds. In addition, there are a few schools that offer German, Russian and other curricula.
3   The ratio of Emiratis to expatriates in the UAE fluctuates greatly depending on economic conditions and regions. For example, the percentage of UAE nationals (Emiratis) varied much more in Dubai compared to other Emirates in the period between 2008 and 2013.
4   The distinction between Classical Arabic and Modern Standard Arabic (MSA) is generally not used in Arabic so when Arabs refer to 'the Arabic language' it implies either, depending on ideology. However, Arab linguists use Classical Arabic to describe the language of the Quran, and classical literature and Modern Standard Arabic to refer to the contemporary variety used in literacy and formal contexts. Differences between these two varieties are lexical, morphological and syntactic, with Classical Arabic being more synthetic and MSA more analytic. Native Arabic speakers acquire another variety of Arabic, referred to as Colloquial or Dialectical Arabic, as their first language, which they use in daily interactions. They are usually introduced to MSA in school for literacy

functions. Each Arab country has its own variety of spoken Arabic but MSA is common to all.

5   English is the medium of instruction in both public and private universities in most disciplines.

6   In private schools, English is introduced as the major language from kindergarten and if Arabic is used, it is the foreign language.

7   No minimum level of proficiency in Arabic is required for admission at both public or private universities in the UAE.

8   Emiratisation is a policy which aims to increase the number of UAE nationals in the workforce particularly in the private sector.

9   UAE nationals in public schools are paid higher than expatriate Arab and South-Asian teachers and receive additional benefits from the government.

10 Each Arab state has its own particular colloquial Arabic dialect. The dialects are usually classified along a geographical continuum: the North African group, the Egyptian group, the Levant and the Gulf groups. Comprehension across these regional dialects is difficult due to phonological, lexical and idiomatic differences.

11 See also Haeri (1997) for similar attitudes towards Arabic in Egypt and elsewhere in the Arab world.

12 The Arabic alphabet represents consonants only, with short vowels symbolised by diacritics that appear on top of the consonantal symbol or under it. Vowels are often not represented and are inferred by the reader from the context. In addition, some consonants are differentiated by the use of diacritics only. For example, the letters b, t, th, n and y are all written in the same way except for the number of dots above or below the letter.

REFERENCES

Abu-Rabia, S. (2001). 'The Role of Vowels in Reading Semitic Scripts: Data from Arabic and Hebrew'. *Reading and Writing: An Interdisciplinary Journal*, 14, 39–59.

ADEC (Abu Dhabi Educational Council) Arabic Subject. www.adec.ac.ae/en/Education/KeyInitiatives/Curriculum-Improvement/Pages/Arabic-Subject.aspx (retrieved May 2014).

ADEC (Abu Dhabi Educational Council) Key Initiatives. www.adec.ac.ae/en/Education/KeyInitiatives/Pages/default.aspx (retrieved May 2014).

Ahmed, A. (2013). 'Islamic and Arab Culture Lost in UAE's Foreign Schools'. www.thenational.ae/news/uae-news/education/islamic-and-arab-culture-lost-in-uaes-foreign-schools ixzz2royC2tRh (retrieved May 2014).

— (2011). 'New Curriculum is a Solution to Low Performance Concerns'. *The National* online (retrieved May 2011). www.thenational.ae/news/uae-news/new-curriculum-is-a-solution-to-low-performance-concerns ixzz31Itgmqhs (retrieved May 2014).

Al Ameri, K. (2013). 'Arabic is Precious, but the English Language is Essential'. www.thenational.ae/thenationalconversation/comment/arabic-is-precious-but-the-english-language-is-essential ixzz2r-18P2Vca (retrieved May 2014).

Al Amiri, A. (2012). 'The Role of National Policies and Legislation in the Development of Education Systems'. In *Essentials of School Education in the United Arab Emirates*. Abu Dhabi: The Emirates Center for Strategic Studies and Research, 19–55.

Al Baik, D. (2008) 'It is Not Acceptable to Drop Arabic Language from our Lives'. *Gulfnews*. 16 March.

Al Kaff Al Hashemi, B. and Underwood, M. (2013). 'Challenges of Learning Arabic in the UAE – Even for Emiratis'. *The National* online. www.thenational.ae/uae/education/challenges-of-learning-arabic-in-the-uae-even-for-emiratis ixzz2r1TPcwOK TRACT (retrieved May 2014).

Al Khan, M.N. (2013). 'Arabic is not Dead but Teaching Must Improve, UAE Report Shows'. *The National* online. www.thenational.ae/news/uae-news/arabic-is-not-dead-but-teaching-must-improve-uae-report-shows ixzz2gLzs6N47 (retrieved May 2014).

Al Lawati, A. and Al Najami, S. (2008). 'In Depth: Sorry, I Don't Speak Arabic'. *Gulf news online*.

Al Matuei, M. (2012). 'UAE Society and the Educational Process'. In *Essentials of School Education in the United Arab Emirates*. Abu Dhabi: The Emirates Center for Strategic Studies and Research (ECSSR), 57–83.

Al Munajjed, M. and Sabbagh, K. (2011). *Youth in GCC Countries: Meeting the Challenge*. Booz and Company, Inc. ideationcenter.com.

Al Najami, S. (2007). 'Bilingual Education Hangs in the Balance for Schools'. *Gulf News* online.

Al Sumaiti, R. (2012). *Parental Involvement in the Education of Their Children in Dubai*. Dubai School of Government. Policy Brief 30.

Badry, F. (2012). 'Education in the UAE: Local Identity and Global Development'. In *Essentials of School Education in the United Arab Emirates*. Abu Dhabi: The Emirates Center for Strategic Studies and Research (ECSSR), 85–106.

— (2004). *Acquiring the Arabic Lexicon: Evidence of Productive Strategies and Pedagogical Implications*. Bethesda, MD: Academica Press.

Badry, F., Baetens Beardsmore, H., Frigols Martin, M., Mehisto, P. and Wagner, D. (2012). Early Dual Language Learning Center. Insight Seminar, Zayed University, 6–8 May, 2012. Unpublished Consultancy Report.

Baker, C. (2003). *Foundations of Bilingual Education and Bilingualism* (third edition). Clevedon: Multilingual Matters.

The National online (2012). 'Balance Arabic and English Curriculum'. Editorial, October 14. www.thenational.ae/thenationalconversation/editorial/balance-arabic-and-english-curriculum ixzz2r-1Rzrwh7 (retrieved May 2014).

Beatens-Beardsmore, H. (1996). 'Reconciling Content Acquisition and Language Acquisition in Bilingual Classrooms'. *Journal of Multilingual and Multicultural Development*, 17: 2–4, 114–122.

Collins, L. (2011). 'Expat Teachers aren't Only Ones Leaving UAE Schools'. *The National* online. www.thenational.ae/news/uae-news/education/expat-teachers-arent-only-ones-leaving-uae-schools ixzz-2rO1jHbXC (retrieved May 2014).

Cummins, J. (2000). *Language, Power and Pedagogy: Bilingual Children in the Crossfire*. Clevedon: Multilingual Matters.

Dickson, M. and Le Roux, J. (2012). 'Why do Emirati Males become Teachers and how do Cultural Factors Influence this Decision?' *Learning and Teaching in Higher Education: Gulf Perspective*, 9: 2.

Emirates 24/7 News online (2012). 'Mohammed unveils Arabic Language Charter', 23 April. www.emirates247.com/news/government/mohammed-unveils-arabic-language-charter-2012-04-23-1.455274 (retrieved May 2014).

Farrell, L. and Fenwick, T. (2007). 'Educating a Global Workforce'. In Lesley Farrell and Tara Fenwick (eds), *Educating the Global Workforce: Knowledge, Knowledge Work and Knowledge Workers. World Yearbook of Education*. London: Routlege. 13–26.

Findlow, S. (2006). 'Higher Education and Linguistic Dualism in the Arab Gulf'. *British Journal of Sociology of Education*, 27: 1, 19–36.

Garcia, O. (2009). *Bilingual Education in the 21st Century: A Global Perspective*. West Sussex: Wiley-Blackwell.

Genesee, F.H. (2009). 'Early Childhood Bilingualism: Perils and Possibilities'. *Journal of Applied Research on Learning*, 2, Special Issue, Article 2, April 2009.

Godwin, S. (2006). 'Globalization, Education and Emiratisation: A Study of the United Arab Emirates'. *The Electronic Journal on Information Systems in Developing Countries*, 27: 1, 1–14.

Gulf News (2014). 'New Award to Encourage Use of Arabic'. Nation A13, 8 May.

Hoff, E. (2006). 'How Social Contexts Support and Shape Language Development'. *Developmental Review* 26, 55–88.

Haeri, N. (1997). 'Symbolic Capital: Language, State, and Class in Egypt'. *Current Anthropology*, 38, 795–816.

Hassan, H. (2007). Talk presented at the Knowledge Conference Held in Dubai, 29–30 October 2007.

Ibrahim, R. and Aharon-Peretz, J. (2005). 'Is Literary Arabic a Second Language for Native Arab Speakers? Evidence from a Semantic Priming Study'. *Journal of Psycholinguistic Research*, 34, 51–70.

Ibrahim, R. (2011). 'Literacy Problems in Arabic: Sensitivity to Diglossia in Tasks Involving Working Memory'. *Journal of Neurolinguistics*, 24, 571–82.

Issa, W. (2013a). 'Lessons in English in UAE schools "violation of constitution" FNC told'. *The National* online, March 6. www.thenational.ae/news/uae-news/education/lessons-in-english-in-uae-schools-violation-of-constitution-fnc-told ixzz2znhhdagH (retrieved May 2014).

— (2013b). 'Tough New Tests for Prospective Arabic Teachers in Dubai'. *The National* online. www.thenational.ae/news/uae-news/education/tough-new-tests-for-prospective-arabic-teachers-in-dubai ixzz2thLuCK6t (retrieved May 2014).

— (2013c). 'Young Emiratis Divided over Calls to Teach Lessons in Arabic'. *The National* online. www.thenational.ae/news/uae-news/young-emiratis-divided-over-calls-to-teach-lessons-in-arabic ixzz-2rovSA5W4 (retrieved May 2014).

Knowledge and Human Development Authority (2014). *Inspection of Private Schools 2013–2014. Key Findings*. www.khda.gov.ae.

Malek, C. (2013). 'UAE Students Show Little Improvement in Arabic'. *The National* online. www.thenational.ae/uae/uae-students-show-little-improvement-in-arabic ixzz2tgx5MozX (retrieved May 2014).

Matthew, F. (2008). 'Shoring Up National Identity'. *Gulf News*. www.archive.gulfnews.com/articles/08/04/17/10206230.html (retrieved May 2014).

Ministry of Education Strategy (2009–2014). الخطة الخمسية لإدارة المنهاج. (Five-year Strategic Planning), 63. moe.gov.ae.

— (2010–2020). الوثيقة الوطنية لمادة اللغة العربية (National Document on the Arabic Language), 13. www.moe.gov.ae/Arabic/Pages/Curriculum.aspx.

Mohammed, E. (2008). 'Arabic is Key to National Identity'. *Gulf News*. www.gulfnews.com/news/gulf/uae/heritage-culture/arabic-key-to-national-identity-1.98255 (retrieved May 2014).

National Bureau of Statistics United Arab Emirates (2013). www.uaestatistics.gov.ae/EnglishHome/ReportDetailsEnglish/tabid/121/Default.aspx?ItemId=1914&PTID=104&MenuId=1. (retrieved May 2014).

National Qualifications Authority (NQA) (2013). *The UAE Education System: Overview of Performance in Education* (fig.5, p. 7). www.nqa.gov.ae.

Nazzal, N. (2013). 'Majority of Teachers in Public School Don't Carry Degrees in Education: Ministry Analyses Results of Assessment Tests'. *Gulf News* special. www.gulfnews.com/news/gulf/uae/

education/majority-of-teachers-in-public-school-don-t-carry-degrees-in-education-1.1205092 (retrieved May 2014).

Pennington, R. (2014). 'Skills are More Important than Formal Qualifications, UAE Educators Told'. *The National* online. www.thenational.ae/uae/education/skills-are-more-important-than-formal-qualifications-uae-educators-told ixzz2rOI4cf5V (retrieved May 2014).

Riches, C. and Genesee, F. (2006). 'Cross-linguistic and Cross-modal Aspects of Literacy Development'. In F. Genesee, K. Lindholm-Leary, W.M. Saunders and D. Christian. *Educating English Language Learners: A Synthesis of Research Evidence*, 64–108. NY: Cambridge University Press.

Rowe, M. L. (2008). 'Child-directed Speech: Relation to Socioeconomic Status, Knowledge of Child Development and Child Vocabulary Skill'. *Journal of Child Language*, 35, 185–205 Cambridge University Press.

Saiegh-Haddad, E. (2005). 'Correlates of Reading Fluency in Arabic: Diglossic and Orthographic Factors'. *Reading and Writing: An Interdisciplinary Journal*, 18, 559–82.

Salama, S. (2012). 'UAE Pupils Top Tests in Arab Region'. *Gulf News* online. http://gulfnews.com/news/gulf/uae/education/uae-pupils-top-tests-in-arab-region-1.1118022.

Singleton, D. (2001). 'Age and Second Language Acquisition'. *Annual Review of Applied Linguistics*, 21, 77–89.

Swain, M. and Johnson, R.K. (1997) 'Immersion Education: A Category within Bilingual Education'. In R.K. Johnson and M. Swain (eds), *Immersion Education: International Perspectives*, 1–16. Cambridge: Cambridge University Press.

Swain, M. and Lapkin, S. (2005). 'The Evolving Sociopolitical Context of Immersion Education in Canada: Some Implications for Program Development'. *International Journal of Applied Linguistics*, 15: 2, 169–86.

Scheele, A., F. Leseman, P.P.M. and Mayo, A.Y. (2010). 'The Home Language Environment of Monolingual and Bilingual Children and their Language Proficiency'. *Applied Psycholinguistics*, 31, 117–40.

Swan, M. (2013). 'UAE Schools and Universities Need to Do More to Bolster National Identity'. *The National* online. www.thenational.ae/news/uae-news/education/uae-schools-and-universities-need-to-do-more-to-bolster-national-identity ixzz2rowDfGv4 (retrieved May 2014).

Taha, H.Y. (2013). 'Reading and Spelling in Arabic: Linguistic and Orthographic Complexity'. *Theory and Practice in Language Studies*, 3, 5, 721–7.

Tairab, H. and Al Shannag, Q. (2013). *Analysis of TIMSS 2011 Results: UAE Perspectives. PowerPoint presentation at the 5th Math, Science, and Technology Education (MSTE) Conference.* UAEU: Department of Curriculum and Instruction, College of Education.

Youssef, M. (2008). 'Use of Arabic will Preserve our Cultural Identity – Intellectuals'. *Gulf News* online. www.gulfnews.com/news/gulf/uae/heritage-culture/use-of-arabic-will-preserve-our-cultural-identity-intellectuals-1.90978 (retrieved May 2014).

FORCES	MECHANISMS
Contextual	**Vehicles**
Recency of educational system	State financing of education
Flexibility to adopt reforms	Wealth of country
Stakeholders desire to transform society	Ministry of Education's 5 year plan and strategies 2010–2020
Demographic factors (88% expats)	Decentralisation
Openness to the outside world	Local educational councils
	Memoranda of understanding with external agencies and educational institutions
Towards English	Model schools
	Private schools
English as a global language	
English as the language of IT and pop culture	
Desire to belong to the advanced world	**Legislation and plans**
Towards Arabic	The Arabic Charter
	Pilot MAG schools (schools of the future)
Rich cultural heritage of Arabic	The ADEC initiatives
Arabic tied to religion	Language-in-education reforms
Ties with rest of the Arab world	Incentivisation for nationals to join the teaching profession
Goals	Teacher training programmes
	Development of teaching materials
Buy-in to a vision of transforming the country into a knowledge society through English	Common European Framework of Reference
Sense of mission related to preserving local culture and identity through Arabic	National standardised assessment tests
	International standardised assessment tests
A desire to take a leading role in protecting Arabic in the Arab world	
Status associated with international standardised tests	

COUNTERWEIGHTS

Fear of corruption of Arabic	Modernising teaching of Arabic
Loss of L1 and learning English	Arabic charter and other government initiatives
Continued dependence on the West	Building a knowledge society
Modernisation of society	Local culture and traditions
Lack of local knowledge	International expertise
Misconceptions about age of exposure to L2	Bilingualism research
Multiglossic nature of Arabic	Cultural, religious values attached to MSA
Localisation of decision-making	Reliance on federal government in less wealthy Northern Emirates
Negative perceptions towards teaching Arabic and teaching through Arabic	Modern approach to teaching

11 MALTA:
Bilingual Education for Self-Preservation and Global Fitness

Antoinette Camilleri Grima (University of Malta)

CHAPTER NAVIGATOR

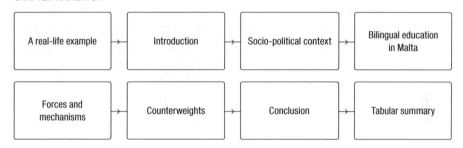

A REAL-LIFE EXAMPLE

The year is 2004. The seminar room is packed with teachers. I had been invited by the principal of a secondary school to give the plenary speech at a staff development conference. I could sense that the teachers were uneasy and wary that I, an academic, would support the principal's belief that code-switching should be banished from the classroom. A few years ago the Ministry of Education in Malta had recommended for the first time that a small group of subjects be taught in Maltese and that the rest be taught exclusively in English without code-switching (i.e. without switching between the two languages). My doctoral research, along with other research, had shown that judicious code-switching between Maltese and English at all levels of the education system, and across subjects, had numerous educational benefits. The authors of the national policy were aware of this research but chose to ignore it, relying instead on their own beliefs.

As I made it clear that I found fault with the new national policy, and that my research had illustrated the marvellous ways in which teachers in Malta used two languages for the maximum benefit of learners, I could hear sighs of relief coming from various corners of the hall. I got the sense that teachers found it affirming to have their bilingual practices acknowledged as an academically powerful way of working with learners.

Shortly before the school development conference, the school principal had implemented a language separation policy. Tuesdays and Thursdays were reserved for the sole use of English. Within a few weeks of launching the new policy, and soon after my presentation at the staff development conference, the principal reported that he accomplished most of his office work on the 'English-only days', as he had no interruptions. On one particular English-only day, an accident took place in the school car park and he was not informed about it. The principal realised that both staff and students simply went silent on the English-only days. That was the end of the language separation approach. He abolished the English-only days, and allowed teachers language freedom in the classroom.

INTRODUCTION

Bilingual education in Malta operates on a national level from kindergarten through to and including post-secondary education. The use of Maltese and English as media of instruction is a result of historical circumstances (Brincat 2011). As a consequence of British colonisation (1800–1964), English took over from Italian as an official language that played a key role alongside the local language, Maltese. Previously, during the time of the Knights of St John in Malta (1535–1798), Italian had been the language of culture and education. After 1800 and prior to 1999, the issue of bilingual education was not discussed. It was officially assumed that the medium of instruction in Malta was English. The 1999 National Curriculum (Ministry of Education 1999) was the first attempt to regulate language use in the classroom. However, the 2012 National Curriculum (Ministry of Education 2012) eliminated all reference to language as a medium of instruction. This reflects a context where bilingualism and bilingual education constitute an integrated stable phenomenon, valued and desired by stakeholders due to the respect for Maltese as a national language on the one hand, and the global capital entrenched in English on the other.

THE SOCIO-POLITICAL CONTEXT

Malta is *de jure* and *de facto* a bilingual state. The Constitution of Malta (1964) in Article 1(5) declares Maltese the national language, and Maltese and English official languages. Maltese is the native language of the people, learned and spoken by the vast majority as a first language (see Table 1). English is acquired in early childhood mostly through education and the media, and is present in all societal domains.

The local media broadcast and publish in both languages: two of the four daily newspapers, and five of the eleven weekly newspapers are in English; all six local television stations broadcast in Maltese with some films, shows and documentaries in English without dubbing; 13 local radio stations broadcast in Maltese, with some programmes presented in English by Maltese or foreign speakers of English (Vella 2013). In public administration, both Maltese and English are used. For instance, the *Gazzetta tal-Gvern ta' Malta / The Malta Government Gazzette* is published in a dual-column format in both languages.

However, in the Law Courts the Maltese version of the law, and not the English one, is binding. Parliamentary verbatim proceedings are reported only in Maltese. When Malta became a member of the European Union in 2004, Maltese became one of the official languages of the European Union (EU). This has given the Maltese language international visibility and a new language industry comprising translation and interpretation services. As a result, Maltese has earned greater value and respect locally and abroad (Sciriha and Vassallo 2006).

According to the *Census of Population and Housing 2011* (National Statistics Office 2014), the population of Malta is 417 432, of whom 5% are non-Maltese citizens. Table 1 summarises the replies of Maltese citizens to the 2011 census question with reference to language use. A high percentage of Maltese citizens reported being bilingual in Maltese and English (around 78%), and trilingual in Maltese, English and Italian (almost 40%). (For further details on trilingualism in Malta see Caruana (2013), and see Vella (2013), for a description of language varieties in Malta).

Table 1: Languages spoken in Malta

speak	well	average	total	% of Maltese citizens
Maltese	352 121	5 571	357 692	90%
English	248 570	61 709	310 279	78%
Italian	93 401	62 863	156 264	39%
French	11 698	18 886	30 584	8%
German	3979	3 987	7966	2%
Arabic	3948	2457	6405	1.6%

(Adapted from the Census of Population and Housing 2011,
National Statistics Office 2014)

Maltese and English are employed by the Maltese population, either one language at a time, or in interacting ways in both written and spoken forms (Camilleri Grima 2013a). Maltese-English bilingualism in Malta is a societal phenomenon thriving on widespread individual bilingualism. The classroom, a sociolinguistic reality, is a microcosm of local society (Camilleri Grima 2001).

BILINGUAL EDUCATION IN MALTA

Bilingualism in education in Malta has been omnipresent since the beginning of schooling in the nineteenth century. Maltese has always had a role to play as the language of communication among learners and between learners and teachers (Camilleri 1994). English replaced Italian slowly at the turn of the twentieth century. Since then Italian has continued to be taught as a subject, while English gained a stronghold as a medium of instruction alongside Maltese from early childhood education to post-secondary level.

All initial teacher training is conducted by the Faculty of Education at the University of Malta while continuing professional development is regularly organised by the Directorate of Education. For admission to the B.Ed. (Honours) courses in Early Childhood Education and Primary Education, as well as for the Diploma for Learning Support Assistants, all candidates must obtain a Pass on a University of Malta proficiency test in both Maltese and English. In order to be employed within the state sector, teachers must be proficient in both languages. This requirement is an important mechanism underpinning the bilingual ethos in education.

The only official requirement with regard to the use of Maltese and English as media of instruction was introduced in the national curriculum of 1999 (Ministry of Education 1999), which recommended that all subjects, except languages, Religion, Maltese History, Social Studies and Personal and Social Education, should be taught in English without code-switching. However, teachers did not follow this requirement and continued to teach in two languages. There are conflicting attitudes, reasonings and recommendations in the 1999 document in so far as, on the one hand, it supports bilingualism, but on the other hand, it recommends monolingual policies and strategies (Camilleri Grima 2003).

However, tradition may at times be a more powerful force than policy as subjects continue to be taught bilingually in Maltese and English. Here, a distinction must be made between written and spoken bilingualism, especially with regard to classroom teaching and examinations. At age 16, when students are in their final year of compulsory education, they sit for the matriculation examinations. Students must pass a minimum of six examinations in different subjects to gain entry to a post-secondary institution. Examinations in Maltese, English and Mathematics are obligatory. High-achieving students tend to take about 11 examinations. All the examinations are in English but students are allowed a choice of language in four of them: Religion, Environmental Studies, Maltese History and Social Studies. In these subjects, students may answer any given examination question in either Maltese or English, but are not allowed to code-switch within the same answer. In other words, both languages can be used within the same examination paper, but each individual answer must be written in only one language. To some extent, this reflects traditional language use at school, which can largely be described as one where translanguaging has been commonplace. For example, textbooks for most subjects are in English but are often discussed in Maltese in the classroom. In the four subjects where answers in Maltese are allowed in the matriculation examinations, textbooks in Maltese are generally available and commonly used in several schools. Therefore, in school, both languages are used separately when used in written form, but they come together when used in spoken discourse.

Although there is a perception among educational administrators and the general public that there has been a subject-specific language-separation approach in Maltese bilingual education in the past decades, in reality this is only the case as far as the written medium is concerned. The spoken medium of instruction has always involved translanguaging as witnessed and expressed in personal communications by teachers and learners. While the term 'code-switching' is used in official documents and by non-linguists who perceive reality through a 'monolingual consciousness' (Camilleri Grima 2003) as a result of language separation in writing, the term 'translanguaging' has been adopted by experts in the field of bilingualism in education who have dissected bilingual classroom discourse and who have explained the pedagogical benefits of a spoken bilingual medium of instruction.

Translanguaging – drawing upon the full spectrum of one's linguistic resources in order to 'make sense' (Garcia 2009) – has been a reality in Maltese classrooms since the beginning of schooling in Malta (Camilleri 1994; Camilleri Grima 2013b). In Maths and Science lessons, for example, where the written medium of instruction is English, teachers and learners still use Maltese for discussions and to sort out their thinking and articulate key concepts. In lessons where the written medium is Maltese, English is sometimes brought into play with reference to extended reading on the subject and to access relevant information available via contemporary media. In the independent, non-state sector, where the medium of instruction is more likely to be English for all subjects in both written and spoken form, Maltese is used by teachers in order to establish rapport with Maltese-speaking learners, and for topic, classroom and discourse management (Borg 2004).

An interesting scenario where a strict English-only policy was implemented in a primary school is documented by Farrugia (2009a; 2009b). Farrugia found that an exclusive use of English during Mathematics lessons was not an educationally beneficial policy. Not allowing the use of Maltese meant that pupils were held back from answering and asking questions, and therefore, participating actively in the lesson. Furthermore, the teacher was unable to relate some of the mathematical concepts to everyday life outside the classroom. These restraints can be considered a form of 'silencing' (Simon 1990), rooted in the language distance between home and school.

FORCES AND MECHANISMS

The economic and other benefits of English locally cannot be overestimated. Over one million tourists, more than double the local population, visit Malta every year. They come largely from Britain and other western European countries. In 2013, tourism accounted for around 35% of Malta's gross domestic product (Trading Economics 2014). Furthermore, 6% of all tourists are foreign students who come to Malta to study English as a foreign language (National Statistics Office 2013). The strong tourism industry requires the local population to be fluent in English and other languages. In addition,

Maltese continues to be held in high esteem by the local population. The language is being constantly developed in academic, technical and scientific fields, largely as a result of the expanding terminological and grammatical resources necessary to translate EU legislation and to facilitate its use by experts when giving evidence in court and by law makers. In education, there is a slow but steady increase in the provision of material for teaching Maltese, and more sporadically in its use as a written text in subjects like Geography and Environmental Education.

In brief, the forces that influence bilingualism and bilingual education are: (1) a belief among the general population in the value of bilingualism; (2) a belief among the general population in the value of Maltese which the vast majority of families continue to use so that children usually first arrive at school as Maltese dominant; (3) the supremacy of Maltese in the courts when interpreting legislation; (4) pragmatism arising out of a lack of Maltese language learning materials and the plethora of English language materials; (5) the prioritisation of learner understanding and participation during lessons over and above any 'monolingualising' strategies advocated by administrators or politicians, and (6) the tradition of teaching certain subjects through Maltese and others through English.

Mechanisms that support bilingualism and bilingual education are: (1) broad-based opportunities (e.g. bilingual media, families, workplace) to use both Maltese and English; (2) the instrumental benefits of English, including its use in tertiary education, and in tourism and international trade; (3) the requirement for teachers to be bilingual; (4) English language learning resources that foster reading and writing in English; (5) the requirement to translate all EU legislation into Maltese and all Maltese legislation into English (this requires highly specialised terminology as well as academic and legal language), and (6) the lack of monolingual state-sector programmes on offer, which means that neither parents, children, nor teachers, have a choice but to persist in a bilingual *habitus.*

The co-existence of Maltese and English has not been without conflict. On the one hand, there are those who believe that: (1) Maltese should gain a greater role as a medium of instruction for the language's own sake, as a language planning option coloured by a nationalistic attitude; coincidentally supported by (2) educationists who believe that the weaker learners would fare better at school if taught through Maltese. On the other hand, others complain about the weakening proficiency in English by all, and the Minister has recently engaged a UK institution to examine and address this issue (*Times of Malta* 2014).

The sociolinguistic reality is very complex in Malta and areas for development and change must include, for instance, acknowledgement of the diverse language backgrounds and proficiency levels of learners and teachers; the range of abilities and learning styles of learners; the discrepancy in attitude to translanguaging between that of experts and non-experts; and the fact that top-down enforcement is bound to fail unless it is heartily backed by all the stakeholders, including teachers, learners and their parents.

COUNTERWEIGHTS AND CONCLUSION

In Malta, bilingual education is not promoted for its own sake, as an option or by choice. Rather, it results from a sociolinguistic reality where each of the two languages is needed and where economic survival and social success cannot be envisaged through proficiency in one language without the other. Maltese is the first language learned at home by around 90% of the population and continues to be used by this large majority as the main spoken language throughout life. There is a strong force in the value accorded to Maltese as a living symbol of national identity at the local, European and global levels. Maltese possesses great historical and cultural significance. It continues to be used not just in the home but in public administration and other workplaces, in the media and for drafting legislation. Therefore, despite having to co-exist with a major world language for the last two centuries, there is no reason to believe that in the foreseeable future Maltese will disappear either from school or society. At the same time, English has tremendous power emanating from its social, economic and other benefits which can accrue to each member of Maltese society.

Hence, the counterweights that continue to support, build and regenerate bilingual education in Malta are the positional power of Maltese as a native language and language of identity on the one hand, and the value placed on the benefits of possessing English on the other. Luckily, what emerges is not only knowledge and proficiency in two languages by the majority of the Maltese, but also the accrued benefits of bilingualism that have recently been much acclaimed in the literature (e.g. Bialystok 2011).

REFERENCES

Bialystok, E. (2011). 'Reshaping the Mind: The Benefits of Bilingualism'. *Canadian Journal of Experimental Psychology*, 65: 4, 229–35.

Borg, G. (2004). *The Impact of Bilingual Education. A Case Study of a Year 2 Class in a Maltese Primary School.* Unpublished B.Ed. (Hons.) dissertation, University of Malta.

Brincat, J. (2011). *Maltese and Other Languages.* Malta: Midsea Books.

Camilleri, C. (1994). *Newspaper Documents Contributed to the History of Education in Malta 1900–1915.* Unpublished B.Ed. (Hons.) dissertation, University of Malta.

Camilleri Grima, A. (2001). 'The Maltese Bilingual Classroom: A Microcosm of Local Society. *Mediterranean Journal of Educational Studies*, 6: 1, 3–12.

— (2003). '"Do as I say, not as I do." Legitimate Language in Bilingual Malta!' In Huss, L., Camilleri Grima, A. and King, K.A. (eds), *Transcending Monolingualism. Linguistic Revitalisation in Education.* Lisse: Swets & Zeitlinger Publishers.

— (2013a). 'Challenging Code-Switching in Malta'. *Revue Française de Linguistique Appliquée*, 18: 2, 45–61.

— (2013b). 'A Select Review of Bilingualism in Education in Malta'. *International Journal of Bilingual Education and Bilingualism*, 16: 5, 553–69.

Caruana, S. (2013). Italian in Malta: A Socio-Educational perspective. *International Journal of Bilingual Education and Bilingualism*, 16: 5, 602–14.

Farrugia, M.T. (2009a). 'Registers for Mathematics Classrooms in Malta: Considering Options'. *For the Learning of Mathematics*, 29: 1, 20–25.

— (2009b). 'Reflections on a medium of instruction policy for Mathematics in Malta'. In Barwell, R. (ed.), *Multilingualism in Mathematics Classrooms*, Bristol: Multilingual Matters.

García, O. (2009). *Bilingual Education in the 21st Century. A Global Perspective.* Oxford: Wiley-Blackwell.

Ministry of Education (1999). *Creating the Future Together. National Minimum Curriculum.* Malta: Ministry of Education.

— (2012). *A National Curriculum Framework for All.* Malta: Ministry of Education and Employment.

National Statistics Office, Malta (2013). *Teaching English as a Foreign Language: 2012.* Malta: NSO.

— (2014). *Census of Population and Housing 2011.* Malta: NSO.

Sciriha, L. and Vassallo, M. (2006). *Living Languages in Malta.* Malta: IT Printing.

Simon, R.I. (1990). 'The Fear of Theory'. In Eagleton, T. (ed.), *The significance of Theory.* Cambridge: Blackwell, 82–5.

Times of Malta (2014). 'Education Ministry in Campaign to Raise Standards of English Language Use;. www.timesofmalta.com/articles/view/20140910/local/education-ministry-in-campaign-to-raise-standards-of-english-language-use.535181 (retrieved September 2014).

Trading Economics (2014). Malta GDP Growth Rate. www.tradingeconomics.com/malta/gdp-growth (retrieved July 2014).

Vella, A. (2013). 'Languages and Language Varieties in Malta'. In *International Journal of Bilingual Education and Bilingualism*, 16: 5, 532–52.

FORCES	MECHANISMS
Key values	**Context**
Freedom to decide (context demands proficiency not curriculum)	Broad-based opportunities to use both languages
Pragmatism (using those learning resources that are available)	**Knowledge building**
Tradition and *habitus*	Research
Beliefs	**Requirements**
A belief in the value of bilingualism	For all teachers and learners to be bilingual
A belief in the value of Maltese	**Vehicles**
	Lack of monolingual state programmes
	Teacher professional development

COUNTERWEIGHTS	
Global capital entrenched in English	Respect for Maltese language, history and traditions
Dominance of English	Use of Maltese in public administration and media

12 COLOMBIA:
Challenges and Constraints

Anne-Marie de Mejía (Universidad de los Andes, Bogotá)

CHAPTER NAVIGATOR

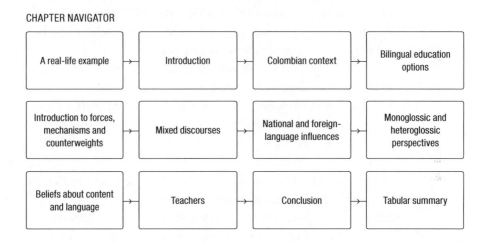

A REAL-LIFE EXAMPLE

Parental demand is the primary reason that schools in Colombia often initiate a transition from a primarily monolingual to a 'full/true' bilingual programme. This was the case with one private Spanish-medium school in Bogotá. The school had previously offered an intensive English programme through language classes, but parents wished to see English used to teach content subjects such as Natural Science, Maths or Social Science. In Colombia, 'bilingual' schools enjoy higher status and can charge higher fees than monolingual schools. In this case, one of the specific reasons given was 'the need to find new contexts to put the students in contact with English' in a manner that did not have a negative impact on content learning (Arango 2010).

While the head teacher of this school supported the bilingual initiative and took an active part in initial group discussions, many of the teachers strongly resisted integrating content from other subject areas (i.e. social sciences) into the English programme. As Arango (2009), who researched the bilingual programme, points out, this resistance often arose from a fear of shifting from just teaching language to teaching Social Science through English. Teachers also believed that this would require more work. Arango was also the school's administrative coordinator. She championed the development of the bilingual programme. Although Arango enjoyed the support of the head teacher and the school's Board of Trustees, her status as an administrator worked against her as some of the teachers saw her 'incursion' into the academic life of the school as unjustified.

In her study, Arango (2009) identified centralist school traditions and the lack of a unified institutional vision of bilingualism and bilingual education as forces impeding the teaching of content matter through English. A common vision and entrenched traditionalism fuelled the resistance of the English teachers to the new approach. Arango highlighted, however, the counterbalancing effect of the head teacher's authority, which facilitated the implementation of decisions taken by the school authorities. Nevertheless, the English teachers maintained their covert resistance to the initiative. One pedagogical implication of Arango's (2010, 85) study was the recognition of 'the need to include more academic objectives in the English class, which implies a greater sensitivity to the need to integrate language and academic content in the teaching of a foreign language'. This sums up one of the latent and very powerful tensions underlying this case – the traditional perspectives of teachers from different disciplines towards the relative importance of both language and subject-area content and their lack of willingness to try a new, expanded approach where teachers take responsibility for teaching both content and language.

INTRODUCTION

In this chapter, some of the tensions, forces, mechanisms and counterweights that have accompanied the development of bilingual education programmes in Colombia are examined. First of all, there is an overview of the linguistic ecology of the country, followed by a description of key legislation on bilingualism and multilingualism. This is followed by a short account of the different bilingual programmes currently available in Colombia, particularly in the private sector, which has a longer tradition of bilingual education than the state sector. Finally, there is a discussion of some of the forces, mechanisms and counterweights that have both facilitated and constrained these developments.

OVERVIEW OF THE COLOMBIAN CONTEXT

In Latin America in general, according to Hamel (2008), it is possible to distinguish two different spaces with their respective educational systems which, in different ways, aim to support students in becoming bilingual or multilingual. These can be classed as regions where Indigenous[1] languages, such as Quechua, Aymara or Nasa Yuwe, are spoken, and regions where foreign languages, many of them originally immigrant languages, such as English, French or German, are used.

Colombia is a case in point. The terms 'bilingualism' and 'bilingual education' appear in two very different contexts: (1) bilingual programmes in international languages offered to majority-language speakers, and (2) ethno-education programmes designed for members of ethnic-minority communities, both Indigenous and Afro-Colombian. This separation can be explained by the radically different historical and economic conditions in which these two types of educational provision have developed. While bilingualism in internationally prestigious languages, such as Spanish-English, Spanish-French and Spanish-German, provides access to a highly visible, socially accepted form of bilingualism, leading to the possibility of employment in the global marketplace, bilingualism in minority Indigenous or Creole languages leads, in most cases, to an invisible form of bilingualism in which the native language is undervalued and associated with underdevelopment, poverty and backwardness (de Mejía 1996).

Spanish is the official language of Colombia and is spoken by the majority of the population as a first language, and it is used in government and education. It is only in the last two decades that the multilingual and pluricultural nature of the country has been officially recognised in the framework of the Colombian Political Constitution of 1991, when Indigenous languages were awarded co-official status with Spanish for the first time, at least in the territories where they are spoken. Currently there are about 69 separate vernacular languages in existence. These include: Indigenous languages, two native Creoles, as well as Colombian Sign Language and Romani. Many speakers of Indigenous languages are bilingual in Spanish and their native language, although the degree of bilingualism varies widely in different parts of the country (Baker and Prys Jones 1998).

The official policy of ethno-education for minority communities, ratified by the Education Law of 1994, recognised the importance of designing curricula that consider educational provisions that reflect the unique characteristics and beliefs of the Indigenous communities themselves, as well as show respect for their cultures and languages. This is in line with the notion of Intercultural Bilingual Education widely disseminated in Bolivia and Peru (López and Sichra 2008). However, despite these efforts, bilingualism in minority Indigenous or Creole languages is often still not recognised by the wider community and is undervalued (de Mejía 2005).

In a later development, in 2004, the Colombian Ministry of Education (henceforth the Ministry) created The National Bilingual Programme, which aimed to offer all school pupils the possibility of reaching a B1 Common European Framework of Reference for Languages (CEFR) level of proficiency in English at the end of their school studies. More specifically, the goal was:

> To have citizens who are capable of communicating in English, in order to be able to insert the country within processes of universal communication, within the global economy and cultural openness, through [the adopting of] internationally comparable standards. (Ministerio de Educación Nacional 2006b)

This objective should be understood within the context of the divide between private and public education in the country insofar as high-status bilingualism had previously been the privilege of students in private schools that catered to families from higher socio-economic strata. In contrast, since 2004, the Ministry has emphasised the improvement of English-language proficiency among all students within a vision of competitiveness and global development; according to the Ministry, 'to be bilingual means to have more knowledge and opportunities to be competent and competitive and to improve the quality of life of all Colombians' (Al Tablero 2005).

As part of this policy, in 2006, a document entitled *The Basic Standards of Competence in Foreign Languages: English*, based on the CEFR, was formulated by the Ministry with substantial input from the British Council. The rationale given for adopting the CEFR was that it was the result of ten years of research and that it would provide a common frame of reference for assessing foreign-language performance throughout the Colombian educational system, particularly in relation to international standards, as the following quotation shows: 'The adoption of a common referent with other countries will allow Colombia to examine advances in relation to other nations and introduce international parameters at the local level' (Ministerio de Educación Nacional 2006a).

More recently, *The Project for the Strengthening of Foreign Language Competences (English)* (2013) has continued to emphasise English, as part of the *Policy for Relevance and Innovation.* This aims to strengthen 'the communicative competences of teachers and students [in the public sector] to encourage the inclusion of human capital within the knowledge economy and the globalized labour market' (Ministerio de Educación Nacional website 2013). This reflects recent developments in Chile and Mexico, which have launched a series of initiatives such as English Opens Doors (Chile), and The National English Programme for Basic Education (Mexico). The Chilean government initiative, inaugurated in 2003, aims to have all students graduating after eight years of basic education with a CEFR A2 level of English language proficiency. Furthermore, those graduating from Grade 10 would be expected to achieve a B1 level. The programme promotes a communicative methodology centered on conversation and argumentation. English teachers receive 'up-skilling' incentives in the form of immersion programmes and internships in English-speaking countries. An additional initiative entitled The National Strategy of English 2014–2030 was launched in response to data from 2012 which showed that only 18% of the student population had achieved government language learning targets. The Strategy set a target for 50% of learners to achieve the prescribed CEFR levels by 2030 (Ministerio de Educación Nacional, Gobierno de Chile 2014).

The Mexican initiative launched in 2008 was based on both the CEFR standards and a Content and Language Integrated Learning (CLIL) approach. Its goal was to begin the teaching of English in kindergarten, and to continue with this until the end of middle school education (from the ages of 5 to 15) (Mexican Ministry of Education 2011, cited on the PNIEB website 2014).

However, the emphasis on English at the expense of other foreign and vernacular languages in Colombia, as well as the use of the CEFR as a benchmarking tool, has been criticised by academics at some of the leading universities and has resulted, in turn, in defensive statements by the Ministry and the British Council, the agency that had worked together with the Ministry to develop the 'Standards' document referred to above (Ministerio de Educación Nacional 2006a).

OVERVIEW OF BILINGUAL EDUCATION OPTIONS

As noted earlier, bilingual education is traditionally associated with education in the private sector in Colombia, although recently there have been several interesting developments in the public sphere, particularly in Bogotá (Abouchaar et al. 2010). This is similar to the situation in Argentina (as well as in other parts of Latin America) where Banfi and Rettaroli (2008) have noted that these so called 'elite' schools were set up to serve immigrant communities in the nineteenth century. All content areas in these school curricula are taught in both Spanish (the national language) and in the immigrants' heritage language. More recently, in 2001, the government of the City of Buenos Aires set up state-run 'plurilingual schools' to provide bilingual programmes in various foreign languages (English, French, Portuguese and Italian) as part of a drive for greater equity and the 'raising of educational standards ... in socially disadvantaged areas' (Banfi and Rettaroli 2008).

According to a survey carried out in 2001 by de Mejía and Tejada, bilingual schools can be divided roughly into two groups. The first consists of schools that have a strong connection with foreign countries (such as the US, France or the UK) and their governments. These schools often receive direct financial support from those countries and/or are offered foreign teachers. The head teachers of these schools are usually foreign nationals. Many of the learning materials are imported from abroad. Students frequently have the opportunity for direct contact with the foreign country through exchanges or supervised visits organised by the schools. They also often take international exams as well as the Colombian High School Diploma, as required by law. This frequently reduces exposure to English in the secondary school curriculum in contrast to the intense exposure experiences in primary schools, where often 80% of subjects are taught in English (de Mejía et al. 2006), as schools try to ensure that students are able to perform well in the Colombian leaving examinations.

The second group of bilingual schools are national institutions that aim for high levels of proficiency in at least one foreign language, usually English, in addition to the pupils' first language, usually Spanish. Most of these establishments were founded by individuals or small groups of people, generally Colombians (Araújo and Corominas 1996). Some of these schools may be classified as bilingual institutions in the sense that they have a high degree of contact with the foreign language and foreign teachers and they use two languages as media of instruction, yet sometimes they do not identify themselves openly as such because they wish to emphasise their role as educators of Colombian citizens. The head teachers are generally Colombian.

In bilingual education programmes in majority-language contexts in Colombia, there is a steady increase in the use of the second language (L2) throughout the pre-primary and primary levels until the secondary or high-school level, where some decrease in the use of the L2 occurs, as noted by de Mejía and Tejada (2001). In Grade 11 or 12, students are often encouraged to take international examinations. This type of programme is generally considered an enrichment form of education (Hornberger 1991) in which the student's first language is valued and supported at the same time as the foreign language is developed.

Because there is great variety in the programmes and practices of private bilingual schools in the country, it is difficult to characterise them in general terms. However, there is some indication recently of a tendency to integrate the planning and development of different areas of the curriculum so that, for example, the approach adopted towards initial literacy is similar in both Spanish and English. Often this is a result of individual initiative on the part of some teachers. On other occasions, schools appoint a bilingual coordinator who helps to harmonise developments in both languages across the curriculum.

Ethno-education programmes, or bilingual education for communities speaking Indigenous and Creole languages, constitute a third type of provision. These are implemented mainly in state schools which depend on the Ministry of Education at the national level and on the local Education Secretariats at the regional level. In some ways these programmes are similar to the Intercultural Bilingual Education programmes that are sanctioned by a special law in Venezuela which authorises the development of 'curricular design, school calendar, didactic materials, teacher training and relevance in the light of this particular modality' (Ley Orgánica de Educación 2009, Art. 27). In some cases, these programmes are partially supported by community organisations that have educational programmes (such as the Indian Regional Council established in the Cauca Department in the South West of the country), and various NGOs, which promote the notion of 'Indigenous' education with the support of international resources. The programmes are few and far between. The families whose children study in these programmes generally come from isolated rural communities (Indigenous and Afro-Colombian), which suffer the consequences of exclusion, marginalisation and/or armed conflict. The programmes are mainly offered at the primary level. The heterogeneous levels of learner language proficiency and the fact that learners often come from different language groups are common sources of difficulty for educators. These programmes are not well resourced and must deal with a shortage of qualified teachers and appropriate learning materials in the native community languages.

INTRODUCTION TO FORCES, MECHANISMS AND COUNTERWEIGHTS THAT HAVE SHAPED BILINGUAL PROGRAMME DEVELOPMENT

The remainder of this chapter is concerned with analysing in more detail some of the forces, mechanisms and counterweights that have been referred to earlier and which have had an influence on the development of bilingual programmes in Colombia. As alluded to earlier, there is a tension between two powerful forces: the belief in the value of English as an instrument of strategic importance in global communication and gaining an economic advantage, on the one hand, and on the other hand, the value of developing intercultural understanding and tolerance of difference and diversity. A further powerful force is the general perception that Spanish, the national language, carries much greater prestige and value than Indigenous languages.

The next section discusses as a negative force the lack of understanding of the nature and value of interculturality and intercultural communication in many bilingual educational institutions. This is followed by a consideration of how contrasting forces characterised by a monoglossic versus heteroglossic understanding of bilingualism plays out in different educational scenarios, both in policy and in practice. In the last two sections, teacher beliefs (major forces) about the relative importance of language and content teaching and learning within bilingual programmes are analysed. Finally, there is a discussion of tensions inherent in counterweights relating to beliefs about the value of employing native English-speaking teachers as opposed to bilingual Colombian staff.

MIXED DISCOURSES

This section focuses on tensions generated by two different forces relating to the linguistic capital of English in a globalised world on the one hand, and on the other hand, to the development of intercultural understanding based on the learning of other languages and cultures. A major force in bilingual education is the value placed by Colombian parents and the Ministry on English as a mechanism for supporting participation in the global marketplace through the development of language and other intercultural skills. The Ministry (2006b) refers to English as an instrument of strategic communication that allows access to grants and study leave abroad as well as greater and better work opportunities and the consolidation of a 'basis on which to construct the competitive capacity of a society'. This is to be achieved by providing people with 'a comparative advantage, an attribute of their competence and competitivity' (Vélez White 2006). At the same time, there is an emphasis on the desire to help individual students learning English to 'open their minds and accept and understand new cultures'. This force is also characterised as a desire to 'promote interchange between different societies' (Ministerio de Educación Nacional 2006b) and 'to diminish ethnocentrism and allow individuals to appreciate and respect the value of their own world, as well as to develop respect for other cultures … and appreciation of plurality and difference' (Ministerio de Educación Nacional 2006b).

A possible counterweight to the tension between these two forces can be seen in the inclusion by the Ministry of the notions of sociolinguistic competence, and linguistic and pragmatic competence, in the descriptors used in *The Basic Standards of Competence in Foreign Languages: English* (2006b) to characterise the levels of English language proficiency required of students at the end of Grades 3, 5, 7, 9 and 11. Thus, teachers and school administrators are reminded that linguistic competence is not the only goal required in the study of English, but that intercultural understanding is necessary as well.

The widespread belief among the majority of the Colombian population in the value of prestigious international languages and the perception by many, including some Indigenous peoples, that Indigenous languages are of little value in the contemporary world are other influential forces. The perceived value of Spanish as a language of power within the wider national and international context serves as a powerful negative counterweight to the preservation and development of Indigenous languages that are currently being marginalised in education and society at large. The fact that these languages are not widely used in national settings, such as in government, the media, education and business, reinforces perceptions of their low status.

NATIONAL AND FOREIGN INFLUENCES

The tensions deriving from the opposing forces of national versus global identity are the focus of this section. It is argued that there is a dearth of teacher education courses in intercultural communication which could function as mechanisms for deepening understanding in this area.

A tension between 'us and them' or between Colombian and foreign influences is reflected in the curriculum of many of the schools that participated in a study carried out by de Mejía et al. (2006). They argued that this tension is reflected in multiple ways. For example, teachers reported that textbooks were commonly imported from the US, even though they acknowledged that many of the references contained in them were culturally alien to their students. The lack of economic incentive on the part of many foreign publishers to produce culturally appropriate material for the Colombian and Latin American markets is an important factor to be taken into account in this respect. There was recognition on the part of some educators of the importance of helping students to become conscious of their Colombian identity, on the one hand, and, on the other hand, of providing them the necessary skills to function in a globalised world. However, generally speaking, there are few mechanisms, such as guidelines, provided to teachers on how to achieve a critical intercultural vision in practice (Buitrago 1997; de Mejía and Tejada 2001). There is a tendency to relegate the treatment of cultural aspects to the celebration of traditional festivities, both foreign and national, without including richer and more nuanced intercultural considerations as a fundamental structuring principle in the curriculum. This effectively eliminates the opportunity for students to confront their cultural assumptions, particularly in the area of the social sciences, through an examination of the cultural beliefs and practices in other countries. Thus, there is evidence of a lack of understanding (a negative force) of interculturality and intercultural communication in many bilingual schools in the country. Mechanisms such as teacher education courses in culture and intercultural communication are not readily available and not considered as important as the development of linguistic competence in the foreign language.

Furthermore, understanding of the concept of culture itself is also often superficial. While there is an appreciation of difference, there is little reflection on the deeper causes or implications of intercultural differences. This brings to mind Fishman's criticism (1977, cited in García 1991) of bilingual programmes in the US, where biculturalism is trivialised by being limited to singing and dancing routines. This negative force can again be attributed, in part, to a lack of mechanisms such as in-service teacher development programmes and mentoring; this is evidenced by Buitrago's (2002) research into a bilingual education programme in Cali where the teachers 'admitted that they did not have the necessary training' to teach the socio-cultural aspects of the programme.

MONOGLOSSIC AND HETEROGLOSSIC PERSPECTIVES

This section considers how different visions of bilingualism result in powerful forces which influence the ways in which the curriculum and classroom practice are conceived and executed. Monoglossic versus heteroglossic views of bilingualism constitute additional powerful opposing forces that have a major impact on how teaching and learning are organised in Colombian schools. Those with a monoglossic view of bilingualism treat each of a 'child's languages as separate and whole', whilst those with a heteroglossic view hold a more 'integrated plural vision' of bilingualism (Garcia 2009).

A diagnostic study on bilingual education, commissioned by the Ministry in 2006 and carried out by Universidad de los Andes in six different regions of the country, was designed to provide an overview of the state of the art of English-Spanish bilingual programmes. It specifically looked at the characteristics of education in seven international and 18 national private bilingual schools, based on questionnaire, interview and document data. The results confirmed that in the seven international bilingual schools the monoglossic view was dominant (de Mejía et al. 2006). As a consequence, content areas taught in English had little or no direct relationship with those taught in Spanish. However, in three of the schools, there was also evidence of points of articulation between the first and foreign languages in the curriculum. In these schools, the concepts and key information taught through English were reinforced in Spanish in other areas of the curriculum.

In spite of the mainly monoglossic approach evident in the seven international bilingual schools, fifty percent of the 18 national bilingual schools in the same study reported that they integrated the teaching of topics taught in the first language and those taught in the foreign language in content areas, characterising this as a type of 'intertextuality' or interrelationship between literacy processes in the two languages. A key mechanism used in two schools to support this interrelationship and to foster cooperation (a force) was the fusing together of the Spanish and English departments to create a Bilingual department. In yet other cases, there was also evidence that some of the schools kept a clear separation between what was taught in the two languages. For example, this is evidenced in the following quotation, where the Head of Department of a school in Bogotá maintained, 'We have a very independent project as regards English and as regards Spanish; they are not independent republics, but they do have their bases very far apart' (de Mejía et al. 2006).

BELIEFS ABOUT CONTENT AND LANGUAGE

This section will examine forces such as a belief in the efficacy of teaching content through a foreign language and a perception that this is superior to simply teaching a foreign language only in language classes. These beliefs are aligned with differing perceptions by teachers from different disciplines as to the relative importance of language learning as opposed to developing understanding of a particular subject area.

As described in the real-life example at the beginning of this chapter, another key force in the spread of bilingual programmes in Colombia is the belief, particularly among parents, that a bilingual school necessarily teaches certain subjects through a foreign language, as opposed to simply offering intensified foreign language instruction. A further related belief is that a bilingual education programme is necessarily more effective than other types of foreign language provision. However, as also discussed in the real-life example, the traditional perspective of teachers from different disciplines regarding the relative importance of language versus subject-area content is a powerful force that needs to be addressed if teachers are to take responsibility for teaching both content and language.

In a recent study at primary school level, Truscott de Mejía et al. (2012) aimed to characterise current practices in the teaching and learning of academic content in eight bilingual primary schools in Bogotá. Using interview data, classroom observation and document analysis filtered through the lens of case study and cross-case analysis, it was evident that there was tension in some of the schools around the relative weighting that should be accorded to language and content instruction. On the one hand, schools acknowledged that it was important to stimulate the use of English beyond the English language class. On the other hand, seven of the eight schools were concerned that 'the achievements in the different curricular areas (should) not be affected by the emphasis on English'. One of the science teachers described this in the following manner:

> I teach Science in English and for me it is a plus that the children can answer me clearly in English, but if I see that there is a child who finds it difficult to reply in English, but who understands the concept and demonstrates this in Spanish, I say, 'this person is doing what I expect him to do', because I am the Science teacher and I have to evaluate Science, not English.

For this teacher, the scientific content of his class was more important than the teaching and evaluation of the vehicular language being used. This indicates that belief in disciplinary boundaries and a reluctance to assume responsibility for the development of bilingualism, which is often conceived of as the responsibility of the foreign languages department in schools, is a powerful force. Such a force would require an equally powerful counter-weight in order to support the development of a new belief in the value of Content and Language Integrated Learning (CLIL).

TEACHERS

This section continues to focus on teacher beliefs, this time in relation to native speakers, which is also a powerful force influencing programme delivery. Many teachers and parents perceive native-speaking teachers of English as superior to bilingual Colombian staff. Foreign teachers are often hired as a counterweight to redress local teachers' difficulties with regard to target language proficiency levels and cultural knowledge. Yet many foreign teachers do not make a long-term commitment to the schools and face challenges in intercultural communication (de Mejía et al. 2006). For example, de Mejía et al. (2006) suggested that some of the students found foreign teachers to be rather distant and would have liked them to develop a more personal relationship with them. The aforementioned points imply that although foreign teachers represent a helpful mechanism in programme development, this mechanism may bring with it its own set of limitations.

In contrast, hiring native Colombian bilingual teachers to teach in English brings with it other challenges. Specifically, while they may be better able to understand students' difficulties in learning a new language and culture, they often lack sufficient competence in English to use it naturally with their students both inside and outside the classroom; in many cases, these teachers would have found it more 'natural' to have used Spanish with their Colombian students.

Another challenge that has been noticed in recent studies (de Mejía et al. 2006; Gonzalez Moncada 2007) is that bilingual schools have not been able to find bilingual teachers who are qualified to teach non-language subjects such as Science in English so they have instead hired language teachers to teach those subjects. This has raised concerns about how successfully a given non-language subject can be taught by a language teacher. For example, Luz Elena Barragán (2005) argued that English teachers teaching Science would undermine the discipline for the students, as language teachers are generally not experts in this field.

CONCLUSION

In Colombia, bilingualism and bilingual education are complex phenomena. Various beliefs constitute powerful forces that compete with one another. The overwhelming perception that English language proficiency is essential to get on in life leads to an underestimation of the value of bilingualism and bilingual education in other languages, both foreign and Indigenous. This is also reflected in the high status that native English-speaking teachers enjoy. Counterweights offered by mechanisms such as government policies and programmes to strengthen bilingualism and multilingualism in the Indigenous and Creole communities are insufficient to counter the value placed on Spanish and English.

At the school level, this chapter has explored some of the tensions and resistance resulting from protectionism and fear of change in response to bilingual initiatives on the part of key administrative personnel. There is also the traditional divide between practitioners who consider themselves primarily language specialists and those who see their expertise and responsibilities in relation to the content areas they teach. This divide is maintained and possibly reinforced by a lack of mechanisms, such as teacher education courses or mentoring, aimed at promoting deeper understanding of the nature of culture and intercultural understanding among administrative staff, teachers and parents. Furthermore, the difference between monoglossic versus heteroglossic views of bilingualism are two powerful opposing forces that have great influence on curricular decisions about whether a separatist or an integrated (bilingual) approach is implemented.

Bilingualism and bilingual education in Colombia, while apparently supported by key stakeholders in the country, on closer examination is seen to enshrine a series of contradictions that need to be resolved if the education system as a whole is to ensure that, 'the capital and wealth produced for a country by plurilingualism may translate into linguistic capital for each individual and that plurilingualism may become an educational priority' (Ministerio de Educación Nacional 1999).

NOTES

1   'Indigenous' is intentionally capitalised to accord these languages a measure of equal status with other languages.

REFERENCES

Abouchaar, A., Fajardo, L.A. and Vargas, N. (2010). *Informe Final Proyecto Bilingüismo Aditivo por Contenidos para el Distrito Capital*. Bogotá: Universidad Nacional de Colombia.

Arango, L. (2009). *Revisión del Programa de Bilingüismo de un Colegio en Transición de un Programa de Inglés Intensivo a un Programa Bilingüe*. Unpublished MA thesis. Bogotá: Universidad de los Andes.

— (2010). 'Revisión del Programa de Bilingüismo de un Colegio en Transición de un Programa de Inglés Intensivo a un Programa Bilingüe'. *Voces y Silencios: Revista Latinoamericana de Educación*, 1: 1, 69–87.

Araujo, M. C.and Corominas, Y. (1996). *Procesos de Adquisición del Inglés como Segunda Lengua en Niños de 5-6 años de Colegios Bilingües de la Ciudad de Cali*. Unpublished MA thesis. Cali: Universidad del Valle.

Baker, C. and Prys Jones, S. (1998). *Encyclopedia of Bilingualism and Bilingual Education*. Clevedon: Multilingual Matters.

Banfi, C. and Rettaroli, S. (2008). 'Staff Profiles in Bilingual Educational Contexts in Argentina'. In C. Hélot and A.M. de Mejía (eds), *Forging Multilingual Spaces*. Bristol: Multilingual Matters.

Barragán, L.E. (2005). 'Las Ciencias Naturales en un Ambiente Bilingüe'. Unpublished MA thesis. Bogotá: Universidad de los Andes.

Buitrago, H. (1997). 'La Cultura en un Programa de Inmersión en la Sección de Primaria de un Colegio Bilingüe de Cali: Políticas y Prácticas Pedagógicas'. Unpublished MA thesis. Cali: Universidad del Valle.

— (2002). 'Aprender de una Cultura vs. Aprender otra Cultura. Un Enfoque Intercultural para Colegios Bilingües'. In A.M. de Mejía and R. Nieves Oviedo (eds), *Nuevos Caminos en Educación Bilingüe en Colombia*. Cali: Universidad del Valle.

de Mejía, A.M. (1996). 'Educación Bilingüe: Consideraciones para Programas Bilingües en Colombia'. *El Bilingüismo de los Sordos*, 1:2, 21-25.

— (ed.) (2005). *Bilingual Education in South America*. Clevedon: Multilingual Matters.

de Mejía, A.M. and Tejada, H. (2001). 'La Construcción de Modalidades Bilingües en Colegios Monolingües de Cali: Colegio Gimnasio la Colina'. Unpublished research report.

de Mejía, A.M., Ordóñez, C. and Fonseca, L. (2006). *Estudio Investigativo sobre el Estado Actual de la Educación Bilingüe (Inglés-Español) en Colombia. Informe de Investigación*. Ministerio de Educación Nacional/Universidad de los Andes.

García, O. (1991). *Bilingual Education: Focusshrift in Honor of Joshua A. Fishman on the Occasion of his 65th Birthday*. Amsterdam/Philadelphia: John Benjamins.

— (2009). *Bilingual Education in the 21st Century: A Global Perspective*. Oxford: Wiley Blackwell.

Gonzalez Moncada, A. (2007). 'Professional Development of EFL Teachers in Colombia: Between Colonial and Local Practices'. *Íkala*, 12: 18, 309–32.

Hamel, R. (2008). 'Plurilingual Latin America: Indigenous languages, Immigrant Languages, Foreign Languages – Towards an Integrated Policy of Language and Education'. In C. Hélot and A.M. de Mejía (eds), *Forging Multilingual Spaces*. Bristol: Multilingual Matters.

Hornberger, N.H. (1991). 'Extending Enrichment Bilingual Education: Revisiting Typologies and Redirecting Policy'. In O. García (ed.), *Bilingual Education: Focusschrift in Honor of Joshua A. Fishman*, 1. Amsterdam/Philadelphia: John Benjamins.

Ley Orgánica de Educación (2009). 'La Asamblea Nacional de la República Bolivariana de Venezuela'.

López, L.E. and Sichra, I. (2008). 'Intercultural Bilingual Education'. In N.H. Hornberger and J. Cummins (eds), *Encyclopedia of Language and Education*, 5. New York: Springer.

Ministerio de Educación Nacional (1999). *Lineamientos Curriculares: Idiomas Extranjeros*. Bogotá: Ministerio de Educación Nacional.

— (2006a). *Educación: Visión 2019*. Bogotá: Ministerio de Educación Nacional.

— (2006b). *Estándares Básicos de Competencias en Lenguas Extranjeras: Ingles*. Bogotá: Ministerio de Educación.

Ministerio de Educación Nacional, Gobierno de Chile (2014). *Programa Inglés Abre Puertas*. www.ingles.mineduc.cl.

Secretaría de Educación Pública (2014). *National English Program in Basic Education*. www.sepbcs.gob.mx.

Truscott de Mejía, A.M., Peña Dix, B., Arciniegas de Vélez, M.C. and Montiel Chamorro, M.L. (eds) (2012). *Exploraciones sobre el Aprendizaje de Lenguas y Contenidos en Programas Bilingües*. Bogotá: Ediciones Uniandes.

Vélez White, M.C. (2006). Carta Abierta. *Estándares Básicos de Competencias en Lenguas Extranjeras: Ingles*. Bogotá: Ministerio de Educación Nacional.

FORCES	MECHANISMS
Key values in human relations	**People**
Equity or lack thereof Cultural understanding or lack thereof	Committed, ambitious parents
	Knowledge building
Principles for cooperation	Research
Stakeholder inclusion Recognition of local expertise Valuing foreign expertise	**Agreements**
	Legislation –National Bilingual Programme Common European Framework of Reference Language proficiency standards Cooperation agreements with British Council
Goals	
A desire to close the gap between private education Provision and public or state education Relationship building Global competitiveness	**Missing vehicles**
	Training programmes in teaching culture and intercultural communication
Beliefs	**Teachers**
A belief in the future instrumental benefits of bilingual education (particularly in English) A belief that Indigenous and Creole languages are Considerably less valuable than Spanish and English A monoglossic versus heteroglossic view Status Prestige	Bilingual local teachers Foreign teachers
	Learning materials
	Culturally suitable or unsuitable materials
	Management structures
	A bilingual department

COUNTERWEIGHTS

Fear of change	Global, governmental and parental pressure
Elitism	Equal language rights for all
Emphasis on one language	Emphasis on a variety of languages
Foreign influence	National orientations
Teaching language and content separately	Integration of content and language

13 SOUTH AFRICA:
Three Periods of Bilingual or Multilingual Education

Kathleen Heugh (University of South Australia)

CHAPTER NAVIGATOR

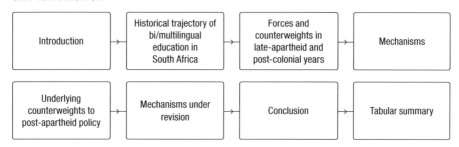

INTRODUCTION

Since the mid-nineteenth century, South African education has been characterised by a series of language education policies in which bilingual and/
or multilingual education have been initiated for socio-political and educational reasons, and then terminated or thwarted for competing socio-political, rather than educational reasons. The education policies and practices of
the country offer those interested in colonial and post-colonial theory an example of how policy may oscillate between a monolingual and a multilingual
view of education depending on which political forces are most powerful at
a particular time. This example sheds light on the residual and reproductive
nature of both a monolingual (Anglocentric) habitus (Gogolin 2009) and a
bi/multilingual resistance to forces of Anglicisation that have been sustained
for two centuries. The South African case also offers a longitudinal, if inter-
mittently broken, history of comparative research on the merits and demer-
its of bilingual and monolingual English-medium education from the 1930s
onwards.

A brief historical discussion of bi/multilingual education in South Africa
provides a background to current forces and counterweights that oscillate

away from and towards bi/multilingual education. Bilingual education first appeared in South Africa in the mid-nineteenth century as a feature of Dutch-settler (Boer) resistance to a British policy of Anglicisation. Residual antipathy towards Anglicisation became a significant contributory force that led to a segregationist conceptualisation of multiple parallel, but separate, forms of mother-tongue education with bilingual and trilingual components between 1948 and 1994. The purpose of multiple parallel mother-tongue-based systems was to separate communities along lines of race, colour, and linguistic affiliation. This site is also one in which ideological change intent on socio-political, economic and educational integration since 1994 has been accompanied by an education policy based on principles of additive bi/multilingual education. Whereas the apartheid regime effected its iteration of multiple parallel mother-tongue education systems with speed and efficacy in order to secure what were thought to be vulnerable interests of the Afrikaans-speaking minority, the current political regime has not yet begun to implement its multilingual policy 20 years after claiming majority rule and interest in equal human (including linguistic) rights. This is even though the most recent policy has been intended to contribute towards socio-political and educational equality, and appears to be supported by significant mechanisms and resources to assist implementation. The first purpose of the following discussion is to offer insights into the historical and contemporary dynamics of policy change and resistance. A second purpose is to utilise the force-counterweight lens in an attempt to peel away the conventional explanations of policy attributed to governmentality (e.g. Foucault 1991; Pennycook 2002) and to turn the gaze towards key agents with interests in policy-making and resistance. A third purpose is to demonstrate that mechanisms put in place to effect policy are only successful when they match both explicit and implicit policy intent and design.

HISTORICAL TRAJECTORY OF BI/MULTILINGUAL EDUCATION IN SOUTH AFRICA

Britain attempted colonisation of territory and Anglicisation of people in what today is South Africa on several occasions in the late eighteenth and early nineteenth centuries, finally succeeding in colonising two coastal regions, the Cape in 1820 and Natal by 1844. Displaced Boer (mainly Dutch, but also German and Huguenot) settlers who had been in the region since the mid-seventeenth century 'trekked' inland, where they established independent territories known as the Orange Free State and Transvaal Republics by 1854. Education and the medium of instruction were of particular importance to the Boers in terms of linguistic, cultural and faith-based identity. Whereas they resisted the English-only regimes for 'white' Dutch and English-speaking settlers in the British territories, the Boers were satisfied with either Dutch (mother tongue)-medium or bilingual Dutch-English medium primary school education in their territories. Secondary education in these areas was provided in bilingual configurations of Dutch-English or English medium. British interest in the discovery of gold in the Boer Republics led to the South African (Anglo-Boer) War of 1899–1902, which concluded with a British victory and annexation of the former republics. The British administration immediately introduced a policy of Anglicisation across the entire region, prohibiting Dutch-medium and bilingual Dutch-English-medium education for children of Anglo or Dutch origin. The education of African children was left to missionary organisations that taught through the medium of local African languages for the first four to six years of primary school, followed by a switch to English-medium instruction. By 1906, the Anglicisation policy began to weaken and, as a result of political negotiations to formalise a Union of South Africa in 1910 in which the two European settler communities were enfranchised, both English and Dutch were declared official languages. This meant that the principle of mother-tongue education was guaranteed and bilingual (dual-medium) Afrikaans-English education was restored in many parts of the country, including for children of European and mixed descent (so-called 'coloured'). However, the psychological and residual damage of linguistic policies of Anglicisation and resistance set in motion a chain of language education policy decisions that continue to exert pressure on the current policies of bilingual and multilingual education. These are discussed below.

By World War II, research demonstrated that the degree of societal bilingualism attained amongst communities using a creolised Dutch (renamed Afrikaans in 1925) and English was highest among those who attended bilingual schools (Malherbe 1946). A study of the academic achievement of 18 000 students in 1938 provided evidence of the educational and socially integrative advantages of bilingual education (Malherbe 1946). Additional research among South African soldiers during World War II confirmed these data and also provided evidence of a correlation between the degree of Afrikaans-English bilingual proficiency and social integration among the speakers of the two languages (Malherbe 1977).

In 1948, a segregationist government, dominated by speakers of Afrikaans who bore historical fear of and resentment towards speakers of English, came into power. Their intent was to secure ethnolinguistic and faith-based protection from Anglo-interests for the white Afrikaans-speaking minority community through a system of separate ethnolinguistic (apartheid) social control. One of the most effective ways to put this into operation was through separate and parallel education systems for children, divided along lines of 'race' and linguistic identity. Although the principle of bilingualism for all school students was upheld, bilingual (dual-medium) schools for speakers of English and Afrikaans were discouraged, and replaced with separate mother-tongue-based primary and secondary schools for all children. In some cases, schools implemented a parallel bilingual system in which children were divided into separate Afrikaans and English cohorts within the same school. All students were nevertheless expected to become bilingual in Afrikaans and English, or trilingual in an African (mother-tongue) language plus Afrikaans and English by the time they exited secondary school, even though they were separated in linguistically ghettoised schools or streams within schools. This was an education system that promoted bilingual and trilingual education for students, but in a segregated and unequally resourced system that advantaged 'white' Afrikaans- and English-speaking children, and provided what appeared to be additional linguistic hurdles for African children. Afrikaans- and English-speaking students were expected to develop bilingual proficiency through 12 years of mother-tongue-medium and 12 years of second language-as-a-subject education. African children, however, were to receive eight years of mother-tongue medium and five years of Afrikaans and English as subjects in primary school (third to eighth year). Then they were expected to continue with three languages as subjects throughout secondary school and to use Afrikaans as a medium of instruction for Mathematics plus one other subject, and English for Science plus one other subject. The African mother tongue was also continued as a medium of instruction for non-academic subjects.

At one level, the education system served to ensure that the requirement to implement the official Afrikaans-English bilingual policy across the country was equally distributed across the education system for each linguistic group. At another, it served the purpose of promoting the principle of mother-tongue education for all groups. Had African parents been offered the opportunity to choose either English- or Afrikaans-medium education for the five years of secondary school, it is likely that most would have opted for English. This is because English had come to signify political and economic liberation within African politics since the early twentieth century (Alexander 1989) and English came to carry the symbolic capital of education. So it is not surprising that African parents viewed the discrepancy in linguistic require-ments (three languages for African students, two languages for others) and the requirement for some subjects to be taught through Afrikaans in sec-ondary, as inequitable and also as a deliberate effort to limit access to English. Thus, the perceived inequity and perceived restriction on educational access to English resulted in robust resistance from African and other disadvan-taged communities against what they understood as an 'Afrikanerisation' of education. In other words, Afrikanerisation of education spawned responses from politically disadvantaged African communities similar to those from the Boer community towards the earlier British policy of Anglicisation. However, whereas the Boers' response had been towards protection and ad-vancement of their own language, African parents turned towards English. The desire for English amongst speakers of African languages coincided with evidence that each of the former British colonies in Southern and Eastern Africa opted for an English-dominant education system, particularly for sec-ondary school education, from the mid-1960s onwards. At the time, few rec-ognised that, although African parents in South Africa were correct and that government policy had been intended to dilute access to English, the educa-tional implementation of policy was to show unintentional advantages for African school students. Between 1955 and 1978, retention rates to the end of secondary school steadily increased (albeit from a low base), and secondary school leaving certificate examination pass rates increased from 43.5% in 1955 to 83.7% by 1976, the highest level in the history of education in the country to date. Unwittingly, the apartheid government, simply because it was intent on a mother-tongue-based approach to education in order to pro-tect the ethnolinguistic identity of Afrikaans-speaking children, happened also to offer African students an educationally sound language policy. It was one most likely to offer prospects of achievement across the curriculum, in-cluding an opportunity to develop strong proficiency in English. However, this only became evident after retrospective analyses of school achievement data that spanned years of apartheid rule (Heugh 1999).

Growing resistance and civil revolt from African-language speaking com-munities who demanded increased access to English-medium education resulted in the government reducing African mother-tongue-medium edu-cation to four years and removing the requirement of Afrikaans-medium education for half of the (non-language) secondary school subjects by 1978. What nobody anticipated at the time was that school-leaving completion and achievement rates for African high-school students from this point on-wards would begin to decline. By 1990, research identified the transition from mother-tongue-medium education at the end of Grade 4 to English-medium education in Grade 5 as a major contributory factor to unprecedented rates of failure, attrition from Grade 5 onwards and low retention to the end of primary school (Macdonald 1990). This was followed by declines in student achievement in secondary school, including in English. The secondary school leaving pass rate for English declined from 78.2% in 1978 to 38.5% in 1984 (Hartshorne 1992). Most parents or leaders of the resistance movements did not understand that the declining achievement of students with African home languages was related to the change of language policy. Most (English speakers) shied away from pointing towards the connection between home language and learning, despite growing evidence in the literature and research from North America at the time (e.g. several authors in Skutnabb-Kangas and Cummins 1988). They were also reluctant to acknowledge an association between declining student achievement and the earlier introduction of English-medium education compared with achievement in the years in which mother-tongue medium had been used for eight years of primary school.

FORCES AND COUNTERWEIGHTS IN LATE APARTHEID AND POST-COLONIAL YEARS

Increasing political resistance through the 1980s led to six years of political negotiations designed to end apartheid and to usher in a post-colonial and democratic order in 1994 within an equality-driven rights-based constitution (Republic of South Africa/RSA 1996). The negotiations included a complex array of stakeholders across the political spectrum, including those affiliated with the politics of: (a) 'white' Afrikaner-ethnolinguistic identity and the apartheid regime; (b) neoliberal Anglocentric identities, and (c) several significant strands of black resistance political movements to the left of the others. Stakeholders with political influence within what was to become a new African National Congress (ANC) government led by Nelson Mandela included those who had either been imprisoned or obliged to live in exile for two to three decades during the apartheid era. Stakeholders who aligned themselves with the ANC included an influential group of English-speaking academics who had occupied senior positions in English-medium universities during the apartheid years. Several of these academics had objected to the hegemony of Afrikaans and the skewing of resources towards Afrikaans-medium universities during apartheid, and anticipated language policy changes that would re-establish the privileged status of English in universities under the new ANC-led government (e.g. Ridge 2000).

Other stakeholders within anti-apartheid groupings, who had been engaged in literacy and alternative education NGOs during the latter years of apartheid, took a different stance towards an English-dominant policy. Researchers connected with two of these NGOs, the National Language Project (NLP) and the Project for the Study of Alternative Education in South Africa (PRAESA, based at the University of Cape Town), found historical and comparative evidence from elsewhere in Africa of the need to build on mother-tongue or home-language literacy within bilingual or multilingual approaches to education. They drew attention to research from the 1930s, which indicated that there were educational advantages to bilingual education. It is notable that this research was conducted prior to the apartheid regime's language education policy changes, which introduced separate systems of mother-tongue-based bilingual education for speakers of Afrikaans and English and separate systems of mother-tongue-based multilingual education for African children. The 1930s research should, therefore, not be conflated with that conducted during apartheid (Heugh 1987, 1999; de Klerk 2002). In 1991, at the end of an international academic boycott against apartheid in South Africa, the NLP under the auspices of the University of Cape Town hosted the first language (policy) conference to include scholars from elsewhere in Africa in order to debate possibilities for post-apartheid language policy. The conference included South Africans who represented a broad spectrum of political and educational stakeholder interests, including those associated with or sympathetic to the ANC, considered to be a government-in-waiting. The scholars from other parts of Africa made it clear to South African participants that after three decades of independence from colonial rule, the English-dominant education systems in Zimbabwe, Zambia, Nigeria, Botswana, Tanzania, Malawi and Kenya had failed to deliver successful outcomes for students. With the exception of Zimbabwe, retention rates of African children to the end of primary school remained low and by secondary it was even lower (several authors in Crawhall 1992). The evidence increasingly pointed towards the need for longer primary education in the local languages plus English – in other words, a multilingual education system that would provide strong bilingual education for each child. There was a fundamental difference between the apartheid system, which utilised mother-tongue-based bilingual and multilingual education, and the proposals for post-apartheid bilingual and multilingual education. In the former, mother-tongue-based bilingual or multilingual education was conceptualised as part of a segregated and unequally resourced education system that would benefit speakers of Afrikaans and English, and simultaneously offer advantages along lines of race or colour. The latter, the proposal for bilingual

and multilingual education in post-apartheid South Africa, was conceptualised as falling within an integrated national department of education and
was designed to ensure equal opportunity for students to receive meaningful
education with equitable educational outcomes.

The ANC and its affiliates simultaneously launched a National Education
Policy Initiative (NEPI) to articulate proposals for post-apartheid education
policy that would achieve equity. This included a focus on language education. Although there was informal collaboration between the NLP and
NEPI, powerful English speakers with respected ANC credentials within
NEPI found it difficult to accept proposals for bilingual and multilingual
education that emphasised extended use of home language (mother tongue)
even if this were to include well-resourced teaching of English (NEPI 1992,
Taylor and Vinjevold 1999). Several senior NEPI members had been in exile
in other African countries and had accepted what seemed to be an inevitable post-colonial position on language education. No other post-colonial
African government had adopted an approach that included extensive use
of multiple African languages as primary languages of instruction. This was
despite the advice of African scholars and long-standing research evidence
in these countries that pointed towards the failure of English-dominant systems. There were nevertheless divided positions on this matter within NEPI.
Members of the NEPI team who had not been in exile were very much aware,
particularly through discussion with the scholars from other African countries at the NLP conference, that student attrition and repeater rates indicated
the failure of English- (or French-, or Portuguese-) dominated education systems in African countries from the mid-1960s onwards. Despite this, senior
NEPI members advising the ANC ahead of a change of government in 1994
were not prepared to accept the substantial use of African languages as part
of a bilingual education system. By the early 1990s, there were two very dif-
ferents sets of language education policy proposals within the anti-apartheid
groups: one that was convinced that the country needed to move towards
an English-dominant education system in order to achieve socio-political
and educational equity; and another that was convinced that the only way to
achieve this would be through a bi/multilingual education system.

Language education policy was also broached in a broader forum. This was
one concerned with constitutional negotiations involving the major political
groupings and which was to lead to a change of government in 1994 and a
human-rights-based constitution in 1996. The NLP-PRAESA language education research team was invited by each of the different political parties to
the political left and right of the ANC to discuss language education research
findings that might contribute towards an inclusive and equitable policy.

The ANC preferred its own internally-driven advisory process. As indicated above, this was favourable to an English-dominant focus, despite the advice of its own language education research task group (led by Zubeida Desai who had also been one of the NEPI group that recognised the research evidence offered by African scholars at The NLP conference discussed above).

In the end, the ANC recognised that a major blockage to a political settlement at the negotiating table was that speakers of Afrikaans were afraid that an ANC government would reduce the status of Afrikaans and, thus, place restrictions on the official use of Afrikaans after 1994. Speakers of Afrikaans were afraid that the ANC were about to usher in a repeat of the British policy of Anglicisation after the Anglo-Boer War. The ANC was wary of a right-wing response that this might unleash. So a compromise agreement was reached to replace the previous policy of two official languages, English and Afrikaans, accompanied by 'official recognition' of nine African languages, with a new policy to include 11 official languages in the Constitution (RSA 1996). Equal official status for 11 languages appeared to head off the emphasis towards and preference of the ANC for English. The constitution also included provision for an 'independent' statutory body, the Pan South African Language Board (PANSALB) to promote multilingualism, to protect minority languages, and to monitor government implementation of the actual policy that was expected to follow. It appeared for a while that the principles included in the constitution paved the way for the articulation of a strong multilingual education policy based on robust support for the home language (mother tongue) plus English for all students.

MECHANISMS

The discussion now turns towards the mechanisms that were put in place during apartheid to implement its version of a multilingual policy and to compare these with those adopted by the post-apartheid system. First, in each historical period, the government introduced new education policy. Second, it introduced specific mechanisms to support and implement that policy. Under apartheid, these mechanisms worked well because policy was clear and the government was determined to carry through policy. Under the ANC-led government, language policy has been treated with ambivalence, in part because it has been understood within the ANC as a compromise to keep right-wing speakers of Afrikaans from engaging in armed resistance to change. The mechanisms initially set in place to support language education policy, however, were systematically undermined through a sequence of decisions that were subsequently taken for reasons that had little to do with implementation of policy. In other words, they arose from a lack of commitment to policy, as will be shown below.

During apartheid, the government put in place particular mechanisms to ensure effective implementation of its language education policy. The first mechanism was to set out language education policy in the Bantu Education Act of 1953. The second was to locate language education planning in a directorate under the National Department of Education. The third was to decentralise language education planning to a number of departments of education for 'white', 'coloured', Indian and African children. Within these directorates, further mechanisms were put in place. The directorate in the National Department of Education included specific units for terminology development and translation for educational purposes in Afrikaans. Mechanisms to implement language policy for African-language-speaking children within the Department of Bantu Education included further devolvement to parallel departments of education in the 'so called' independent homelands for seven African-language-speaking groups. These language planning mechanisms led to an expansion of a chain of support services for language education in the seven African languages, including state-run services for translation and terminology development. Independent language boards established to standardise orthographies from the early twentieth century were co-opted to work alongside the Department of Bantu Education and/or each language's designated education department. This gave the language boards expanded responsibilities but also partly compromised their political independence. Their role was to participate in lexicographic and terminology development, to promote the writing of literacy materials and literary texts, and to monitor teams of textbook writers who were commissioned by the Department of Bantu Education in association with textbook publishers. Scholars of African languages located within universities led the lexicographic endeavour required for dictionaries, usually in collaboration with language boards. Publishers of school textbooks and reading materials in each of the recognised languages were required to adhere to quality-control mechanisms in liaison with the language boards and university-based language experts (e.g. Mahlalela-Thusi and Heugh 2010). The government-allocated expenditure per school student was on a sliding scale in which the highest allocations favoured white students. Despite relatively minimal expenditure on African education and relatively archaic technologies for translation, parallel sets of textbooks, dictionaries and readers were made available in each of the designated languages within the first few years of policy initiation in 1955, and these continued until the late 1970s. Under apartheid then, the implementation of policy was followed through with a series of mechanisms and strategies that involved government departments and effective collaboration with groups of language professionals outside government (i.e. language boards, university-based academics and publishers).

After apartheid, mechanisms to support multilingual education were initially established that would align with the 1996 constitutional provisions. These were swiftly undermined, however, as shall be discussed below, and whereas a chain of interconnected support services flourished during apartheid and a plethora of literary materials in African language were developed and published, this has not happened during the post-apartheid years.

Post-apartheid mechanisms that were to support the policy were located within three agencies: an 'independent' statutory body, the Pan South African Language Board (mentioned earlier), the Department of Arts, Culture, Science and Technology, and the Department of Education. The constitution provided for the establishment of a watchdog body, the Pan South African Language Board (PANSALB), to monitor government's articulation of and implementation of national language policy, including language education policy. The new national Department of Education (DOE) was to assume overall responsibility for language education policy. However, overall responsibility for language policy and implementation was shifted from the DOE, where it had been during apartheid, to the Department of Arts, Culture, Science and Technology (DACST, later Department of Arts and Culture, DAC). Thus, the directorate responsible for language planning and language services was removed from the DOE to the DACST. This directorate was given more responsibilities with regard to the expansion of language planning, translation and terminology development services. The relocation of the directorate, however, served to remove a significant mechanism required for language education policy implementation from the DOE. It therefore left a structural gap within the DOE. This gap was amplified by a lack of co-operation between the two departments, DOE and DACST, with key officials in each refusing to co-operate with one another (Heugh 2003). Although PANSALB was originally established as an independent statutory body in 1996, legislative amendments in 1999 brought the board under the financial and administrative control of the DAC. This restricted its capacity to fulfil its 'watchdog' function over government language policy and implementation, and thus prevented it from executing its constitutional obligations (Heugh 2003, Makoni 2003). This coincided with a change of leadership within the ANC-led government when Nelson Mandela stepped down as President of the country in 1999. He was followed by Thabo Mbeki, who was less inclined to be concerned about the language-related sensitivities of the

Afrikaans-speaking community and more inclined to favour an English-only policy. Mbeki appointed a new Minister of Education, Kader Asmal, in 1999, who was expected to follow suit. The new Minister of Education refused to meet with PANSALB, by then regarded as a responsibility of the Minister of Arts and Culture. PANSALB made numerous attempts to meet Minister Asmal about the (non-)implementation of the policy on language in education during his term of office, 1999–2004, to no avail.[1] The refusal of the Minister to meet with PANSALB underscored the structural fragility of mechanisms that had initially been intended to support the implementation of language education policy in the post-apartheid years. From 2000 onwards, PANSALB has been able to contribute very little by way of support, protection or monitoring of government policy development and implementation. What PANSALB did do, however, was disband or render illegitimate the old language boards that had contributed toward the resourcing of multilingual policy of the previous government. PANSALB replaced these old boards with new substructures responsible for each language, but these have not been able to fulfil their responsibilities, while the expertise held in the old boards withered. Thus PANSALB has failed as a useful mechanism to acquit its responsibilities, largely because of legislative changes which stripped it of its power, and because it was placed under a government department at odds with the department responsible for education. It further unwittingly disempowered other structures that had been supporting the development of resources for the use of African languages in education prior to the political changes of the mid-1990s.

Meanwhile, once the directorate for language planning had been moved from the DOE to DACST, the DOE proceeded with language education policy on its own and without the support of DACST, and within a few years also without the support of PANSALB. It appointed two advisory teams in 1995, one to focus on curriculum and assessment transformation, and one to focus on new language-in-education policy. The curriculum team was led by those who had held senior positions in the ANC and NEPI process, while the language policy group included the former director of the NLP and then current director of PRAESA, Neville Alexander, who by this time was also a member of PANSALB. Thus, the curriculum team was one which was more comfortable with the idea that English should be the main language of education across the country for African children after the third year of education. This view is in line with practice in other post-colonial countries. Alexander, although not having been directly involved in the language education research or policy proposals submitted to the constitutional assembly, was invited to lead language education policy discussions with the DOE. His presence and contribution to the policy discussions turned out to have mixed consequences, as will be discussed. In other words, in the absence of a directorate responsible for language education in the DOE, in the absence of adequate co-operation between DOE and DACST, and in the division of responsibilities for the advisory groups on language and curriculum policy, it was inevitable that contradictions and theoretical mismatches would arise.

As might be predicted, curriculum and assessment policy (DOE 1997a) reverted to previous versions with an early transition to English-medium education for the majority (78%) of school students, i.e. African-language speaking students. The language-in-education policy (DOE 1997b) followed an additive approach to bilingual and multilingual education based on the principle of extended use of the mother tongue/home language plus systematic provision of English, as consistent with the research available at the time. The theoretical contradiction between the two policies was papered over in the introduction to the curriculum document, which claimed alignment. Since there was no structural home for the implementation of language education policy within the DOE, the directorate responsible for curriculum development was left to implement curriculum and language policy. It did this through a narrow interpretation of policy designed to lead African school students from three years of home-language medium education to an early transition to English in Grade 4 in successive iterations of curriculum policy and revision (DOE 1997a, 2002; DBE 2011). Not only this, but this directorate was responsible for destroying all of the archived educational materials developed in African languages during the apartheid period (Mahlalela-Thusi and Heugh 2010). In other words, it destroyed resources that could have been used to build upon, revise and inform the development of new materials in the current period.

What we can say is that policy and mechanisms for policy implementation were aligned during apartheid and that multilingual education was established, resourced and maintained during this period, albeit for the wrong reasons of inequitable segregation. In contrast, policy and the mechanisms put in place in the years after the change of government in the mid-1990s are characterised by misalignment and inconsistency, and have either not supported or have undermined multilingual education, even to the point of destroying resources that could be used to implement policy. This is the case even though policy was intended to ensure equitable educational opportunity, to ensure social integration and to offer African children a meaningful education in which they could achieve educational success.

UNDERLYING COUNTERWEIGHTS TO POST-APARTHEID POLICY

There have been numerous arguments offered as counterweights to post-apartheid language education policy. These have been voiced particularly by those committed to the English-dominant education paradigm and who are also key advisors to the DOE. One argument offered is that the 1997 multilingual education policy either cannot work or does not work (e.g. Taylor and Vinjevold 1999; Murray 2002; Fleisch 2008). However, to date no serious attempt has been made to implement the policy (e.g. Desai 2013; Heugh 2013), and thus it cannot be evaluated as if it had been implemented. While the weak mechanisms for implementation discussed above and the proponents of an English-dominant argument are part of the reason for this failure, there are additional counterweights which provide further explanation.

The first additional explanation relates to longstanding ideological differences between various anti-apartheid political movements, from the 1960s onward, specifically between the more moderate ANC and more radical left-wing Neville Alexander. Alexander was in prison with the ANC leadership, and his political views overlapped with those of the ANC on many matters. However, they differed in relation to their views on the political-economy and on the role of African languages in a post-apartheid South Africa. This led to different stances towards a multilingual education system as proposed by researchers in the two NGOs that were led by Alexander (the NLP and PRAESA) and the more English-dominant paradigm of the ANC. Alexander's disagreements with some key ANC officials therefore coloured the organisation's view of the language education research conducted within the NLP and PRAESA, confirmed by scholars from other African countries in the NLP's 1990 conference, and as influenced the DOE's 1997 language-in-education policy. This underlying tension contributed to a marginalisation of the language-in-education policy after it had been officially adopted by the Ministry of Education in 1997.

A further counterweight relates to an ongoing cycle of reasons advanced by government officials to explain why the policy cannot be implemented. These include a number of residual misconceptions that have little evidential support. The first entails the proposition that parents refuse bilingual education based on the home language because, allegedly, they associate it with the mother-tongue education policy intended to segregate society under apartheid. The second is a claim that the costs of developing teaching and learning materials in 11 languages is prohibitive. The third is a claim that there are insufficient, or no, teaching and learning materials in African languages, and that there is an insufficient pool of personnel with the expertise to develop materials and to translate these into the African languages. A fourth is that there is limited, or no, terminology in African languages suitable for educational contexts. A fifth is that school students use hybridised or evolving languages rather than conventionally conceptualised language systems, and that this therefore makes it impossible to teach African languages in schools (e.g. Taylor and Vinjevold 1999). The first four claims are ones that have been circulating in African countries more widely for the last six decades.

PANSALB, although not able to intervene directly in the failure to implement policy, undertook research that demonstrated that some of the above claims had little evidential foundation in the South African context. For example, a National Sociolinguistic Survey of the country was commissioned by PANSALB. It established that 88% of South Africans across all groups and over the age of 15 support well-resourced home-language instruction and strong English-language instruction, i.e. bilingual education for students from each language background (PANSALB 2000). Only 12% of respondents favoured an English-only education system. At the time of data collection, approximately 9% of the respondents were speakers of English, suggesting that a very small percentage of speakers of languages other than English believed that English-dominant education was most desirable. These data conflict with the unsubstantiated claims made by government sources regarding the support for English-dominant education. Studies of the costs and benefits of various types of language education policy indicate that investment in strong home-language medium instruction plus strong teaching of English are likely to be recovered through lower repeater costs over five years (Cole 2005). To date, there has been no research data to show that bilingual or multilingual education is more costly than monolingual education in a former colonial language over the medium to long term in any African country (Ouane and Glanz 2011). The PANSALB survey also found that the majority of respondents identified closely with one or two languages. Although they may very well engage in multilingual practices of code-switching and the use of new urban varieties, this does not necessarily negate their identification with more conventionally understood language varieties (Heugh 2007).

MECHANISMS UNDER REVISION

Some of the mechanisms set in place to implement language education policy appear to be under revision. This is because student achievement, particularly in relation to literacy and numeracy, has been of serious concern for the last two decades. Despite considerable resources directed towards educational transformation in the country, there have not yet been noticeable returns on this investment (DBE 2010; DBE 2013a). While there have been several attempts at curriculum revision (e.g. DOE 1997a, 2002; DBE 2011), curriculum documents continue to assume a maximum of three years of home-language-medium instruction for African children, followed by transition to English by or before the fourth year of primary. Subsequent to a series of reports on the failure of primary education across the system (e.g. DBE 2013a), it seemed as if the department was intending to revise language policy and its implementation in a draft document, *The Incremental Introduction of African Languages in South African Schools* (DBE 2013b). However, since the release of the document, the focus on revision has been limited to expanding the teaching of African languages as subjects to speakers of Afrikaans and English (approximately 22% of students in the system). The document appears to have lost sight of extending the use of African languages as media of teaching and learning beyond Grade 3. In other words, there has been no effort directed toward extending the teaching and learning of African languages to the 78% majority of students in the country who need this the most. Where there are innovative approaches that explore multilingual school-based education, these have been initiated by educators who work either within the NGO sector or within universities (e.g. Benson and Plüddemann 2010; Desai 2013; Probyn 2009). While government agencies are aware of these interventions, they avert their gaze. In the absence of a dedicated directorate for language policy and planning within the national education system, there is an inability to devise a mechanism to ensure that there is alignment between policy, planning and implementation. There is also an inability or unwillingness to collaborate with stakeholders in and outside the country who have the expertise to contribute towards policy implementation.

CONCLUSION

The South African case demonstrates the residual knock-on effects of implementation of a discriminatory language policy. Anglicisation and Afrikanerisation of education were each implemented in order to subjugate at least one section of society. The apartheid system identified a single mechanism to oversee the planned implementation of its policy. This was a directorate within the National Department of Education, replicated in the Department of Bantu Education, and also partially devolved to parallel departments of education for 'independent homelands'. Implementation was effective and strengthened through collaboration with various sets of stakeholders engaged in several aspects of language development and service provision, literary authorship, linguistic scholarship and the publishing industry. However, the regimented implementation of this policy and its association with mother-tongue education and limited access to English resulted in a stigmatisation of the use of African mother tongues in education and advanced the trajectory, particularly in the minds of ANC aligned stakeholders, towards English. On the one hand, this example demonstrates the prospects for successful implementation of policy when policy and implementation are aligned; it receives unambiguous support of government structures; and it collaborates with multiple agencies outside of government. On the other hand, this case also demonstrates that it was not intended as a socially just and equitable policy.

The post-apartheid government was accompanied in 1996 by what was thought to be one of the most enabling and progressive human rights constitutions and a number of mechanisms, including PANSALB, to support the promotion of multilingualism in education. However, administrative decisions removed the key directorate for language policy and planning from the newly unified national Department of Education, thereby leaving a significant administrative gap. PANSALB's capacity to monitor government language policy was rendered ineffective by 1999 and although it had set up numerous substructures to replace the more productive and useful old language boards, the new structures have floundered along with PANSALB. PANSALB meanwhile managed to de-legitimise the former language boards and this has resulted in a dissipation of expertise in literary writing, translation and language-development activities, which are necessary to support multilingual education. The limitations of the post-1994 mechanisms together with political differences among key stakeholders have contributed to a misrepresentation of bilingual and multilingual education within government as a ruse for a return to apartheid-style mother-tongue education. This has been to the detriment of the majority of students in the school system. What this example shows is that unless policy and implementation are aligned and followed up with unambiguous mechanisms to ensure implementation, policies conceived with good intent flounder in the face of political forces and counterweights that have little to do with the concerns of equitable education. This is a process which may be termed 'reverse planning'.

NOTES

1 The author was a member of the Pan South African Language Board during this period and was the member tasked with making repeated requests for a meeting with the Minister.

REFERENCES

Alexander, N. (1989). *Language Policy and National Unity in South Africa / Azania*. Cape Town: Buchu Books.

Benson, C. and Plüddemann, P. (2010). 'Empowerment of Bilingual Education Professionals: The Training of Trainers Programme for Educators in Multilingual Settings in Southern Africa (ToTSA) 2002–2005. *International Journal of Bilingual Education and Bilingualism*, 13: 3, 371–94.

Cole, P. (2005). 'The Economics of Language in Education Policy in South Africa'. In N. Alexander (ed.), *Mother-Tongue-based Bilingual Education in South Africa. The Dynamics of Implementation*. Frankfurt: Multilingualism Network, and Cape Town: PRAESA.

Crawhall, N. (ed.) 1992. *Democratically Speaking*. Cape Town: National Language Project.

Department of Basic Education (DBE) (2011). *National Curriculum Statement (NCS) Curriculum and Assessment Policy Statement (CAPS): Intermediate Phase Grades 4–6. English First Additional Language*. Pretoria: DBE.

— (DBE) (2013a). *National Report 2012: The State of Literacy Teaching and Learning in the Foundation Phase*. Pretoria: DBE.

— (DBE). (2013b). *The Incremental Introduction of African Languages in South African Schools: Draft Policy*. Pretoria: DBE.

Department of Education (DoE). (1997a). *Curriculum 2005: Lifelong Learning for the 21st Century*. Pretoria: DoE.

— (DoE). (1997b). *Language in Education Policy*. Pretoria: DoE.

— (DoE). (2002). *Revised National Curriculum Statement Grades R–9 (Schools). Languages English – Home language*. Pretoria: DoE.

Desai, Z. (2013). 'Local Languages: Good for the Informal Marketplace but Not for the Formal Classroom?' *Education as Change*, 17: 2, 193–207.

Fleisch, B. (2008). *Primary Education in Crisis: Why South African Schoolchildren Underachieve in Reading and Mathematics*. Cape Town: Juta.

Foucault, M. (1991). 'Governmentality'. In G. Burchell, C. Gordon and P. Miller, (eds), *The Foucault Effect: Studies in Governmentality*. Hemel Hempstead: Harvester Wheatsheaf.

Gogolin, I. (2009). Linguistic habitus. In J.L. Mey (ed.), *Concise Encyclopedia of Pragmatics*. Oxford: Elsevier.

Hartshorne, K. (1992). *Crisis and Challenge: Black Education 1920–1990*. Cape Town: Oxford University Press.

Heugh, K. (1987). 'Underlying Ideologies of Language Medium Policies in Multilingual Societies with Particular Reference to Southern Africa'. Unpublished M Phil Thesis, University of Cape Town.

— (1999). 'Languages, Development and Reconstructing Education in South Africa'. *International Journal of Educational Development*, 19, 301–13.

— (2003). 'Can Authoritarian Separatism give way to Language Rights?' *Current Issues in Language Planning*, 4: 2, 126–45.

— (2007). 'Language and Literacy Issues in South Africa'. In N. Rassool (ed.), *Global Issues in Language, Education, and Development: Perspectives from Postcolonial Countries. Linguistic Diversity and Language Rights,* 4, 187–218). Clevedon: Multilingual Matters.

— (2013). 'Multilingual Education Policy in South Africa: Constrained by Theoretical and Historical Disconnections'. *Annual Review of Applied Linguistics,* 33, 215–337.

Heugh, K., Siegrühn, A. and Plüddemann, P. (eds), 1995. *Multilingual Education for South Africa.* Johannesburg: Heinemann Pearson.

Macdonald, C. (1990). *Crossing the Threshold into Standard Three: Main report of the Threshold Project.* Pretoria: Human Sciences Research Council.

Mahlalela-Thusi, B. and Heugh, K. (2010). 'Terminology and School Books in Southern African Languages. Aren't There Any?' In B. Brock-Utne, Z. Desai, M. Qorro and A. Pitman (eds), *Language of Instruction in Tanzania and South Africa – Highlights from a Project,* 113–31.

Makoni, S. (2003). 'From Misinvention to Disinvention of Language: Multilingualism and the South African Constitution'. In S. Makoni, G. Smitherman, A. Ball, and A.K. Spears (eds), *Black Linguistics: Language, Society, and Politics in Africa and the Americas,* 132–53. New York, NY: Routledge.

Murray, S. (2002). 'Language Issues in South African Education: An Overview'. In R. Mesthrie (ed.), *Language in South Africa.* Cambridge: Cambridge University Press.

National Education Policy Investigation (NEPI) 1992. *Language.* Cape Town: National Education Co-ordinating Committee and OUP.

Ouane, A., and Glanz, C. (eds) (2011). *Optimising Learning, Education, and Publishing in Africa: The Language Factor: A Review and Analysis of Theory and Practice in Mother-tongue and Bilingual Education in Sub-Saharan Africa.* Hamburg, Germany: UNESCO Institute for Lifelong Learning (UIL) and the Association for the Development of Education in Africa (ADEA)/African Development Bank. http://unesdoc.unesco.org/images/0021/002126/212602e.pdf (retrieved January 2015).

PANSALB. (2000). *Language Use and Language Interaction in South Africa: A National Sociolinguistic Survey.* Pretoria: Pan South African Language Board.

Probyn, M. (2009). '"Smuggling the Vernacular into the Classroom": Conflicts and Tensions in Classroom Codeswitching in Township/Rural Schools in South Africa'. *International Journal of Bilingual Education and Bilingualism,* 12: 2, 123–36.

Republic of South Africa (RSA) (1996). *The Constitution of the Republic of South Africa.* Pretoria: RSA.

Ridge, S. (2000). 'Mixed Motives: Ideological Elements in the Support for English in South Africa'. In T. Ricento (ed.), *Ideology, Politics, and Language Policies: Focus on English.* Amsterdam, the Netherlands: John Benjamins.

Skutnabb-Kangas, T. and Cummins, J. (eds) (1988). *Minority Education: From Shame to Struggle.* Cleveland: Multilingual Matters.

Taylor, N., and Vinjevold, P. (eds) (1999). *Getting Learning Right. Report of the President's Education Initiative Research Project.* Johannesburg: Joint Education Trust.

FORCES	MECHANISMS
Socio-political	**People / stakeholders**
Colonial dominance through Anglicisation	Political party allegiances and differences
Boer resistance through Afrikanerisation	NGO interventionists
African resistance to Afrikanerisation and apartheid use of 'mother tongue', bilingual and multilingual education	University-based educators, teachers, researchers, lexicographers
English-speakers resentment towards Afrikanerisation of civil service	Uncooperative officials in different government departments
	Legislation
Division within anti-apartheid politics	
(Un)stated political intent	Bantu Education Act 1953
	Constitution of the Republic of South Africa 1996
Goals	Pan South African Language Board Act 1996
	Language-in-education policy 1997
English-dominant education system	Curriculum policy 1997
Ethnolinguistically separated education system to protect speakers of Afrikaans, and for purpose of divide & rule	**Instruments of implementation**
Post-apartheid nation-building to be strengthened with promotion and development of multilingualism	1955–1994:
	National Department of Education
	• Directorate responsible for language policy implementation
Beliefs	Bantu Education Department
	• Directorate responsible for language education policy implementation
English understood as (aspirational access to) education, political & economic mobility by speakers of African languages	Language Board for each ethnolinguistic group
	1994– present:
English understood as an instrument of symbolic violence against speakers of Afrikaans	Parliamentary establishment of Pan South African Language Board
Afrikaans representative of cultural & faith-based identity	• Language boards disbanded; new PANSALB sub-structures established with limited capabilities
Afrikaans representative of oppressive & divisive apartheid regime	Relocation of Language Planning Directorate from Education to Department of Arts, Culture, Science and Technology (DACST)
Multilingualism (mis) understood as a problem in terms of:	Structural gap for Directorate of Language Education Planning in national Department of Education
• resourcing implementation	Dysfunctional relationship among Department of Education, DACST & PANSALB
• expertise/training	
• parental support	**Research**
• association with discriminatory apartheid policy of mother-tongue education	1930s–1940s:
	Evidence of educational & socially integrative advantages of bilingual education
	1980s– present:
	Evidence from across sub-Saharan Africa of advantages of bilingual/ multilingual education
	PANSALB 2000 – 88% people express preference for bilingual/ multilingual education

COUNTERWEIGHTS	
Socio-political ideologies	Competing socio-political ideologies
Anglicisation and colonial domination	Afrikanerisation and resistance to British colonisation
Afrikanerisation and ethnolinguistic division	Anglocentrism as a rejection of ethnolinguistic division
Post-colonial Anglocentricism and monolingual habitus	Post-apartheid constitutional multilingualism
Recursive fear of linguistic domination	Research-based evidence in support of and successful provision of bi/multilingual education

VOICES FROM THE FIELD:
Brunei Darussalam

Abd Rhaman Nawi (Director, Curriculum Development Department, Ministry of Education, Brunei Darussalam) and colleagues

INTRODUCTION

Linguistically, Brunei Darussalam is relatively homogeneous, with the majority of its inhabitants speaking Malay. The Malay ethnic group is the predominant group and Brunei Malay is the mother tongue of more than 50 percent of the population. Bahasa Melayu has been the official language of Brunei Darussalam since 1959. Brunei Malay and Bahasa Melayu are largely mutually intelligible. However, the country has long been more ethnically diverse with at least eight other Austronesian languages being used.

English has played an important role in Brunei Darussalam since the start of the British Residency period in 1888. As the country was once a British Protectorate, there was awareness of the importance of English and exposure to the British system of education. This has had its influence on the previous education system and continues to do so in the present system.

LINGUISTIC SITUATION/CONTEXT

The evolution of Brunei Darussalam's language policy and education system bears testimony to the importance accorded to both the Malay and English languages. The sovereignty of Bahasa Melayu as the national language of the country is safeguarded and upheld in the constitution and promoted through the ongoing efforts of the Language and Literature Bureau. At the same time, English as an international language of communication and commerce is widely recognised and promoted through the school curriculum, which uses both Bahasa Melayu and English as media of instruction. In addition, there is increasing awareness of the need to develop other languages as well.

The first school in Brunei Darussalam was a Malay-medium primary school established in 1914. The first non-government English-medium primary school was established in 1931. By 1941, there were 32 Malay-, Chinese- and English-medium primary schools. At the time, only primary education was available in Brunei.

With the establishment of the Education Department in 1951, the first Government English Preparatory School was set up in 1952. English-medium preparatory pupils, who graduated in 1953, were able to proceed to secondary education with the establishment of the first English-medium secondary school the same year. In 1966, Malay-medium secondary education became available in Brunei with the establishment of the First Malay Secondary School.

A Bilingual Education Policy was formulated in 1984. The existing Malay-medium and English-medium school systems were reorganised in 1985 to ensure that learners would achieve sufficient proficiency in both Malay and English to study through these languages at the tertiary level. Under this new policy, all government schools followed a common national curriculum from pre-school until pre-university. The policy was later extended to private schools (except international schools) in 1992.

In 1993, the 9-Year Compulsory Education Act was augmented with the 12-Year Education Order. Every student is now encouraged to have at least 12 years of formal education. Additional policies adopted between 1997 and 2007 sought to foster the development of an effective, efficient and equitable system of education consonant with the national philosophy of a Malay Islamic Monarchy and the needs of a modern and increasingly ICT-dependent era. The success of educational policy changes is evident in Brunei's rising rate of literacy which was 69% in 1971, rising to 89.2% in 1991 and 96.1% in 2011.

FORCES

The actual motivation to shift to using a different language can be attributed to economic or pragmatic factors, or to social psychological factors such as attitudes and identity. The learning of English in the Bruneian education system arises from a belief in the value of students continuing their studies in English-speaking countries. Equally, it is viewed as essential for the modernisation, internationalisation and diversification of the economy.

Over the years, Brunei Darussalam has formulated a strategic plan to advance its educational reforms. This mechanism focuses on three strategic concepts or forces for change: a professional, accountable and efficient organisation; quality education; and teaching and learning excellence. The introduction of the National Education System for the 21st Century (SPN21) in January 2009 serves as the mechanism for realising the vision that drives the MoE's strategic plan. SPN21 also addresses concerns such as the need to sustain and strengthen performance in the Malay language, in English, and in Mathematics and the Sciences.

The phenomena of globalisation and digitalisation in the twenty-first century have brought about new educational challenges. Instead of purely focusing on cognitive and skills development, other aspects of a holistic education are now deemed important forces in education. These include the inculcation of spiritual, moral, social and cultural attitudes and values.

MECHANISMS

In the early twentieth century, Brunei's education system focused on the development of the three Rs' and the provision of general knowledge through subjects such as Geography, Health Science, Physical Education, Handicraft and Gardening.

With independence, the lower primary to lower secondary curriculum became more general in nature. All subjects at the pre-school up to Primary 3 levels were taught in Malay except English Language. In 2009, Science was introduced from Primary 1 onwards. Also as of 2009, the medium of instruction for Primary 1-3 Mathematics is English. In Primary 4-6, all subjects are taught in English except Bahasa Melayu, Islamic Religious Knowledge, Social Studies, Physical Education and Art, which are all taught in Bahasa Melayu.

At the secondary level, new subjects such as Computer Studies and Design & Technology were introduced in 1993 and 2002 respectively and Information Technology (IT) was emphasised through Information and Communications Technology (ICT) across the curriculum.

Other value-added mechanisms introduced included the Reading Language Acquisition project (RELA) in 1989, the thinking skills programme Cognitive Research Trust (CoRT) in 1993/2008, Learning Programme Styles (LEAPS) in 1994, Specialist Mathematics and Science Teachers projects for Primary Schools in 1994, and the Active Mathematics in the Classroom project (AMIC) in 2004.

Increasing awareness of the potential 'synergy' between the Malay and English languages has led to collaboration on phonics instruction between Malay and English teachers in the consultant-led literacy programme, The Integrated Approach to Reading Acquisition (TIARA), for pre-school pupils in government primary schools. Bahasa Melayu teachers now lay the groundwork by teaching the 18 common phonemes in the first half of the pre-school year.

The introduction of the 12-year education system, and the widespread use of English as a medium of instruction, alongside a shortage of qualified local teachers, have led to the recruitment of teachers from Malaysia, Singapore, Australia, New Zealand, the United Kingdom, Canada and the Indian sub-continent. The Ministry of Education employs CfBT Educational Services (Brunei) to recruit some of these teachers.

Over the years, the Ministry has widened the scope of CfBT from mere recruitment of teachers to a capacity enhancer. The CfBT contract is now linked to performance targets. It must now deliver measurable short- and medium-term outcomes (e.g. improved student attainment in individual schools and nationally).

COUNTERWEIGHTS

Three decades after the bilingual education system was introduced, various issues raised by opponents have been allayed, including the following:

Nationalism vs Nationism

The nationalistic fervour of a newly independent Brunei in the 1980s has now been countered with economic realism requiring the education system to produce students capable of obtaining better employment and generating economic growth for the nation.

Identity loss vs Enriched uniform identity

The fear that learning another language might be at the expense of one's own culture and identity is increasingly being supplanted by the realisation that national cultures could be enriched by taking on an international identity, promoted by the spread of English. In Southeast Asia, countries are seeking to retain their national identities, expressed in terms of religious, artistic and cultural differences, whilst becoming more comfortable with internationalism.

Education in English vs in Bahasa Melayu

Like Malaysia and Singapore, Brunei Darussalam is trying to protect the identity of the nation while still widely using English as a medium of instruction. English in education is crucial in preparing the nation to face local and international challenges. While there is concern that a predilection for speaking English will result in lost status and identity related to the national culture and mother tongue, the use of English throughout the education system has resulted in additional educational opportunities and economic opportunity.

Two high-status languages vs diversity of languages

Increased mobility, the effects of intermarriage, and the influence of the supra-regional languages have resulted in the emergence of new patterns of communication that are threatening an increasing number of Indigenous languages. It is also likely that the use of these Indigenous languages is being further eroded through Malay and English-medium education. This awareness has induced certain groups within the community to step up efforts to remedy the situation.

SUGGESTED FURTHER READING

Jones, G. M. (1996). 'The Bilingual Education Policy in Brunei Darussalam'. In P.W. Martin, C. Ozog, and G. Poedjosoedarmo (eds), *Language Use and Language Change in Brunei Darussalam*. Athens, Ohio: Ohio University Center for International Studies, 123–32.

— (2003). 'Bilingual Education Equals a Bilingual Population? The Case of Brunei Darussalam'. In W.C. Daniel and G. Jones (eds). *Education and Society in Plurilingual Contexts*. VUB Brussels University Press: Brussels.

Ministry of Education, Brunei Darussalam (1998). *General Information Concerning the Education System*.

— (1998). *Educational profile of Brunei Darussalam document prepared for the International Bureau of Education*.

Sammons P., Davis S., Bakkum L., Hessel G. and Walker C. (2014). *Bilingual Education in Brunei: The Evolution of the Brunei Approach to Bilingual Education and the Role of CfBT in Promoting Educational Change: Summary Report*.

CONCLUSION:
Forces, Mechanisms and Counterweights

Peeter Mehisto (Institute of Education, University College London)

CHAPTER NAVIGATOR

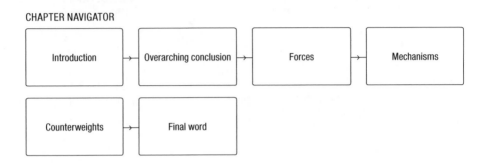

INTRODUCTION

This chapter revisits the paradigm of forces, mechanisms and counterweights. It does this by first by making one overarching conclusion. Then it proceeds to discuss core forces, mechanisms and counterweights that are common to and worthy of consideration in most bi/trilingual education contexts. In particular, the ways in which constituent forces and mechanisms interact with themselves and each other will be analysed (see Figure 1). The emergent or dynamic nature of context and the fact that forces, mechanisms and counterweights are a by-product of and filtered through the perceptions of people will be discussed throughout the chapter.

ONE OVERARCHING CONCLUSION

The complexities of leading and managing bi/trilingual education have featured prominently in this book. These complexities have been presented through the prism of forces, mechanisms and counterweights (herein jointly referred to as 'factors'), as well as through the concept of reciprocal co-evolution. Even if, through an exhaustive multi-disciplinary research process, one were to map out in an organised fashion the majority of factors that have

Figure 1: Forces, mechanisms and counterweights paradigm

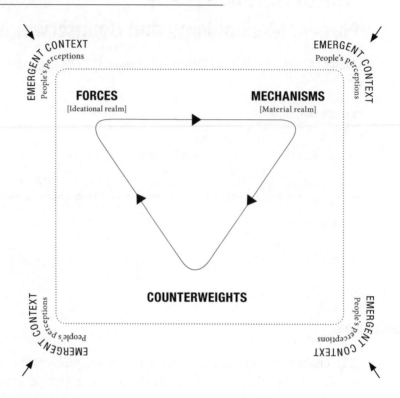

an impact on bi/trilingual education, maintaining a focus on all of these multiple factors would be a challenge at both the individual and systemic levels. Moreover, virtually all of these factors have been created by and filtered through the hearts and minds of people – and people are unpredictable.

Therefore, it is my belief that the greatest complexities of building bilingual and trilingual education systems originate to a large extent in the multiple perceptions, understandings and actions of stakeholders. Stakeholders are any individual, group or organisation that can affect or be affected by a bi/trilingual programme. Effective leaders and managers of bi/trilingual education work systematically to identify and engage stakeholders. Central to engaging stakeholders is the ability to understand, synthesise and navigate the diversity and commonalities inherent in individual views and beliefs, procedures, organisations and systems at large, while being able to influence and support stakeholder learning, the building of common narratives and co-constructed change at all these levels.

This ability needs to be underpinned by a strong knowledge base in bi/trilingual education, which in part has been distilled in the chapters of this book and the voices from the field. Some of these core factors will be discussed in the next sections of this chapter. In addition to understanding, synthesising, navigating and using knowledge about the various factors inherent in successful bi/trilingual programmes in diverse contexts in thoughtful ways, it is essential to incorporate knowledge and skills from other fields. These include planning, change management, communication, lobbying, psychology (e.g. decision-making), education in general, and the scaling up of reforms. Also, central to effectively working with others is being self-aware on the meta-cognitive, meta-affective and meta-social levels. High levels of self-awareness can help leaders and managers to better understand and navigate stakeholder concerns and group dynamics, and to support others in doing the same. Bi/trilingual education often requires stakeholders to step outside of their comfort zone. Stakeholders need support in reflecting on, adjusting and adding to their understandings, practices and plans, and in sharing power.

It is helpful if stakeholder inclusion is declared as a principle and that the principle is agreed upon with stakeholders. The agreement needs to be codified in a public document. Stakeholder inclusion can then take on a form of moral authority that can be called upon by any stakeholder who does not feel consulted. It is also helpful if certain mechanisms such as annual roundtables and committees are created to foster consultation. Effective stakeholder consultations and relationships are respectful yet open, frank and constructive. They regularly engage stakeholders with evidence, facts, plans, decision-making, analysis of progress and risk, and the taking of responsibility as stakeholders are encouraged to work toward achieving a common good. **Ultimately stakeholder relationships make or break any new programme.**

FORCES

The above conclusion points to constructive **stakeholder inclusion** as a major force in driving any bi/trilingual programme. Stakeholder inclusion is a principle, an idea or a concept. If one believes in the principle of stakeholder inclusion, and has the knowledge, skills, and moral and positional authority to engage stakeholders as partners in bi/trilingual education, the nature of the bi/trilingual programme one creates is bound to also reflect the vision of those stakeholders. In other words, stakeholder inclusion, as is the case with other forces, can take on a performative or constructive 'generative-productive' (Scott 2010) role. Equally importantly, if one were not to map out stakeholders and if one were to choose unknowingly, unconsciously or deliberately to exclude stakeholders from substantive discussions, these individuals, groups or organisations could later work against bi/trilingual education. Consequences arising from opposition could be as severe as legislation against bi/trilingual education or less severe, such as not incorporating aspects unique to bi/trilingual education into assessment policies and practices. Ignoring students as a stakeholder could contribute to student attrition from bi/trilingual programmes. For example, one Canadian study (Wesely 2010) identified a divide between student beliefs about good teaching and actual teaching as a primary reason for student attrition. In addition, if boys and girls are not seen as separate stakeholder groups, more of one gender may enter or drop out of a bi/trilingual programme. Yet all stakeholders may not wish to engage in discussion, let alone in open, frank and constructive dialogue. For example, certain local or national government officials may simply ignore or refuse to engage with stakeholders calling for bi/trilingual education. Here, synergy can play an important role, where several stakeholder groups such as academics, parents, business people and educators can together lobby officials. In Canada, educated and active parents working with academics succeeded in lobbying for and obtaining bilingual education, whilst by and large in South Africa parents have yet to succeed in doing so. At the very least, excluded stakeholders can be seen as a lost opportunity to gain further participation in, support for and enrichment of a programme.

Certain forces appear to be key to leading and managing any major bi/trilingual programme or education system. Other forces are also worthy of consideration and some of these will be discussed below. Establishing priorities is essential to allow one to concentrate efforts on those forces that will give the greatest return. Forces that are core to the development of bi/trilingual education are depicted at the heart of Figure 2, while additional forces for consideration are displayed around these. Although the forces described below often play an important role in successful bi/trilingual programmes, no claim is made that a programme cannot be successful without taking these into account. Also, although the list of forces is extensive, it is not exhaustive, nor can it take into account the diversity inherent in all contexts.

Cognitive fluency (rapid and easy cognitive processing) is a term coined by Unkelbach (2006). Research into human cognition and into the cognitive load that the average person can carry informs us of the limits of short-term or working memory. It tells us that knowledge is stored in schema, and that once we manage to store information, retrieval of that information may be imperfect. The large number of factors associated with the development of bi/

Figure 2: Forces

FORCES

[Ideational realm]

A sense of mission	**Cognitive fluency (clarity)**	Love of a language and culture
A vision	•	Status of a language
Status quo	**An interest in national security and social cohesion**	Hard work
Respect	•	Buy-in
Trust	**A belief in or a lack of belief in the value of bi/trilingual education**	Status of supporters
Autonomy		Commitment
Globalisation	•	Caring
Clarity	**A belief in the value of a wide evidence base**	Stamina
Reiteration	•	Leadership
Recognition of local concerns and expertise	**High expectations for all stakeholders including students**	Teamwork
	•	Xenophobia
Social and political pressure	**Open access to information**	Learning for all
Fear	•	Meta-affective,
Hegemony	**Power sharing**	meta-cognitive
Learning for all	•	and meta-social awareness
	Justice or injustice	

trilingual education implies that as one is planning for bi/trilingual education, fostering stakeholder dialogue and creating mechanisms such as plans, policies, curricula, reports, guides, learning resources and research projects, precision in thought will facilitate programme development. A lack of **precision in thought**, and in particular in plans and policies, will make it difficult for those involved to understand and implement the intentions of those leading the initiatives. Written and verbal messages need to be (1) articulated in concise and unambiguous manner; (2) organised in a fashion that allows for their easy processing, storage and retrieval; (3) be part of a coherent whole; and finally (4) aligned with practices. If practices are not aligned with policies, the practices will nullify the policies. All too often, precision of thought and the way information is organised in key documents does not foster cognitive fluency in the reader. This can easily lead to unnecessary tensions, the inefficient use of resources and the non-realisation of potential.

Fostering cognitive fluency through precision of thought takes time and special skill. In addition to stakeholder inclusion, which has already been discussed, fostering cognitive fluency also requires that one draw on other forces such as **a belief in the value of a wide evidence base and open access to information**. Research evidence can help people avoid counter-factual thinking such as assuming that Spanish-speaking young people in California will learn to speak English and be more successful in schools if they are quickly transitioned from bilingual Spanish-English to monolingual English-medium education. As discussed in Chapter One (USA), the research evidence shows this is not the case. Open access to plans and reports exposes those plans and reports to the scrutiny of others who may find the weaknesses in them. Their feedback can be used to improve them, and improve the precision of thought and expression in them.

However, not everyone is willing to or feels compelled to review the evidence. **'Wilful blindness'**, the act of ignoring challenging issues or research facts, buoyed by a sense of feeling that one's intuition is correct, can be a major negative force (Heffernan 2011). This involves being seduced by one's own surface-level thinking, as opposed to investigating one's initial thoughts through deeper-order thinking and against a wide range of available evidence. In California, wilful blindness has led to legislation restricting access to bilingual education. Politicians have ignored the benefits of bilingual education and the potential negative consequences of placing Spanish-speaking students in primarily monolingual programmes. In South Africa, government officials have not fostered the development of bilingual education and biliteracy despite the well-documented negative consequences of their current education practices, as discussed in the previous chapter. They persist in making several unsubstantiated claims about why bilingual education cannot be further developed, ignoring research results that would undermine their arguments.

National security concerns have led the US to create numerous mechanisms such as reports and strategies that have led to the creation of yet more mechanisms. These include the General Accountability Office's report entitled *Foreign Languages: Human Capital Approach Needed to Correct Staffing and Proficiency Shortfalls*; the Department of Defense's *Defense Language Transformation Roadmap*, and the *National Security Language Initiative* launched by the Departments of Education, Defense and State, and the National Intelligence Agency. These mechanisms have led to other mechanisms such as increasing the number of Language Designated Positions in the federal government; STARTTALK, which offers summer immersion programmes for students; and the National Security Language Initiative for Youth, which offers scholarships for students and recent graduates to study abroad in countries where languages designated as critical to US interests are spoken. These mechanisms have all been created as a result of a major force – concern for national security. They have fostered language learning. On a different scale, Estonia's desire to shore up national security and **social cohesion** has led to efforts to integrate the Russian-speaking communities in order to leave these communities and the country less open to manipulation by Russia. Language learning through bilingual education is seen as a key vehicle for integration and national security. Fostering social cohesion has also been a key motivation for fostering trilingual education in Kazakhstan.

A **belief in the value of one's ancestral language** is at the core of bilingual programmes in Basque, Estonian, Hawaiian, Māori, Mohawk and Welsh. This force has been so strong that the Mohawks have established full-time immersion programmes for adults. Māori families in one school have committed to having one parent always speak Māori with their children and with other children in the Māori-medium programme. This is also the case with one Hawaiian programme. The belief in the value of an ancestral language has also combined with a desire to right past **injustices**, as has been the case in New Zealand and the Basque Country. A belief in the value of Hebrew led to the establishment of a Hebrew immersion programme in the 1890s, which contributed to the eventual revitalisation of Hebrew as a national language. The **belief in the value of bi/trilingual education** has also been a major force in establishing both small- and large-scale bi/trilingual education programmes in the Basque country, Canada, Estonia, Kazakhstan, the Netherlands, the United States, Wales and in many other countries not profiled in this book. In other circumstances such as Malta, despite an initial lack of policy supporting bilingual education, teachers have long chosen to use two languages to teach as they and society at large have believed in the value and importance of bilingualism. The **sense of mission** of parents who believe in the value of bilingualism has been such a strong force that sceptical or uninformed government officials in countries such as Canada, Estonia and the United States have eventually chosen to support these programmes.

In contrast, the value placed on English in many nations and the value placed on other major high-status languages such as Spanish in Colombia have become major forces that undermine the learning of Indigenous languages. Finding counterweights and creating sufficiently attractive mechanisms against high-prestige languages has been a problem for Indigenous peoples in North and South America, and Africa. The UAE has been unable to find a force or create sufficient mechanisms that could counter the draw of English so that Arabic could flourish on co-equal footing with the *lingua mondo*. In South Africa, it is the unfounded beliefs of government officials regarding the value of English alongside misconceptions regarding the challenges of providing native-language education that appear to be acting as an obstacle to the provision of bilingual education, despite the fact that bilingual education is the preferred option of most surveyed parents.

Finally, in a dynamic co-evolutionary world of competing priorities one should never assume prevailing forces will remain constant and that the continuation of a bilingual education programme is assured. In Estonia, some 10 years ago, the Estonian Language Immersion Centre, which coordinated the programme nationally, was briefly threatened with closure. It had one influential opponent in government who did not believe in the value of early immersion programmes. Fortunately, stakeholder beliefs were so strong that stakeholders rallied with great speed and aplomb to protect the Centre and that threat dissipated.

In the UK, the devolution of powers from the United Kingdom to Wales led to the adoption of the Government of Wales Act 2006. Through this Act the National Assembly for Wales gained the power to make laws for Wales in certain defined areas. This includes the area of education and training. One could falsely assume that this would be a boon to Welsh-English bilingual education. However, the government's own Welsh-medium Education Strategy Annual Report for 2013–14 indicates that the government is far from meeting its targets for the period 2010–15 for the provision of Welsh-medium education. Furthermore, some government officials inside the Welsh Department for Education and Skills appear to believe that some aspects of the value of bilingual education have not been proven. Furthermore, they do not appear to have been taking advice from experts in the field of bilingual education or co-operating with a wide range of stakeholders in bilingual education. The government now has full responsibility for the marketing of bilingual education and there have been complaints that their new marketing campaigns have been very low-key, with more emphasis on the availability of bilingual education than on its advantages. This may well change. This criticism may help the officials involved to continue their journey in bilingual education, improve their understanding of it, build belief in it and become better able to support it.

MECHANISMS

Forces are insufficient for action. Forces must lead to the creation of mechanisms. Mechanisms belong to the material realm. They are tangible. An effective mechanism is part of a system that interacts with other parts and leads to something being done or created. Mechanisms receive their energy from a force or a combination of forces. Not only do forces bring life to mechanisms, but they direct how mechanisms are used. In other words, even if mechanisms are created with a causal purpose in mind, mechanisms are not in and of themselves causally efficacious. For example, a new curriculum document can be an important mechanism, but that document will need to be brought to life. Getting teachers to accept and believe in the value of that document will likely require professional development that gives teachers ample opportunities to discuss their understandings in relation to the curriculum. They will also likely need to learn and try out new strategies for the implementation of the curriculum, and discuss these experiences with colleagues, students and/or a mentor.

In the ideal world, numerous mechanisms could be developed to support bi/trilingual education. However, the number of core mechanisms required may vary greatly from context to context. In the Netherlands, a **central body** was created **to lead, manage and coordinate the bilingual programme**. That in and of itself is a key mechanism. A similar central programme management/co-ordinating body or mechanism has been created in the Basque Country, Estonia and Kazakhstan, yet Canadian programmes have developed and flourished without such a mechanism. Also, fluency in English among teachers in the Netherlands is more widespread than is the case in the Basque Country, Estonia and Kazakhstan. When it comes to hiring teachers this makes the establishment of a Dutch-English bilingual programme in the Netherlands easier than establishing a Basque-Spanish-English, Estonian-Russian-English or Kazakh-Russian-English programme. As is the case with several countries, the Dutch have organised **professional development**, created **networking opportunities** for educators, and developed **learning resources**, **public relations materials** and **teacher guides**. However, the leaders of the Dutch bilingual programme often stress the seminal role of two additional mechanisms. These are their **programme accreditation standards** and **quality indicators** (see the Tools section of this book). Importantly, these were created through a stakeholder-inclusive process that has led to a high-level of buy-in and commitment to their bilingual programme.

Core mechanisms are depicted at the heart of Figure 3 while some additional mechanisms are displayed around these. The list is extensive, but not exhaustive. Although successful programmes have not used all of these mechanisms, the core mechanisms depicted below are, I believe, likely to support programme development in most contexts. In almost any context, it would likely be helpful to have **an agreement on what is meant by terms** such as bilingualism, trilingualism, bilingual education, trilingual education, biliteracy, triliteracy and culture. The professional literature abounds with diverse definitions of those terms, and points to the fact that the understandings of those terms can vary greatly among academics, officials and educators. I have met officials from several parts of the world who feel that any school teaching a second language (L2) in only language classes, or all subjects in the students' L2 with the first language (L1) only in language classes, is bilingual. These are interpretations of bilingual education that would not have occurred to me, had I not entered into a discussion about the meaning accorded those terms by those officials. It is thus helpful to debate and agree on key terminology.

In addition, it is important to agree on **programme goals** that are tangible and measurable. For example, if one does not state that one is seeking to have students achieve 'grade-appropriate levels of academic achievement in non-language school subjects, such as Mathematics, Science or History taught primarily through the L2 and in those taught primarily through the L1', some may mistakenly assume that the curriculum may need to be simplified for those subjects taught through the L2. There would be no public commitment to ensuring that students in bilingual programmes learn as much academic content as is learnt in monolingual programmes. That would likely place a programme at risk. Instead, the goal described above provides a clear benchmark against which to evaluate a programme. In addition, clear goals are also required for language learning such as grade- and age-appropriate levels of advanced proficiency in L2 reading, writing, listening and speaking. A pan-European mechanism, the *Common European Framework of Reference for Languages* is a helpful tool for describing what constitutes advanced L2 proficiency, but further descriptors are needed for the learning of academic language in diverse content subjects if educators and students are to know what is expected of them. Similarly, if supporting students in developing 'the capacity for and interest in intercultural communication' is not a publically declared goal, it is less likely that intercultural knowledge, skills and dispositions will be a focus of learning resources and learning activities. The clearer the targets, the easier it is to teach to them, and for learners to consciously work towards them.

Figure 3: Mechanisms

MECHANISMS
[Material realm]

Planning year

Teacher attestation/school accreditation criteria and process

Overview of the economic, cognitive and cultural benefits of bi/trilingualism and bi/trilingual education

Teacher selection criteria and process that take into account language skills and attitudes toward bi/trilingualism

Public reports

Job descriptions

Public displays of support

Electronic networking opportunities

Visions and mission statements

Steering committee

Visible short-term wins

Rewards and recognition policy and plans

Communications plan

National strategy

Professional associations

Professional development policy

A leadership and management body
•
Mutually agreed-upon definitions of key terminology
•
Mutually agreed-upon programme goals including language targets
•
Committed and knowledgeable leaders
•
Results-based planning documents with timelines
•
Political and social capital
•
Local, national and international agreements
•
Local, reigonal and national financing
•
Local research and a solid literature review of research
•
An agreement on core pedagogical principles and values
•
School selection criteria and process
•
Criteria for learning resources development
•
Assessment policies and instruments
•
Learning materials
•
Professional development programmes for key stakeholders
•
Incentives to draw in and keep people in bi/trilingual education
•
Well-qualified teachers, principals, government official and parents
•
Face-to-face networking opportunities

School evaluation criteria

Websites

Student admissions/withdrawal policy

Minutes of meetings

Public relations materials

Conferences, forums and seminars

Parents' association

Public discourse

National and international legislation

Agreement on values

Parent information brochures

The European Charter

The Common European Framework

Extra-curricular activities

Study visits

Mentoring programmes

High-level correspondence with plenty of CCs

Various social networking accounts

Research into bi/trilingual education has been a seminal mechanism in supporting the expansion of bi/trilingual programmes in Canada, the Basque country, Estonia, the United States and several other countries. Having several **reviews of the professional literature on bi/trilingual education research** widely available can be a helpful mechanism as well. Programme managers and leaders need to draw on a solid knowledge base. This knowledge is useful in providing reference points for discussions about establishing a bi/trilingual programme. It can be used to move discussion about bi/trilingual education away from the affective and onto the rational plane. In addition, having access to a literature review on the potential cognitive, economic and other benefits of bi/trilingualism and bi/trilingual education would also be a valuable mechanism. This knowledge base can be used to inform and lobby people in positions of power, such as opinion leaders or politicians. Literature reviews are a key mechanism used by those leading the trilingual programme in Kazakhstan. Equally importantly, **high-status and well-informed individuals** such as the Belgian countess described in Chapter Two (Europe) is an example of someone who helped to change government policy in regards to bilingual education. Such individuals were also called upon in Estonia in the early days of its bilingual programme to build public awareness of and support for the initiative.

Ultimately it takes **committed leaders** who believe in the value of bilingualism to launch and develop programmes. The governor of Utah, who had personal experience in bilingualism, became a champion for bilingual education, but it would take better-informed officials to develop the vision and the mechanisms needed to actually allow for the launch of the state's bilingual programme. President Nazarbayev's vision of a trilingual Kazakhstan has helped launch a systemic approach to developing trilingual education in that country, and helped direct substantial resources to the realisation of his vision. That vision seems to have tapped into a vision supported by ethnic Kazakhs and seems to mitigate possible opposition from ethnic Russians. However, in other countries **parents** have been the leaders or pivotal mechanism in initiating bilingual programmes. Parents in Canada, New Zealand, the United States and Wales have displayed exceptional stamina in building the social and political capital, and the knowledge base needed to launch and expand bilingual education.

Policy prescriptions are other core mechanisms. The Welsh Language Strategy, the Official Languages Act of Canada and the Kazakhstan 2050 Strategy, all of which call for high levels of societal bi/trilingualism, are examples of mechanisms that have been used as a basis and an inspiration for further action leading to the development of bi/trilingual education. On their own, these policies would have been insufficient. They have combined with other mechanisms such as plans, and a force such as a deep-seated belief in the value of bi/trilingualism to create synergy for working toward the policy goals. In contrast, the UAE Arab Charter is an example of a policy prescription that aims to promote Arabic through numerous initiatives, but which to date has not had the desired effect. There are currently insufficient counterweights against the widespread belief in society that fluency in English is more valuable than fluency in Arabic, and against the omnipresence of English in society. Similarly, in Colombia, despite having a constitution that since 1991 gives co-official status to Indigenous languages along with Spanish in those territories where Indigenous languages are spoken, and despite the Education Law of 1994, which stresses the importance of respecting Indigenous cultures and languages, provision of bilingual education in Indigenous languages remains undervalued and often unavailable.

Planning documents are crucial mechanisms. Results-based planning frameworks can help stakeholders to organise the complexities of bi/trilingual programme/systems development. They can also compensate for the fact that human working memory cannot hold at the same time the large number of elements contained in these frameworks. By mapping out these elements in an organised fashion, a results-based planning framework makes the complexities navigable and increases the likelihood that they will be taken into account during bi/trilingual programme development. Here the interrelated nature of forces and mechanisms come to the forefront. If stakeholder inclusion, cognitive fluency, and precision of thought and expression are key values, then cooperation with stakeholders should lead to plans both at the systemic and institutional levels that are more likely to be grounded in the realities of a given context. If intended impacts, outcomes, outputs, indicators and risks are clearly articulated and presented in a well-organised and easily processed manner, all stakeholders are more likely to understand what is planned and suggest changes. They are also more likely to understand what measures need to be taken, what financial and human resources are required, who is responsible for what, how success will be measured, what the risks are and how these can be dealt with. There is an old adage in the management world that says 'if you cannot measure it, you cannot manage it'.

Negotiating for clarity and having stakeholders sign off on plans also means that results-based plans can act as a group decision-making instrument. Sharing power may be a difficult force to manage, but stakeholders who have helped develop and sign off on plans are more likely to understand

and support their implementation. Also, the initial investment in time into planning with stakeholders should facilitate programme implementation. In addition, programme research and public reports are essential mechanisms that need to go hand-in-hand with planning instruments. Human nature being what it is, people are more likely to deliver on the public promises contained in plans when they are expected to report publically on the achievement of planned targets at regular intervals. **Research** results and **public reports** also lead to the sort of analysis required to keep plans alive by keeping them somewhat flexible and grounded in contextual realities.

Several interrelated mechanisms that need to support one another can also help to support teachers and students in learning in bilingual education contexts. It was several years into the Estonian immersion programme, which I helped to co-manage during its initial years, before we moved away from speaking in generalities (to which people impute their own meaning) to being more specific when discussing best practices in teaching and learning. In-depth **professional development** was provided on various strategies such as how to encourage critical thinking or scaffold the simultaneous learning of content and language, but we had not articulated concisely what we believed were **core teaching and learning practices** that were **central to bilingual education**. Agreeing on a limited number of core pedagogical practices helps to focus attention, guide lesson analysis, develop professional development programmes, and explain to stakeholders the nature of teaching and learning in a bilingual education context. By limiting the number of teaching and learning practices that are designated as 'core', it is possible concomitantly to also respect and encourage teacher autonomy. Equally importantly, **criteria for learning materials development** can help ensure that learning materials are suitable for a bilingual or trilingual education context. For example, criteria can encourage authors to have students reflect both on content and language, make cross-linguistic connections and build the knowledge, skills and attitudes that foster intercultural communication. With criteria in place it is easier for authors and publishers to understand and address needs. This is particularly important in bilingual education contexts, where the number of students engaged in the programme may be so low that the market forces of competition that lead to improvements in the quality of products do not operate. Other core mechanisms are formative and summative **assessment policies and instruments** that take into account the particularities of assessment in bi/trilingual education contexts, such as the extent to which students know and can use strategies for learning content, language and learning skills; student attitudes toward each language and toward learning through each language; and individual student progress in learning the academic language in each content class (to avoid 'plateauing').

A **new curriculum** for a bilingual programme is a rare mechanism. Instead, schools are usually expected to teach based on the existing regional or national curriculum. However, as bilingual education is not simply a matter of switching the language of instruction, other mechanisms can be of great help. These include special **teacher guides** which, for example, help content teachers to set language objectives and show how they can teach the academic language of their subject. **Textbooks, student workbooks, electronic learning materials** and professional development are often discussed mechanisms that can support programme development. Less discussed is **professional development for government officials, inspectors, principals, vice-principals, teaching assistants and parents**. Each group needs mechanisms for learning. If government officials do not understand the nature of bi/trilingualism and bi/trilingual education they may make ill-informed decisions that can have a negative impact on programmes. If inspectors are not well versed in bi/trilingual education they may begin to undermine those practices being encouraged through teacher professional development. Principals who do not understand the need for cooperation among teachers teaching through different languages, the need for bi/trilingual extra-curricular activities or for creating opportunities for students to have contact and communication with speakers of the students' L2 or L3 may not facilitate such activities. Parents are key partners in bilingual education. Helping parents to understand how they can support children's language learning and how they might unintentionally undermine it is also worthy of specific mechanisms.

These and other mechanisms are best maintained in a well-planned and coordinated process of guided reciprocal co-evolution to ensure that they reinforce rather than undermine one another. For example, if teacher salaries are tied to an attestation process, and attestation criteria foster competition among teachers instead of cooperation, teachers may not share their experience and learning resources with their colleagues. It is also noteworthy that research in Canada has found that novice teachers are more likely to leave immersion programmes where more experienced colleagues do not share their materials and experience with them (Karsenti et al. 2008). Mechanisms that foster cooperation over competition are likely to be most effective. Also, if professional development initiatives do not take into account the particularities of bi/trilingual education, they may end up undermining the bilingual or trilingual aspect of these programmes. For example, if professional development for teachers emphasises critical thinking about content being learnt in subjects such as Maths and Science, and ignores how students can be taught to think critically about language, then Maths and Science teachers and their students are less likely to focus on both content and language learning. If universities set fluency in a second or third language as one entrance criterion, and/or offer content courses through several languages, then students are less likely to drop out of bilingual and trilingual programmes in high school.

Any new mechanism may have unintended consequences, and therefore it is wise to always first think through the consequences of a planned change. Recently in Wales, for example, mechanisms that fostered the learning and use of Welsh such as the Welsh Language Board have been abolished and their responsibilities shifted to mechanisms within the government and to the new Welsh Language Commissioner – a politically independent body, established to promote and facilitate use of the Welsh language. These changes have apparently led to the centralisation of responsibility for language issues, including education, in the hands of government. There is anecdotal evidence suggesting that stakeholders in bilingual education now have fewer contact points to discuss issues relevant to them with authorities, and that stakeholder inclusion on this issue is not a government priority. Moreover, the tabling of the Welsh-medium Education Strategy Annual Report on 17 July 2014 on the last day before the Welsh Assembly adjourned for holidays indicates the possible lack of status that the government accorded the report. In other words, it may initially appear that new mechanisms may better serve the interests of bilingual education, but there is no guarantee that new mechanisms will be instituted by people who have the same knowledge-base and interest in bilingual education or that those mechanisms are fully fit for purpose. As it is impossible to always foresee all the strengths and weaknesses of a new mechanism or how people will react to and use it, asking for stakeholder input in the planning stages will likely help to ensure that a planned mechanism also meets stakeholder needs. Furthermore, while new mechanisms are being created, it is in the interest of bi/trilingual education to build future opportunities for stakeholder consultations and cooperation into the mechanisms to ensure that unintended forces, such as the lack of belief in the value of bilingual education, do not gain an undue power base.

COUNTERWEIGHTS

In a complex system of bi/trilingual education no one person or group of people has all of the power, answers to questions, or solutions to problems. No one mechanism or force can guarantee quality programming. A complex system is emergent and dynamic. As the various elements of complex systems co-evolve, they can be said to interact with, and at times counteract, one another. For example, newly introduced mechanisms have been known to have unintended consequences in education systems. High-stakes testing has been introduced in several nations to improve the quality of education, but it has in some jurisdictions led to consequences such as a reduction in the scope and richness of learning for students as teachers teach to the test. It is also known that even when student test scores improve an over-emphasis on preparing for examinations may lead to a decline in student motivation to learn. In some jurisdictions, bilingual education has drawn high-achieving students away from regular programmes, in turn creating less stimulating learning environments for lower performing students. Highly successful bilingual programmes have been known to lead to declining enrolment in nearby primarily monolingual programmes, thereby also feeding opposition to bilingual education.

This section focuses primarily on potentially negative forces and mechanisms, or on forces and mechanisms that may become too influential in bi/trilingual education, and it suggests how these can be tempered with positive counterweights (see Figure 4). Several counterweights have already been discussed in the above sections on forces and mechanisms. Here again this section will focus on key counterweights that have been successfully used in some of the jurisdictions discussed in this book. For example, opposition to bilingual education in Estonia was countered through raising awareness among a wide range of stakeholders about the benefits of bilingualism and bilingual education, and about research facts. Opposition was reduced by building political and social capital, by holding public meetings in Russian-medium schools where experts in the field such as researchers, and students and parents with personal experience of a bilingual programme answered questions, and by including teachers teaching through Russian (the schools' primary language of instruction) in professional development programmes offered to teachers teaching through Estonian (the students' second language).

Figure 3: Counterweights

COUNTERWEIGHTS

Stability as a default position	versus	Well-justified and well-planned change
Fear	versus	Expert testimony of students
Resistance to major change	versus	A pilot project
Too many priorities	versus	Plans agreed upon with stakeholders
Over-emphasis on benefits of immersion	versus	Challenges of immersion and ways of addressing these
Results-based plans	versus	Iterative approach
Strong pull	versus	Measured push
Short-term student achievement	versus	Many indicators of success
Status quo in monolingual schools	versus	Benefit to students and society of bilingual education
Pressure to deliver more and more	versus	Agreed-upon priorities
Lack of experience	versus	Expert advice, commitment, desire to learn
Frankness	versus	Constructive dialogue
Guidelines taken as prescriptions	versus	Professional development and action research fostering autonomy
Wilful blindness / faith in one's own intuition	versus	A belief in the value of research and the regular use of research findings

A rapidly evolving bi/trilingual education system intends to increase its share of the education market. That fact alone is going to cause tension as a bi/trilingual programme seeks to obtain time on people's agendas, money and other resources, and as it potentially displaces or otherwise affects people or priorities. Fears and concerns surrounding the planned bi/trilingual change need to be countered. An often-used positive counterweight in bi/trilingual education has been the pilot project. A pilot project can use its own counterweights, such as expert (parent, researcher, student) testimony, a promise to engage closely with parents, involvement of foreign experts and substantial professional development in order to mitigate fears and concerns. If the pilot is well planned, implemented and researched, people can see from the research and from parent and student feedback that a proposed model works. At that point, others will be more likely to accept such programmes. However, some government and education officials might still resist introducing bi/trilingual programmes. Parental demand and grassroots movements have in such circumstances been successful in driving programme creation and/or expansion in countries such as Canada, the Netherlands, New Zealand and the United States.

It is noteworthy that rapid and constant change is inherent in ambitious pilot projects as they seek to develop a new and complex system. In such projects many mechanisms need to be created and forces dealt with in a short timeframe. The rapid and constant pace of change needs to be tempered with counterweights that offer a certain degree of stability in dynamic and emerging contexts. Priorities, in particular when they have been agreed upon with stakeholders, can temper the pace of development to ensure it is reasonable so that agreed upon priorities do not become obscured under pressure to deliver yet more value for stakeholders. If everything is a priority, nothing is. Expert internal and external advice by way of reports can also act as a counterweight to pressure to deliver more. Defining short-term wins such as the selection of schools through an open and transparent process, the opening of a management centre, the creation of policies, the delivery of a certain number of hours of training to teachers, the development of new learning materials and parent approval of progress can all help stakeholders understand what is being accomplished and realise that external pressure on the project to deliver more may be untimely or unwise. Stability can also be found in core mechanisms such as foundation agreements (e.g. a national government strategy, a four- or five-year results-based plan with a 'ring-fenced' budget approved by stakeholders, core pedagogical values and principles, criteria for learning materials development, curriculum documents, a relatively autonomous body to lead the project). By investing heavily in core mechanisms to ensure that their purpose is clear, and by ensuring that the rights and responsibilities of stakeholders involved in developing and using those mechanisms are well defined and by making related documentation concise and user-friendly, it is possible to counter the waste arising from frenetic activity directed at meeting vague targets. For example, if criteria for learning resources are in place, it is more likely that newly created learning materials will meet programme needs. If a powerful individual has an additional interesting idea that would require significant effort to implement, existing plans can be used to demonstrate a lack of capacity to implement the idea in the here and now, but also to plan for it at a future date.

Finally, once a pilot has been successful, immense pressure may be applied to scale up a bi/trilingual programme for implementation in a large part of the education system. Once again, expert advice can be a valuable counterweight. Stakeholders need advice on change management, and on how scaling up a reform effort from a pilot project to a system at large differs. For example, establishing a sustainable bi/trilingual education programme in a K-12 education system is at minimum a 14-year change process that will have an impact on, among others, business; cultural institutions; educational publishing; educator professional organisations such as teacher associations and unions; local and national government; libraries; the media; national examinations; parents; politicians; students; teacher and school principal pre-and in-service education, and the research community. The challenges faced in many schools embarking on a large-scale reform may differ from those faced by pilot schools; preparedness for reform may be different; and educator understandings may vary, as will levels of support for or resistance to the proposed change.

A FINAL WORD

The rewards of bi/trilingualism are potentially manifold for the individual, for a nation and for the world at large. On a personal level, they include potential cognitive, financial, health and social benefits. On a societal level, bi/trilingualism can lead to greater national stability, social cohesion, increased competitiveness in the global marketplace and prosperity. On a global level, they may lead to an increase in the number of people who are better able to understand one another, and avoid and navigate conflict. A lot is known about how to develop bi/trilingual programmes in diverse contexts and how successful these programmes can be. Still, these programmes are not to be entered into lightly by simply assuming that one must change the medium of instruction. If stakeholders are prepared to co-operate, to learn about best practices in leadership, management and pedagogy as they relate to bi/trilingual education, and if they are prepared to commit their time and other resources to develop these programmes, then by all means, they should start planning for programme implementation. Hopefully this book can serve as one tool, among others, to enable them to move forward with bi/trilingual education.

> *The world we have created is a product of our thinking; it cannot be changed without changing our thinking.* (Albert Einstein)

REFERENCES

Heffernan, M. (2011). *Willful Blindness: Why We Ignore the Obvious at Our Peril*. London: Simon & Schuster.

Karsenti, T., Collin, S., Villeneuve, S., Dumouchel, G. and Roy, N. (2008). *Pourquoi les nouveaux enseignants d'immersion ou de français langue seconde quittent-ils la profession? Résultats d'une enquête pancanadienne*. Ottawa: Association canadienne des professeurs d'immersion.

Scott, D. (2010). *Education, Epistemology and Critical Realism*. London: Routledge.

Unkelbach, C. (2006). 'The Learned Interpretation of Cognitive Fluency'. *Psychological Science*, 17: 4, 339–45.

Wesely, P. (2010). 'Student Attrition from Traditional and Immersion Foreign Language Programs'. *Language and Linguistics Compass*, 4: 9, 804–17.

APPENDIX: Tools

The following tools introduced below have been used for planning, constructing and implementing bi/trilingual education in countries profiled in this book. When co-constructed and/or used with stakeholders, the tools have served to build stakeholder understanding, shape behaviour and build context favourable to bi/trilingual education.

Tool 1: National or regional-level planning considerations for bi/trilingual education

This series of cards distils key considerations for those planning national or regional bi/trilingual programmes. These considerations can be analysed by groups. Those cards/considerations that do not pertain to the users' context can be crossed out and additional points written in (see pages 292–5).

Tool 2: A bilingual education continuum

The continuum summarises individual and group practices, beliefs and assumptions that support or undermine learning in bilingual education contexts. The continuum is intended to serve as a basis for structuring stakeholder dialogue about bilingual education (see pages 296–7).

The following tools are available online at:
education.cambridge.org/buildingbilingual

Tool 3: School-level planning considerations for trilingual education

This series of cards distils school-level considerations for those planning to establish a trilingual programme. These considerations can be analysed by groups. Those cards/ considerations that do not pertain to the users' context can be crossed out and additional points written in.

(Note: this tool can easily be adapted for **bilingual education**)

Tool 4: CLIL essentials

The CLIL essentials distil those practices that are at the core of Content and Language Integrated Learning (CLIL). Several practical examples of CILL best practices are included.

Tool 5: A results-based management (RBM) framework for early immersion (Estonia)

Initially, this RBM document was used to distil potential complexities associated with the development of the Estonian early immersion programme. At the same time, the framework became a group decision-making instrument that was used to plan and implement the Estonian early immersion programme.

Tool 6: A results-based management framework for late immersion (Estonia)

Initially, this RBM document was used to distil potential complexities associated with the development of the Estonian late immersion programme. At the same time, the framework became a group decision-making instrument that was used to plan and implement the Estonian late immersion programme.

Tool 7: A national level strategic plan for immersion (Estonia)

This strategic plan was developed by a broad range of stakeholders in Estonia not just to plan for the expansion of the immersion programme but to help increase stakeholder engagement in programme development. The plan fits on one sheet of A4 paper (folded in 3 as a flyer) to help ensure ease of processing (cognitive fluency) by its readers and the primacy of key goals and strategies.

Tool 8: Standards for bilingual education in English for general academic secondary education and pre-university secondary education (The Netherlands)

The standards serve as a guide for Dutch secondary schools wishing to establish a bilingual education programme and to join the national Network of Bilingual Schools. Equally importantly, they serve as guidelines for those who are already part of that network. The standards align with the national curriculum, but draw out targets particular to bilingual education.

Tool 9: Bilingual education quality indicators for the pre-university level (The Netherlands)

These quality control indicators (45 in all) are part of a framework instrument used in the accreditation of schools in Dutch national Network of Bilingual Schools. They are based on the standards (Tool 8). The quality control indicators include categories such as student achievement, international orientation, CLIL, organisational preconditions, and individual and team-based professional development.

Tool 10: Nazarbayev Intellectual Schools (NIS) core values and pedagogical principles (Kazakhstan)

This tool draws out core values and pedagogical principles of the trilingual schools of the NIS network. The document provides examples of how these principles would be applied by educators and students.

Tool 11: Dual Language Immersion Program Fidelity Assurances Grades 1–6 (Utah)

These fidelity assurance criteria constitute a list of requirements that schools joining Utah's state Dual Language Immersion Program must meet.

National level planning considerations for bi/trilingual education

Suggested use: Print each box on a separate card. Participants prioritise each card for years 1, 2 and 3 of their planned programme. They can add or delete points and/or cards as they see fit.

Public

- identify common fears, and explain:
  - goals of bi/trilingual programme
  - research facts on bi/trilingual education
  - that it is suitable for all students
  - typical learning process
  - expected short-term and long-term results

Public (continued)

- share success stories including parent and student stories
- give examples from other countries
- explain:
  - how teachers and principals will be trained
  - how students will be supported

Ministry officials

- need to be aware of:
  - programme types
  - needed investments
  - research facts on bi/trilingual education
- suggest ways of achieving government goals
- establish regulatory framework

Curriculum issues

- language curriculum is content based and supports content learning (includes content objectives)
- content (e.g. maths) curriculum also includes language objectives
- extra-curricular programme is also trilingual (e.g. outdoor learning, museums)

Universities

- develop capacity to teach and research bi/trilingualism, bi/trilingual education and language shift
- train teachers in bi/trilingual education
- train principals and vice-principals in leading bi/trilingual schools

Learning resources

- have criteria for learning resources development
- ensure criteria provide guidelines on language and culture, e.g. define culture and intercultural competence, and identify useful ways of translanguaging

Whole system view

- ensure that bi/trilingualism is supported from pre-school through to secondary, vocational education and post-secondary education
- be aware of how high-stakes assessment decisions will influence bi/trilingual goals

Teacher competences

- define competences unique to working in bi/trilingual environments e.g. knowing how to draw out and teach academic language
- agree on language requirements for teachers

In-service professional development

- teachers need:
  - ongoing support, not just two weeks of courses
  - in-class support and mentoring
  - networking opportunities
- foster inter-school cooperation

Managing risks

- analyse possible risks
  - lack of public support
  - some officials that may not support the programme
- make plans, goals and success indicators transparent
- foster stakeholder dialogue
- work with politicians and other leaders

Research

- be aware of existing research findings
- establish long-term research programme to measure student achievement in language and content classes
- ensure research is independent
- research out-of-school language use

Libraries

- create bi/trilingual digital and print-based collections
- librarians need to be bi/trilingual
- school librarians need to support students in doing research in two or three languages
- teachers and librarians team teach

Bilingual exchanges

- establish financing mechanisms
- create an agency that manages knowledge and facilitates exchanges
- research their effectiveness
- cooperate with media

Good pedagogy

- more can be learned in less time
- be aware of high-impact teaching and learning strategies that foster content and language learning
- train teachers, vice-principals, principals and local government officials in high-impact teaching and learning strategies
- identify strategies unique to bi/trilingual education

Principal and vice-principal competences

- key role is to support teachers
- understand what changes in leading a bi/trilingual school, e.g. the need for teachers teaching through different languages to cooperate
- language requirements

Extra-curricular activities

- provide financing mechanisms to encourage extra-curricular activities in L2 and L3 (also in L1 if it is disadvantaged)
- create L1, L2, L3 sports, science and art camps
- also use L2 and L3 for outdoor learning, museums and projects

Internationalisation

- create international partnerships to exchange experience
- use ICT to connect with L2 and L3 speakers
- undertake international assessments to measure success, identify problems, find solutions and reduce opposition

Common European Framework of Reference (CEFR)

- build your own descriptors for operationalising CEFR for L2 and L3
- do not use CEFR for L1
- train teachers and administrators in using new descriptors

Assessment 1

- agree regionally or nationally on assessment guidelines that take into account aspects unique to bi/trilingual education (e.g. students learning through L2 and L3 not over-penalised for language errors)
- national examinations also test ability to write in L2/L3
- students are not afraid to make mistakes in speaking
- celebrate short-term wins

Assessment 2

- foster the use of formative assessment in both content and language classes to support ongoing improvement of fluency in L1, L2 and/or L3
- train content teachers in providing feedback on language and encourage students to always reflect on language and content learning in all classes

Facilitating cooperation

- encouraging inter-school cooperation so lessons learnt can be shared (e.g. by financing small projects)
- encouraging inter-regional networking (e.g. conferences)
- financing teacher visits to other schools

Working with stakeholders

1 What does each stakeholder group want or expect from the Ministry?
2 How does the stakeholder group assess the Ministry's performance?
3 From the stakeholder's perspective, how well is the Ministry doing?

Working with stakeholders (continued)

4 How would the stakeholder group like to work with the Ministry?
5 What do you need from stakeholders to be successful?

Questions used by Penny Lawler and Maureen Edgar, Ontario Ministry of Education and Training

School financing

- provide schools meeting bi/trilingual criteria with 10% more budget (will help drive expansion)
- finance extra-curricular activities such as exchanges and language camps
- create a project fund for schools to innovate (include requirement to share learning)

Working with ethnic groups

- respect languages and cultural differences
- listen to their concerns
- have experts respond to those concerns
- help each group understand how they can benefit from bi/trilingualism

Establishing voluntary L2 early immersion

- early immersion is a fast way of increasing the number of L2 speakers
- if voluntary, and also fosters L1 learning, parents are more likely to support it
- teachers and school leaders need to be trained and learning resources created
- later can add 3rd language

L1/L2 terminology and materials

- if L1/L2 is a threatened language:
  - set up a national translation and terminology centre
  - provide online access to terminology
  - work to improve status of threatened language
  - create very high quality learning resources in threatened language

Giving the disadvantaged language an advantage

- make learning materials in the disadvantaged language particularly interesting and attractive
- ensure teachers teaching through this language are well trained
- actively manage its status
- provide public information about the benefits of learning the disadvantaged language

Avoiding the folklorisation of the disadvantaged language

- use this language to teach high-status subjects such as Science and ICT
- continue to develop the language corpus
- provide incentives for using the language
- showcase successful individuals who speak the disadvantaged language, like sports or movie stars, and business people

Creating legislative & regulatory framework

- ensure that laws, regulations and programmes support bi/trilingual education and the use of two/three languages in daily life

Creating key policy documents

- create a bi/trilingual policy for schools to follow or require schools to develop their own policy (to be signed off)
- provide schools guidelines (not just regulations)
- analyse existing policy documents to see if they support bi/trilingual education

Identifying stakeholders

- Nationally: Parliament, ministries of education, finance, justice and foreign affairs; government; prime minister; vice prime minister; boards; universities, teacher unions; media
- Locally: local departments of education; city mayors; authors and designers of learning materials; students; parents; media; libraries; museums

Broadband Internet access in all schools

- key for using authentic materials and for contact and communication with L2 and L3 speakers
- key tool in developing autonomous language learners

Pilot projects

- test out various options
- provide seed money
- identify, capture and distribute knowledge
- define context in which pilot took place
- take into account changed contexts when applying knowledge from pilot elsewhere

Knowledge management

- the process of capturing, distributing and effectively using knowledge
- capture and distribute learning from pilot projects
- distribute results of research and help people interpret these

What would you change, remove from or add to these cards?

A BILINGUAL EDUCATION CONTINUUM

FACTORS UNDERMINING MEANINGFUL LEARNING OF CURRICULUM

BELIEFS

- Challenging content cannot be taught/learnt through L2
- Socially disadvantaged and low-achieving students cannot learn challenging content through L2
- Teaching either through L1 or L2 is superior
- Teachers just teach their subject(s)
- Intuition is always right
- Working alone is best

ASSUMPTIONS

- Native speakers of L2 can teach through L2 without training
- Teachers will do what a principal asks
- Appearances and assumptions can be taken at face value
- Someone who has successfully taught one Grade can teach another
- Parents should not interfere in school education

INEFFECTIVE PRACTICE ⬅

(In classes taught through L2) extensive, non-judicious use of L1 and translation[1] ⬅

Teacher-talk and activities dominate lessons ⬅

Initiation-response-feedback pattern and answers for display dominate lessons ⬅

Component parts of academic language are not drawn out ⬅

Insufficient scaffolding of language or its complete absence ⬅

Insufficient scaffolding of content or its complete absence ⬅

Unclear or unstated intended learning outcomes (language, content, learning skills) ⬅

No teaching or modelling of learning skills ⬅

Low expectations in relation to content and language learning and in relation to socially disadvantaged students ⬅

Strong sense of teacher and student disassociation from one another ⬅

Aggressive, psychologically unsafe climate where many students do not experiment with content and language ⬅

High level of teacher attention to control ⬅

No cross-curricular or cross-cultural links ⬅

Cognitively unchallenging tasks and low level of student engagement in learning ⬅

No authentic materials or communication with L2 speakers ⬅

NOTES

1   L1 = first language *L2 = second language
2   ZPD = zone of proximal development (Vygotsky 1978)

EFFECTIVE PRACTICE

(In classes taught through L2) limited and judicious use of L1 and translation

Student-talk, and engagement in individual and peer-cooperative work dominate lessons

Dialogic discourse dominates lessons

Component parts of academic language are drawn out

Ample and detailed scaffolding of language while maintaining students in their ZPD[2]

Ample and detailed scaffolding of content while maintaining students in their ZPD

Clearly stated intended learning outcomes (language, content, learning skills) and regularly discussing progress against these

Teaching and modelling of learning skills (content and language)

High expectations in relation to content and language learning and in relation to socially disadvantaged students

Constructive, psychologically safe climate where all student freely experiment with content and language

High level of student decision-making and self-control (autonomy and agency)

Critical thinking as driver of learning (content, langauge, learning skills)

Rich cross-curricular and cross-cultural links

Cognitively challenging tasks and high level of student engagement in learning

Authentic materials used in authentic ways and guided communication with L2 speakers

FACTORS FOSTERING MEANINGFUL LEARNING OF CURRICULUM

BELIEFS

- Challenging content can be taught through L2
- Socially disadvantaged and low-achieving students can learn challenging content through L2
- Teaching through L2 is valuable if L1 also developed through L1 subject classes
- Teachers teach both content and language
- Bilingual education is on occasion counterintuitive
- Working in cooperation with others is a key value

ASSUMPTIONS

- Native speakers of L2 need training in teaching through students' L2
- Teachers will make their own decisions based on their own beliefs, but these can be modified through PD and other forms of cooperation
- Appearances and assumptions need to be questioned/explored
- Challenges faced by teachers change from Grade to Grade
- Parents are partners in education

© Mehisto, Peeter (2012). *Excellence in Bilingual Education: A Guide for School Principals.* Cambridge University Press.

INDEX